2026
중등영어 교사임용

권영주 임용 전공
영어 교육론

TEACHING ENGLISH

PREFACE
머리말

　임용 영어교육론은 우리 선생님들이 새내기 교사가 되어 교직에 첫발을 내딛게 될 때 가장 필요한 과목이 될 것이다. 초임 교사가 되어 교실현장에서 사용하게 될 영어교수법이나 학생의 수준 등이 그동안 책에서 배운 내용과 다르고 교직에 대한 평소의 기대와는 다르게 나타나는 면이 있을 수는 있다. 하지만 영어교육에 대한 기본 철학이 있고 어떠한 문제점이 나타날 것이라는 것을 예상하고 대비할 수 있다면 아무런 준비가 되지 않은 상태에서 어려움을 만나는 경우와는 다르게 잘 헤쳐 나갈수 있을 것이다.

　2024년과 2025년 임용 영어시험에서 영어교육론은 80점 만점에 각각 38점과 36점이 출제되면서 임용 합격을 위해서는 높은 점수를 받아야 하는 필수 요소가 되고 있다. 영어교육론에서 다루어지는 내용들은 효과적인 2언어 습득을 위한 기본 원리로 시작하여, 실러버스와 교과서의 이용, 평가의 종류와 목적, 그리고 4기능과 문법·어휘지도까지 영어 교육을 위한 전반적인 내용을 다음과 같이 구성하고 있다.

1. 2언어습득 및 학습이론
2. 영어교재론 및 교육과정
3. 영어평가
4. 영어교수법
5. 4기능、어휘/ 문법지도및 ICT 활용지도

　2014년부터 중등교사를 위한 전공영어 시험이 1차 서답형 (기입형과 서술형)으로 개정되면서 그를 위한 방식의 학습방법이 필요하게 되었다. 이에 따라 정확한 답을 서술해야 하는 서답형에 따른 학습방법이 요구되고 있다. 우리나라 교육과정 평가편에 따르면 서답형 문항의 목적은 크게 다음과 같이 분류될 수 있다.

- 창의적인 문제해결력을 갖춘 인재 양성
- 자기주도적 학습능력 신장

서답형 문항을 풀기 위해서는 다음과 같은 필수사항이 고려되어야 할 것이다.

- 제시되는 지문의 양 증가로 빠른 독해
- 직접 서술해야 하는 문제를 위한 정확한 지식 필요
- 종합적 사고력을 기반으로 한 문제 해결 방법 강화

이러한 문제점을 해결하고 합격하기 위해서 다음과 같은 학습단계를 실천해볼 수 있다.

1. ELT 아티클과 원서교재 읽기를 통해 내용을 전체로서 이해한다.
2. 글쓰기 문제연습과 첨삭을 통해 본인의 장점과 단점을 이해하고 수정해간다.
3. 기출문제를 풀어보며 실제문제 안에서 답을 찾아간다.
4. Mindmap을 통해 내용의 구조화를 수행한다.
5. Keywords의 반복연습으로 답안이 되는 요소를 정리한다.

기초를 잘 닦고 시작하는 공부는 어떠한 문제가 출제되거나 다른 새로운 영역으로 적용해야 할 때 강한 생존력을 나타낼 수 있다. 새롭게 시작하는 선생님과 다시 한번 도전하는 선생님 모두, 이제 영어교육론의 이론을 처음 대하는 마음으로 차근차근 시작해 보기로 하자.

CONTENTS
목차

▶▶▶ 기출분석 ········· x

PART 1 Teaching and Learning in Classroom Practices _ 27

chapter 01 Teaching by Principles ········· 28
- 01 Cognitive Principles ········· 30
- 02 Socioaffective Principles ········· 34
- 03 Linguistic Principles ········· 36

chapter 02 Motivation ········· 41
- 01 Theoretical Background of Motivation ········· 43
- 02 Methodological Perspectives ········· 49

chapter 03 Context of Learning and Teaching ········· 51
- 01 연령에 따른 학습 ········· 52
- 02 언어 능숙도에 따른 학습 ········· 53

PART 2 Second Language Acquisition _ 57

chapter 01 Second Language Acquisition ········· 59
- 01 Behavioristic Learning ········· 61
- 02 Innatism ········· 64
- 03 Cognitivism ········· 71
- 04 Interaction Hypothesis ········· 73
- 05 Social Constructivist Model ········· 80

chapter 02 Learner Language ········· 86
- 01 Learner Language ········· 88
- 02 Error Analysis ········· 90

chapter 03　Learning Strategies　98
01 Individual variability　100
02 Styles & Strategies　104

PART 3　Teaching Methodology _ 115

chapter 01　Teaching Methodology　116

chapter 02　Grammar Translation Method　120

chapter 03　The Direct Method　123
01 Teaching and Learning　124
02 Classroom Techniques　125

chapter 04　Audiolingual Method　127
01 Teaching and Learning　128
02 Selection of Materials　129
03 Language in Audiolingual Method　130

chapter 05　Community Language Learning　136
01 Principles　137
02 Lesson Design　138
03 Instructional Roles　140

chapter 06　The Silent Way　142
01 Principles　143
02 Learning and Teaching　144

chapter 07　Suggestopedia　146
01 Principles　147

CONTENTS 목차

    02 Procedure ··· 148

chapter 08 Total Physical Response ·· 150
    01 Principles ··· 151
    02 Teaching Principles ·· 153

chapter 09 The Natural Approach ·· 155
    01 Principles ··· 155
    02 Learning Procedure ·· 157

chapter 10 Communicative Language Teaching ··· 159
    01 Communicative Language Teaching ··· 161
    02 Task-Based Instruction ··· 170
    03 Content-Based Instruction ··· 183
    04 Whole Language Approach ··· 186
    05 Participatory Approach ··· 189
    06 Lexical Approach ··· 190
    07 Multiple Intelligences ·· 192

PART 4   Teaching Language Skills _ 195

chapter 01 Integrated Skills ·· 196
    01 Integrated Lesson ··· 197

chapter 02 Teaching Listening ·· 203
    01 Features of Listening ·· 206
    02 Procedures of Listening ··· 208

chapter 03 Teaching Speaking and Pronunciation ·· 214
    01 Integration of Listening and Speaking ·· 217

02 Principles of Speaking ·······219
03 Conversational Analysis ·······222
04 Discourse Analysis ·······224
05 Teaching Pronunciation ·······226

chapter 04 Teaching Reading ······· 231
01 Principles for Reading ·······232
02 Teaching Reading ·······235
03 Classroom Applications ·······243

chapter 05 Teaching Writing ······· 249
01 Writing Approaches ·······250
02 Writing Assessment Tasks ·······253
03 Principles for teaching Writing Skills ·······255
04 Feedback on writing ·······258

chapter 06 Form-focused Instruction ······· 260
01 Classroom Applications ·······262
02 Teaching activities ·······267
03 Focus-on-form and Focus-on-formS Approaches ·······270

chapter 07 Teaching Vocabulary ······· 274
01 Principles for Teaching Vocabulary ·······275
02 Classroom Instruction ·······277
03 Lexical Approach ·······284

CONTENTS
목차

PART 5　Language Curriculum _ 287

chapter 01　Curriculum Design ·········· 288
　01 Concepts of Curriculum ·········· 290
　02 Procedure of Curriculum ·········· 291

chapter 02　Syllabus ·········· 295
　01 교수 과정의 발달 ·········· 295
　02 Types of Syllabus ·········· 298

chapter 03　Lesson Planning ·········· 302
　01 Guidelines for Lesson Planning ·········· 302
　02 Sample Lesson Planning ·········· 305

chapter 04　Material Development ·········· 310
　01 Classroom materials ·········· 311
　02 Authentic Materials in Classrooms ·········· 314
　03 Adaptation for Teaching Materials ·········· 319

chapter 05　Classroom Activities ·········· 325
　01 Classroom Activities ·········· 325
　02 Interactive Language Teaching ·········· 326

chapter 06　ICT 지도 ·········· 333
　01 ICT in the classroom ·········· 334
　02 Methods of using ICT ·········· 336

PART 6   Language Assessment _ 343

chapter 01   Assessment Principles 344
     01 Categories in Assessment 348
     02 Principles of Assessment 352
     03 Classroom Language Tests 356

chapter 02   Assessing Language Skills 364
     01 Assessing Listening 365
     02 Assessing Speaking 368
     03 Assessing Reading 372
     04 Assessing Writing 376
     05 Assessing Grammar and Vocabulary 380

부록   Glossary _ 383

기출문제 분석표

2002년-2025년 영어교육론 기출문제 분석표

▌2025학년도 ▌ 영어교육론 기출문제 내용분석표 (36점)

기입형

A3	(교재론) 자료를 학생들의 동기를 높이기 위하여 modifying하여 개정한다.
A4	(영어 평가) 평가원리에서 interrater reliability의 중요성을 이해한다.

서술형

A8	(중간언어) semantic deviation & number of arguments 오류를 서술한다.
A9	(말하기평가) clarity & authenticity를 말하기 평가 항목을 위해 서술한다.
A11	(수업목표) reception & production의 수업목표를 서술한다.
A12	(읽기전략) 문제점을 파악하고 그에 대한 읽기전략을 제시하여 서술한다.
B6	(PBL) 프로젝트교수법 과정에서 잘 못 수행한 목표 & 평가에 대하여 서술한다.
B7	(듣기지도) 듣기활동에서 intensive듣기와 창조적활동에 대하여 서술한다.
B10	(문화지도) reflecting, comparing, interacting과정을 선택하여 서술한다.
B11	(ICT지도) 디지털 도구를 사용하는 원리에 어긋나는 내용을 서술한다.

▌2024학년도 ▌ 영어교육론 기출문제 내용분석표 (38점)

기입형

A1	(영어평가) 평가원리에서 시간과 경제성을 중시하는 practicality를 이해한다.
A2	(2언어습득) 언어의 빈도나 특정언어의 salience을 높여서 언어습득에 도움을 준다.
B1	(말하기지도) 의사소통에서 함축된 의미인 illocutionary acts를 이해한다.

서술형

A8	(듣기지도) 듣기의 macro와 micro전략을 구별하여 서술한다.
A9	(말하기지도) 의사소통을 위한 활동을 구별하고 서술한다.
A11	(교수요목) 다양한 항목을 위한 교수요목과 교사의 수업방식을 비교·서술한다.
A12	(교수도구) 학습자들의 요구에 따라 맞는 디지털 도구를 서술한다.
B6	(영어평가) item analysis를 위한 구체적 항목을 서술한다.
B7	(과업수행) 언어의 난이도와 수행조건을 변화시키는 과업수행을 서술한다.
B10	(문화지도) 유형의 문화산물을 위한 문화교수원리를 서술한다.
B11	(문법지도) 귀납법과 연역법을 통한 교수방법을 서술한다.

▍2023학년도 ▍ 영어교육론 기출문제 내용분석표 (38점)

기입형
A1	(2언어 습득) 언어습득과정에서 backsliding되는 과정을 이해한다.
A4	(평가) computer adaptive test의 특성을 이해한다.
B1	(연구) action research를 통한 교사의 연구 활동을 이해한다.

서술형
A8	(교수법) 실제 삶과 연관된 수업과 cognitive skill을 높이는 수업을 서술한다.
A9	(읽기지도) word master와 graphic organizer를 활용한 읽기 수업을 서술한다.
A10	(언어습득과정) 언어습득과정의 실제 사례를 서술한다.
A12	(문화지도) culture를 지도하기 위한 다양한 방법을 서술한다.
B6	(말하기지도) speaking 활동의 문제점과 해결 방법을 서술한다.
B7	(쓰기지도) content와 organization을 향상시킨 방법을 서술한다.
B10	(어휘지도) collocation과 grammar 향상을 위한 방법을 서술한다.
B11	(평가) multiple choice평가를 만드는 guideline을 이해하고 서술한다.

▍2022학년도 ▍ 영어교육론 기출문제 내용분석표 (36점)

기입형
A1	(평가) 평가 유형과 평가 원리에서 washback이 미치는 영향을 이해한다.
A2	(교수법) 두 교사의 대화를 통해 효과적인 integrated approach을 이해한다.

서술형
A8	(듣기지도) comprehension-based 학습을 위한 processing 방법을 서술한다.
A9	(개별전략) 개별적인 언어학습 전략에 대하여 추천하고 특성을 서술한다.
A10	(실용언어) 학습자 언어의 pragmatic 측면을 구체적으로 서술한다.
A12	(교재론) online 교재에 근거하여 speaking과 발음연습의 방법을 서술한다.
B6	(언어지도) lexical cohesive devices의 쓰임과 내용을 서술한다.
B7	(쓰기지도) genre를 가르치기 위한 쓰기지도의 방법을 구체적으로 서술한다.
B10	(평가) 교사가 목표로 하는 쓰기의 평가방법을 찾아 서술한다.
B11	(문법지도) focus on form으로 목표 언어를 가르치는 방식을 서술한다.

기출문제 분석표

▎2021학년도 ▎영어교육론 기출문제 내용분석표 (36점)

기입형
A1	(교재론) 실제 교실활동에서 사용되는 realia를 찾아 쓴다.
B1	(평가) 쓰기평가에서 intrarater reliability를 이해한다.

서술형
A8	(말하기지도) 말하기지도에서 fluency와 complexity중심으로 진행되는 방법을 서술한다.
A9	(통합지도) 통합교육의 성취기준을 이해하고 활동과 연결하여 서술한다.
A10	(2언어습득) foreigner talk에서 나타나는 언어의 수정과정을 서술한다.
A12	(어휘지도) collocation과 context의 사용을 사전에 대비하여 서술한다.
B6	(쓰기지도) 글쓰기의 grammar, mechanics, organization을 이해하고 지도방법을 서술한다.
B7	(2언어습득) 언어의 발달단계, fronting & inversion를 서술한다.
B8	(문화활동) culture capsule과 culture island 활동의 특성을 서술한다.
B9	(통합활동) information transfer와 partial dictation의 특성을 서술한다.

▎2020학년도 ▎영어교육론 기출문제 내용분석표 (28점)

기입형
A1	(어휘학습) 어휘를 익힐 때 depth의 중요성을 서술한다.
A2	(curriculum) 교육과정 작성시에 가장 시작이 되는 needs analysis를 이해한다.
A3	(언어지도) 언어의 적절성을 맞추기 위해서 formality의 필요성을 이해한다.
B2	(교재론) 교재작성의 필수요소에서 authenticity의 중요성을 이해한다.

서술형
A5	(담화론) 대화에서 사용되는 전략중에서 cataphoric words와 hedges의 쓰임에 대하여 예시와 함께 서술한다.
A10	(학습전략) outlining 방법에 대하여 이해하고 본문의 내용을 요약하여 서술한다.
B4	(2언어습득) 의사협상을 하는 과정인 trigger, indicator, response, reaction을 이해하고 각 과정의 예시를 찾아 방법을 서술한다.
B6	(영어평가) 평가에서 이론과 다르게 시행된 두 단계, internal consistency, item discrimination과 concurrent validity를 찾아 그 이유를 서술한다.
B10	(수업활동) 수업활동에서 language와 delivery가 잘 시행되지 않은 이유를 찾아 서술한다.

▎2019학년도 ▎ 영어교육론 기출문제 내용분석표 (32점)

기입형

A1	(2언어습득) 학습자의 유형분류: auditory, visual, kinesthetic
A2	(영어평가) 통합기술을 위한 c-test, rational/ random deletion: cloze
A3	(2언어습득) 의사소통을 위한 피드백의 종류: elicitation

서술형

A11	(2언어습득) 오류의 기원 interference와 overgeneralization을 분류하고 특히 한국어 학습자에게서 나타나는 특성을 interlingually 설명할 수 있다.
A12	(task 활동) purpose, time allocation, scoring의 교사 수업 방법을 설명한다.
A14	(writing 지도) process-based 수업에서 recursive vs linear와 meaning vs form focused feedback의 비교를 통해 서술한다.
B4	(2언어습득) 의사소통 전략을 쓸 때 구체적인 예시를 통해 avoidance, appeal to authority, word coinage를 설명한다.

논술형

B8	(수업과정) 두 교사의 수업을 비교하여 curriculum, objectives, formative assessment 에서 일치하는 것과 그렇지 않은 것을 선택하여 설명할 수 있다.

▎2018학년도 ▎ 영어교육론 기출문제 내용분석표

기입형

A1	(영어교수법) 학습의 차이 이해: incidental & intentional
A3	(CALL) 기존의 수업과 반대방향의 새로운 학습법의 시도: flipped learning
A7	(영어교수법) sociocultural theory에서 zone of proximal development 안에서 scaffolding을 통해 학습이 나아가는 방향을 이해한다.

서술형

A10	(영어교수법) TBLT를 syllabus차원에서의 문제점을 쓰는 것이므로 synthetic/ analytic의 비교로 언어를 separate하지 않고 whole로 가르친다는 내용을 서술한다.
A13	(영어평가) diagnostic 평가의 특성으로 before the class, 학습자의 장단점을 확인할 수 있으며 나아갈 방향에 대한 guide를 제시할 수 있다는 것을 서술한다.
B5	(2언어습득) 실제상황에서 학습자의 own ideas를 이용하여 target form을 사용하고 meaning negotiation으로 interaction을 하는 활동을 서술한다.

논술형

B8	(영어교수법) 선임교사의 조언에 따라 잘 수행되는 활동과 그렇지 못한 활동을 구별하여 설명할 수 있다. objective request라는 function에 대한 활동과 strategies, approximation과 body language와 local error, explicit correction feedback의 설명이 포함된다.

기출문제 분석표

▌2017학년도 ▌ 영어교육론 기출문제 내용분석표

기입형

A1	(통합수업) Ss 스스로 탐구하고 수행하는 활동: portfolio(s)
A6	(읽기지도) reading skills: skimming과 scanning

서술형

A9	(영어평가) criterion-related validation에서 predictive validity를 알아내고 입학점수 CEE와 학업성적 GPA와의 positive association을 서술한다.
A13	(읽기지도) phonics approach에 나타난 문제점을 이해하고, sound value 중심읽기 에서의 이해도의 부족을 context로 보충해야 한다고 서술한다.
B1	(문법지도) form-focused instruction의 두 종류, formS와 form를 이해하고 그 특성을 서술한다.
B2	(교재분석) material adaptation을 하는 이유, personalize를 찾고 adding과 reordering의 기법을 서술한다.
B4	(2언어습득) meaning negotiation strategies를 두 학생의 대화 속에서 찾아 clarification requests와 comprehension checks를 각각 서술한다.

논술형 B

B8	(영어교수법) 두 교실을 비교하여 각 교사의 다른 roles와 seating arrangement에서 나타난 class management차이를 비교 서술한다.

▌2016학년도 ▌ 영어교육론 기출문제 내용분석표

기입형

A1	(2언어습득) 학습 방법: strategies
A3	(말하기활동) 활동 기법: jigsaw
A7	(화용론) 다양한 영어의 발전: world Englishes
A8	(화용론) communicative competence를 기르기 위해 social context안에서 습득되는 요소: sociolinguistic competence & speech act

서술형

A12	(2언어습득) feedback 종류에 대한 설명과 효과적인 방법 분석한다.
A13	(영어평가) 효과적인 평가원리와 부족한 원리를 분석한다.
B1	(영어평가) 수업에서 summative test의 문제점과 formative test 개선점을 서술한다.
B3	(쓰기지도) schema활성화와 writing방법에 대한 서술한다.
B5	(문법수업) deductive와 inductive learning에 대하여 서술한다.

논술형 B

B8	(영어교수법) mechanical/ meaningful drills활동에서 communicative competence를 기를 수 있는 활동에 대하여 설명할 수 있다.

▌2015학년도 ▌ 영어교육론 기출문제 내용분석표

기입형
A2	(2언어습득) output modification: lexical & syntactic
A3	(영어평가) item analysis: facility, discrimination & distractor
A4	(말하기지도) speaking function의 두 가지 종류: interpersonal & transactional
A5	(읽기지도) pleasure, within the level, own choice를 위한 방법: extensive reading

서술형
A1	(통합수업) culture-integrated수업의 objectives 서술한다.
A2	(2언어습득) feedback에 따른 학생의 uptake와 그를 위한 strategy 관계를 서술한다.
B1	(교재론) 가장 적합한 CMC자료를 선정하여 그 이유를 서술한다.

논술형
B2	(영어교수법) 수업 observation에서 나타난 문제점과 해결책을 제시할 수 있다.

▌2014학년도 ▌ 영어교육론 기출문제 내용분석표

기입형
A7	(영어평가) 평가의 유형과 신뢰도의 종류: interrater & intrarater reliability
A8	(2언어습득) 학습자 오류의 근원: overgeneralization
A9	(쓰기수업) 과정중심에서 revising 단계: time expression와 peer-feedback
A10	(읽기지도) 전략의 종류: inferencing

서술형
B2	(화용론) request에 대한 interactional moves에서 discourse의 문제점과 전략을 서술한다.
B3	(교재론) 수업 활동과 과업을 위한 교과서의 특성을 분석한다.
B6	(문법지도) meaning과 form 수업을 위한 input processing을 설명한다.

논술형
B2	(영어교수법) 수업의 강점과 약점을 이해하고 그룹안에서 낮은 레벨의 학생을 위한 해결방법을 제시한다.

기출문제 분석표

▌2013학년도 ▌ 영어교육론 기출문제 내용분석표

객관식 문항

15	학습자 중심의 문법 교수법
16	어휘의 collocation을 가르치는 수업절차 이해
17	2언어 습득 및 학습에 대한 이론을 이해
18	두 가지 다른 syllabus에 대해 비교 분석
19	듣기 수업 절차를 읽고 각 단계 특징들을 이해
20	교재 분석 및 평가를 분석
21	online blog를 활용한 수업을 이해
22	각 수업활동의 역할과 기능을 이해
23	교사의 쓰기지도 능력을 평가
24	쓰기지도를 위한 피드백의 유형을 이해
25	multiple-choice items 제작시 유의점을 이해
26	과거시제를 익히기 위한 form-focused 수업절차
27	문항분석표를 보고 문항난이도와 변별도를 올바르게 해석
28	process-writing의 진행단계와 문제해결을 위한 협동과업

▌2012학년도 ▌ 영어교육론 기출문제 내용분석표

객관식 문항

15	교사의 교수방법과 학생의 학습전략의 차이에서 오는 문제점
16	structure-based & experiential-based Syllabus
17	교사의 다양한 피드백
18	교재분석에 따른 평가표 이해
19	평가의 기본적 원리와 특징
20	듣기의 topdown processing을 통한 교실활동적용
22	말하기평가 유형분석으로 방법이해
23	deductive teaching 방법
24	suprasegmental (prominence)강세발음 지도
25	product-oriented Writing유형
26	읽기수업의 교수접근방법
27	통합수업의 수업계획표 분석
28	TPR과 communicative language teaching 수업 비교분석
29	collocation 수업 과정 분석

2011학년도 | 영어교육론 기출문제 내용분석표

객관식 문항

15	수업에서의 교재론의 활용성
16	대조분석학과 상황중심교수법에서의 언어습득
17	읽기의 pre-, while, post-활동의 절차
18	Focus on FormS와 Focus on Form의 차이 이해
19	교사의 Teaching Log를 통한 교수방법
20	수업활동의 행동주의, Input, Output Hypothesis
21	Multiple choice시험에서 항목분석표 이해
22	듣기수업의 과정이해
23	Task based Language Teaching 절차이해
24	교수요목의 차이점 이해
25	semantic mapping 어휘 활동의 이해
27	ICT Web Quest활동을 통한 쓰기수업
28	교실활동의 다양한 Feedback 분석
29	발음지도의 활동방법

2010학년도 | 영어교육론 기출문제 내용분석표

객관식 문항

15	learning log를 통한 학습전략 이해
16	Conferencing을 통한 쓰기 평가
17	최근 영어 교수법 ESP 활용방법
18	Task based Language Teaching 과업 종류
19	문법 Garden Path Strategy 지도의 원리
20	말하기 활동 Jigsaw activity 이해
21	Cloze Test와 C-Test에 대한 원리이해
22	쓰기 활동 Dicto-comp
23	Content based Instruction의 종류
24	Input enhancement 활동의 특징이해
25	읽기수업에서 자기 평가표 분석하기
26	쓰기지도를 위한 수업설계와 절차
27	말하기활동에 대한 교수학습법 이론 적용
29	교재분석의 다양한 영역 이해

기출문제 분석표

▎2009학년도 ▎

(1) 영어교육론 기출문제 내용분석표

객관식 문항	
14	쓰기 활동에서의 Feedback
15	Post-reading 그룹 활동
16	Integrated Teaching의 수업 방안
17	ALM 활동의 원리이해
18	Multiple choice시험에서 항목분석표 이해
19	semantic network를 활용한 어휘지도 수업
20	학습을 위한 학습자전략과 동기 원리
21	Form vs Meaning의 교수법
22	수업의 담화 방법
23	교재의 구성방법
24	Pushed output – Interaction Hypothesis
25	reading의 다양한 활동이해
26	ICT를 활용한 Process Writing
28	글의 register를 이해하는 듣기 지도

(2) 평가원모의고사 내용분석표

객관식 문항	
11	쓰기 활동을 통한 정의적인 학습자 전략
12	중간언어발달 – Interaction Hypothesis
17	meaning negotiation에 따른 학습 효과
18	듣기와 문법학습 통합지도
19	Internet Conferencing을 통한 쓰기활동
20	타당도의 종류 이해
21	중간언어발달 – Negotiation of Meaning
22	성격유형을 통한 학습전략
23	Bottomup과 topdown을 활용하는 읽기전략
26	교수학습 활동의 종류
27	교재에서 각 활동별로 의미와 언어형식의 방법
28	어휘중심과 과업중심교수법의 교수요목 이해
29	어휘 학습방식의 이해 (어원분석과 word family)
32	교수요목(Competency-based)의 특징이해
33	말하기 연습방법이해 (기계적방법 vs 인지적방법)

2008학년도

(1) (서울, 인천) 영어교육론 기출문제 내용분석표

	서술형 문항
8 (4점)	synthetic & analytic syllabus의 차이와 특성을 이해하여 차이를 세단어 구문으로 서술한다.
9 (3점)	constructivist가 주장하는 scaffolding의 개념을 이해하고 지문에 나타나는 dialogue에서 보이는 내용을 참조하여 본문의 내용을 채워 넣는다.
10 (3점)	authentic한 글의 특성을 이해하기 위하여 두 가지의 text를 비교분석하여 authentic text가 가지고 있는 특성의 기제를 설명하고 예를 찾는다.
11 (4점)	authentic material이 가져야 하는 특성을 서술한다. 내용의 단순화보다는 학생들이 하는 과업을 단순화시키는 것이 더 효과적이다.
12 (3점)	CAI 활동의 종류와 특성을 연결한다.
13 (4점)	어휘지식에 포함되어야 하는 내용들을 상세하게 이해한다.
15 (4점)	cloze test의 실제 평가하는 내용항목들을 파악하여 그 예들을 이론에 맞게 연결한다.
16 (3점)	process-writing의 과정을 수업활동에 맞추어 나열한다.

(2) (전국) 영어교육론 기출문제 내용분석표

	서술형 문항
6 (4점)	computer-adaptive test의 특성을 이해하고 본문을 완성한다.
7 (3점)	문법요소를 평가하기 위한 평가지의 필수요소에 대한 내용을 채워넣는다.
8 (3점)	글의 style에 대한 설명을 읽고 그를 잘 표현하는 내용정리를 연결한다.
9 (4점)	interaction hypothesis에서 negative evidence와 modified output의 예를 dialogue에서 찾는다.
10 (3점)	쓰기활동에서 introduction을 미루지 말아야하는 이유에 대하여 요약한다.
11 (3점)	structured word net에서 배울 수 있는 내용을 지문을 통해 파악하고 요약한다.
12 (4점)	교실상황에 맞는 수업 활동과 적절치 못한 수업활동을 파악하고 이유를 설명한다.
13 (4점)	문법지식의 declarative & procedural knowledge에 대한 차이를 이해한다.

기출문제 분석표

2007학년도

(1) (서울, 인천) 영어교육론 기출문제 내용분석표

서술형 문항

문항	내용
6 (3점)	읽기에서 interactive compensatory model의 특성을 이해하고 두 단어로 요약정리한다.
7 (4점)	학생의 발화에 대한 교사의 적절한 피드백을 연결한다.
8 (4점)	interaction hypothesis에서 학생의 발화와 언어습득의 관계를 이해한다.
9 (4점)	input processing instruction에서 나타나는 특성을 전통식 문법수업과 비교하여 이해한다.
10 (3점)	학교 project를 통한 활동내용의 본문을 읽고 글의 제목을 7자로 표현한다.
11 (3점)	self-report 자료에 대한 본문을 읽고 그 특성을 8자로 표현한다.
15 (4점)	수업활동과 teaching principles에 대한 연결을 요구하는 내용으로 각 하나의 단어로 표현한다.
21 (9점)	교실에서 학습능력에 따라 나누어지는 ability grouping에 대한 본인이 생각하는 장점이나 단점을 두 가지 이유로 설명한다. 100 단어로 서술한다.

(2) (전국) 영어교육론 기출문제 내용분석표

서술형 문항

문항	내용
2 (4점)	authentic material & media 사용의 장단점을 본문에서 찾아 우리말로 서술한다.
5 (3점)	문법지도활동 4가지를 놓고 가장 accuracy에서 fluency oriented 된 활동을 순서대로 배열한다.
7 (3점)	form-focused approach의 효과적인 교수 방법을 본문내용에 맞게 요약 서술한다.
9 (4점)	언어학습에서 문학교육의 의의와 전통적 수업에서 문학작품을 대하는 태도를 읽고 이해하여 우리말로 서술한다. (20자와 50자)
10 (3점)	Suggestopedia 영어교수법의 수업현장과 수업원리를 읽고 명칭을 작성한다.
11 (3점)	영어 교재론에 대한 문제로서 독해지문의 성격을 파악하고 각 문항에서 요구하는 이해도의 수준을 연결한다.
14 (3점)	communication strategy를 이해하고 대화상에 나타난 실제의 예와 전략을 연결한다.
15 (4점)	읽기교수방법에서 쓰이는 활동들의 이름과 활동내용을 연결한다.
18 (3점)	performance objectives의 구성요소와 구체적인 예를 연결한다.
19 (4점)	interaction hypothesis를 이해하고 본문의 내용에 맞는 단어를 채워넣고 30자 단어의 요약문을 작성한다.

2006학년도

(1) (전국) 영어교육론 기출문제 내용분석표

	서술형 문항
3 (3점)	comprehensible output hypothesis의 개념을 토대로 본문의 내용을 요약한다.
5 (2점)	adjacency pairs의 개념을 이해하고 적절한 발화의 예를 본문에서 요구하는 발화와 매칭 시킨다.
8 (2점)	syllabus의 변천을 이해하고 alternative syllabus를 찾아 서술한다.
13 (4점)	concordance 프로그램의 특징을 이해하고 이 프로그램을 통해서 얻을 수 있는 어휘정보와 어휘 지도 활동을 고른다.
14 (5점)	task의 특성과 유형을 파악하고 각 class activity에 해당하는 task유형을 본문에서 찾아서 작성한다.
15 (2점)	Sapir-whorf hypothesis의 개념을 정확히 이해하고 이 이론을 비판하는 입장의 글을 찾는다.
16 (3점)	materials, classroom methods, lessons를 만들기까지의 과정을 본문을 통해 파악하고 빈칸을 채워넣는다.
17 (4점)	본문에서 설명하는 수업상황을 파악하고 그에 해당하는 수업목표를 찾는다.
18 (4점)	두 가지 drill 유형을 보고 audio-lingual method와 communicative language teaching중 어디에 속하는지 구분하고 각각의 특징을 파악하라.
20 (3점)	컴퓨터를 활용한 쓰기수업이 예를 보고 각 수업에서 적용된 쓰기 활동 유형을 찾는다.
21 (2점)	신뢰도 추정방법의 두 가지 설명이 intrarater reliability인지 interrater reliability인지 선택한다.

(2) (서울) 영어교육론 기출문제 내용분석표

	서술형 문항
2 (4점)	cohesion과 coherence의 차이와 특성을 참조하여 본문의 내용을 채워 넣는다.
7 (4점)	heterogeneous class가 가지고 있는 장점과 단점을 본문에 근거하여 서술한다.
8 (4점)	두 명의 교사가 어디에 초점을 맞추고 수업을 진행하는지 accuracy, substitution, meaningful한 이 세 가지 측면에서 25자 내외로 서술하시오.
10 (3점)	multiple-choice question을 만들 때의 주의사항을 본문의 내용을 통해 숙지하고 빈칸을 채운다.
15 (3점)	Ss의 level을 고려한 pre-reading / pre-listening activity의 특성을 이해하고 본문에서 보이는 내용을 참조하여 빈칸을 채워넣는다.
16 (3점)	explicit correction, recasts, clarification requests를 본문의 내용을 통해 숙지하고 예를 찾아 매칭 시킨다.

기출문제 분석표

2005학년도

(1) (서울) 영어교육론 기출문제 내용분석표

서술형 문항

문항	내용
2 (3점)	motherese와 foreigner talk의 차이점을 본문을 통해 이해하고, 특징단어를 채워 넣는다.
3 (2점)	vocabulary learning에서 explicit/ incidental learning의 중요성을 요약한다.
4 (4점)	explicit vocabulary learning의 약점 2가지를 본문에서 찾아 각각 25자 이내로 서술한다.
8 (2점)	예시를 통해 발화의 modification의 개념을 이해한다: negotiation of meaning & comprehensible input
9 (2점)	교사의 modified input의 특징을 두 단어로 쓴다.
12 (2점)	본문에서 설명된 material adaptation의 특성을 이해하고 빈칸을 채워 넣는다.
16,7 (4점)	sociolinguistic competence를 예를 통해 특성을 이해하고 빈칸을 채워 넣는다.
18 (3점)	online learning의 특성을 이해하고 장점과 단점을 각각 서술한다.
19 (2점)	Ss의 composition을 읽고 teacher's written feedback의 빈칸을 완성한다.
20 (2점)	Ss의 composition에서 function words사용의 mistake를 고르고 correction을 제공한다.
22 (2점)	교실 상황에서 결여된 validity type: content validity
24 (2점)	본문을 통해 authentic materials 사용의 잠재적 문제점을 7단어로 쓴다.
25 (3점)	authentic materials 사용에 관한 교사의 충고를 15자로 쓴다.

(2) (전국) 기출문제 내용분석표

서술형 문항

문항	내용
6 (3점)	교실 수업상황을 보고 lesson plan의 빈칸에 적절한 활동과 목차를 작성한다.
7 (3점)	unplaned and unrehearsed spoken language에서 사용된 발화의 유형을 보기에서 연결한다.
8 (4점)	지문에서의 교실 영어의 예를 보고 선생님이 사용하는 수업 활동의 이름을 작성한다.
9 (3점)	concordancing, MUDs & MOOs, and voice recognition & production을 이해하고 그 특성을 보기에서 찾아 쓴다.
10 (2점)	문항내용을 이해하고 주어진 데이터의 IF(difficulty)와 ID(discrimination)를 계산한다.
12 (4점)	collocation과 lexical chunk를 이해하고 관련된 approach와 특성을 작성한다.
13 (3점)	평가에 중요한 6가지 개념 (reliability, construct validity, interactiveness, authenticity, practicality)를 이해하고 그 개념들을 요약된 그림에 연결한다.
14 (3점)	Chomsky가 주장하는 LAD의 개념과 second language acquisition의 관계에 관한 글을 요약하고 adult와 children의 차이를 이해한다.
17 (4점)	item analysis에서의 주의해야 할 상황들과 특히 context의 중요성을 이해하고 주어진 본문을 요약한다.

20 (2점)	ESL/EFL class에서 문학을 사용하는 이유를 이해하고 관련된 세부내용을 연결한다.
22 (4점)	measure of speech rate에 관한 본문을 통해 2~4단어를 사용하여 table의 제목을 쓰고 발화속도를 단어 단위로 측정하는 방법과 음절 단위로 측정하는 방법의 장·단점에 대하여 4줄이내의 우리말로 쓴다.

2004학년도

(1) (서울) 기출문제 내용분석표

서술형 문항	
2 (4점)	지문을 읽고 학생들에게 동기부여를 할 수 있는 multimedia tools를 작성한다.
6 (5점)	교사와 학생간의 interaction을 분석한 다음 교사와 학생간의 교실현상으로 빈칸을 채워 넣는다.
7 (4점)	Gestalt Approach에 대해 이해하고 그에 파생하는 2가지 method와 key word를 찾는다.
9 (5점)	주어진 teaching material과 procedure을 분석하여 빈칸 채워 넣는다.

(2) (전국) 기출문제 내용분석표

서술형 문항	
4 (3점)	self-talk의 특성에 대해 이해하고 빈칸을 채워 넣는다.
6 (4점)	읽기에서 connotation의 의도를 알고 이해하여 짧은 phrase로 서술한다.
10 (2점)	errors에 대한 글을 읽고 오류의 근원에 대하여 짧은 phrase로 서술한다.
11 (4점)	implied meaning에 대한 대화를 읽고 분석하여 채워 넣는다.
13 (4점)	class instruction procedure를 분석하여 이 수업의 장점과 예상되는 문제점을 쓴다.
14 (3점)	immersion 수업에 쓰인 teaching strategy를 분석하여 채워넣는다.
15 (3점)	pre-reading activities의 종류에 대해 이해하고 적용하여 구별 짓는다.
17 (3점)	giving feedback in writing class에 대해 이해하고 주요개념을 채워 넣는다.

기출문제 분석표

▎2003학년도 ▎

(1) (서울) 기출문제 내용분석표

	서술형 문항
2 (3점)	implied meaning의 개념을 이해하고 본문에서 밑줄 그어진 부분의 implied meaning을 분석한다.
3 (5점)	time creating, facilitation, and compensation devices를 분류하고 3가지 장치들의 공통된 기능을 서술한다.
6 (4점)	cohesion과 coherence를 이해하고 주어진 문장을 conjunction, pronouns & article을 사용하여 수정한다.
8 (3점)	recast를 사용하여 지문 속의 학생에게 줄 feedback을 서술한다.
9 (6점)	on-line non-interactive & on-line interactive technologies의 관점에서 문화지도 방법을 각각 설명한다.
10 (4점)	주어진 발화에 적용된 foreigner talk의 4가지 특성을 서술한다.
12 (5점)	본문에서 설명하는 alternative test method (dialogue journal)을 적고 학생들의 journal에 대한 response를 할 때 무엇을 해야 하는지 서술한다.
13 (4점)	norm-referenced measurement와 criterion-referenced measurement의 특성을 서술한다.

(2) (전국) 기출문제 내용분석표

	서술형 문항
8 (4점)	본문에서 input hypothesis를 이해하고 comprehensible input과 silent period 명칭을 작성한다.
9 (2점)	지문의 어휘력 평가의 distractors가 적절치 못한 이유를 서술한다.
10 (3점)	지문의 설명과 교수법에 사용된 integrated approach의 한 교수법의 명칭을 작성한다.
11 (2점)	지문의 학생들이 사용하는 communication strategies를 보기에서 연결한다.
12 (2점)	영어 청취 수업에서 느린 속도보다 보통 속도로 된 자료의 활용을 권장하는 이유를 우리말로 2가지 서술한다.
13 (4점)	지문을 잘 이해하기 위해 필요한 담화능력 요소를 찾고, 그 예를 지문에서 찾는다.
14 (4점)	교사의 feedback을 보기의 feedback유형과 연결하고 그 유형의 특성을 서술한다.

2002학년도

(1) (전국) 기출문제 내용분석표

	서술형 문항
8 (4점)	empathic listening의 특성과 방법을 알고 예시문을 서술한다.
9 (3점)	문화가 언어에 미치는 영향을 이해하고 key word 찾는다.
10 (4점)	'dicto-comp' 수업의 특징을 이해하고 그 process를 서술한다.
11 (5점)	total physical response의 일종인 audio-motor unit과 draw the picture 기법의 공통점과 차이점을 작성한다.
12 (4점)	constructive view of language testing에 관해 이해하고 빈칸 넣는다.
13 (4점)	CALL을 사용한 지문의 수업계획안을 분석하고 이 수업의 긍정적 효과를 4가지 측면 (교재활용, 교수법, 학습자, 쓰기학습)에서 기술한다.
14 (4점)	두 대화지문을 분석하고 더 authentic한 대화를 찾고 근거를 서술한다.

(2) (서울) 기출문제 내용분석표

	서술형 문항
2 (4점)	sociocultural competence의 오류를 파악하고 적절한 표현으로 수정한다.
3 (4점)	curriculum의 차이를 파악하여 그 차이점을 요약 서술한다.
6 (4점)	학생의 작문에 나타난 의미와 문법의 오류를 찾아 바르게 수정한다.
7 (5점)	syllabus의 종류와 문제점을 알고 근거 두가지를 서술한다.
8 (4점)	한국 환경에서 instrumental과 intrinsic/ extrinsic motivation의 실례를 서술 한다.
9 (4점)	어휘 수업의 implicit/ explicit 방법을 읽고 요약 정리한다.
10 (4점)	TPR의 방법에 대한 본문을 읽고 그를 위한 실제 교실활동의 예를 서술한다.
11 (5점)	multimedia 사용의 종류와 장점을 각각 3개씩 서술한다.
13 (5점)	듣기수업에서 topdown과 bottomup 방식특징을 서술하고 활동의 종류를 구별한다.
14 (3점)	읽기전략에서 사용되는 topdown 방식의 한 예를 읽고 맞는 방법을 찾아낸다.
15 (3점)	portfolio 평가를 수행하는데 필요한 기준을 두 가지 서술한다.

PART 1

Teaching and Learning in Classroom Practices

01. Teaching by Principles
02. Motivation
03. Context of Learning and Teaching

CHAPTER 01 Teaching by Principles

> **단원 길라잡이**
> - 여러 학습법과 교수법을 통합하는 기저에 깔린 교육적 원리를 이해할 수 있다.
> - 각 원리들에 있는 여러 측면을 교실수업에 적용시킬 수 있다.
> - 내적 동기와 외적 동기를 이해하고 내적 동기가 수업 내에서 어떻게 구현되는지 이해할 수 있을 것이다.

Introduction

이제 영어 선생님이 되기 위한 임용시험을 위하여 전공 영어에서 영어교육론의 이론과 실제를 이해하는 여행을 시작해 보기로 한다. 영어교육론이라는 과목은 교육의 전반적인 이론을 이해하고 교실 안에서 우리 학생들에게 적용하는 방법들을 고민하는 학문이다. 정확히 표현하면 학문이라기보다는 실천 이론이라고 하는 것이 더 정확할 수 있겠다. 이것은 어딘가 멀리 있는 이상향의 이야기가 아니라 영어선생님이 되어서 만나게 될 학생들을 가르치면서 당면하게 될 문제에 관한 이야기이다. 더 가까이는 전공영어에서 40~50%에 달하는 높은 배점에서 좋은 점수를 받기 위하여 공부하게 되어야 할 것이다. 영어교육론은 1차 시험의 합격을 위해서만 필요할 것이 아니라 수업시연을 하는 2차 시험을 위한 준비를 제공하게 될 것이다. 즉, 지금부터 읽고 공부하는 모든 내용들이 교실 현장에서 수업을 할 때 학생들에게 적용하는 내용이 되어야 할 것이다.

그 출발점으로 영어교육론의 교수 기본이론에 들어가 보기로 하겠다. 가장 먼저 무엇을 보아야 하는지 생각해 보자. 학습자들이 2언어습득을 하는데 도움을 주기 위해서 가장 중요한 것이 무엇이 될까? 선생님으로써 끊임없이 고민해야 할 내용이다. 우선적으로 learning과 teaching의 원리를 이해하고 그 원리에 따라 교육을 실시하는 것이 필요하다. 이론과 실제를 이해하고 내재화함으로써 교육을 발전시킬 수 있다는 것이다. 그래서 가장 기본이 될 수 있는 교수 원리 12가지에 대하여 알아보기로 하자. 이 원리는 cognitive, affective, linguistic principles로 크게 나뉘고 다시 그 안에서 12개의 세부 개념으로 나뉠 수 있다. 이제 이 기본 개념이 영어교육론의 중추가 되어 계속 통합되고 연관될 것이니 꼭 기억해 놓고 가도록 해야겠다.

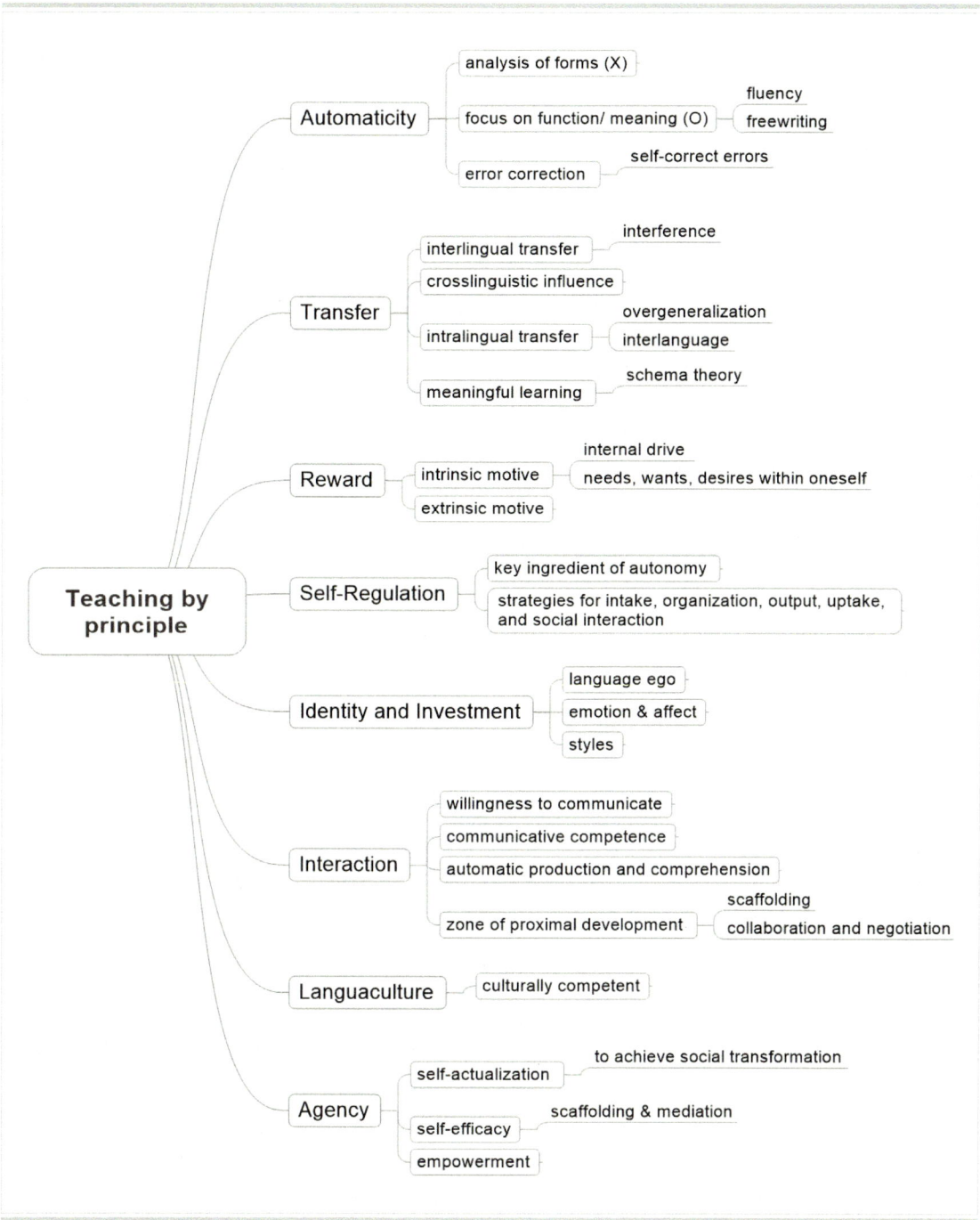

01 Cognitive Principles

1. Automaticity

Efficient second language learning involves a timely movement of the control of a few language forms into the automatic processing of a relatively unlimited number of language forms. Overanalyzing language, thinking too much about its forms, and consciously lingering on rules of language all tend to impede this graduation to automaticity.

(1) Attention-Processing Model

- The childlike, subconscious processing: automatic processing with peripheral attention to language forms
- In order to manage the incredible complexity and quantity of language, one must move away from processing language unit by unit, focusing closely on each, and graduate to a form of high-speed, automatic processing in which language forms are only on the periphery of attention.

(2) Automaticity Principles

- Subconscious absorption of language through meaningful use
- Efficient and rapid movement away from a focus on the forms of language to a focus on the purposes of language
- Efficient and rapid movement away from a capacity-limited control of a few bits and pieces to a relatively unlimited automatic mode of processing language forms
- Resistance to the temptation to analyze language forms

(3) Classroom Applications

- Make sure that a major proportion of classroom activity is focused on the use of language for purposes that are as authentic as a classroom context will permit. 예 task-based activity, group and pair work, and involvement in topics that are relevant to students' lives
- Practice exercises and explanations dealing with grammar, vocabulary, phonology, discourse, and other forms have a place in the adult classroom, but don't overwhelm your students with a focus on form. 예 Short, five-minute grammar-focus exercises may be more helpful than long explanations or lectures from you.
- When you focus your students on form, your goal is to help them to notice forms, to modify or correct errors when appropriate, and ultimately to incorporate that information into their language use. 예 Error correction is more effective if students are

- made aware of an error and are encouraged to self-correct.
- Fluency activities, in which you deliberately do not focus on forms, may help students to attend to meaning or to accomplishing a task, and to unblock their overattention to form. 예 freewriting, in which students are asked to write about a topic of interest with virtually no attention, at this stage, to correctness
- Automaticity is a slow and sometimes tedious process; therefore, you need to exercise patience with students as you slowly help them to achieve fluency. Don't expect your students to become chatterboxes overnight in their new language.

2. Transfer

(1) Types

① Interlingual transfer (interference) : Any difficulty in learning an L2 could be equated to the differences between a learner's first and second languages.
　※ Crosslinguistic influence: The difference between influence, rather than prediction is important to capture the range of syntactic, lexical, discourse, and pragmatic interference that can occur.

② Intralingual transfer (overgeneralization) : It is a hot topic in analyzing sources of error in learners' output, and in describing interlanguage of learners.

③ Meaningful learning : Cognitive psychologists revolutionized educational psychology by stressing the importance of meaningful learning for long-term retention. Transfer underlies all meaningful learning. If a task in a group activity puts learners into a familiar context, new grammatical, lexical, and discourse forms will be more easily embedded into students' L2 competence. And in learning to read and write, schema theory encourages students to relate existing knowledge, of both content and skills, to new material.

(2) Classroom Applications

- If topics and context for tasks are associated with something students already know, then linguistic features will be more easily learned. Become acquainted with your students' backgrounds, interests, personalities, occupations, hobbies, likes and dislikes, and ground classroom activities on those individual characteristics.
- When introducing new grammar, vocabulary, or discourse features, review previously learned material on which the new material is based through brainstorming or clustering activities.
- As you teach one skill area, connect what students are learning to other skills such as speaking or reading. Avoid the pitfalls of rote learning. Base your teaching as much as possible on content that learners can identify with, as opposed to grammar-driven teaching.

3. Reward

(1) B. F. Skinner: The anticipation of reward is the most powerful factor in directing one's behavior. Human beings are universally driven to act, or behave, by the anticipation of some sort of reward, tangible or intangible, short term or long term, that will ensue as a result of the behavior.

(2) Disadvantages
- Conditioning by rewards can lead learners to become dependent on short-term rewards.
- Conditioning by rewards can coax them into a habit of looking to teachers and others for their only rewards.
- Conditioning by rewards can forestall the development of their own internally administered, intrinsic system of rewards.

(3) Classroom Applications
- Provide an optimal degree of immediate verbal praise and encouragement to students as a form of short-term reward.
- Encourage students to reward each other with compliments and supportive action. Display enthusiasm and excitement yourself in the classroom.
- Encourage learners to see the intrinsic, long-term rewards in learning an L2 by pointing out what they can do with the language, the benefits of being able to use it, jobs that require it, and so on.
- Give your students some choices in types of activities, content, or subject matter so that they feel some 'ownership' of their language development. Encourage students to discover for themselves certain principles and rules, rather than simply giving them an answer.

4. Self-Regulation

(1) The key to successful language learning is self-regulation, 'deliberate goal-directed attempts to manage and control efforts to learn the L2'. One of the key foundation stones of effective L2 pedagogy today is to create a climate in which learners develop autonomy, 'the capacity to control one's learning' and self-regulation is cited as a key ingredient of autonomy.

(2) Classroom Applications
- Teachers can help beginners to be able to develop a sense of autonomy through guided practice, strategy training, and allowing some creative innovation within limited forms.

- As learners gain confidence and begin to be able to experiment with language, implement activities in the classroom that allow creativity.
- Encourage students to set some goals for their self-regulated learning.
- Help your students to become aware of their own preferences, styles, strengths, and weaknesses, so that they can then take appropriate [self-regulated] action in the form of strategies for better learning.
- Pair and group work and other interactive activities that are focused on tasks provide opportunities for students to practice language, and to be creative in their choices of vocabulary, grammar, and discourse.
- Praise students for trying language that's a little beyond their present capacity. Provide feedback on their speech – just enough to be helpful, but not so much that you stifle their creativity. Suggest opportunities for students to use their language outside of class.

5. Identity and Investment

(1) The language ego concept is more elegantly refined and expanded into as identity: the extent to which L2 learners do not perceive themselves merely as individual entities but, more importantly investment of time, effort, and attention to the second language in the form of an individualized battery of strategies for comprehending and producing the language. The methods that the learner employs to internalize and to perform in the language are as important as the teacher's methods.

(2) Classroom Applications

Overtly display a supportive attitude to your students. Your patience, affirmation, and empathy need to be openly communicated: the need for attention to each separate individual in the classroom.

(3) Difficulty of Applications

- There are a variety of learning styles among learners. Learners also employ a multiplicity of strategies for sending and receiving language and one learner's strategies for success may differ markedly from another's.
- A variety of techniques in your lessons will at least partially ensure that you will reach a maximum number of students. So you will choose a mixture of group work and individual work, of visual and auditory techniques, of easy and difficult exercises.

(4) Strategies-Based Instruction

You can solve some aspects of the dilemma surrounding variation and need for individualization in a classroom.

- Am I seizing whatever opportunity I can to let learners in on the secrets to develop and use strategies for learning and communication?
- Do my lessons and impromptu feedback adequately sensitize students to the wisdom of their taking responsibility for their own language?
- How can I ensure that my students will want to put forth the effort of trying out some strategies?

6. Autonomy Principle

(1) Successful mastery of a foreign language will depend to a great extent on learners' autonomous ability both to take initiative in the classroom and to continue their journey to success beyond the classroom and the teacher.

(2) Classroom Applications
- Learners at the beginning stages of a language will be somewhat dependent on the teacher but teachers can help beginners to develop a sense of autonomy through guided practice.
- Don't forget that pair and group work and other interactive activities provide opportunities for students to do language on their own.
- Encourage creativity and praise students for trying language that's a little beyond their present capacity.

02 Socioaffective Principles

1. Willingness to Communicate

(1) Principles

Willingness to Communicate combines concepts of self-confidence and risk-taking and two other related constructs: anxiety, that is, the extent to which learners may worry about themselves; and self-efficacy, a person's belief in his or her ability to accomplish a task. Successful language learners generally believe in themselves and in their capacity to accomplish communicative tasks, and are therefore willing risk takers in their attempts to produce and to interpret language that is a bit beyond their absolute certainty. Their willingness to communicate results in the generation of both output and input.

(2) Classroom Applications

- Give ample verbal and nonverbal assurances to students, affirming your belief in the student's ability.
- Sequence techniques from easier to more difficult. As a teacher you are called on to sustain self-confidence where it already exists.
- Create an atmosphere in the classroom that encourages students to try out language.
- Provide reasonable challenges in your techniques – make them neither too easy nor too hard.

2. The Language-Culture Connection

(1) Principles

Whenever you teach a language, you also teach a complex system of cultural customs, values, and ways of thinking, feeling, and acting. Especially in second language learning contexts, the success with which learners adapt to a new cultural milieu will affect their language acquisition success, and vice versa, in some possibly significant ways.

(2) Classroom Applications

- Discuss cross-cultural differences with your students, emphasizing that no culture is better than another.
- Include among your techniques certain activities and materials that illustrate the connection between language and culture.
- Teach your students the cultural connotations, especially the sociolinguistic aspects of language. Screen your techniques for material that may be culturally offensive.
- Make explicit to your students what you may take for granted in your own culture.

(3) Acculturation

- Help students to be aware of acculturation and its stages.
- Stress the importance of the second language as a powerful tool for adjustment in the new culture.
- Be especially sensitive to any students who appear to be discouraged, then do what you can to assist them.

03. Linguistic Principles

1. The Native Language Effect

(1) Principles

The native language of learners exerts a strong influence on the acquisition of the target language system. While that native system will exercise both facilitating and interfering effects on the production and comprehension of the new language, the interfering effects are likely to be the most salient.

(2) Effects

① Interfering effects: The most salient, observable effect appears to be one of interference; the majority of a learners' errors in producing the L2, especially in the beginning levels, stem from the learners' assumption that the target language operates like the native language.

② Facilitating effects: powerful element in the process of L2 acquisition
- Less observable in learners' errors
- Give teachers something observable to react to.
- It is natural that your feedback should most often focus on interference.

(3) Classroom suggestions

- Regard learners' errors as important windows to their underlying system and provide appropriate feedback on them.
- Help your students to understand that not everything about their native language system will cause error.
- Thinking directly in the target language usually helps to minimize interference errors; try to coax students into thinking in the second language to avoid the first language clutch syndrome.

2. Interlanguage

(1) Principles

Second language learners tend to go through a systematic or quasi-systematic developmental process as they progress to full competence in the target language. Successful interlanguage development is partially a result of utilizing feedback from others.

(2) Interlanguage

Just as children develop their native language in gradual and systematic stages, adults manifest a systematic progression of acquisition of sounds and words and structures and discourse features. In the mind's eye of learners, a good deal of what they say or comprehend may be logically correct even though, from the standpoint of a native speaker's competence, its use if incorrect.

(3) Teacher Roles

Allowing learners to progress through such systematic stages of acquisition poses a delicate challenge to teachers as classroom instruction makes a significant difference in the speed and success which learners proceed through interlanguage stages of development.

(4) Distinction between affective and cognitive feedback

① Affective feedback: the extent to which we value or encourage a student's attempt to communicate
② Cognitive feedback: the extent to which we indicate an understanding of the message itself
③ Teachers should provide sufficient positive affective feedback to students and at the same time give appropriate feedback to students about whether or not their actual language is clear and unambiguous.

(5) Classroom Applications

- Try to distinguish between a student's systematic interlanguage errors and other errors. Teachers need to exercise some tolerance for certain interlanguage forms. Don't make a student feel stupid because of an interlanguage error.
- Give students the message that mistakes are not bad but that most mistakes are good indicators that innate language acquisition abilities are alive and well; mistakes are often indicators of aspects of the new language that are still developing.
- Try to get students to self-correct selected errors; the ability to self-correct may indicate readiness to use that form correctly and regularly. Provide ample affective feedback — verbal or nonverbal — to encourage students to speak.
- As you make judicious selection of which errors to treat, do so with kindness and empathy so that the students will not feel thwarted in future attempts to speak.

3. Communicative Competence

(1) The Components of Communicative Competence

Given that communicative competence is the goal of a language classroom, instruction needs to point toward all its components: organizational, pragmatic, strategic, and psychomotor. Communicative goals are best achieved by giving due attention to language use and not just usage, to fluency and not accuracy, to authentic language and contexts, and to students' eventual need to apply classroom learning to previously unrehearsed contexts in the real world: Grammatical competence, Discourse competence, Strategic competence and Sociolinguistic competence. Communicative Competence is reacting to other paradigms that emphasized attention:

- to grammatical forms
- to correct language forms
- to artificial, contrived language and techniques in the classroom
- to a finite repertoire of language forms and functions that might not have lent themselves to application in the world outside the classroom

(2) Classroom Rules

- Remember that grammatical explanations or drills or exercises are only part of a lesson or curriculum; give grammar some attention, but don't neglect the other important components of communicative competence. Some of the pragmatic aspects of language are very subtle and therefore very difficult. Make sure your lessons aim to teach such subtlety. In your enthusiasm for teaching functional and sociolinguistic aspects of language, don't forget that the psychomotor skills (pronunciation) are an important component of both. Intonation alone conveys a great deal of pragmatic information.

- Make sure that your students have opportunities to gain some fluency in English without having to be constantly wary of little mistakes. They can work on errors some other time. Try to keep every technique that you use as authentic as possible: use language that students will actually encounter in the real world and provide genuine, not rote, techniques for the actual conveyance of information of interest. Someday your students will no longer be in your classroom. Make sure you are preparing them to be independent learners and manipulators of language out there.

문헌읽기　**Processes of Intercultural language learning**

Intercultural language learning can be enriched through the processes of noticing, comparing, reflecting, and interacting.

1. Noticing
① This step involves learners becoming aware of cultural aspects and linguistic features in the target culture. This is the stage of exposure and observation.
② Example Activity
- Task: Watch a video of a Japanese tea ceremony.
- Student Experience: Students observe the gestures, language, and rituals involved, such as bowing, the use of polite expressions, and specific movements for pouring tea.
- Outcome: A student might notice, "People bow several times and use honorific language during the ceremony. It seems very formal."

2. Comparing
① Learners compare the target culture to their own, identifying similarities and differences. This stage fosters critical thinking and cultural awareness.
② Example Activity
- Task: Compare birthday celebrations in Korea and the U.S. using videos and group discussions.
- Student Experience: Korean students might share their experience of "eating seaweed soup and having family gatherings" versus "cutting a birthday cake with friends at a party" in the U.S.
- Outcome: A student might reflect, "In Korea, birthdays often emphasize family, while in the U.S., friends play a bigger role. Both cultures value sharing food, though."

3. Reflecting
① Learners think deeply about their personal reactions to the observed cultural differences and similarities, considering how they relate to their own beliefs and values.
② Example Activity
- Task: Write a journal entry about how language reflects cultural values.
- Student Experience: After learning about the use of formal and informal pronouns in French (tu and vous), students reflect on the cultural significance of politeness and hierarchy.
- Outcome: A student might write, "I think it's fascinating how the French language has specific words to show respect. In Korean, we also use honorifics, but it's more about the age difference than formality."

4. Interacting
① Definition: Learners communicate their ideas and experiences, actively engaging with others to share and reshape their understanding of cultural diversity.
② Example Activity:

- Task: Participate in a classroom debate about cultural stereotypes and how they affect cross-cultural communication.
- Student Experience: One student shares, "I used to think Americans were too direct, but now I realize it's their way of being honest." Another responds, "That's interesting! In my culture, we avoid direct comments to keep harmony."
- Outcome: Through dialogue, students reshape their interpretations, realizing that cultural norms are situational rather than universally rigid.

CHAPTER 02 Motivation

> **단원 길라잡이**
> - 2언어 습득에서 과업을 성공적으로 성취하는데 필수요소인 동기의 중요성을 이해한다.
> - 도구적-통합적 동기와 내재적-외재적 동기의 특성을 이해한다.
> - 내적 동기를 활용한 효과적인 2언어 학습방법을 연구한다.

Introduction

다음과 같은 대화가 한 한국의 중학교 교실에서 이루어질 수 있을 것 같다.

> 소영: 영어로 말하기가 너무 떨리고 제가 실력이 없어서 참여하기가 어려워요.
> 선생님: 그러면 네가 좋아하는 BTS에 대해 영어로 이야기해보면 어떨까?
> 소영: 뭐요?(신나함) 영어로 자꾸 틀리게 말하는데 어쩌죠?
> 선생님: 전혀 문제가 없어. 다 틀릴 수 있는 거야. 네가 특히 BTS 뷔에 대해 잘 알고 있으니까 다른 친구들과 선생님에게 이야기해줄거 많을거 같은데... 나도 궁금한데...

이럴 때 선생님은 소영이를 학습의 능동적 주체로 인식하고 소영이가 어려워 하는 점을 받아들이고 말하고 싶은 내용을 표현할 수 있게 도와주고 있다. 또한 틀려도 괜찮다는 이야기로 affective filter를 과감하게 낮추고 있다. 학습자의 needs를 이해하고 개개인의 현재 상태를 출발점으로 설정하여 다양한 동기 유발 방법과 학습 활동을 구안함으로써, 자신들의 언어 학습에 더 적극적으로 참여하게 할 수 있다. 학습자 스스로 학습 과정 및 내용을 결정하게 하는 등 가능한 학습 선택권을 많이 부여함으로써 잠재적 가능성이 최대한 발현될 수 있도록 하여야 한다. 이제 motivation의 종류가 무엇이며 어떻게 하여 긍정적인 motivation이 발달하여 영어학습에 도움이 될 수 있는지를 알아보도록 하자.

motivation에 대한 이야기는 고대 교육으로부터 현재까지 다양한 방식으로, 하지만 모두 가장 중요한 영역으로 생각하고 다루어지고 있다. 우리나라 개정 교육과정에 따르면 학습자의 능력, 흥미, 인지 수준에 맞추어 다양한 동기 유발 방법과 학습 활동을 구안하여 learner-centered의 수업이 이루어지도록 할 때 최적의 교육을 할 수 있다고 인정하고 있다. 그래서 오늘날 교육의 중요한 원리 중의 하나로서 제시될 수 있는 것이 개인차를 고려한 individualized learning이 되고 있다. 학습 목표를 달성하기 위해서는 학습자의 개인차를 인정하는 교수 방법이 필요하며, 학습자의 개인차를 고려한 학생 중심의 교수-학습은 학습의 개별화를 통해 가장 효율적으로 이루어질 수 있다는 것이다. 학생들의 cognitive ability나 학업 성취도 차이뿐 아니라 cognitive, affective, social 다양성 등의 개인차를 고려한 다양한 주제와 활동을 포함하는 학생 중심의 수업으로 개개 학생의 잠재력을 개발하고 교육의 효율성도 높일 수 있다. 학업 성취 수준 및 능력에 따라 난이도가 다른 과제를 부여하는 수준별 교육의 기반 위에 학생의 관심과 흥미에 따라 학생이 원하는 주제를 선택하도록 하고, 학생이 선호하는 학습 양식 및 multiple intelligence이론 등을 고려한 학습 활동을 고안하는 것이 바람직하다. 또한, 학습자 훈련을 통해 스스로 학습할 수 있는 learning strategy을 길러 주는 것도 필요하다. 교사는 학생들이 교실수업에서 self-reward를 찾을 수 있도록 흥미롭고, meaningful하고, 도전적인 과제를 제공하여 intrinsic motivation를 유발시킴으로써 성공적인 영어 학습에 이를 수 있도록 도와주어야 한다.

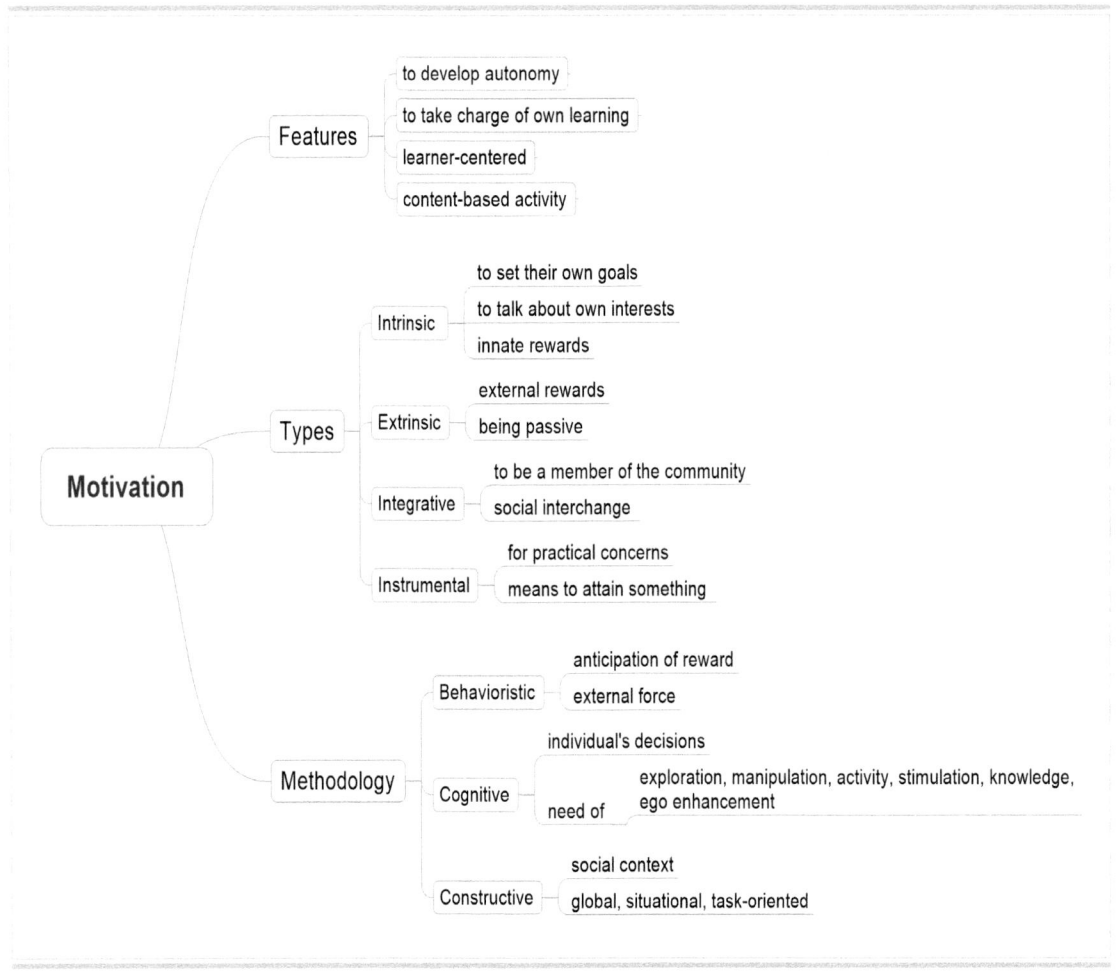

01. Theoretical Background of Motivation

1. Definitions of Motivation

In general, motivation is the driving force in any situation that leads to action. In the field of language learning a distinction is sometimes made between an orientation, a class of reasons for learning a language, and motivation itself, which refers to a combination of the learner's attitudes, desires, and willingness to expend effort in order to learn the second language.

Other theories of motivation emphasize the balance between the value attached to some activity and one's expectation of success in doing it (expectancy-value theory), goal setting, the learner's attributions of success and failure (motivation attribution theory), the role of self-determination and learner autonomy, and the characteristics of effective motivational thinking. Motivation is generally considered to be one of the primary causes of success and failure in second language learning. Guidelines for motivating learners are as follows:

- Teachers are enablers: when you teach, focus more on how to get students to tune in to their potential and to be challenged by self-determined goal.
- Learners need to develop autonomy: administer praise selectively and judiciously, helping students to recognize their own self-satisfaction in having done something well.
- Help learners to take charge of their own learning through setting some personal goals and utilizing learning strategies.
- Learner-centered and cooperative teaching is intrinsically motivating. Therefore, give students opportunities to make choices in activities, topics, discussions, etc.
- Content-based activities and courses are intrinsically motivating. Test, with some special attention from the teacher, can be intrinsically motivating. Allowing some student input to the test, giving well-thought-out classroom tests that are face-valid in the eyes of students, and giving narrative evaluations can contribute to intrinsic motivation.

2. Types of Motivation

(1) Intrinsic Motivation

Intrinsic motivation is characterized as more of a self-determined event where learners take responsibility for their own learning and have more of a sense of control. Enhanced motivation is reliant on innate (intrinsic) factors that cause people to challenge themselves, just as young children do when exploring or encountering a new object for the first time. In the second language acquisition field, intrinsic motivation can be stimulated when teachers become more a manager or facilitator of language learning and relinquish their traditional centerstage authoritarian position. According to Dickinson, intrinsically motivated students become more inclined to set their own goals and monitor their own progress which benefits not only themselves, but the other language learners in the class with whom they interact in small group and paired work. Intrinsically motivated students therefore tend to be more creative and resourceful in using a second language because they are less reliant on the teacher and rather personalize their own learning because the learning involves their natural interest.

① Second Language Classroom
- Teaching writing as a thinking process in which learners develop their own ideas freely and openly
- Showing learners strategies of reading that enable them to bring their own information to the written word
- Language experience approach in which students create their own reading material for others in the class to read
- Oral fluency exercises in which learners talk about what interests them and not about a teacher-assigned topic
- Listening to an academic lecture in one's own field of study for specific information that will fill a gap for the learner
- Communicative language teaching, in which language is taught to enable learners to accomplish certain specific functions
- Grammatical explanation, if learners see their potential for increasing their autonomy in a second language

② Intrinsically Motivating Techniques
- Does the technique appeal to the genuine interests of your students? Is it relevant to their lives?
- Do you present the technique in a positive, enthusiastic manner?
- Are students clearly aware of the purpose of the technique?

- Do students have some choice in:
  - choosing some aspect of the technique?
  - determining how they go about fulfilling the goals of the technique?
- Does the technique encourage students to discover for themselves certain principles or rules (rather than simply being told)?
- Does it encourage students in some way to develop or use effective strategies of learning and communication?
- Does it contribute to students' ultimate autonomy and independence?
- Does it foster cooperative negotiation with other students in the class? Is it truly interactive?
- Does the technique present a reasonable challenge?
- Do students receive sufficient feedback on their performance (from each other or from you)?

As a teacher, think of yourself as a facilitator of learning whose job it is to set the stage for learning, to start the wheels turning inside the heads of your students, to turn them on to their own abilities, and to help channel those abilities in fruitful directions.

(2) Extrinsic motivation

Those who believe that motivation to learn is prompted by external rewards believe that people are basically passive. Behaviorist philosopher Barry Schwartz notes that students will usually respond only when the environment tempts them with the opportunity to get rewards or avoid punishments. When a learner receives an incentive or tangible reward to participate or to complete an activity, this is referred to as extrinsic motivation. When someone is extrinsically motivated, the individual spends time to complete an activity as a means to an end or to receive a reward of some type. However, Bowman has conducted research which appears to show decreased motivation among college students who were offered only extrinsic rewards. Bowman claims that rewards are too controlling, do not lead to learner autonomy and serve to undermine self-determination. He argues that extrinsically motivated students eventually become "de-motivated" which is a state characterized by the belief on the part of the student that their efforts are inconsequential to accomplish a specific task and that they lack the ability to do so.

In the field of second language learning and motivation, Park and Kim claim that Korean students are more motivated by social tradition, an extrinsic or an external source of motivation in learning English. Park and Kim suggest that while memorization of grammar and English vocabulary among Korean ESL students is above average, the students' long term ability to stay motivated to master English over a life-time will be inhibited if they are only motivated by social tradition. Cluck points out that language learning will be inhibited if it relies solely on external controls such as parental approval. This seems to confirm what other studies have shown regarding the use of extrinsic rewards as the main motivational strategy in learning a language. Cluck suggests that since students need to be self-motivated in learning English as a second language, the teacher who deemphasizes extrinsic rewards such as grades and verbal praise may foster a better language learning environment.

▶ Intrinsic and Extrinsic Motivation in Education

Extrinsic Pressures	Intrinsic Innovations	Motivational Results
school curriculum	learner-centered personal goal-setting individualization	self-esteem self-actualization decide for self
society's expectations (conformity)	family values	love, intimacy, acceptance, respect for wisdom
tests & exams	security for comfortable routines task-based teaching	community, belonging, identity, harmony, security
immediate gratification	long-term goals the big picture things take time	self-actualization
make money!	content-based teaching: ESP (vocational, education, workplace)	cooperation, harmony
competition never fail!	cooperative learning group work, risk-taking, innovation, creativity	manipulations of strength, status, security, learn from mistakes, nobody's perfect

(3) Integrative orientation

- It is characterized by a willingness to be like-valued members of the language community.
- The construct of integrative motivation (most prominently associated with R. C. Gardner) includes the integrative orientation, positive attitudes towards both the target language community and the language classroom and a commitment to learn the language (socio-educational model).
- Integrative motivation refers to students who wish to integrate into the target culture. Integrative motivation as defined by Brown's (1994) is where learners have the desire to integrate into the target language community, culture and become part of that society. Learners learn the second language because they wish to socialize or participate in the target language group (Saville, 2006)

(4) Instrumental orientation

- The learner's desire to learn a language for utilitarian purposes in the context of language learning; Towards more practical concerns and purposes such as getting a job or passing an examination, reading technical material and translation, etc
- If a student is instrumentally motivated, his/her goals are to achieve a certain reward such as promotion or good grades.

 KEY NOTE

Types of Motivation

	Intrinsic	Extrinsic
Integrative	L2 learner wishes to integrate with the L2 culture 예 for immigration or marriage	Someone else wishes the L2 learner to know the L2 for integrative reasons 예 Japanese parents send kids to Japanese language school
Instrumental	L2 learner wishes to achieve goals utilizing L2 예 for a career, promotion	External power wants L2 learner to learn L2 예 corporation sends Japanese businessman to US for language training

 문헌읽기 **Instrumental and Integrative Motivation**

Gardner and Lambert (1972) introduced the notions of instrumental and integrative motivation. Instrumental motivation refers to the learner's desire to learn a language for utilitarian purposes (such as employment or travel or exam purposes) in the context of language learning. On the other hand, integrative motivation refers to the desire to learn a language to integrate successfully into the target language community. In later research studies, Crookes and Schmidt (1991), and Gardner and Tremblay (1994) explored four other motivational orientations: (a) reason for learning, (b) desire to attain the learning goal, (c) positive attitude toward the learning situation, and (d) effortful behavior.

Many theorists and researchers have found that it is important to recognize the construct of motivation not as a single entity but as a multi-factorial one. Oxford and Shearin (1994) analyzed a total of 12 motivational theories or models, including those from socio-psychology, cognitive development, and socio-cultural psychology, and identified six factors that impact motivation in language learning:

- Attitudes (i.e., sentiments toward the learning community and the target language)
- Beliefs about self (i.e., expectancies about one's attitudes to succeed, self-efficacy, and anxiety)

- Goals (perceived clarity and relevance of learning goals as reasons for learning)
- Involvement (i.e., extent to which the learner actively and consciously participates in the language learning process)
- Environmental support (i.e., extent of teacher and peer support, and the integration of cultural and outside-of-class support into learning experience)
- Personal attributes (i.e., aptitude, age, sex, and previous language learning experience)

Based on this brief discussion, we believe that teachers are able to drive the students to learn the language and to sustain students' interest in language learning if they can provide activities that are:

- interrelated between in-class and out-of class language activities
- communicative (game type) integrative (short/small activities form larger activities)
- pleasant, safe and non-threatening
- enthusiastic
- group-based
- meaningful or relevant
- challenging

These activities help promote:

- self-confidence
- experiences of success
- learning satisfaction
- good relationships among learners and between teacher and students

02 Methodological Perspectives

(1) Behavioristic perspective
- The behaviorist perspective is concerned with how environmental factors (stimuli) affect observable behavior (response). The behaviorist perspective proposes two main processes whereby people learn from their environment: classical conditioning and operant conditioning.
- Students know what they want or desire, and their wants or desires may not always correspond to what a teacher chooses to reinforce or ignore. Approaches that are exclusively behavioral are not sensitive enough to students' intrinsic, self-sustaining motivations.
- Anticipation of reward: Our acts are likely to be at the mercy of external force.

(2) Cognitive perspective
emphasis on the individual's decisions: the choices people make as to what experiences or goals they will approach or avoid, and the degree of effort they will exert in that respect; Six needs undergirding the construct of motivation (D. Ausubel)
- need of exploration
- need for manipulation
- need for activity
- need for stimulation
- need for knowledge
- need for ego enhancement

(3) Constructive perspective
emphasis on social context as well as individual personal choices; each person is motivated differently, and will therefore act on his/her environment in ways that are unique within a cultural and social milieu

① The needs concept of motivation: Belongs to all three schools of thought: the fulfillment of needs is rewarding, requires choices, and in many cases must be interpreted in a social context. Depending on whether a learner's context or orientation was (a) academic or career-related (instrumental orientation) (b) socially or culturally oriented (integrative orientation), different needs might be fulfilled in learning a foreign language because within either orientation, one can have either high or low motivation, it is important to distinguish orientation from motivation.

② There is no single means of learning a second language: Some learners in some contexts are more successful in learning a language if they are integratively oriented; Others in different contexts benefit from an instrumental orientation. Two orientations are not

necessarily mutually exclusive; most situations involve a mixture of each orientation.
- Integrative orientation: a moderate desire to socialize with speakers of the target language
- Assimilative orientation: a more profound need to identify with the target language culture
- An academic orientation or a career or business orientation

③ Motivation can be global, situational, or task-oriented: a foreign language learner may possess high global motivation, but low task motivation to perform well on the written mode of the language.
- Jean Piaget: Human beings universally view incongruity, uncertainty, and disequilibrium as motivating.
- Abraham Maslow: Intrinsic motivation is superior to extrinsic; we are ultimately motivated to achieve self-actualization once our basic physical safety, and community needs are met; we strive for self-esteem and fulfillment.
- Jerome Bruner: autonomy of self-reward: One of the most effective ways to help both children and adults think and learn − to free them from the control of rewards and punishments. Extrinsically driven behavior has the addictive nature.

KEY NOTE

Three Perspectives

Behavioristic	Cognitive	Constructivist
• Anticipation of reward • Desire to receive positive reinforcement • External, individual forces in control	• Driven by basic human needs; (exploration, manipulation…) • Degree of effort expended • Internal, individual forces in control	• Social context • Community • Social status • Security of group • Internal, interactive forces in control

CHAPTER 03 Context of Learning and Teaching

단원 길라잡이
- 연령과 능숙도 수준에 따른 2언어 습득과정을 파악한다.
- 다양한 2언어 학습기관을 이해한다.
- Sociocultural 교수방법을 교실현장에 적용하여 이해한다.

Introduction

학습이 이루어질 때 고려해야 할 내용은 다양하다. 학습자중심으로 하여 살펴볼 때 첫 시작은 나이라고 할 수 있다. 나이라고 하는 것은 지적인 것과도 밀접한 관계가 있기 때문에 가장 일반적인 분류라고 볼 수 있다. 그리고 또 다른 개인차는 언어의 능숙도에 따른 다른 교수방법이 나올 수 있다. 교사의 발화, 언어의 난이도, 활동의 방법과 함께 fluency와 accuracy가 달라 질 수 있을 것이다.

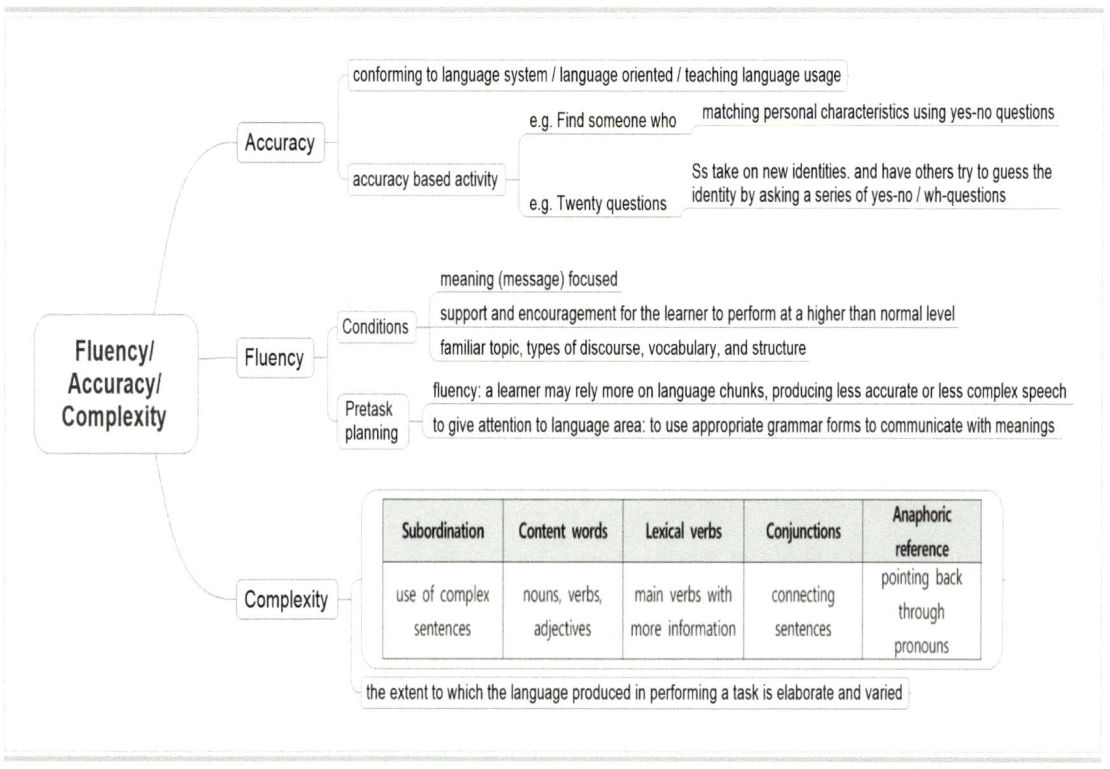

01. 연령에 따른 학습

Intellectual development	(C) 어린이의 지적 단계는 "concrete operations"이므로 언어의 기능적 목적에 중점을 두고 문법용어, 추상적 용어 사용 지양한다. 언어 개념을 설명하는 metalanguage는 사용하지 않고 특정 pattern과 예를 제시한다. 문형의 반복은 뇌와 귀의 협응을 촉진시키므로 지겹지 않게 성인의 양에 비해 많이 반복한다. (T) 'here and now' 맥락에서 벗어나 문법과 어휘를 이용 하여 즉각적인 의사 소통의 맥락으로 확장 시킬 수 있는 능력을 지니게 된다. 학습자가 관심 주는 대상 파악이 중요하고 적절치 않은 주제는 지적 과업의 성취를 방해한다. (A) 추상적인 규칙과 개념사용이 가능하지만 지나친 usage 사용이나 reality가 부족해서는 안된다.
Attention span	(C) 아동의 attention span 확장을 위해서는 흥미롭고 다양한 활동 제공하고 주제나 과목에 대해 교사는 열정을 보여주어 아동의 호기심을 이끌어 낼 수 있어야 한다. 유머감각은 학생들이 웃으면서 학습할 수 있도록 해준다. (T) attention span이 길어지는 과정이지만, 주위 환경에 따라 때때로 짧아진다. (A) Attention span이 길지만, 짧고 재미있는 activities가 중요하다.
Sensory input	(C) 아동의 5감각을 모두 자극해야 한다. kinesthetic 활동이 되는 역할극, 게임, TPR 활동과 프로젝트, sensory aids 활용하는 꽃향기, 식물과 과일 만져보기, video, music, picture, realia, nonverbal language 활용등이 중요하다. (T) 감각 입력은 중요하지만 추상적 개념이 확장된다. (A) 감각 입력을 강조할 필요 없지만 다양한 감각 입력은 활기찬 수업을 가져온다.
Affective factor	(C) 아동은 동료에 대해 극도로 민감하며, 성인보다 정의적으로 민감하다. "Be patient and supportive to build self-esteem!" 가능한 많은 oral participation을 이끌어 낸다. (T) ego, self image, self-esteem이 최절정에 이르는 때이므로 학생을 당황케 하지 않으며 개개인의 재능을 파악하고 경쟁을 부추기지 않고 그룹 활동에서 적극적으로 위험 감수를 하도록 한다. (A) 정서적 요인도 고려한다.
Authentic, meaningful language	(C) 즉각적인 보상이 뒤따르는 authentic 하고 meaningful한 언어를 제시: context를 제시하여 새로운 언어 학습을 하여 장기파지에 도움이 된다 (story lines, familiar situations and characters, real-life conversations, meaningful purpose in using language). whole language approach가 중요하고 전체적인 연관성을 파악케 한다. (T) 부자연스럽고 지나치게 분석적 언어사용은 자제한다. (A) context-reduced한 언어도 받아들일 수 있지만 authenticity와 meaningfulness 중요하다.

Note: C=children, T=teens, A=adults

02 언어 능숙도에 따른 학습

Cognitive learning process	(B) focal & controlled mode에 속함 : 유의미한 목적 위해 언어를 사용케 함으로써 peripheral processing을 유도한다. (I) 얼마간의 automatic processing 을 갖게 된다. 구, 문장, 문형 그리고 대화규칙 들이 꾸준히 연습되고, 수적으로 증가되는 과정이다. 교사는 산재되어 있는 언어의 모든 조각들을 자동성을 이용하여 분류해야 한다. (A) automaticity화 : focal과 peripheral attention간의 미묘한 상호작용을 계속한다.
Teacher role	(B) 교사에게 많이 의존 : 교사는 학생 스스로 계속 학습할 수 있도록 하도록 한다. 짝이나 그룹 활동을 통해 학습자 중심 수업을 유도할 수 있다. (I) 교사가 유일한 initiator가 아니다 : Learner-centered work가 지속될 수 있다. (A) 학생 pace에 말려들거나 활동이 무의미하게 느껴질 수 있으므로 계획 철저 : 언어를 automatic해가는 학습자들의 계속적인 노력을 도와주고, 언어의 요소들에 대한 focal & peripheral한 attention사이에서 적절한 상호작용을 돕는다.
Teacher talk	(B) 이해를 돕기 위해 천천히 하는 것은 좋지만, 말의 자연성을 잃지 않게 한다. articulation 이 명확하기만 하면, 초보 단계라고 해서 더 크게 말할 필요 없다. (I) articulation만 명확하면 자연스런 속도를 유지할 수 있다. (A) natural language와 speed가 필수 : feedback 제공자로서 교사 역할 중요하므로 학생에게 기회를 많이 주고 L1의 사용은 자제한다.
Authenticity of language	(B) 간단한 인사나 소개 등의 authentic language를 사용해야 한다. (I) 학습자가 문법의 미묘한 점에 집착할 수도 있는데 이를 금지한다. 분석적 성향이 실제 언어와 동떨어지게 만들 가능성이 있으므로 교사는 이를 견제 한다. (A) 모든 authentic language 자료 사용 가능 : 실제 언어가 아닌 것은 부적합하다.
Fluency and accuracy	(B) fluency를 목표로 하지만 발화 길이는 한정되고 flow of language를 위한 accuracy, 문법적 음운론적 실수는 수정한다. fluency의 기초가 되는 pronunciation work가 중요하다. (I) accuracy나 fluency에 집착 현상 발생 가능 : 교사의 개별적 관심이 요구되며 fluency 향상에 도움 되는 범위 내에서만 오류수정을 한다. (A) error가 비교적 드물고, 교사나 동료의 수정이 도움 된다.
Student creativity	(B) 언어 학습의 궁극목표는 unrehearsed situation에서 수용적이고 생산적인 창조력을 모두 요구하는 의사소통이다. 단, 학습자의 창조성을 너무 기대치는 말라. (I) interlanguage errors는 창조적 언어체계를 보여주는 단서 : 긍정적으로 보고 unrehearsed situation에 적용 가능한 교실언어와 다양한 media와 written word 사용 (A) 학습자는 수업교재를 실제 상황에 활용할 수 있다.

Techniques	(B) ① 반드시 짧고 단순한 technique과 다양한 activities를 사용하고 짧은 mechanical 학습 (반복, 연습)이 필요하다. ② Listening & speaking goals: 유의미하고 사실적인 의사소통 과업이다. 회화적 기능보다는 문법, 어휘, 말의 길이에 의해 목표가 제한된다. ③ Reading & writing goals: 학습자의 L1 필독 수준(literacy)을 간파해야 한다. ④ Grammar: EFL 상황 : 간단한 문법 설명은 L1를 이용하고 적절한 예와 pattern을 사용한다. (I) ① 복잡한 techniques 사용 가능: chain stories, story telling, paired interview, group problem solving, role play. ② Listening & speaking goals: 사용 언어 형태의 다양화 도모: short conversation, ask & answer question, find alternative ways to convey meaning. ③ Reading & writing goals: skimming과 scanning 사용: writing은 좀 더 정교화 ④ Grammar: 일부 문법 설명은 2언어를 이용하고 문법의 "sore spots"에 관심을 두고 지나친 문법 사용을 금지한다. (A) ① sociolinguistic, pragmatic competence 사용 가능하고 group debate, argumentations, complex role play, skimming and scanning, essay writing ② Listening & speaking goals: sociolinguistic적 미묘한 차이에 초점: register, style, the status of the interlocutor ③ Reading & writing goals: critical reading, schemata, writing a document related to profession ④ Grammar: functional forms, sociolinguistic/ pragmatic phenomena, strategic competence에 관심을 두고 metalanguage사용과 deductive수업도 가능하다.

Note: B=beginner level, I=intermediate level, A=advanced level

문헌읽기　When to Start Language Learning

Most experts believe that when a child is introduced to a second language at an early age their chances of becoming more proficient in the target language will be higher. However, it is not necessarily true to say "the earlier the better". It is suggested that the most efficient time to learn another language is between 6 and 13. However, children who learn in pre-to-early teens often catch up very quickly with children who learn from an earlier age. Also this does not mean that languages cannot be learnt later in life. The experience and environment at school and how language is taught and practiced play a vital role in language acquisition, regardless of how young or old the child is. Whatever the age, when children learn a second language they develop skills that will help to create opportunities in their future. They acquire the lifelong ability to communicate with others under diverse circumstances. Indeed, regardless of the level of proficiency, learning a second language and learning about different cultures generally broadens a child's outlook on life. It also opens up alternative educational and career opportunities.

언어를 배우기 어려운 상황

- Feeling uncomfortable, distracted or under pressure
- Feeling confused by abstract concepts of grammar rules and their application which they cannot easily understand
- Activities which require them to focus attention for a long time
- Boredom
- Being over-corrected

Reading the list above, you may be surprised at the number of items that remind you of traditional educational practices. In fact, research does suggest that traditional classroom teaching may have the effect of preventing rather than helping children to learn better. You cannot force a child to learn. You can only provide a conducive environment, useful resources, and carefully structured input and practice opportunities.

언어를 배우는 방법

- Having more opportunities to be exposed to the second language
- Making associations between words, languages, or sentence patterns and putting things into clear, relatable contexts
- Using all their senses and getting fully involved; by observing, copying, doing things, watching and listening
- Exploring, experimenting, making mistakes and checking their understanding
- Repetition and feeling a sense of confidence when they have established routines
- Being motivated, particularly when their peers are also speaking/learning other languages

학습자의 전체적인 면을 포함시키기

Children have highly inquisitive minds and enjoy learning through play and using their imagination by observing and copying, doing things, watching and listening. Children also learn a lot of their first language by physically responding to their parents' instructions in real and meaningful contexts. The parent says, "Look at that dog" or "Give me the ball" and the child does so. These interactions between parent and child always have a clear reason for the communication. This is very a different learning situation from asking, "What is the past tense of 'give'?" The only reason for this question is to test the child's memory. It is not fun and it does not involve the child's senses.

언어적 실수에 대한 처리 방법

For children, making mistakes is part of the natural process of learning.

- A five-year-old-speaking his mother tongue may still make grammar mistakes.
- They will frequently 'invent' their own rules and over-generalisations like "my car breaks", or "my friend camed to the party yesterday". So, learning another language will also involve a lot of mistakes.
- This is a natural part of learning. In fact, for effective communication it is a good idea to concentrate on learning words, not grammatical accuracy. If a foreigner comes up to you and asks, "Train station where please?" you can understand and help, even though the grammar is awful. Now, imagine if he says, "Can you please tell me where to find… uh… er… oh?"
- There's plenty of time later for learning the grammar; but knowing the words will help your child communicate now, and help them in learning the grammar later — Don't correct, 'model' the correct form of the language. So if your child says "The boy wented home," you can say, "Yes. The boy went home. What did he do then?"
- Encourage children to correct themselves, this will build confidence and deepen the learning process. Say "Almost right, try again…" or show the child where the mistake is but do not give them the answer.
- Some correction is okay but be careful not to over-correct. A page full of crossing out and corrections can be very demotivating, as is always being told, "Wrong! Do it again!"
- Particularly in speech it is much better to let the child develop their ideas and fluency than to keep interrupting with corrections. The ideas are more important than the grammar.
- Keep their age and level of English in mind. Give lots of praise and encouragement for every effort.
- They can't know everything.

2

Second Language Acquisition

01. Second Language Acquisition
02. Learner Language
03. Learning Strategies

KEY NOTE

Theories of Learning

	Behavioristic Learning Structural Linguistics "Say what I say"	Cognitivism (Innatism) Generative Linguistics "It's all in your mind"	Constructivism (Interactionist position) "a little help from my friends"
연대	1940s ~ 1950s	1960s ~ 1970s	1980s
연구 대상	공식적으로 관찰측정 가능한 반응	관찰 가능한 자극반응의 측면이나 언어학자들에 의해 수집된 언어 자료를 통해서 언어를 살필 수 없다.	협동 그룹이나 커뮤니티에 근거한 사회적 행동
주창자 & 전제	Bloomfield, Sapir, Fries • 각 언어들은 상호간 무한히 상이하다. • 인간의 인지과정은 연구대상에서 제외된다. • 언어는 각기 언어항목들로 세분화될 수 있다.	Chomsky • 언어는 표층구조와 심층구조로 이루어져 있다. • 심층구조에서 관찰 가능한 표층 구조가 생성된다.	Vygotsky 사회적 상호작용이 인지발달의 기본이며 predetermined stages의 개념을 부정한다.
관련 심리 학파	Behavioral Psychology • Pavlov, Skinner • 객관적인 관찰기록이 가능한 반응에만 초점 • 과학적 방법이 엄격히 준수 • 인지, 사고, 개념형성, 지식습득, 직관 등의 이성적 분야는 제외	Cognitive Psychology • Ausubel • 의미, 이해, 지식 • 조직과 기능의 심리학적 원리 • 인간행동의 내면에는 기저구조와 동기가 있다. • 인간행동의 기술뿐만 아니라 설명도 중요하다.	Interactionist Theory 수정된 상호작용이 input을 comprehensible하게 만들며 그 comprehensible input이 습득을 촉진시킨다.
학습 이론	Programmed Instruction • 단계적인 강화프로그램 • 즉각적 feedback이 주어짐으로써 향후 학습 방향/장단점 파악하여 능동적 학습 가능 • punishment 지양하고, 바람직하지 못한 행동을 소거하며 alternative response에 reinforcement 부여하는 방식을 제시 했다.	Meaningful Learning • 학습자들의 관심, 필요, 목적에 부합한 의미 있는 학습 상황 설정 • 새로운 주제 학습은 학습자들의 기존 학습과 관련하여 함 • 지나친 문법 설명이나 drill은 자제	Whole Language Approach • 언어를 자연스럽게 이용 • 모든 학습자가 참여할 수 있는 group 활동 이용 • one skill이상을 활용할 때 학습의 효율성 최대화 • interaction 역할의 중요성

CHAPTER 01 Second Language Acquisition

단원 길라잡이
- 2언어 습득의 역사와 유형을 이해하고 실제 교실에서 활용할 수 있도록 한다.
- 2언어 학습자의 중간 언어 형태를 분석하고 발전시킬 수 있다.
- 효과적인 의사소통을 위한 학습유형과 전략을 이해할 수 있다.

Introduction

이제까지 영어 학습의 기본 원리를 살펴보았다. 이러한 기본 원리들은 그냥 만들어진 것이 아니라 2언어 습득의 이론들을 바탕으로 하여 가장 효과적인 영어교수원리를 만들어 낸 것이다. 그래서 이제부터는 2언어습득이론이 어떻게 이루어졌으며 무엇인지를 알아보기로 하겠다. 이것을 통해서 우리의 영어교육의 방향성을 확고하게 할 수 있을 것이다. 과거 behaviorism의 영어교육은 암기와 단순연습이 학습의 중심에 있었다. 그래서 학습자들은 자신의 생각을 표현하고, 말하기 보다는 주어진 문장구조를 연습하여 완벽하게 말하는 데 중점을 두었다. 그런데 이러한 교수방법이 효율적으로 이루어지지 않는다는 것을 발견한 cognitivists들이 언어습득의 내재적 요인을 설명하기 시작했다. 특히 Stephen Krashen이 주장하는 input hypothesis는 2언어습득도 어린아이가 모국어를 습득하는 과정처럼 natural하게 이루어 질 때 가장 효과적이라는 기본이론을 바탕으로 하고 있다. 그런데 input hypothesis는 input만을 강조하다 보니 output이 만들어지지 않는다는 비판을 받으면서 output hypothesis와 interaction hypothesis가 만들어지는 계기를 주었다.

현재는 위의 교수법들의 문제점을 극복하고 social interaction이 교육의 중심이 되는 social constructivism이 영어교육론의 전체적인 흐름을 만들어주고 있다. Social constructivism은 teaching과 learning에 대한 많은 연구가 이루어져왔다. Social constructivism은 Vygotsky's sociocultural perspective에 근거하여 심리적 기제를 설명하고 있다. 대표적 교육적 전략은 collaborative learning으로서 communication, knowledge sharing, critical thinking 등을 social context안에서 연습할 수 있도록 하는 것이다. 교실 안에서 discussion을 확장시키면서 가질 수 있는 장점이 많다. group discussion에 참여함으로써 교실학습에서 생긴 지식을 일반화하고 전이시키고 생각을 말로써 전달하기 위한 기초를 다질 수 있다. discussion은 자신의 아이디어를 test하고 다른 사람의 아이디어를 synthesize하고 배운 것에 대한 더 깊은 이해를 세울 수 있도록 학생의 능력을 발달시키는데 중요한 역할을 한다. 크고 작은 group discussion은 학생들이 self-regulation이나 self-determination을 연습할 기회를 제공하고 tasks를 계속 해나갈 수 있도록 한다. discussion은 학생들의 motivation, collaborative skills와 문제해결 능력을 증가시킨다.

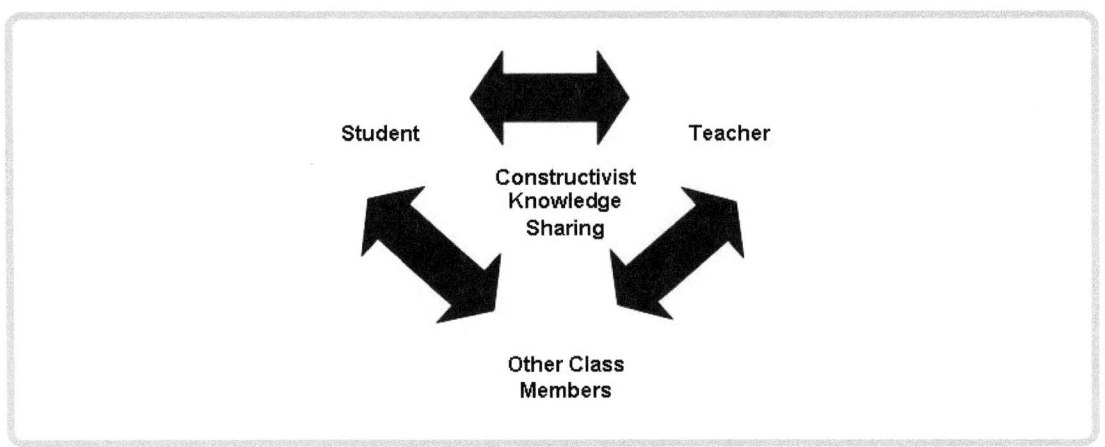

구성주의에서는 discussion과 interactive discourse을 통하여 학생들에게 자신들의 독립적인 생각을 나타내는 기회로서 L2를 사용할 기회를 제공함으로써 학습을 촉진하려고 하고 있다. 현재 우리 교육에서 discussion이 중시되는 데 그 이유는 discussion이 meaning-making을 만들어내는 sustained responses를 끌어낼 수 있기 때문이다. 이러한 활동은 교실 안에서 다른 동료들과의 ideas를 서로 negotiating하면서 생겨날 수 있으며, 이러한 유형의 학습은 retention과 information의 인지적 발달과 연관되어 있는 in-depth processing을 촉진할 수 있다는 믿음하에서 진행되고 있다.

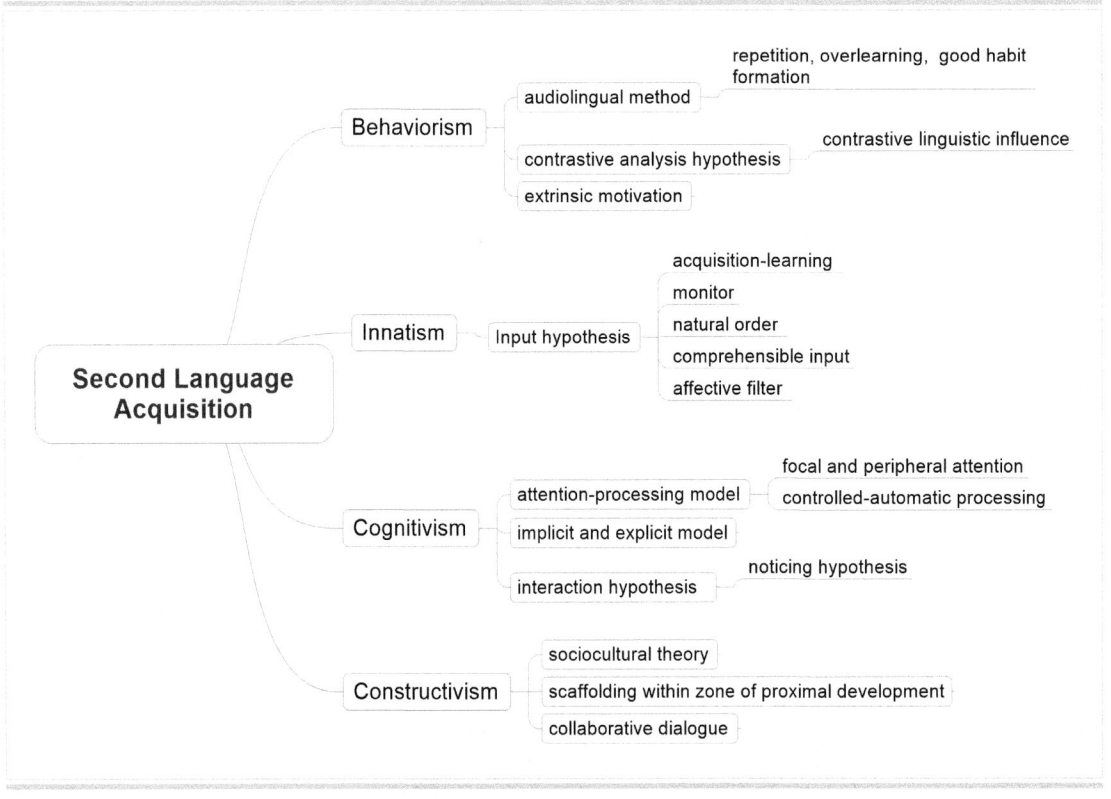

01 Behavioristic Learning

1. Behaviorism to language

As Skinner turned from experimental work to concentrate on the philosophical underpinnings of a science of behavior, his attention turned to human language with verbal behavior and other language-related publications; verbal behavior laid out a vocabulary and theory for functional analysis of verbal behavior, and was strongly criticized in a review by Noam Chomsky.

Skinner did not respond in detail but claimed that Chomsky failed to understand his ideas, and the disagreements between the two and the theories involved have been further discussed. In addition; innate theory is opposed to behaviorist theory which claims that language is a set of habits that can be acquired by means of conditioning. According to some, this process that the behaviorists define is a very slow and gentle process to explain a phenomenon as complicated as language learning. What was important for a behaviorist's analysis of human behavior was not language acquisition so much as the interaction between language and overt behavior. In an essay republished in his 1969 book Contingencies of Reinforcement, Skinner took the view that humans could construct linguistic stimuli that would then acquire control over their behavior in the same way that external stimuli could. The possibility of such "instructional control" over behavior meant that contingencies of reinforcement would not always produce the same effects on human behavior as they reliably do in other animals.

The focus of a radical behaviorist analysis of human behavior therefore shifted to an attempt to understand the interaction between instructional control and contingency control, and also to understand the behavioral processes that determine what instructions are constructed and what control they acquire over behavior. Recently, a new line of behavioral research on language was started under the name of Relational Frame Theory.

Behaviorism focuses on one particular view of learning and a change in external behaviour achieved through a large amount of repetition of desired actions, the reward of good habits and the discouragement of bad habits. In the classroom this view of learning led to a great deal of repetitive actions, praise for correct outcomes and immediate correction of mistakes. In the field of language learning, this type of teaching was called the audio-lingual method, characterized by the whole class using choral chanting of key phrases, dialogues and immediate correction.

2. Contrastive Analysis Hypothesis

(1) Principles

- Deeply rooted in the behavioristic and structuralist approaches, the CAH claimed that the principal barrier to L2 is the interference of L1 system with the 2nd system.
- A scientific-structural analysis will develop a taxonomy of linguistic contrasts between them which will enable the linguist to predict the difficulties a learner would encounter.
- Clifford Prator (1967) captured the essence of the grammatical hierarchy (Stockwell, Bowen, and Martin, 1965) in six categories of difficulty was applicable to both grammatical and phonological features of language.

▶ **Hierarchy of Difficulties**

단계	정의	한국어와 영어의 대조 비교
Level 0 : Transfer	No difference or contrast is present between the two languages. The learner can simply transfer a sound, structure, or lexical item from the native language to the target language.	영어의 /m/은 한국어의 /ㅁ/과 같아 발음에 어려움을 느끼지 않는다.
Level 1 : Coalescence	Two items in the native language become coalesced into essentially one item in the target language.	한국어의 입다, 쓰다, 신다 등이 영어에서는 모두 wear로 합병된다. (ㅂ/ㅃ:p).
Level 2 : Underdifferentiation	An item in the native language is absent in the target language. The learner must avoid that item.	한국어에는 존재하는 존칭어미 -시, -옵 등이 영어에 없다. (으:∅).
Level 3 : Reinterpretation	An item that exists in the native language is given a new shape or distribution.	국어의 'ㅅ'과 영어의 's'는 다르다.
Level 4 : Overdifferentiation	A new item entirely, bearing any similarity to the native language item, must be learned.	한국어에는 없는 허사 there가 영어에는 존재한다. (∅ : θ, f, v).
Level 5 : Split	One item in the native language becomes two or more in the target language requiring the learner to make a new distinction.	한국어의 /ㄹ/은 영어에서 /l/과 /r/로 나타난다.

(2) From Contrastive Analysis to Cross-linguistic Influence

① Predictions of difficulty by means of contrastive procedures had many shortcomings. The process could not account for all linguistic problems or situations not even with the 6 categories. And the predictions of difficulty level could not be verified with reliability.

- The attempt to predict difficulty by means of contrastive analysis was called the strong version of the CAH (Wardaugh, 1970), a version that he believed unrealistic and impracticle.
- Wardaugh also recognized the weak version of the CAH in which the linguistic difficulties can be more profitably explained a posteriori by teachers and linguists. When language and errors appear, teachers can utilize their knowledge of the target language and native language to understand the sources of error.

② The so-called weak version of the CAH is what remains today under the label cross-linguistic influence (CLI) suggesting that we all recognize the significant role that prior experience plays in any learning act and the influence of the native language as prior experience must not be overlooked. Syntactic, lexical, and semantic interference show far more variation among learners than psycho-motor-based pronunciation interference.

(3) Learner Language

① CAH stressed the interfering effects of L1 on L2 learning and claimed, in its strong form, that L2 learning is primarily a process of acquiring whatever items are different from the L1.

② This narrow view of interference ignored the intralingual effects of learning. Learners are consciously testing hypotheses about the target language from many possible sources of knowledge.
- knowledge of the native language
- limited knowledge of the target language itself
- knowledge of communicative functions of language
- knowledge about language in general
- knowledge about life, human beings, and the universe

Learners act upon the environment and construct what to them is a legitimate system of language in its own right.

02 Innatism

1. Krashen's Input Hypothesis

(1) The Acquisition-Learning

This distinction is the most fundamental of all the hypotheses in Krashen's theory and the most widely known among linguists and language practitioners. According to Krashen, there are two independent systems of second language performance: the acquired system and the learned system. The acquired system or acquisition is the product of a subconscious process very similar to the process children undergo when they acquire their first language. It requires meaningful interaction in the target language – natural communication – in which speakers are concentrated not in the form of their utterances, but in the communicative act. The learned system or learning is the product of formal instruction and it comprises a conscious process which results in conscious knowledge about the language, 예 knowledge of grammar rules. According to Krashen, learning is less important than acquisition.

(2) The Monitor hypothesis

This hypothesis explains the relationship between acquisition and learning and defines the influence of the latter on the former. The monitoring function is the practical result of the learned grammar. According to Krashen, the acquisition system is the utterance initiator, while the learning system performs the role of the 'monitor' or the 'editor'. The monitor acts in a planning, editing and correcting function when three specific conditions are met: that is, the second language learner has sufficient time at his/her disposal, he/she focuses on form or thinks about correctness, and he/she knows the rule. It appears that the role of conscious learning is somewhat limited in second language performance. According to Krashen, the role of the monitor is – or should be – minor, being used only to correct deviations from 'normal' speech and to give speech a more polished appearance.

(3) The Natural Order hypothesis

This hypothesis is based on research findings which suggested that the acquisition of grammatical structures follows a 'natural order' which is predictable. For a given language, some grammatical structures tend to be acquired early while others late. This order seemed to be independent of the learners' age, L1 background, conditions of exposure, and although the agreement between individual acquirers was not always 100% in the studies, there were statistically significant similarities that reinforced the existence of a Natural Order of language acquisition. Krashen, however, points out that the implication of the natural order hypothesis is not that a language program syllabus should be based on the order found in the studies. In fact, he rejects grammatical sequencing when the goal is language acquisition.

(4) The Input hypothesis

This hypothesis is Krashen's attempt to explain how the learner acquires a second language. According to this hypothesis, the learner improves and progresses along the 'natural order' when he/she receives second language input that is one step beyond his/her current stage of linguistic competence. 예 If a learner is at a stage 'i', then acquisition takes place when he/she is exposed to comprehensible input that belongs to level '$i + 1$'. Since not all of the learners can be at the same level of linguistic competence at the same time, Krashen suggests that natural communicative input is the key to designing a syllabus, ensuring in this way that each learner will receive some '$i + 1$' input that is appropriate for his/her current stage of linguistic competence.

(5) The Affective Filter hypothesis

This hypothesis embodies Krashen's view that a number of affective variables play a facilitative role in second language acquisition. These variables include: motivation, self-confidence and anxiety. Krashen claims that learners with high motivation, self-confidence, a good self-image, and a low level of anxiety are better equipped for success in second language acquisition. Low motivation, low self-esteem, and debilitating anxiety can combine to raise the affective filter and form a mental block that prevents comprehensible input from being used for acquisition. In other words, when the filter is up, it impedes language acquisition. On the other hand, positive affect is necessary, but not sufficient on its own, for acquisition to take place.

2. Against Input Hypothesis

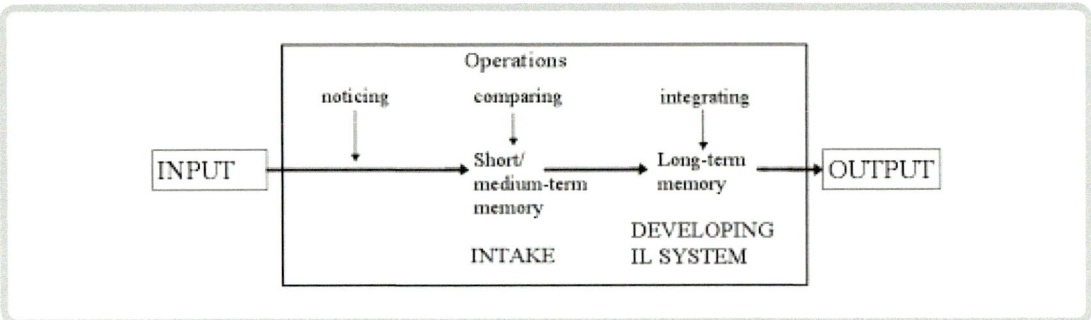

(1) **Intake :** subset of the input that is comprehended and attended to in some way: It contains the linguistic data that are made available for acquisition. Conditions to become 'intake' are as follows;
- Complexity : Items should be at an appropriate level of difficulty.
- Saliency : Items should be noticed or attended to in some way.
- Frequency : Items must be experienced with sufficient frequency.
- Need : The item must fulfill a communicative need.

(2) **Role of Input**
① High Input Generators: HIGs are those who are good at initiating interaction, thereby generating conversation with people and increasing their opportunities to speak and to learn.
② Low Input Generators: LIGs are the opposite - passive learners who prefer to stay in the shadows. Studies show, unsurprisingly, that HIGs make much more progress.

(3) **Importance of Output**
Krashen's comprehensible input must at the very least be complemented by an 'output hypothesis' that gives extensive credit to the role of the learner's production' (ibid: 282). Output hypothesis was tested directly in a study of second language learners of English. In a study investigating the acquisition of English questions, three groups carried out communicative tasks. The groups focused on enhancement and opportunity to modify following feedback. Developed by Merrill Swain, the comprehensible output (CO) hypothesis states that learning takes place when encountering a gap in the linguistic knowledge of the L2. By noticing this gap the learner becomes aware of it and might be able to modify his output so that he learns something new about the language. Although Swain does not claim that comprehensible output is solely responsible for all or even most language acquisition, she does claim that under some conditions, CO facilitates second

language learning in ways that differ from and enhance input due to the mental processes connected with the production of language. This hypothesis is closely related to the Noticing hypothesis. Swain defines three functions of output:

① Noticing function: Learners encounter gaps between what they want to say and what they are able to say and so they notice what they do not know or only know partially in this language.

② Hypothesis-testing function: When learners say something there is always a hypothesis underlying about grammar. By uttering something, the learners test this hypothesis and receive feedback from an interlocutor.

③ Metalinguistic function: Learners reflect about the language they learn and hereby the output enables them to control and internalize linguistic knowledge.

문헌읽기 Output Hypothesis

The comprehensible output (CO) hypothesis states that we acquire language when we attempt to transmit a message but fail and have to try again. Eventually, we arrive at the correct form of our utterance, our conversational partner finally understands, and we acquire the new form we have produced. The originator of the comprehensible output hypothesis, Merrill Swain (Swain, 1985), does not claim that CO is responsible for all or even most of our language competence. Rather, the claim is that "sometimes, under some conditions, output facilitates second language learning in ways that are different form, or enhance, those of input" (Swain and Lapkin, 1995, p. 371). A look at the data, however, shows that even this weak claim is hard to support.

Insights into Learner Output

The aim of this article is to provide useful techniques for teaching in the language classroom and address three issues crucial in learner output: negotiation of meaning, learner production, and repair work. The first two sections explain the theoretical background based on research findings. The third section suggests ways in which some of these findings may be applied to classroom situations. The fourth section summarizes the main points of the article, in particular, their implications in classroom teaching.

Learner Production and Language Learning

Recently, several second language acquisition (SLA) researchers have systematically argued that the function of L2 learners production is not only to enhance fluency and indirectly generate more comprehensible input, but also to facilitate second language learning by providing learners with opportunities to produce comprehensible output (Krashen 1985, 1989, 1994; Long 1983, 1990; Van Patten 1990). Learners achieve this by modifying and approximating their production toward successful use of the target language (Swain 1985, 1993, 1995).

Swain and Lapkin (1995:373) maintain that in the process of modifying their interlanguage (IL) utterances for greater message comprehensibility, L2 learners undertake some restructuring that affects their access to their knowledge base. "…the assumption is that this process of modification contributes to second language acquisition" (Swain and Lapkin 1995:373). Many scholars have concluded that opportunities for comprehensible input and output are equally important in language learning (Swain 1985, 1995).

Similarly, many of these studies have shown that interactions, where the negotiation of meaning between native speakers/nonnative speakers (NSs/NNSs) and nonnative speakers/nonnative speakers (NNSs/NNSs) is prevalent, are also important for the production of comprehensible output. It is through the negotiation of meaning that both learners and their interlocutors work together to provide comprehensible input and produce comprehensible output.

Pica, Holliday, et al., (1989:65) pointed out that "although… research has focused mainly on the ways in which negotiated interaction with an interlocutor helps the learner to understand unfamiliar L2 input, we believe that it is also through negotiation that learners gain opportunities to attempt production of new L2 words and grammatical structures as well." Negotiated interactions are important not only because they provide NNSs with an opportunity to receive input, which they have made comprehensible through negotiation, but also because these interactions provide NNSs with opportunities that enable them to modify their speech so that the output is more comprehensible (Long 1983; Varonis and Gass 1985, Gas and Varonis, 1985, 1994; Doughty 1988, 1992; Deen 1995; Loschky 1994).

Repair Work and Language Learning

According to Schegloff et al., (1977) and Schegloff (1979), there is a cline in convertsations. In normal conversation, the norm is self-initiated and self-completed repair. In non-normal conversation, the proportion of other-initiations and other-completions is higher than would be expected. In situations where there is a constant failure to repair, interlocutors will eventually cease to converse. It has also been observed that in NS/NS discourse (Schegloff et al., 1977) and NS/ advanced NNS discourse (Kasper 1985), the vast majority of repair is content and pragmatic repair rather than linguistic (phonological, lexical, morpho-syntactic) repair.

These observations suggest the thesis that success in L2 learning may be measured by the proportion of self-initiated, self-completed repair in relation to other-initiated, other-completed repair, and by the proportion of content and pragmatic repair in relation to linguistic repair. Thus, the more self-initiated, self-completed content and pragmatic repair, the more native-like the interaction will be. However, the more other-initiated, other-completed linguistic repair, the less native-like the interaction will be. Hence, the optimal L2 learning environment is one in which self-initiated, self-completed content and pragmatic repair dominates.

Research that investigated NS/NNS and NNS/NNS negotiated interaction has confirmed the importance of self-initiated, self-completed repair over other-initiated, other-completed repair (Kasper 1985, Shehadeh 1991). Shehadeh (1991) found that self-initiated clarification attempts occurred in significantly greater proportions than other-initiated clarification requests (70 percent versus 30 percent, respectively). Instances of self-initiated comprehensible output occurred in significantly greater proportions than instances of other-initiated comprehensible output (73 percent versus 27 percent, respectively). These findings confirmed that to have conversations that require the kind of performances associated with successful language learning, students need to focus on self-initiated, self-completed repair.

Pedagogical Implications on Negotiation of Meaning and Learner Interaction

The results of these empirical studies and observations may provide some useful insights into classroom teaching. This section will suggest two different but closely related sets of pedagogical implications: those that relate to negotiating meaning and learner/ learner interaction, and those that relate to repair work.

One of the main underlying principles of the studies on negotiating meaning is that all data emphasize task-based instruction and learner/learner interaction. Thus, the first set of pedagogical implications for language learning relates to activities that involve the negotiation of meaning in dyadic and group interactions. In terms of classroom practice, this means that educators should introduce such activities as problem solving, decision making, opinion exchange, picture dictation, and jigsaw tasks. These types of activities provide an ideal atmosphere for negotiating meaning in appropriate contexts. Learners have opportunities to receive input that they have made comprehensible through negotiation and at the same time, to produce comprehensible output, an output which learners have made comprehensible to other learners through negotiations.

The implications of the studies on the negotiation of meaning match paradigms such as the communicative language approach, which centers on learner/learner interactions. Indeed, this teaching approach emphasizes interactions that involve problem solving, decision making, and opinion exchange, picture dictation, and jigsaw tasks—all standard communicative exercises for developing fluency in the target language (TL) (Johnson 1982, Brumfit 1984, Hunter and Hofbauer 1989, Widdowson 1990).

Teachers who use the communicative approach can justify these types of activities because they encourage learners to produce comprehensible output in the direction of TL-like performances. The findings of interactional studies support the importance of interaction and the negotiation of meaning in developing proficiency in the target language, thus confirming the importance of negotiated interactions in the production of comprehensible output, one of the basic principles of the communicative language approach.

Repair Work

The second set of pedagogical implications relates to repair work in the language classroom. The main conclusion here is that if repair leading to comprehensible output is integral to successful language learning, then not only are clarification requests (other-initiations) important, but more importantly, the extent to which self-repair is used.

Therefore, self-initiated clarification attempts and self-initiated comprehensible output should be encouraged as preferred classroom strategies, which are strategies in NS/NS interaction (Schegloff et al., 1977).

Since the main goal of learning an L2 is to approximate NS/NS interaction, creating situations that encourage the production of self-initiated comprehensible output is a motivating teaching strategy. In conversations, these situations give the learner more opportunities to use the TL and are significantly more frequent than other-initiated clarification requests and instances of other-initiated comprehensible output (Gaskill 1980, Kasper 1985, and Shehadeh 1991).

It must be cautioned that in the monolingual classroom, there is the possibility that students, in the process of their negotiated interactions and repair work, might resort to their shared mother tongue (MT) to complete the task or the activity required. Nonetheless, assuming that learners are motivated and desire to learn the TL, it is possible to argue that learner-use of the MT in performing the activities required is a more remote possibility than might be expected.

In Shehadeh's (1991) study, the two NNS subjects (ages 24 and 32) who shared one MT background (Arabic) interacted completely in English (the TL) rather than resorting to their shared MT to complete the tasks. This supports Long and Porter's (1985:224) conclusion that "the findings concerning mixed first language groups do not mean, of course, that group work will be unsuccessful in monolingual classrooms, which is the norm in many EFL situations... the research clearly shows that the kind of negotiation work of interest here is also very successfully obtained in the group of the same first language background." Studies on the negotiation of meaning and repair work may provide many other useful insights into classroom teaching. In particular, pedagogical research may look at what types of tasks and activities might be used, what their distinguishing cognitive characteristics should be, how activities might be graded to match the proficiency levels of learners, and how teachers can create situations that encourage self-initiated, self-completed repair and learner/ learner negotiated interactions.

03 Cognitivism

1. Attention-Processing Model

 KEY NOTE

Information processing

Attention	Controlled	Automatic
Focal	Performance based on formal rule learning • Grammatical explanation of a specific point • Word definition • Copy a written model • The first states of memorizing a dialog • Prefabricated patterns • Various discrete-point exercises	Performance in a test situation • Keeping an eye out for something • Advanced L2 learner focuses on modals, clause formation, etc. • Monitoring oneself while talking or writing • Scanning • Editing, peer-editing
Peripheral	Performance based on implicit learning or analogic learning • Simple greetings • The later stages of memorizing a dialog • TPR/ Natural Approach • New L2 learner successfully completes a brief conversation	Performance in communication situations • Open-ended group work • Rapid reading, skimming • Free writes • Normal conversational exchanges of some length

(1) Based on cognitive theory, second language learning is a mental process and assumes a hierarchy of complexity of cognitive skills. McLaughlin's assumptions:
- Second language learning is a skill to require automatization of component sub-skills.
- Humans have a limited capacity to manage controlled processes.
- Second language processing skills become more efficient via automatization.

(2) Structured practice leads to automatization and integration of linguistic patterns. Processing mechanisms are:
- Controlled processing mechanisms: capacity limited and temporary
- Automatic processing mechanisms: relatively permanent
- An ultimate communicative goal for language learners: peripheral, automatic attention-processing of language

2. Implicit and Explicit models

- Implicit linguistic knowledge: information automatically or spontaneously used like children's language
- Explicit linguistic knowledge: linguistic knowledge

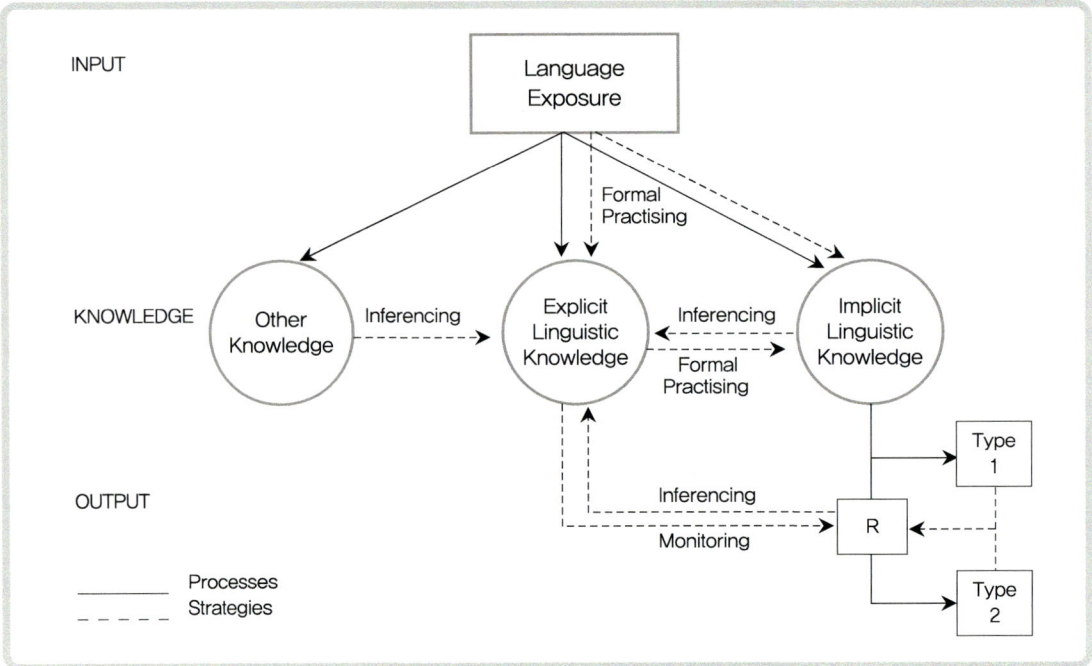

04. Interaction Hypothesis

1. Principles of Interaction Hypothesis

(1) The Interaction Hypothesis, proposed by second language acquisition expert Michael Long, offers an explanation of one way in which ESL or EFL students can best succeed at learning a target language. It posits that interaction between a non-native speaker (NNS) and a native speaker (NS), or non-native speaker of a higher level, creates a naturalistic second language acquisition environment where the NNS learns through negotiation of meaning and/or becoming aware of gaps in their target language knowledge.

(2) The Interaction Hypothesis has taken as basic the notion that conversation is not only a medium of practice, but also the means by which learning takes place, more specifically when it comes to the negotiation of meaning (Gass p.234). Especially negotiation work that triggers interactional adjustments by the native speaker or more competent interlocutor, facilitates acquisition because it connects input, internal learner capacities, particularly selective attention, and output in productive ways. (Long 1996, pp. 451-2).

핵심플러스   Trigger-Signal-Response-Reaction

According to Doughty, the essential feature of the negotiation sequence is the opportunity that is provided to the learner to process utterances in the L2 which become more comprehensible. Her negotiation model incorporates a trigger, a signal, a response, and a reaction. A trigger is an utterance or part of an utterance that is not understood. A signal is used by the interlocutor to express a lack of comprehension. A response then comes from the first speaker trying to repair the problem. A reaction is an extension or a response to the repair. This model is similar to the one employed by Gass and Varonis (1985), although they use the term "indicator" instead of "signal." Gass and Varonis also included two types of responses: direct (often wh-questions) and indirect (repetition, use of intonation). Direct and indirect responses are considered without further differentiation since both are part of the negotiation process.

Negotiation process

Trigger	⇨	Signal(indicator)	⇨	Response	⇨	Reaction / follow-up
• lexical/phonetic error • language complexity • task complexity		• clarification request • confirmation check		• repetition • expansion • reformulation		• exclamation • non-verbal correction

Negotiation을 통한 교수-학습원리
① Use of L2 in interaction: L2 acquisition (Long's Interaction Hypothesis)
② Negotiation of meaning: vocabulary acquisition (Long, 1990)
③ Negotiation of vocabulary meaning: deeper understanding of meaning & use of new vocabulary in new contexts (Nation, 2000)
④ Meaningful output: necessary to language learning as meaningful input (Swain's Output Hypothesis)

(3) The Interaction Hypothesis posits that when a language learner is attempting to negotiate conversation in the target language, the gaps in their abilities are revealed to them. These abilities can include but are not limited to pronunciation, syntax, grammar and vocabulary. The Interaction Hypothesis concludes that this self-realization, brought about by authentic interaction, will encourage the second language learner to produce target language output to negotiate meaning and seek out the knowledge they lack. This interaction between the language learner and other students or the learner and the teacher, results in language acquisition on the part of the learner, meaning they have internalized this chunk of language and will be able to produce it later when needed.

(4) The Interaction Hypothesis supports the use of authentic situations in the classroom. Through natural interaction with language classmates, their teacher and native speakers the student gains self awareness that facilitate advancement in the target language. The Interaction Hypothesis reveals to us that 'checks' are the key to the second language acquisition process. One way the language learner realizes the gaps in their knowledge is by checking with the person they are having a conversation with. The simplest of which are known as modification checks. There are several different types of interaction modification checks that take place during a natural conversation which help the learner advance in the target language:

Clarification requests:	The learner recognizes a word that they are unfamiliar with and they ask for clarification.
Confirmation checks:	The learner reacts to a sentence uttered by the other speaker and uses the L2 to confirm that they understood correctly.
Comprehension checks:	The learner asks a question to the other person in the conversation to affirm that they understood the meaning of the learners' sentence or sentences. This production of checks provides the language learner with opportunities build positive affective feelings of confidence and learning opportunities.

Repairing: When the speaker repeats/ paraphrases some part of the other speakers utterance in order to overcome a communication problem

Reacting: When the speaker repeats/ paraphrases some part of the other speakers utterance in order to help establish or develop the topic of conversation.

 문헌읽기 **Input, Interaction, and Second Language Development**

(1) Long's Interaction Hypothesis

Long's (1996) updated version of the interactionist hypothesis claims that implicit negative feedback, which can be obtained through negotiated interaction, facilitates SLA. Similar claims for the benefits of negotiation have been made by Pica (1994) and Gass (1997). Some support for the interaction hypothesis has been provided by studies that have explored the effects of interaction on production (Gass & Varonis, 1994), on lexical acquisition (Ellis, Tanaka, & Yamazaki, 1994), on the short-term outcomes of pushed output (see Swain, 1995), and for specific interactional features such as recasts (Long, Inagaki, & Ortega, 1998; Mackey & Philp, 1998). However, other studies have not found effects for interaction on grammatical development (Loschky, 1994).

Long's interaction hypothesis (1983a, 1983b, 1985, 1996) evolved from work by Hatch (1978) on the importance of conversation to developing grammar and from claims by Krashen (1985) that comprehensible input is a necessary condition for SLA. Long argues that interaction facilitates acquisition because of the conversational and linguistic modifications that occur in such discourse and that provide learners with the input they need. Through one type of interaction, termed negotiation by Long, Pica, Gass and Varonis, and others, nonnative speakers (NNSs) and their interlocutors signal that they do not understand something (Gass & Varonis 1989, 1994; Long, 1983a, 1983b, 1996; Pica, 1994). Through the resulting interaction, learners have opportunities to understand and use the language that was incomprehensible. Additionally, they may receive more or different input and have more opportunities for output (Swain, 1985, 1995).

Various empirical studies have considered the effects of different input and interactional conditions on SL production and acquisition. Pica's comprehensive review of work on negotiated interaction suggests that interaction may facilitate conditions and processes that are claimed to be important in second language learning. As linguistic units are rephrased, repeated, and reorganized to aid comprehension, learners may have opportunities to notice features of the target language. Pica showed how, through interaction, syntactic elements may be perceived as units because they are segmented or manipulated and certain features can be given prominence through stress, intonation, and foregrounding. The hypothesis has been further refined and developed by Gass (1997), who stressed that the effects of interaction may not be immediate, pointing out the importance of looking for delayed developmental effects of interaction. Other summaries of interaction hypothesis claims and reviews of recent empirical work can be found in Gass, Mackey, and Pica (1998). 예 shows how negotiated interaction may be operating to facilitate L2 development. In this example the NNS does not understand the word glasses. The word is repeated by the native speaker (NS), the original phrase is extended and rephrased, and finally a synonym is given.

NS: There's.. there's a.. a pair of reading glasses above the plant.
NNS: A what?
NS: Glasses, reading glasses to see the newspaper?
NNS: Glassi?
NS: You wear them to see with, if you can't see. Like magnifying glasses.
NNS: Ahh.. glasses.. glasses.. to read you say reading glasses.
NS: Yeah.

(2) Output and Comprehension in the Context of Interaction

Swain (1995) has argued that it is having to actually produce language that forces learners to think about syntax. Swain argued for the importance of comprehensible output in the SLA process. What she means by this is that learners, in their effort to be understood in the target language, are pushed in their production and may try out new forms or modify others. To explore output, Swain and Lapkin (1995) used think-aloud procedures during dictogloss tasks that they suggested may tap into some of learners' introspective processes. Swain and Lapkin (1998) discussed what they termed "collaborative dialogues" in "language-related episodes," in which the learners talk about the language they are producing or writing. They suggested that such conversations may be a source of second language learning. 예 of a learner being pushed to produce more comprehensible output (see also Pica et al., 1989) can be seen below (data are from the current study), where the NNS rephrases the original sentence in an effort to be understood and produces a simile of his partial production of the lexical item that seems not to be understood by the native speaker. Example shows the learner restructuring output to facilitate native speaker understanding of the utterance.

NNS: And one more weep weep this picture.
NS: Huh?
NNS: Another one like gun to shoot them weep weepon.
NS: Oh ok... yeah.. I don't have a second weapon though so that's another difference.

Based on the output hypothesis, it would seem that, for interaction to facilitate SLA, learners need to have opportunities for output during interaction. In many second language classrooms as well as naturalistic contexts, however, learners often observe the output of others without producing their own output. Is it helpful for learners to observe output without actually taking part in it? In terms of comprehension, Pica (1992) found no significant differences between learners who observed interaction and learners who took part in interaction. She therefore suggested that it may not be necessary for learners to take part in interaction for it to have a beneficial effect on comprehension; simply observing interaction may be sufficient. Ellis, Tanaka, and Yamazaki (1994) compared the developmental outcomes for learners who were in the same class and carried out the same task. Some learners actively participated in interaction and some learners listened. Scores for vocabulary acquisition and comprehension were not significantly different for these learners. Ellis et al. concluded that active participation may be less important for acquisition than has been claimed, but they noted that it is not detrimental either. Although the processes involved in production and comprehension and the relationship between them obviously preclude direct comparison, these two studies can be considered supportive of the need for further research on the outcomes of observation of interaction, as well as the outcomes of taking part in interaction.

(3) Premodified Input in the Context of Interaction

Premodified input has also been studied by Pica and her colleagues (see Pica, 1994) in the context of interaction. Premodified input is generally operationalized as input that has been carefully targeted at the level of the learner in order to facilitate learner comprehension. Negotiation is generally not necessary when input is premodified. The linguistic structures are ordered in a supposed difficulty hierarchy. 예 The simple present tense is usually presented early on in most ESL texts: dialogues, and surrounding text are often premodified so that learners will not have difficulties with comprehension.

Conversational interaction that utilizes premodified input — 예 partially scripted role plays— may yield better comprehension in that learners do not have to negotiate for meaning and make adjustments. However, in terms of the interaction hypothesis, premodified input may be less beneficial for learners because their opportunities to listen for mismatches between their own output and the target language are obviously limited when the input has been premodified to ensure comprehension. Premodified input is sometimes termed "scripted" (Gass & Varonis, 1994). of premodified input similar to example (B) might consist of the native speaker taking the questioning role and asking, "Do you have a gun in your picture? A gun is like a weapon. A gun shoots bullets." When input is premodified in the context of interaction, learners seldom have occasions to misunderstand, negotiate for meaning, and produce errors; and therefore opportunities for language learning as a result of their mistakes are limited. The interaction hypothesis suggests that conditions and processes for second language learning are met by negotiation for meaning and the resulting interactional modifications that take place. Thus, premodified input, such as that obtained through scripted interaction, which results in few or no opportunities for negotiation or misunderstandings, may not be helpful for SLA. Learners who participate in negotiation in the context of interaction may have more learning opportunities.

(4) Feedback, Interaction, and Noticing

Long's (1996) claim in the interaction hypothesis was that there is an important role in the SLA process for negotiated interaction that elicits negative feedback. According to Long, this feedback may induce noticing of some forms: "it is proposed that environmental contributions to acquisition are mediated by selective attention and the learner's developing L2 processing capacity… negative feedback obtained in negotiation work or elsewhere may be facilitative of SL development" (p.414). Negative feedback obtained through negotiation for meaning has been discussed above. Another source of negative feedback currently receiving attention in the SLA literature is recasts.

Recasts have been generally defined as being a targetlike way of saying something that was previously formulated in a nontargetlike way (see also Farrar, 1992; Long, Inagaki, & Ortega, 1998; Mackey & Philp, 1998; Oliver, 1995). Thus, in example, from data in the current study, the NS interlocutor responds to the NNS's ill-formed utterance with a reformulation, modifying the NNS's utterance by supplying the copula, adding a plural marker, and adding a preposition. The central meaning of the NNS's original utterance is retained.

NNS: Your picture.. how many.. how many.. cat your picture?
NS: How many cats are there in my picture?
NNS: Yeah... how many cats?

Long (1996) pointed out that recasts are often ambiguous; a learner might not be able to determine whether negative feedback is a model of the correct version or a different way of saying the same thing. Recent work by Lyster (1998a, 1998b) in the classroom context has also pointed to the idea that negative feedback may be perceived or reacted to differently in dyadic and classroom contexts. The focus of the current study was interaction containing negotiation rather than recasts, although in some cases recasts and negotiation cooccur.

If interaction containing negotiation or recasts can lead to SL restructuring, how may this come about? Some researchers have suggested that input must be internalized in some way in order to affect the acquisition process. If learners are to make use of the possible benefits of interaction, for example, because it provides SL data at the appropriate time for them and it provides feedback on their production, they must not only comprehend this SL data but must also notice the mismatch between the input and their own interlanguage system (Gass, 1991, 1997). Ellis (1991) also claimed that the acquisition process includes the procedures of noticing, comparing, and integrating, and that interaction that actually requires learners to modify their initial input may facilitate the process of integration.

Thus, researchers have claimed that if interaction is to affect the learners' interlanguage, learners may need to notice the gap between their interlanguage (IL) form and the second language alternative. Gass (1991) pointed out that "nothing in the target language is available for intake into a language learner's existing system unless it is consciously noticed" (p.136). Noticing or attention to form may be facilitated through negotiated interaction. It has been argued that during negotiation for meaning, when learners are struggling to communicate and are engaged in trying to understand and to be understood, their attention may be on language form as well as meaning. White (1991) has also suggested that, for some SL structures, it may be necessary for there to be incomprehensible input – that is, for there to be a problem in order for learners to develop.

(5) Interaction

The study was designed to investigate the connection between interaction and SL development. Interaction was operationalized following Long (1996), who claimed, as discussed above, that it is beneficial because it can provide implicit reactive negative feedback that may contain data for language learning. Such feedback can be obtained through interactional adjustments that occur in negotiated interaction.

(Interactional modifications/ negotiation sequences)

Description	(a) Negotiation/ Recast	(b) Negotiation
The initial utterance that is not understood	NNS: So your dogs are in space ... vee er vee er ship?	NNS: I have a kind dog man.
Implicit reactive negative feedback: The utterance that lets the first speaker know that her message was not understood.	NS: Are my dogs in a spaceship or space vehicle you mean?	NS: You have a what?
The first speaker's reaction to the feedback; responses can be modified, as in (a), or unmodified, as in (b).	NNS: Yes, are your dog in space ship?	NNS: A kind dog man.

05 Social Constructivist Model

Introduction

가장 중요한 constructivist에 들어가기 전에 한번 쉬고 생각하고 들어가기로 하겠다. 영어교육론에서 가장 중요하게 이야기되는 social constructivist의 주장을 생각해 보자. 이 학자들은 knowledge를 social context안에서 다른 사람과의 interaction속에서 만들어진다고 주장하는 이론에서 시작한다. Vygotsky의 이론에 영향을 받아 일어난 교육사조로서 학습을 active하고 social 과정으로 본다. constructivist의 정신을 이루는 근거는 collaborative elaboration으로서, 지식 형성 과정은 혼자서는 이룰 수 없는 것을, 다른 사람들과의 견해를 서로 나누는 과정에서 함께 만들어 갈 수 있도록 한다.

또 하나 constructivism의 위치를 생각해 보자. cognitive와 humanistic이론을 함께 가지고 있는 교육이론이다. 이전의 behaviorism에서는 organism을 하나의 black box를 중심으로 기능한다고 보았고, cognitivism에서는 그와 반대로 mind의 중요성을 인식하기 시작했다. 하지만 여전히 학습자의 역할은 교사가 제시하는 것을 받아들여야 한다고 보고 있었다. 이러한 개념들이 사회적 유형인 constructivism에 와서 학습자는 교사가 새로운 의미를 만들어낼 때 함께 참여하여 만들어 내는 joint enterprise 로서 보기 시작하고 있다. 이러한 개념들이 constructivism을 위대하게 만들었고 지금은 다른 어느 이론에 비교될 수 없을 만큼 중요한 이론으로 자리잡게 되었다. 그래서 Vygotsky(1978)의 학습이론이 다음과 같은 형태로 정리될 수 있다.

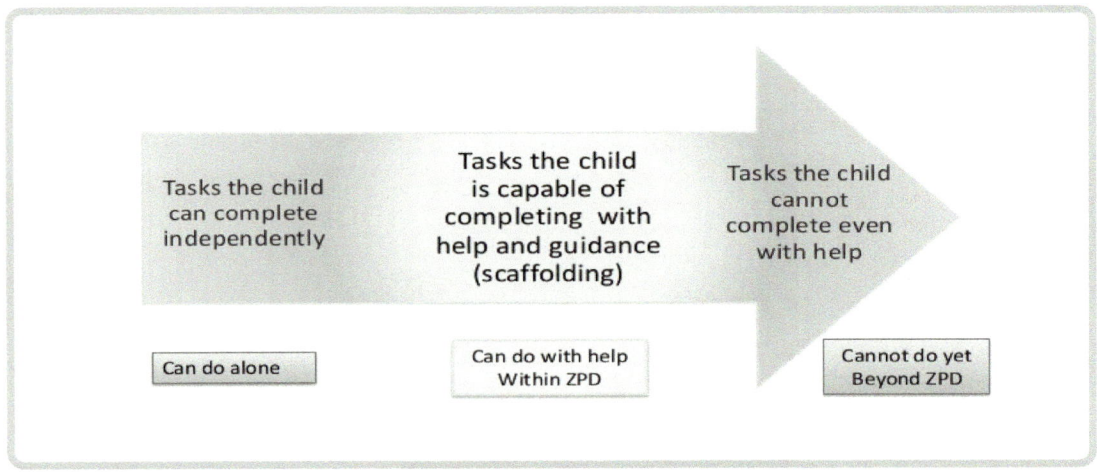

1. Backgrounds of Constructivist Theory

① We can distinguish between 'cognitive constructivism' which is about how the individual learner understands things, in terms of developmental stages and learning styles, and 'social constructivism', which emphasizes how meanings and understandings grow out of social encounters. In this sense, conversational theories of learning fit into the constructivist framework. The emphasis is on the learner as an active 'maker of meanings'. The role of the teacher is to enter into a dialogue with the learner, trying to understand the meaning to that learner of the material, and to help her or him to refine their understanding until it corresponds with that of the teacher.

② Constructivism influences instructional theory by encouraging discovery, experiential, collaborative, project-based, and task-based learning. Constructivist epistemology, as a branch of the philosophy of science, offers an explanation of how human beings construct knowledge from information generated by previous experiences. It has roots in cognitive psychology and biology and is an approach to education that lays emphasis on the ways knowledge is created while exploring the world.

2. Constructivism in Learning

(1) Teaching approaches

① Constructivism, a perspective in education, is based on experimental learning through real life experience to construct and conditionalize knowledge. It is problem based and adaptive learning that challenges faulty schema, integrates new knowledge with existing knowledge, and allows for creation of original work or innovative procedures.

② The types of learners are self-directed, creative, innovative, drawing upon visual / spatial, musical / rhythmic, bodily / kinesthetic, verbal / linguistic, logical / mathematical, interpersonal, intrapersonal, and naturalistic intelligences.

③ The purpose in education is to become creative and innovative through analysis, conceptualizations, and synthesis of prior experience to create new knowledge.

(2) Teacher Roles

① Instructors have to adapt to the role of facilitators and not teachers (Bauersfeld, 1995). Whereas a teacher gives a didactic lecture that covers the subject matter, a facilitator helps the learner to get to his or her own understanding of the content. The emphasis thus turns away from the instructor and the content, and towards the learner (Gamoran, Secada, & Marrett, 1998). A teacher tells, a facilitator asks; a teacher lectures from the front, a facilitator supports from the back; a teacher gives answers according to a set curriculum, a facilitator provides guidelines and creates the environment for the learner to arrive at his or her own conclusions; a teacher mostly gives a monologue, a facilitator is in continuous dialogue with the learners (Rhodes and Bellamy, 1999). A facilitator should also be able to adapt the learning experience 'in mid-air' by taking the initiative to steer the learning experience to where the learners want to create value.

② The educator's role is to mentor the learner during heuristic problem solving of ill-defined problems by enabling quested learning. The learning goal is the highest order of learning: heuristic problem solving, metacognitive knowledge, creativity, and originality that may modify existing knowledge and allow for creation of new knowledge.

③ The learning environment should also be designed to support and challenge the learner's thinking (Di Vesta, 1987). While it is advocated to give the learner ownership of the problem and solution process, it is not the case that any activity or any solution is adequate. The critical goal is to support the learner in becoming an effective thinker. This can be achieved by assuming multiple roles, such as consultant and coach. A few strategies for cooperative learning include (Woolfolk 2010):

Reciprocal Questioning:	Students work together to ask and answer questions.
Jigsaw Classroom:	Students become "experts" on one part of a group project and teach it to the others in their group.
Structured Controversies:	Students work together to research a particular controversy.

3. Learning Process

① Learning is an active social process. Social constructivism, strongly influenced by Vygotsky's (1978) work, suggests that knowledge is first constructed in a social context and is then taken up by individuals (Bruning et al, 1999; M. Cole, 1991; Eggan & Kauchak, 2004). The process of sharing each person's point of view – called collaborative elaboration (Meter & Stevens, 2000) – results in learners building understanding together that wouldn't be possible alone (Greeno et al., 1996). Scholars view learning as active, where learners should learn to discover principles, concepts and facts for themselves. They support guesswork and intuitive thinking in learners (Brown et al.1989; Ackerman 1996). For the social constructivist, the real is not there to be found: it does not pre-exist, but we invent it in a social context.

② We make meanings through acting with each other and the environment. Knowledge is thus a product of humans and is a product of our social nature, and of our culture (Ernest 1991; Prawat and Floden 1994). McMahon (1997) agrees that learning is a social process. He further states that learning is neither a private thing, nor a passive shaping by outside forces. Instead, meaning occurs through social actions.

③ Vygotsky (1978) also highlighted the convergence of the social and active roles in learning. He said that the greatest moment in our mind's development occurs when speech and action converge. Before, these were seen as independent lines of development. Through actions a child constructs meaning for itself, while speech connects this meaning with the common world of her/his culture.

④ Dynamic interaction between task, instructor and learner: A further characteristic of the role of the facilitator in the social constructivist viewpoint, is that the instructor and the learners are equally involved in learning from each other as well (Holt and Willard-Holt 2000). This means that the learning experience is both subjective and objective and requires that the instructor's culture, values and background become an essential part of the interplay between learners and tasks. Learners compare their version of the truth with that of the instructor and fellow learners to get to a new, socially tested version of truth (Kukla 2000). The task or problem is thus the interface between the instructor and the learner (McMahon 1997). This creates a dynamic interaction between task, instructor and learner. This entails that learners and instructors should develop an awareness of each other's viewpoints and then look to their own beliefs, standards and values, thus being both subjective and objective at the same time (Savery 1994).

⑤ Some studies argue for the importance of mentoring in the process of learning (Archee and Duin 1995; Brown et al. 1989). The social constructivist model thus emphasizes the importance of the relationship between the student and the instructor in the learning process. Some learning approaches that could harbour this interactive learning include reciprocal teaching, peer collaboration, cognitive apprenticeship, problem-based instruction, web quests, anchored instruction and other approaches that involve learning with others.

4. Theory of Vygotsky

The most significant bases of a social constructivist theory were laid down by Vygotsky (1962), in his theory of the Zone of Proximal Development (ZPD). Proximal simply means next. He observed that when children were tested on tasks on their own, they rarely did as well as when they were working in collaboration with an adult. It was by no means always the case that the adult was teaching them how to perform the task, but that the process of engagement with the adult enabled them to refine their thinking or their performance to make it more effective. Hence, for him, the development of language and articulation of ideas was central to learning and development. The common-sense idea which fits most closely with this model is that of stretching learners. It is common in constructing skills check-lists to have columns for 'cannot yet do', 'can do with help', and 'can do alone'. The ZPD is about 'can do with help', not as a permanent state but as a stage towards being able to do something on your own. The key to stretching the learner is to know what is in that person's ZPD that comes next, for them.

(1) Vygotsky's Zone of Proximal Development:

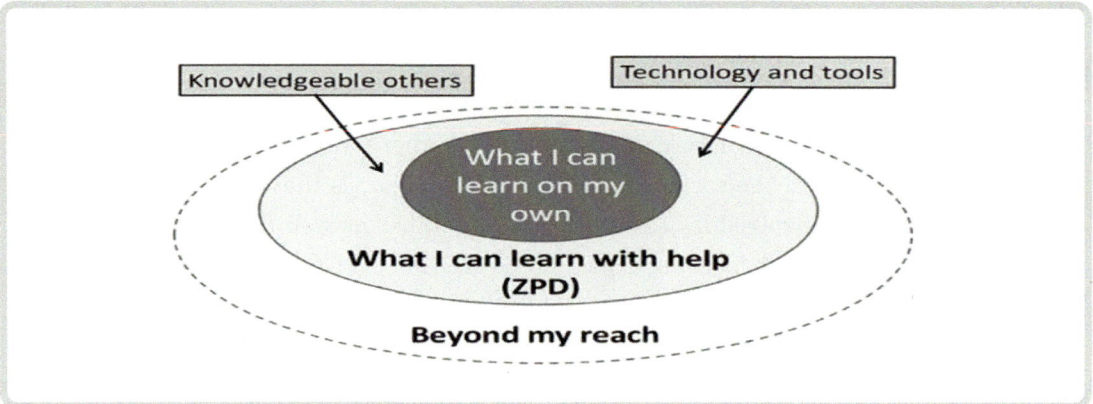

① Definition: the distance between a child's actual cognitive capacity and the level of potential development: Principles of awareness, autonomy and authenticity lead the learner to zone of proximal development where learners construct the new language through socially mediated interaction.

② Approaches based on Constructivism
- Interactive Learning
- Cooperative Learning
- Discovery Learning
- Content and Task-Based and Process-Oriented Learning
- Teacher as a Guide or Facilitator
- Performance-Based Assessment

 KEY NOTE

Summary of L2 Acquisition

Innatist	Cognitive	Constructivist
• Subconscious acquisition superior to learning and monitoring • Comprehensible input • Low affective filter • Natural order of acquisition • Zero option for grammar instruction	• Controlled/ automatic processing • Focal/ peripheral attention • Restructuring • Implicit/explicit • Unanalyzed/analyzed knowledge • Form-focused instruction	• Interaction hypothesis • Intake through social interaction • Output hypothesis • High Input Generators • Authenticity • Task-basked instruction

문헌읽기 **Sociocultural Context in Language Teaching**

The sociocultural element in learning is particularly sensitive in EFL because in acquiring a language there is, to some extent, an appropriation of a cultural identity too. This article looks at the social entity of learning among children. It looks at how as teachers we are social agents and how we are managing the cultural contexts of our classrooms. We prescribe socially appropriate ways of participation, which we need to be aware of. As a teacher I see my classroom through 'Vygotsky eyes', every thing is social. The educational psychologist Vygotsky believed that once children acquired language, language structured thought. From this perspective the child can gradually, through interaction with others come to have an awareness of herself or capacity for reflection. In this way we can see development coming from the social to the individual.

사회적 현상

The zone of proximal development (ZPD) or scaffolding is the gap between what a child can achieve individually and what they can achieve together with others. This may be a peer or an adult. Communication is human, interpersonal and social. Within an activity or social exchange is a construction of knowledge, rather like brick laying, where the child is also learning how to learn, using language as a tool. The interactive process therefore becomes the social product. Learning a language, learning through language and learning to be a particular person are closely related.

상호 교환의 유형

Often a teacher can fall into a role or pattern where they control the legitimate flow of knowledge between the teacher and the pupil. This has been identified by Edwards and Mercer as Initiation, Response, Feedback (IRF). For example, the teacher will ask the class a question, knowing the answer already, and then control the legitimate feedback of answers from the children. If this pattern of exchange is overused in the classroom it can limit;

- the potential of a 'handover' (an autonomous learner)
- individual agency (being able to challenge and negotiate a concept)
- expression of identity (bringing their home culture or cultural 'niche' into their classroom participation)

Fairclough, The author of *Language and Power* describes how through the patterns of exchange in school, over a period of time, will determine what sort of people the pupils will become. Finding out what the teacher wants to hear rather than the real pursuit of understanding is due to the asymmetrical relationship between pupil and teacher. However, peer to peer talk is symmetrical and can promote cognitive development. One of the greatest importances of communication is when an idea has to be formulated and expressed, sharing the idea among essential partners who will test their assumptions

CHAPTER 02　Learner Language

> **단원 길라잡이**
> - 2언어 학습자의 언어 발달단계를 이해한다.
> - 오류 분석의 원인과 종류를 파악한다.

Introduction

　언어습득을 이해하기 위해서는 학습자들이 어떻게 언어를 발달시켜가는지를 살펴봐야 하겠다. 이 과정은 2언어 학습자들도 모국어학습자들이 언어습득을 위해서 겪어가는 과정과 유사점을 가지고 있다. 특히 새로운 언어를 배워가는 과정에서 단순하게 암기했던 언어규칙이 어느 순간에 가면 overgeneralization로 일어날 수 있다. 그리고 그 과정을 거쳐 규칙을 내재화하게 된다. 학습자 언어의 4단계를 거쳐 언어를 습득하게 된다고 할 수 있다. 이전의 behaviorism에서는 오류를 제거해야 할 대상으로 보아왔지만 learner language에서는 영어교육론적인 가치가 있는, 즉 developmental process에 있는 하나의 단계로서 그 자체의 의미를 중시하고 있다. interlanguage로서의 learner language를 이해할 때 그 후에 따르는 error correction, feedback, uptake도 이해할 수 있게 된다.

　현재 영어교육론에서 learner language를 강조하는 것은 교수법의 체계가 많이 변화되었기 때문이다. 학습자가 직접 output으로 시도한 언어를 이용하여 학습하는 것이 가장 효과적이라고 믿는 focus on form의 영역이 확장되면서 동시에 learner language영역이 발달하게 되었다. 이것은 language 자체가 중요하다기 보다는 learners의 needs나 proficiency level을 중시하여 needs analysis에서 학습과정이 시작된다는 것과 같은 맥락에서 이해될 수 있다.

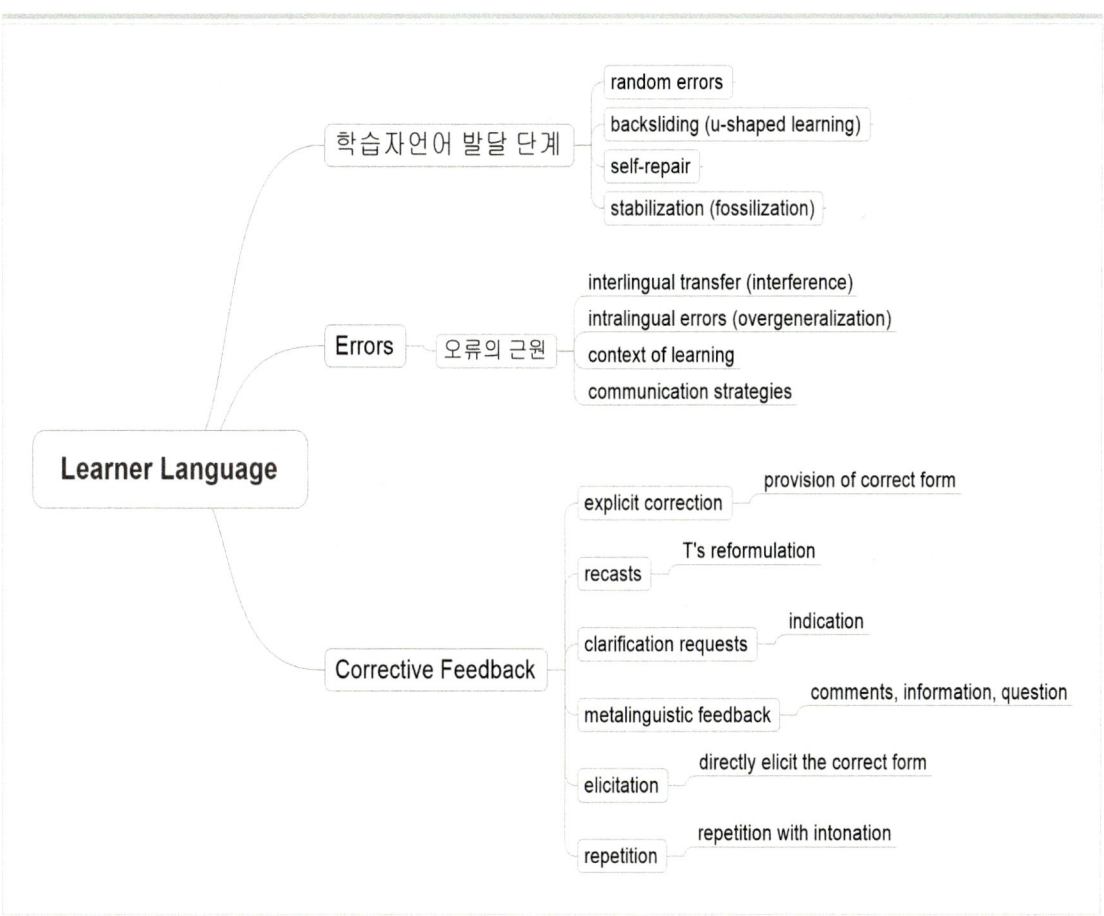

01 Learner Language

1. Stages of Learner Language Development

(1) Presystematic stage

① The stage of random errors : when the learner is unaware of the existence of a particular rule in the target language. These are random.

② "The different city is another one in the another two." Inconsistencies like "John cans sing," "John can to sing," and "John can singing," all said by the same learner within a short period of time, might indicate a stage of experimentation and inaccurate guessing.

(2) The emergent stage of learner language

① Backsliding (U-shaped learning): This phenomenon of moving from a correct form to an incorrect form and then back to correctness: The learner seems to have grasped a rule or principle and then regresses to some previous stage.

② The learner is still unable to correct errors when they are pointed out by someone else. Avoidance of structures and topics is typical.

③ The learner has begun to discern a system and to internalize certain rules. These rules are legitimate in the mind of the learner, although they may not be correct by target language standards.

L:	I go to New York.
NS:	You're going to New York?
L:	[doesn't understand] What?
NS:	You will go to New York?
L:	Yes.
NS:	When?
L:	2007
NS:	Oh, you went to New York in 2007.
L:	Yes, I go 2007.

Note: L=learner, NS=native speaker

(3) The systematic stage

① The learner is now able to manifest more consistency in producing the second language.

② The most salient difference between the second and third stage is the ability of leaners to correct their errors when they are pointed out — even very subtly to them.

> L: Many fish are in the lake. These fish are serving in the restaurants near the lake.
> NS: [laughing] The fish are serving?
> L: [laughing] Oh, no, the fish are being served in the restaurants.
>
> *Note:* L=learner, NS=native speaker

(4) The stabilization (postsystematic) stage

① The learner has relatively few errors and has mastered the system to the point that fluency and intended meanings are not problematic.

② Fossilization: At this point learners can stabilize too fast, allowing minor errors to slip by undetected, and thus manifest fossilization of their language.

③ Self-correct: The system is complete enough that attention can be paid to those few errors that occur and corrections be made without waiting for feedback from someone else.

02 Error Analysis

1. Errors

(1) Meaning of Errors

In the speech or writing of a second or foreign language learner, the use of a linguistic item (예 a word, a grammatical item, a speech act, etc.) in a way which a fluent or native speaker of the language regards as showing faulty or incomplete learning. A distinction is sometimes made between an error, which results from incomplete knowledge, and a mistake made by a learner when writing or speaking and which is caused by lack of attention, fatigue, carelessness, or some other aspect of performance. Errors are sometimes classified according to vocabulary (lexical error), pronunciation (phonological error), grammar (syntactic error), misunderstanding of a speaker's intention or meaning (interpretive error), production of the wrong communicative effect, 예 through the faulty use of a speech act or one of the rules of speaking (pragmatic error). In the study of second and foreign language learning, errors have been studied to discover the processes learners make use of in learning and using a language.

(2) Sources of Errors

① Interlingual transfer (interference)

Students who learn English as a second language already have a deep knowledge of at least one other language. Where that L1 and the variety of English they are learning into contact with each other, there are often confusions which provoke errors in a learner's use of English. In error analysis, an error which results from language transfer, that is, which is caused by the learner's native language. 예 The incorrect French sentence "Elle regarde les" (She sees them), produced according to the word order of English, instead of the correct French sentence "Elle les regarde" (Literally, "She them sees").

② Intralingual errors (overgeneralization)

An intralingual error is one which results from faulty or partial learning of the target language, rather than from language transfer. Intralingual errors may be caused by the influence of one target language item upon another. 예 A learner may produce *He is comes*, based on a blend of the English structures *He is coming, He comes*.

▶ **Types of learners' overgeneralization**

Types	Example
past tense form of verb following a modal	*could taught*
present tense –s on a verb following a modal	*can sings*
–ing on a verb following a modal	*may driving*
are (for be) following will	*will are*
–ing on a verb following do	*do studying*

③ Context of learning

Context refers to, for example, the classroom with its teacher and its materials in the case of school learning or the social situation in the case of untutored second language learning. In the classroom, students often make errors because of:

- misleading explanation from the teacher
- faulty presentation of a structure or word in a textbook
- a pattern that was rotely memorized in a drill but improperly contextualized two vocabulary items presented contiguously, 예 *pointed at* and *pointed out* – might in later recall be confused simply because of the contiguity of presentation.
- A teacher may provide incorrect information by way of misleading definition, word, or grammatical generalization.

Another manifestation of language learned in classroom context is "the occasional tendency on the part of learners to give uncontracted and inappropriately formal forms of language. We have all experienced foreign learners whose bookish language give them away as classroom language learners. The sociolinguistic context of natural untutored language acquisition can give rise to certain dialect acquisition that may itself be a source of error. 예 A Japanese learner who lived in a Mexican-American area in USA produced an interesting language that is a blend of Mexican-American and Standard English colored by Japanese accent.

④ Communication strategies

The fourth source of errors is communication strategies. They are related to learning styles. Learners use production strategies in order to enhance getting their messages across but at times these techniques can themselves become a source of error.

2. Error Analysis

(1) Definition

Error analysis is the study and analysis of the errors made by second language learners. Error analysis may be carried out in order to the following reasons:

- identify strategies which learners use in language learning
- try to identify the causes of learner errors
- obtain information on common difficulties in language learning, as an aid to teaching or in the preparation of teaching materials

(2) Backgrounds

Error analysis developed as a branch of Applied Linguistics in the 1960s, and set out to demonstrate that many learner errors were not due to the learner's mother tongue but reflected universal learning strategies. Error analysis was therefore offered as an alternative to Contrastive Analysis. Attempts were made to develop classifications for different types of errors on the basis of the different processes that were assumed to account for them. A basic distinction was drawn between intralingual and interlingual errors.

Intralingual errors were classified as overgeneralizations (errors caused by extension of target language rules to inappropriate contexts), simplifications (errors resulting from learners producing simpler linguistic rules than those found in the target language), developmental errors (those reflecting natural stages of development), communication-based errors (errors resulting from strategies of communication), induced errors (those resulting from transfer of training), errors of avoidance (resulting from failure to use certain target language structures because they are thought to be too difficult), or errors of overproduction (structures being used too frequently). Attempts to apply such categories have been problematic however, due to the difficulty of determining the cause of errors. By the late 1970s, error analysis had largely been superseded by studies of interlanguage and second language acquisition.

(3) Practical Uses of Error Analysis

Student's performance	Teacher's comments
*a. My friend and a teacher likes it very much. b. My friend and a teacher like it very much.	a.는 주어와 동사의 일치가 이루어지지 않아 올바른 문장으로 만들려면 b.처럼 동사의 수를 복수형태로 재구성해야 한다는 것을 쉽게 알 수 있다.
*c. She went in the traffic. d. She went into the traffic.	c.는 목표언어인 영어에서 가능한 문장이지만 선호되는 문장이 아니지만 'in the traffic'이 비문법적인 것은 아니다.
*e. The big of them contained a snake. f. The bigger of them contained a snake. g. The big one contained a snake.	e.의 경우는 학습자가 의도하는 것이 무엇인지 확실하지 않기 때문에 문장을 재구성하는 것이 어려운 경우이다. e.를 정확한 문장으로 재구성하기 위해서 f. 나 g.를 이용할 수 있다.

(4) Corrective Feedback in Classroom

① Explicit correction : refers to the explicit provision of the correct form. As the teacher provides the correct form, he or she clearly indicates that what the student has said was incorrect. (예 'Oh, you mean···', 'You should say···')

② Recasts : involve the teacher's reformulation of all or part of a student's utterance, minus the error.

③ Clarification requests : indicate to students either that their utterance has been misunderstood by the teacher or that the utterance is ill-formed in some way and that a repetition or a reformulation is required. (예 'Pardon me..', 'What do you mean by···?')

④ Metalinguistic feedback : contains comments, information, or question related to the well-formedness of the student's utterance, without explicitly providing the correct form. (예 'Can you find your error?')

⑤ Elicitation : refers to at least three techniques that teachers use to directly elicit the correct form from the students.
- Teachers elicit completion of their own utterance. (예 'It's a···')
- Teachers use questions to elicit correct forms. (예 'How do we say X in English?')
- Teachers occasionally ask students to reformulate their utterance.

⑥ Repetition : refers to the teacher's repetition, in isolation, of the student's erroneous utterance. In most cases, teachers adjust their intonation so as to highlight the error.

문헌읽기   Corrective Feedback in Second Language Acquisition

Over the last few years, the role played by corrective feedback in language acquisition has become a highly controversial issue. In the field of First Language Acquisition (FLA), researchers express strong reservations concerning the effect that negative evidence has on FLA, if there is any at all. In the field of Second Language Acquisition (SLA), however, there appears to be a growing consensus among the majority of researchers concerning the significance of the role played by negative evidence in the process of SLA. This literature review will focus mainly on the role played by corrective feedback in SLA. While corrective feedback clearly relates to both oral and written discourse, the focus of this discussion will center on oral production, since the preponderance of research has largely focused on this aspect. In the following sections of this review, the meaning of corrective feedback will be discussed, and the different theoretical stances towards its role in SLA examined. Empirical studies that explore the impact corrective feedback has on SLA will be reviewed, followed by a discussion of some of the issues that loom large in research in the area of corrective feedback and its role in SLA.

(1) Definition Of Terms

There are various terms used in identifying errors and providing corrective feedback in the SLA literature, the most common being corrective feedback, negative evidence, and negative feedback. Because of possible confusion arising from the use of this terminology, a brief review of the definitions of terms and of the different types of feedback is presented below. Chaudron (1988) has pointed out the fact that the term corrective feedback incorporates different layers of meaning. In Chaudron's view, the term "treatment of error" may simply refer to "any teacher behavior following an error that minimally attempts to inform the learner of the fact of error". The treatment may not be evident to the student in terms of the response it elicits, or it may make a significant effort "to elicit a revised student response". Finally, there is "the true" correction which succeeds in modifying the learner's interlanguage rule so that the error is eliminated from further production.

Lightbown and Spada (1999) define corrective feedback as: Any indication to the learners that their use of the target language is incorrect. This includes various responses that the learners receive. 예 When a language learner says, 'He go to school everyday', corrective feedback can be explicit, 'no, you should say goes, not go' or implicit 'yes he goes to school every day', and may or may not include metalinguistic information, 'Don't forget to make the verb agree with the subject'.

According to Schachter (1991), corrective feedback, negative evidence, and negative feedback are three terms used respectively in the fields of language teaching, language acquisition, and cognitive psychology. Different researchers often use these terms interchangeably. The feedback can be explicit (예 grammatical explanation or overt error correction) or implicit. Implicit correction includes, but is not limited to, confirmation checks, repetitions, recasts, clarification requests, silence, and even facial expressions that express confusion. Long (1996) offers a more comprehensive view of feedback in general. He suggests that environmental input can be thought of in terms of two categories that are provided to the learners about the target language (TL): positive evidence and negative evidence. Long defines positive evidence as providing the learners with models of what is grammatical and acceptable in the TL; and negative evidence as providing the learners with direct or indirect information about what is unacceptable. This information may be: Explicit (예 grammatical explanation or overt error correction) or implicit (예 failure to understand, incidental error correction in a response, such as a confirmation check, which reformulates the learners' utterance without interrupting the flow of the conversation, in which case, the negative feedback simultaneously provides additional positive evidence and perhaps also the absence of the items in the input.

Long (2001) more recently has offered the following framework incorporating the different types of positive and negative evidence in relation to the linguistic environment, i.e., input. According to the above classification, negative evidence and positive evidence constitute the only two types of evidence available to the language learner. Each type is further divided into subtypes. The frequency of occurrence in different second language (L2) learning contexts as well as the differential effects of different types of negative evidence on interlanguage (IL) development will be discussed in the following sections of this literature review.

(2) **Theoretical Stances On The Role Of Corrective Feedback In SLA**

The theoretical pendulum has swung back and forth regarding the role assigned to negative evidence in the process of SLA. There is a debate on the nature of the driving force behind SLA, i.e., whether it is positive evidence or negative evidence that has the greater impact. According to nativist theory, advocated by Chomsky (1975), negative evidence hardly plays any role at all. This is due to the fact that, for the nativists, what makes language acquisition possible is Universal Grammar (UG), "the system of principles, conditions, and rules that are elements of properties of all human languages". That is to say, in this view of language learning, what makes the acquisition of language possible is UG, and the innate linguistic mechanism that is available to all humans. UG advocates have argued that instruction, including negative evidence, has little impact on forms within UG anyway, since it will temporarily change only language behavior and not IL grammars (Carroll, 1996; Cook, 1991; Schwartz, 1993). In this view, changes in the IL grammar are the result of positive linguistic evidence. In addition, Krashen (1982, 1985) believes that SLA is the result of implicit processes operating together with the reception of comprehensible input. Conscious learning can only act as a monitor that edits the output, after it has been initiated by the acquired system. From this, then, it follows that explicit data, whether in the form of negative evidence or in the form of explicit instruction, can only affect the learning rather than the acquisition of the target language.

Krashen's input hypothesis posits that it is subconscious acquisition that gains dominance, and that learning cannot be converted into acquisition, even though adults can both subconsciously acquire languages and consciously learn about languages. In short, for Krashen, as for the nativists, negative evidence has a barely discernable effect on SLA. Krashen's views and theories of language learning have been challenged on the grounds that while comprehension is essential for language acquisition, such acquisition does not entail unconscious or implicit learning processes; and that noticing is indispensable for the acquisition process (Ellis, 1991; Gass, 1988, 1990, 1991; Gass & Varonis, 1991; Schmidt, 1990, 1994; Schmidt & Frota, 1986). According to the noticing hypothesis, in order for input to become intake for L2 learning, some degree of noticing must occur, and that it is corrective feedback that triggers that learners' noticing of gaps between the target norms and their IL, and thus leads to subsequent grammatical restructuring. According to Schmidt (1990), "subliminal language learning is impossible, and that intake is what learners consciously notice. This requirement of noticing is meant to apply equally to all aspects of language". Language learners, however, are limited in what they are able to notice. The main determining factor is that of attention. As Schmidt (1994) points out, "while the intention to learn is not always crucial to learning, attention to the material to be learned is". Attention, in addition, also controls access to conscious experience, thus allowing the acquisition of new items to take place. Gass (1988, 1990, 1991), moreover, has argued against the notion that learners, with the mere presentation of comprehensible input, would convert it to intake and subsequently to output.

According to her, for learners to be able to internalize input in order to affect the acquisition process, they must not only comprehend this input, but also must notice the mismatch between the input and their own IL system. She points out that "nothing in the target language is available for intake into a language learner's existing system unless it is consciously noticed" (1991). Corrective feedback, for Gass, functions as an attention getting device. She further argues that without direct or frequent corrective feedback in the input, which would permit learners to detect discrepancies between their learner language and the target language, fossilization might occur. Gass and Varonis (1994), moreover, point out that "the awareness of the mismatch serves the function of triggering a modification of existing L2 knowledge, the results of which may show up at a later point in time".

Similarly, Ellis (1991) shares the view that the acquisition process includes the steps of noticing, comparing, and integrating. There is further evidence of the role of corrective feedback in the hypothesis testing models of acquisition. In these models, the learner is assumed to formulate hypotheses about the TL, and to test these hypotheses against the target norm. In this model of learning, corrective feedback, or negative data, plays a crucial role (Bley-Vroman, 1986, 1989). Ohta (2001) takes corrective feedback a step further by showing that if the correct form is provided, learners may have the chance to compare their own production with that of another. In this way, corrective feedback may stimulate hypothesis testing, giving the learner the opportunity to grapple with form-meaning relationships. Corrective feedback that does not provide the correct form, on the other hand, may force the learners to utilize their own resources in constructing a reformulation. In either case, corrective feedback may facilitate L2 development. According to Chaudron (1988), the information available in feedback allows the learners to confirm, disconfirm, and possibly modify the hypothetical, transitional rules of their developing grammars. These effects, however, depend on the learners' readiness for and attention to the information available in feedback. That is, learners must still make a comparison between their internal representation of a rule and the information about the rule in the input they encounter. Finally, Schachter

(1991), with reference to the above views, points out that it is due to the corrective feedback the learners receive that they abandon their wrong hypotheses and immediately switch to formulating new ones. On the question of what kind of evidence can disconfirm incorrect hypotheses about the L2, White (1988) states that positive evidence alone is insufficient.

Concerning whether or not L2 acquisition can progress on the basis of positive evidence alone, she further suggests that it cannot, and that "there will be cases where change from X to Y will require negative evidence". There are certain situations, she argues, which entail negative evidence, i.e., drawing learners' attention to the fact that certain forms are not allowed in the target language. According to White (1988), negative evidence is particularly required when learners adopt grammars that generate a superset of the grammars actually allowed in the target language. In other words, negative evidence is necessary when the learners need to go from a broader grammar (superset) to a narrower grammar (subset). A case in point is that there is no positive evidence that highlights that English does not allow null subjects. Corrective feedback, in cases like the ungrammaticality of null subjects in English, she argues, will help put L2 learners on the right track.

This brings us to the view of SLA as cognitive skill acquisition. In this view of learning, language acquisition includes interaction between input, the cognitive system, and the learner's perceptual motor system. According to this model of language learning, feedback is essential (Johnson, 1988, 1996). This is due to the fact that "it has the properties of informing, regulating, strengthening, sustaining, and error eliminating" (Han, 2001). Given the considerable research on the role of corrective feedback in SLA from the various models of acquisition discussed in this review, it seems that there is a growing belief that interaction between innate and environmental factors is necessary for language acquisition. This leads to Long's (1996, 1998) updated version of the interactionist hypothesis. In this model, Long (1996) proposes that: "Environmental contributions to acquisition are mediated by selective attention and the learner's developing L2 processing capacity, and that the resources are brought together most usefully, although not exclusively, during negotiation for meaning. Negative feedback obtained during negotiation work or elsewhere may be facilitated of SL development, at least for vocabulary, morphology, and language specific syntax and essential for learning certain specifiable L1–L2 contrasts. According to this model of acquisition, interaction that includes implicit corrective feedback is facilitative of L2 development. Interest in the impact that corrective feedback has on IL development, and in the roles of both teachers and students in corrective feedback episodes, has spawned a number of recent studies on the topic. This research has been most prolific in ESL and immersion classrooms."

CHAPTER 03 Learning Strategies

> **단원 길라잡이**
> - 학습자의 다양한 스타일과 전략을 파악한다.
> - 학습전략과 의사소통전략의 종류를 이해한다.

Introduction

학습자 언어를 이해하기 위해서는 우리가 학습자 중심의 수업을 한다는 것은 그들의 언어의 수준과 요구를 이해하는 것이 출발점이 될 것이다. 그들의 다양한 학습 유형과 전략을 알아야 한다. 학습유형은 일반적으로 지속적이며 내재적인 것이며 학습전략은 상황이나 과제에 따라 바꾸어 나갈 수 있는 것으로 설명될 수 있다. 또 다른 종류의 전략으로 의사소통 전략은 의사소통을 하는 과정에서 의사소통에 문제가 발생했을 때 그를 보상하기 위하여 대체하면서 생겨나는 방법이다. 우선 우리나라의 교육과정에서 요구하는 의사소통 전략이 무엇인지를 살펴보고 교실 안에서 가장 효과적으로 활용 가능한 방법들에는 어떤 것들이 존재하는지 알아보기로 하자.

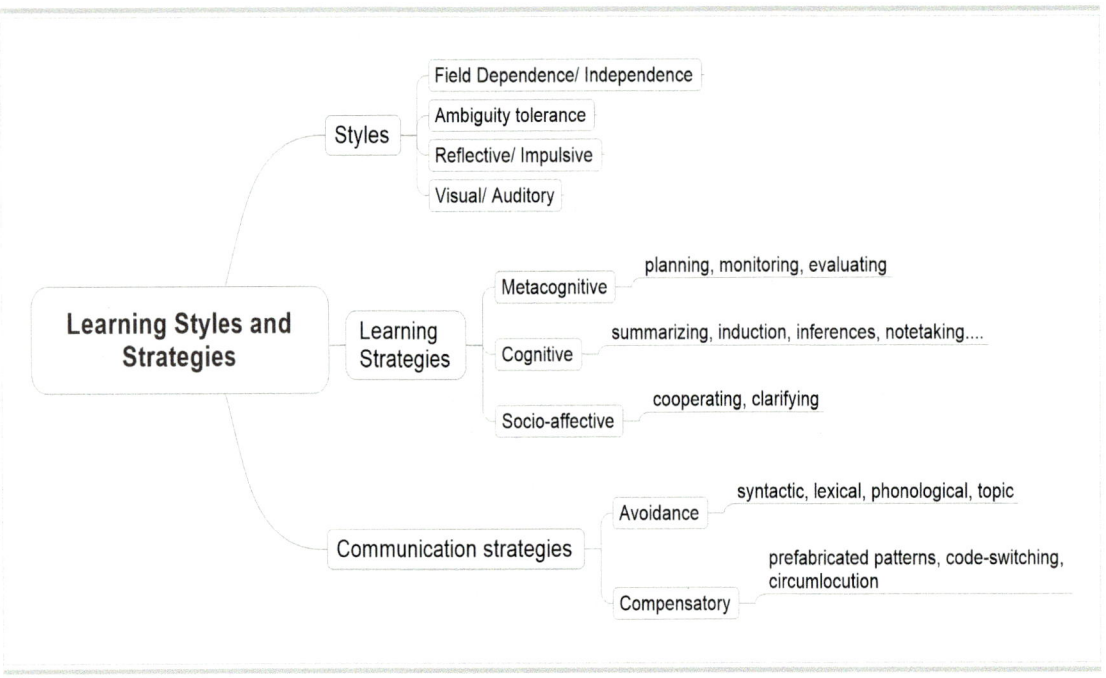

교육과정

교육과정에서의 의사소통전략은 학생들이 효과적인 의사소통을 할 수 있도록 다양한 의사소통전략을 적절히 사용하게 한다. 효과적인 의사소통이란 주어진 상황에서 알고 있는 언어 지식을 최대한 활용하여 상대방이 전달하고자 하는 의미를 이해하고, 자신의 의사를 적절히 표현함으로써 대화를 지속하는 것이다. 이러한 전략은 대화 중 적절한 표현이 떠오르지 않거나 상대방의 의미를 잘못 이해하는 등의 의사소통 위기를 효과적으로 대처하는 데 도움이 된다. 의사소통전략은 개인이 정보의 생산적인 소통을 위해 세우는 의식적인 계획으로서 다음의 유형이 있다.

① 회피(avoidance) : 회피 전략에는 잘 알지 못하는 화제를 자신이 친숙한 다른 화제로 자연스럽게 전환하여 대화를 유지하는 화제 회피와, 주어진 화제는 유지하면서 의미 범주 내에 포함되어 있는 통사적 혹은 어휘적 항목의 회피가 있다.

② 바꾸어 말하기(paraphrase) : 바꾸어 말하기 전략은 근사어(approximation)나 신조어(word coinage) 또는 우회적 표현을 사용하는 것이다. 보다 구체적인 어휘 항목(예 waterpipe)을 대신하여 그 항목을 포함하는 더 넓은 범주의 어휘(예 pipe)를 사용하거나, 필요한 개념을 전달하기 위해 새로운 표현(balloon 대신 airball)을 만들어 사용하고, 적절한 어휘나 구조를 찾지 못할 때 해당 물건이나 행동의 특징 및 요소를 묘사하는 것이다.

③ 권위에의 호소(appeal to authority) : 권위에 직접 호소하는 전략은 전달하고자 하는 의미에 대한 적당한 표현이 떠오르지 않을 때, 원어민이나 자신보다 우수한 언어 사용자에게 정확한 용어, 구문 등을 직접 묻거나 문제해결에 도움을 요청하고, 이따금 자신의 표현이 옳은지를 확인하는 질문을 하는 것이다.

④ 직역(literal translation) : 모국어 표현을 그대로 목표어로 직역하여 표현하는 전략은 목표어의 구조나 어휘로는 어색하지만, 의사소통 중단 위기를 피할 수 있게 해준다. 따라서 제한된 언어 능력이나마 적절히 활용할 수 있는 의사소통전략을 가르친 다음, 이러한 수단이 필요한 상황을 대화로 구성한 활동을 통해 학생들이 의식적으로 전략을 사용하도록 연습시킬 필요가 있다.

⑤ 마임(mime)이나 얼굴 표정 등의 비언어적 전략이 있다.

다양한 정보통신기술(ICT) 자료를 활용하여 의사소통전략이 실제로 사용되는 대화 장면을 보여주면, 전략이 필요한 상황, 사용하는 방법 및 그 효과 또는 중요성 등을 보다 쉽게 인식시킬 수 있다.

01 Individual variability

Individual variability consists of such factors as the age of students, their motivation for learning the target language, and their personality. All of which affect their language learning style. It is essential to recognize that there are individual differences between learners. As a result different learning and studying approaches are exhibited by different cultures and individuals from those cultures.

Additionally certain variables that affect language learning operate on individuals to different degrees. 예 'Transition anxiety' may generally hit one ethnic group more so than another. Developing this point further, the need for a secure and stable family life that provides support to the student, may not be present or present only to a limited degree. This sort of learning base for a student would impinge upon their ability and prove detrimental to their language acquisition. ESL teachers should be aware that students possessing this background may not progress quickly.

1. Foreigner Talk

While native speakers plainly adjust their speech to accommodate non-native speakers on syntactic and prosodic levels, they are also making adjustments on the level of discourse. It has been argued that these interactional adjustments are the crucial ones to the promotion of language learning. The present study compared the proportion of nine interactional features used in the speech of four ESL teachers as they taught beginners and advanced level adult classes. As predicted, display questions and self-repetitions were used much less often with advanced students. The lack of other differences in interactional adjustments may be an artifact of the lesson content or teacher style. High variability in teacher behaviour was discovered. The marked reduction in use of display questions at the advanced level provided encouraging evidence that the ESL classroom is, in fact, preparing students for the real, communicative world. Implications for teacher training are pointed out.

Until recently, second language acquisition research has focused on the learner's production, and attempted to document the stages of development in the acquisition process. Some contemporary studies have shifted the focus to an examination of the learner's linguistic environment, that is, the target language available to the learner and how it affects the learning process. It has been observed that native speakers (NS) adjust their speech in conversation with non-native speakers (NNS) in various ways. This modified register has been termed foreigner talk (FT) by Charles Ferguson (1971), and defined as a register of simplified speech used by speakers of a language to outsiders who are felt to have very limited command of the language or no knowledge of it at all. In the earlier studies, Ferguson and others investigated adjustments at the phonological, prosodic, lexical, and, mainly, syntactic levels of linguistic analysis. In comparison to speech between NSs, FT is characterized by the following:

- slower rate of delivery
- increased loudness
- clearer articulation
- exaggerated pronunciation
- more pauses
- more emphatic stress
- shorter utterances
- lower syntactic complexity
- more avoidance of low frequency items and idiomatic expressions

The focus of research shifted once again when Michael Long (1981a) made an important distinction between input modifications to the linguistic forms used, and interactional modifications to the functions served by those forms, which occur at the level of discourse. Discourse modifications include such phenomena as increased numbers of self-repetitions and confirmation checks. An example (Long 1983a) will serve to illustrate both what is meant by this distinction, and the fact that input and interaction modifications can occur independently.

(1) NS–NS speech	NS:	When did you finish?
	NS:	Ten.
(2) Foreigner Talk–modification in form only	NS:	What time you finish?
	NNS:	Ten o'clock.
(3) Foreigner Talk–modification injunction only	NS:	When did you finish?
	NNS:	Urh?
	NS:	When did you finish?
	NNS:	Ten clock.
	NS:	Ten o'clock?

Exchanges like example (2) are often found in pidginized forms of English (예 between migrant workers and their NS supervisors). The input modifications (uninverted WH-question, deletion of do, and lack of verb inflection) allowed the NNS to understand and complete the exchange in only two turns. Example (3) is typical of conversations in studies between speakers of similar social status (예 the NS and NNS university students in Freed 1981). The utterance form has not deviated from NS–NS norms, but the interactional structure of the conversation has. The NS has added a self-repetition and a confirmation check, resulting in a six-turn exchange to accomplish what the NS–NS exchange does in two. As is apparent from this example, examining interaction involves utterances in context, that is, takes into account the surrounding utterances of both speakers. For instance, the confirmation check in (3) can only be recognized in light of the NNS' preceding utterance. It should also be noted that interactional aspects of foreigner talk are all phenomena found in NS-NS speech. The greater frequency of use of these features in FT is what distinguishes it from NS-NS speech. Presumably, this simplified register of speech provides comprehensible input to the learner at an appropriate level to allow for communicative interaction as well as language learning.

But Long suggests it is the interactional rather than the input modifications which are essential to producing comprehensible input for the NNS (Long 1983b). Evidence in support of this claim is found in Long's comparison of the speech of NSs to NSs and NNSs in conversations generated by six different tasks (1981a). There were no significant differences in the two types of NS speech on 4 out of 5 measures of input modification. NSs did use significantly shorter utterances in addressing the NNSs, but measures of syntactic complexity, and lexical density and frequency were not significantly different in the two groups. However, frequencies on 10 out of 11 interactional measures were significantly different. NS speech to foreigners as compared to that of other NSs contained, 예 more expansions, self- and other-repetitions, comprehension checks, confirmation checks, and clarification requests.

While other studies of foreigner talk have treated subjects as equally good representatives of a common NS behaviour construct, here that assumption was tested in the treatment of teacher as a separate variable. Each teacher was observed teaching one beginner level and one advanced level class, making a total of eight observations. Observing each teacher at both proficiency levels provided control of the teacher variable. Dependent variables were:

Types	Definitions	Examples
Display Questions	Display questions are typically closed-ended and aim to confirm students' understanding of the presented information.	• How do you say this word? • Can you give me __? • What do we call that money back, money back?
Referential Questions	These questions are more open-ended and encourage discussion and exploration.	• What did you read about? • What is a democratic way? • What do you think?
Comprehension Checks	The NS attempts to determine whether their previous utterance has been understood.	• So past tense is, from yesterday, come-came, right? • OK? (rising intonation) • Do you understand 'leave'? Do you know what that means?

Types	Definitions	Examples
Confirmation Checks	The NS requests confirmation that they have correctly understood the NNS.	• Did they leave from Vancouver? Is that what you said? • X does it mean? • What does it mean? (rising intonation)
Clarification Requests	The NS indicates that the NNS's utterance has not been understood and requests clarification.	• Could you please explain it again? • Could you clarify what 'equilibrium' means in this context? • Sorry, I didn't catch that. Could you repeat what you just said?"

The subjects were one male and three female ESL teachers, each with at least 5 years experience. There were no extremes in teaching style or method. The average class size was 16. The students were all adults and all classes contained both · males and females from a variety of first language backgrounds. Oriental backgrounds (Chinese, Japanese, Korean or Vietnamese) were predominant, however, with seven of eight classes having between 64% and 92% Oriental L1 speakers. The NNS's first language may significantly affect a conversational partner's FT, but the present study does not control for this factor, nor has this interesting question been addressed in the literature to date.

The researcher audiotaped all of the observations in as unobtrusive a manner as possible. None of the subjects knew the purpose of the study, but they were told that teacher-student interaction was under scrutiny. They were asked to carry out a regular lesson, but told that any group work or non-teacher-fronted activity would not be recorded. Forty-five minutes of instruction per class (following warm-up conversation) were transcribed and coded to reflect instances of the nine interactional features. Fixed two-factor analyses of variance were performed on the frequency counts to address nine research hypotheses.

The hypotheses can be summarized as follows: the ESL teachers' speech to advanced students, as compared to beginner students, will contain significantly more referential questions and significantly fewer of all the other interactional features studied. Considered together, and in a broader framework, these hypotheses mean it was expected that teachers would approach a NS-NS teacher talk register as their students approached NS proficiency.

02 Styles & Strategies

Style	consistent and rather enduring tendencies or preferences within an individual; general characteristics of intellectual functioning that pertain to you as an individual, and that differentiate you from someone else; characterize a general pattern in your thinking or feeling
Strategies	specific methods of approaching a problem or task, modes of operation for achieving a particular end, planned designs for controlling and manipulating certain information; may vary from moment to moment; vary intra-individually.

1. Styles

학습자의 learning style이 2언어습득에 미치는 영향에 대하여 알아보기로 하자. learning style은 학습자 고유의 성질로서 지속적으로 나타나는 특성이라고 할 수 있다. 그 중에서 가장 대표되는 style이 field dependence/ independence로서 학습자가 학습의 장을 어떻게 인식하고 새로운 학습내용이 들어왔을 때 그 정보를 어떻게 처리하느냐에 관련된 문제이다. 그것을 기본으로 하여 다른 learning style이 함께 작동되므로 아래에 정리된 내용으로 이해할 수 있겠다. 하지만 learning styles은 고정된 성격이라기보다는 변화되는 학습자 성격을 나타내는 것이므로 context안에서 이해하는 자세가 필요하다고 할 수 있다.

Field	Independence	전체 안에서 개별규칙에 대한 인식가능: 2언어 교실학습에 성공 가능 큼
	Dependence	세부보다는 전체사항에 집중: 2언어 의사소통적 성공 가능 큼
Brain Functioning	Left	지적, 분석적, 논리적 경향: 연역적 교수형태 선호
	Right	직관적, 정서적, 종합적 경향: 귀납적 교수형태 선호
Ambiguity	Tolerance	자신의 신념에 반하는 주장에 관용적: 혁신적, 창의적
	Intolerance	자신의 신념에 반하는 주장에 비관용적: 가능성 없는 것 안 다룸
Personality	Reflective	깊이 생각하여 결단 내림: 읽기 느리지만 정확, 오류 잘 간과
	Impulsive	속단적, 투기적 추측 경향: 빨리 읽고 육감으로 해결점 도달
AV	Visual	시각적 입력 선호 경향: 독서차트, 그림 등 도식정보 선호
	Auditory	청각적 입력 선호 경향: 강연, 녹음테이프 등의 청취 선호

(1) Field Independence/ Dependence in Second Language Learning

Field, in psychological terms, refers to a set of thoughts, ideas, or feelings from which your task is perceive specific relevant subsets. A person tends to be dominant in FI or FD, and FI/D is a relatively stable trait in adulthood; the extent of the development of a FI/D style as children mature is a factor of the type of society and home. FI and FD styles are important. Natural language learning in the field requires a FD style; empathy is related to language learning (Guiora et al.) The classroom type of learning requires a FI style; FI correlated negatively with informal oral interviews of adult English learners in the U.S. FI/D might provide one construct that differentiates classroom second language learning from natural second language learning. FI/D is a valuable tool for differentiating child and adult language acquisition. Children, more predominantly FD, may have a cognitive style advantage over the more FI adult. FI/D is variable within one person; depending on the context of learning, individual learners can vary their utilization of FI or FD.

① Field independence style: the ability to perceive a particular, relevant item or factor in a field of distracting items: FI is closely related to classroom learning involving analysis, attention to details, and mastering of exercises, drills, and other focused activities.

② Field dependence (field sensitivity): the tendency to be dependent on the total field so that the parts embedded within the field are not easily perceived, although that total field is perceived more clearly as a unified whole: FD persons will be successful in learning the communicative aspects of a second language. Little empirical evidence because of the absence of a true test of FD.

Field independence	Field dependence
• FI enables you to distinguish parts from a whole, to concentrate on something, to analyze separate variables without the contamination of neighboring variables • Too much FI: "tunnel vision"; see only the parts and not their relationship to the whole • FI increases as a child matures to adulthood. • FI is related to the analytical factor. • A democratic, industrialized, competitive society tends to produce more FI persons: more independent, competitive, and self-confident	• FD perceives the whole picture, the larger view, the general configuration of a problem or idea or event • Authoritarian societies tend to produce more FD. • Persons: more socialized, to derive their self-identity from persons around them, and more empathic and perceptive of the feelings and thoughts of others

(2) Left-brain and Right-brain Functioning

① Left hemisphere: logical, analytical thought, with mathematical and linear processing of information: Left-/right-brain construct with implications for second language learning and teaching

② Right hemisphere: perceives and remembers visual, tactile, and auditory images; more efficient in processing holistic, integrative, and emotional information: Right-brain-dominant learners deal better with whole images, with generalizations, with metaphors, and with emotional reactions and artistic expressions. A greater need to perceive whole meanings in the early stages, and to analyze and monitor oneself more in the later stages.
- Left-brain-dominant learners are better at producing separate words, gathering the specifics of language, carrying out sequences of operations, and dealing with abstraction, classification, labeling, and reorganization.
- Left-brain-dominant second language learners preferred a deductive style of teaching; right-dominant learners more successful in an inductive classroom activities

(3) Ambiguity tolerance

① One of the language learning variables is ambiguity tolerance which can be defined as an attitude to understand the target structure with insufficient knowledge and to what extent learners tolerate the unknown items in the target language. Tolerance for ambiguity can be defined as the degree to which an individual is comfortable with uncertainty, unpredictability, conflicting directions, and multiple demands. Tolerance for ambiguity is manifest in a person's ability to operate effectively in an uncertain environment.

② Ambiguity-tolerant learners learn most effectively when they are given chance of experiences, risks and interactions. On the contrary, ambiguity-intolerant learners learn best in more rigid, more certain, and more structured situations. Intolerance can close the mind too soon, too narrow to creative and harmful in second language learning.

(4) Reflectivity and Impulsivity

① Implications for language learning
- Conceptually reflective children tend to make fewer errors in reading than impulsive children. Reflective students tend to remain longer at a particular stage with larger leaps from stage to stage.
- Impulsive children are usually faster readers, and eventually master the "psycholinguistic guessing game" of reading, which not necessarily deter comprehension. Students with impulsive styles may go through a number of rapid transitions of semigrammatical stages of SLA.

② Research related to second language learning
- Reflective students are slower but more accurate than impulsive students.
- Reflection was weakly related to performance on a proof-reading task.
- Fast-accurate learners or good guessers are better language learners but impulsivity doesn't always imply accuracy.
- Reflectivity/ impulsivity are closely related to systematic and intuitive styles.

(5) Visual, Auditory, and Kinesthetic Styles

① Visual learners tend to prefer reading and studying charts, drawings, and other graphic information. They think in pictures and detail and have vivid imaginations. When extensive listening is required, they may be quiet and become impatient. Neat in appearance, they may dress in the same manner all the time. They have greater immediate recall of words that are presented visually.

② Auditory learners prefer listening to lectures and audiotapes. They rely on speaking and listening as their primary way of learning. 예 An auditory learner may remember everything that was said during a work meeting but has a hard time recalling the information that was outlined in a work report.

③ A kinesthetic-tactile learning style requires that you manipulate or touch material to learn. Kinesthetic-tactile techniques are used in combination with visual and/or auditory study techniques, producing multi-sensory learning.

2. Strategies

(1) **Learning strategies**: related to input processing, storage, and retrieval, i.e., to taking in messages from others

① Types

Types	Definitions
Metacognitive strategies: a term used in information-processing theory to indicate an executive function, strategies - planning for learning, thinking about the learning process, monitoring of one's production or comprehension, and evaluating learning after an activity is completed	
Planning	Previewing main ideas Making plans to accomplish a task Paying attention to key information Seeking out and arranging for conditions to promote successful learning
Monitoring	Self-checking ones comprehension
Evaluating	Developing the ability to determine how well one has accomplished the task
Cognitive strategies: more limited specific learning tasks, and more direct manipulation of the learning material itself	
Summarizing	Saying or writing the main idea
Induction	Figuring out the rules from samples of language
Imaginary	Being able to visualize a picture and use it to learn new information
Auditory	Mentally replaying a word, phrase, or piece of information
Making inferences	Using information in the text to guess the meaning
Using resources	Developing the ability to use reference materials
Grouping	Classifying words, terminology, quantities, or concepts
Note-taking	Writing down key words & concepts in verbal, graphic, or numerical form
Prior Knowledge	Relating new to known information and making personal associations
Social/ Affective strategies: social-mediating activity and interacting with others	
Cooperating	Learning how to work with peers-completing a task, pooling information, solving a problem, and obtaining feedback
Clarifying	Learning how to ask question to get additional explanation or verification from the teacher or someone else who might know the answer
Self-talk	Reducing anxiety by talking positively to oneself

② Methods to teach Learning Strategies

Strategies-based instruction and autonomous self-help training; SBI and autonomous learning are viable avenues to success, cultural differences notwithstanding.

다양한 활동과 자료 이용	Learning style profiles are different for everyone. Students will also have different needs relative to learning strategies depending in their collective goals and objectives. Teacher lesson plans and select activities and tasks to match their learning styles.
learning styles의 가치를 중립적으로 하기	The students in classes will all have different learning styles. Some styles will better than others in different learning situations, but no one learning style is better than another one. One way that you can show that you value all learning styles is to make certain that you vary your lesson plans so that they include activities that address the different styles.
교사의 교수법을 검토하기	Focus in either styles or strategies, and on one or two specific styles or strategies at a time. Before you begin making changes in your approach to teaching relative to learning styles and strategies, you should always make certain that you have clear understanding of what it is that you routinely do.
학생들의 learning styles 확장	Rather than think of each learning style as very separate and unique, it is useful to think of learning styles on a continuum. By thinking of learning styles on a continuum, teacher can see more clearly what styles students are using in the classroom and can get a clearer picture of how to help them stretch their learning styles—particularly for students at the extremes of the continuum.
learning styles과 strategies을 연결	Learning styles and strategies are closely related; therefore, it is important to find ways to link these two concepts in course curricula.

(2) **Communication strategies** : They pertain to output, how we productively express meaning, how we deliver messages to others; elements of an overall strategic competence in which learners bring to bear all the possible facets of their growing competence in order to send clear messages in the second language; may or may not be "potentially conscious"

① Strategy of avoidance

When speaking or writing a second language, a speaker will often try to avoid using a difficult word or structure, and will use a simpler word or structure instead. This is called an avoidance strategy. 예 A student who is not sure of the use of the relative clause in English may avoid using it and use two simpler sentences instead: *That's my building. I live there.* instead of *That's the building where I live.*

Syntactic or Lexical avoidance (within a semantic category)	The learner avoided the lexical item road entirely, not being able to come up with the word way at that point. L: I lost my road. NS: You lost your road? L: Uh, ⋯ I lost. I lost. I got lost.
Phonological avoidance	Avoid using some words because of their phonological difficulty
Topic avoidance	A whole topic of conversation might be avoided entirely; changing the subject, pretending not to understand, simply not responding at all, and so on

② Compensatory Strategies

Prefabricated patterns	the memorization of certain stock phrases or sentences without internalized knowledge of their components 예 pocket bilingual phrase book
Code-switching	the use of a first or third language within a stream of speech in the second language
Direct appeal for help	ask a native speaker, a teacher, or a bilingual dictionary for help
Paraphrase	An expression of the meaning of a word or phrase using other words or phrases, often in an attempt to make the meaning easier to understand. Dictionary definitions often take the form of paraphrases of the words they are trying to define. 예 To make (someone or something) appear or feel younger is a paraphrase of the English verb 'rejuvenate'.
Circumlocution	When learning a language, you use to describe a word or phrase when you don't know it in English. If you have good circumlocution strategies they will stop you hesitating too much or getting blocked when you are speaking.

③ Research

- Successful learners use word association and generating their own rules.
- Strategies represent reported instances of self talk.
- Strategies are asking for repetition and seeking various forms of clarification.
- Strategies include functional practice (using language for communication) and reading practice.

(3) Strategies-Based Instruction

"Teaching learners how to learn" is crucial. Learner strategies are the key to learner autonomy - the one of the most important goals of language teaching: the facilitation of the autonomy. Students will benefit from SBI if they (a) understand the strategy itself, (b) perceive it to be effective, and (c) do not consider its implementation to be overly difficult.

① Different Models of SBI

A. Teachers help students to become aware of their own style preferences and the strategies that are derived from those styles.

B. Teachers can embed strategy awareness and practice into their pedagogy; teachers can help students both consciously and subconsciously to practice successful strategies.

C. Certain compensatory techniques are sometimes practiced to help students overcome certain weaknesses.

D. Textbooks include strategy instruction as part of a content-centered approach.

② Compensatory Techniques for Learning

Weakness in Learning Styles	Compensatory Techniques
Low tolerance of ambiguity	brainstorming, retelling stories, role-play, jigsaw techniques
Excessive impulsiveness	making inferences, scanning for specific information, syntactic or semantic clue searches, inductive rule generalization
Excessive reflectiveness	small group techniques, role-play, fluency techniques, syntactic or semantic clue searches, information gap techniques
Too much field independence	integrative language techniques, fluency techniques, retelling stories, skimming tasks

문헌읽기 **Metacognitive awareness of reading strategies**

Metacognitive awareness of reading strategies refers to a reader's ability to plan, monitor, and evaluate their reading process. The three main categories of strategies —Global Reading Strategies (GLOB), Support Reading Strategies (SUP), and Problem-Solving Strategies (PROB) —serve distinct functions in enhancing reading comprehension.

1. Global Reading Strategies (GLOB): These are high-level, generalized strategies that readers use to plan and manage their reading process. They help readers establish a purpose for reading, maintain focus, and understand the broader structure or intent of the text.
   ① Examples:
   - Previewing the text: Looking at titles, headings, subheadings, or images to get an overview of the content.
   - Setting a purpose: Deciding why the text is being read (e.g., for information, pleasure, or analysis).
   - Using context clues: Trying to understand meaning through surrounding text.
   - Skimming for the main idea: Quickly identifying the central theme before reading in detail.
   - Relating prior knowledge: Connecting the text to what the reader already knows to enhance understanding.
   ② Teaching Tip: Encourage students to practice pre-reading activities, like generating predictions or brainstorming what they know about the topic.

2. Support Reading Strategies (SUP): These strategies involve using external aids or tools to facilitate understanding and retention of the text. They provide additional scaffolding to assist readers in comprehending complex or unfamiliar material.
   ① Examples:
   - Highlighting or underlining important text: Marking key ideas or terms for better focus and review.
   - Taking notes: Summarizing or jotting down important points while reading.
   - Using dictionaries or glossaries: Checking the meaning of unknown words or terms.
   - Rereading for clarification: Going over a passage multiple times to ensure comprehension.
   - Reading aloud: Verbalizing the text to engage auditory processing and improve focus.
   ② Teaching Tip: Model effective use of these tools in class and provide opportunities for students to practice using note-taking templates, glossaries, or highlighting tools.

3. Problem-Solving Strategies (PROB): These are reactive strategies used to overcome comprehension difficulties encountered while reading. They help readers address challenges such as confusing language, unclear meaning, or unfamiliar vocabulary.
   ① Examples:

- Guessing the meaning of unfamiliar words: Using contextual clues to infer the meaning without relying on a dictionary.
- Adjusting reading speed: Slowing down for difficult sections and speeding up for easier parts.
- Pausing and rereading: Taking a moment to reflect and revisit unclear parts of the text.
- Visualizing: Creating mental images to better understand descriptions or narratives.
- Breaking down sentences: Parsing complex sentences into smaller parts for clarity.

② Teaching Tip: Teach explicit strategies for tackling difficult text, such as chunking, visualizing, or underlining confusing parts for later discussion.

4. Integrating the Strategies in Classroom Practice

Teacher can incorporate these strategies into her teaching by:
- Explicit Instruction: Teach each strategy explicitly, with examples and guided practice.
- Modeling: Demonstrate how to apply the strategies during reading. For example, think aloud while reading a challenging text to show how to use context clues or adjust reading speed.
- Practice and Feedback: Allow students to practice the strategies independently or in groups and provide constructive feedback on their use.
- Reflection: Encourage students to reflect on which strategies they found helpful and when they applied them effectively.

By combining GLOB, SUP, and PROB strategies, students develop a holistic approach to reading, equipping them with the tools to navigate texts effectively and independently.

3

Teaching Methodology

01. Teaching Methodology
02. Grammar Translation Method
03. The Direct Method
04. Audiolingual Method
05. Community Language Learning
06. The Silent Way
07. Suggestopedia
08. Total Physical Response
09. The Natural Approach
10. Communicative Langauge Teaching

CHAPTER 01 Teaching Methodology

> **단원 길라잡이**
> - 영어 교수법의 역사를 이해하고 전체 흐름도를 파악할 수 있다.
> - 각 교수법을 바탕으로 교실 현장에서 이용할 수 있는 수업 방법을 만들어 낼 수 있다.
> - 교수법이 심리학, 언어학, 교육학에서 받은 영향력과 관계들을 이해할 수 있다.
> - 의사소통 교수법의 원리들을 상호작용의 수업이해에 적용시킬 수 있다.
> - 다양한 다른 교수법들을 비교분석하고 이해적용할 수 있다.

Introduction

우리가 영어교육에서 적용해 온 역사적인 변화는 영어교수법의 변화와 함께 이루어지고 있다. 영어교수법에서 중요한 부분은 그러한 변화를 바탕으로 현재 어떠한 교수법으로 학습이 효과적으로 일어나고 있는가에 대한 고찰이 되어야 하겠다. 앞서 2언어 습득이론과 교수방법의 원리에서 어떻게 언어가 습득이 되며 그것을 위해서 어떠한 원리들이 있어야 하는지에 대하여 알아보았다. 이제는 그 내용들을 더 확고하게 해줄 수 있는 영어교수법에 대하여 공부하기로 하자. 영어교육론이 그 자리를 확고히 하기 전에는 영어교수법이 그 이름을 대신하고 있었을 정도로 영어교육을 이루고 있는 핵심이라고 할 수 있다. 영어교수법은 영어교육의 역사가 어떻게 흘렀으며 현재는 어떤 영어교수법이 가장 중요한 위치를 차지하고 있는지 이해하게 해준다. 또한 우리가 영어교사로서 교실 안에서 어떠한 방식으로 수업할 때 가장 효과적일 수 있는지에 대한 단단한 이론의 뒷받침을 만들어 주게 될 것이다.

영어교수법에서는 Grammar translation method에서 시작하여 Task-based language teaching으로 발전되어 왔다. 영어교수법은 크게 세가지 흐름으로 나눌 수 있다. 첫 파트는 전통적 언어학습으로서 GTM, ALM, Direct method가 이에 속한다. 이때는 언어습득을 language에 초점을 맞추어서 본 시기가 된다. 두번째 파트는 designer-method 교수법으로서 위의 전통식 교수법에서 나타나는 language중심의 교수법의 반발로 나타났으며, Silent way, Suggestopedia, Community language learning, Natural approach, TPR등이 이에 속한다. 여기에서는 학습자를 중심으로 하는 교수법이 나타나고 인간의 cognitive이고 humanistic적인 측면이 중시되기 시작했다고 볼 수 있다. 세 번째 파트는 Communicative language teaching의 시대로서 지금의 영어교수법의 토대를 이루고 있다. Task-based, Content-based, Whole-language, Experiential teaching 등이 이에 해당되고 학습자중심, 과정중심, 그리고 전체를 중시할 때 학습이 효과적으로 이루어질 수 있다.

교육과정의 교수-학습 방법

교육과정의 영어과 교수-학습 방법은 다음과 같이 요약할 수 있다. 첫째, 학생 중심의 수업을 운영하는 교사의 역할을 강조하고, 둘째, 학생의 의사소통능력을 개발할 수 있는 수업이 되기 위한 교수-학습 방안을 제시하며, 셋째, 수준별 수업에 대한 개념을 명료하게 하며 수준별 수업에 활용할 수 있는 학급 조직, 학습 유형, 학습 활동 등을 예시하여 학교 여건에 따라 적용할 수 있도록 한다. 넷째, 언어의 네 가지 기능에 대한 교수-학습 방법을 제시한다.

가. **학생 중심의 수업을 계획하여 학생들이 수업 활동에 적극적으로 참여할 수 있도록 하고, 교사는 학생들의 협조자가 되도록 한다**: 학생 중심 학습의 특징은 학생들의 필요를 반영하고, 학생들이 학습 내용 및 방법에 영향을 미칠 수 있으며, 학생들의 창의력을 신장하고 성취감, 자존심을 고취시키는 데 역점을 둔다는 것이다. 이러한 학생 중심의 수업을 위해 교사는 학습 목표라는 큰 구조 속에서 학생들의 능력, 필요, 흥미를 고려하여 개인별, 짝별, 조별, 분단별 학습 활동이나 과제를 고안해야 한다.

나. **교사와 학생, 학생 상호간의 활발한 의사소통을 위하여 다양한 활동을 전개한다**: 의사소통능력 신장을 위한 수업에는 학생들이 해 볼만한 재미나 가치가 있다고 느낄만한 실제적인 과제를 부여하여 학습 과정에서 유의미한 의사소통을 목적으로 영어를 사용하는 다양한 의사소통 활동의 경험을 포함해야 한다.

다. **학생들이 효과적인 의사소통을 할 수 있도록 다양한 의사소통전략을 적절히 사용하게 한다**: 효과적인 의사소통이란 주어진 상황에서 알고 있는 언어 지식을 최대한 활용하여 상대방이 전달하고자 하는 의미를 이해하고, 자신의 의사를 적절히 표현함으로써 대화를 지속하는 것이다. 의사소통전략은 개인이 정보의 생산적인 소통을 위해 세우는 의식적인 계획으로, 회피(avoidance), 바꾸어 말하기(paraphrase), 권위에의 호소(appeal to authority), 직역(literal translation) 등의 언어적 전략과 마임(mime)이나 얼굴 표정 등의 비언어적 전략이 있다.

라. **듣기는 시청각 자료를 활용하여 학습 효과를 높이고, 영어 음성 언어에 자연스럽게 노출되도록 지도한다**: 듣기 능력은 말하기를 통해 자동적으로 습득되는 기능이 아니라 말하기 능력보다 우선적으로 학습되어야 하는 기능으로 이해되고 있다. 듣기는 상대방이 말한 것을 소리와 함께 자신의 경험을 바탕으로 화자의 의도를 파악하려고 노력하는 과정이다.

마. **말하기는 유의적이고 의사소통 중심적인 연습 활동을 통해 유창성과 정확성을 기를 수 있도록 하고, 실제 상황에서 적용할 수 있는 언어 능력을 기를 수 있도록 지도한다**: 유의미한 의사소통 중심의 학습활동이란 학습자들이 문제를 해결하기 위해 의사소통에 적극적으로 참여하는 활동을 의미한다.

바. **읽기는 다양한 전략을 사용하여 과업 중심의 활동을 하도록 지도한다**: 읽기 전략은 읽기 학습 분야에서 꾸준히 연구되어 왔다. 이러한 읽기 전략을 훈련하는 것은 학습자 스스로 원하는 전략을 선택하여 자기 주도적인 학습 습관을 기르도록 하는 데 그 목적이 있다. 그러므로 교사가 다양한 읽기 전략을 소개하고 훈련시키는 것은 의미가 크다고 할 수 있다.

사. **쓰기는 목적에 맞는 다양한 형태의 글을 쓸 수 있도록 지도한다**: 쓰기 능력은 단순히 지식이나 원리를 배움으로써 향상되는 것이 아니며 글을 쓰는 과정에서 단어의 선택, 문장의 구조 및 연결 관계, 글의 구성, 통일성과 명료성 등을 글의 목적과 독자의 반응을 예상하고 분석해야 하는 복합적인 능력이다. 따라서 쓰기 능력을 향상시키기 위해서는 과정 중심의 쓰기 지도 방법이나 전략 중심의 지도 방법이 활용되어야 할 것이다.

아. **영어권 및 비영어권의 다양한 문화를 학습하여 타문화에 대한 이해를 높이고, 문화에 대한 올바른 판단력과 가치관을 기르도록 한다**: 영어가 사용되는 사회의 문화를 이해하는 것은 영어로 그 사람들과 의사소통하는 능력을 기르는 데 필수적이며, 현대사회에서는 다양한 문화에 속한 사람들과 영어로 의사소통할 기회가 늘어나기 때문에 다양한 문화를 이해하는 것이 폭넓은 의사소통능력을 기르는 데 도움이 될 것이다.

자. **수업은 가급적 영어로 진행한다**: 외국어 수업을 영어로 진행하는 것은 학생들이 목표언어에 집중하여 그 언어로 생각할 수 있는 기회를 제공할 수 있도록 도와주며, 학습자의 자신감을 증대시키는 효과가 있다고 알려져 있다. 또한, 학생들이 영어 과목에 흥미를 느낄 수 있도록 하며, 유창성을 기르는 데도 도움이 된다. 교실에서 교사가 사용하는 언어는 학생들이 해당 언어를 배우는 데 중요한 입력(input)이 되므로 교사의 올바른 언어 사용이 매우 중요하다.

차. **다양한 멀티미디어 자료와 정보통신기술(ICT) 도구를 활용하여 학생들의 흥미를 높이고 성취감을 느낄 수 있도록 한다**: 우리나라에서는 영어를 외국어로서 학습하므로 학생들이 실제로 영어를 접하고 사용할 기회가 많지 않기 때문에 의사소통 중심의 활동만으로 교실에서 학생들의 영어 사용

능력을 향상시키는 데는 한계가 있다. 요즘에는 실생활에서 쓰이는 영어 문서자료 (written document), 비디오, DVD, CD, 뉴스 등과 같은 다양한 주제에 대한 멀티미디어 자료를 쉽게 구할 수 있어 교사가 이를 활용하여 실제와 매우 흡사한 의사소통 상황을 제시하고 학습 활동을 비교적 다양하게 구성하며, 학습자가 원하는 만큼의 반복 학습을 할 수 있도록 수업을 계획할 수 있다.

카. **학교 실정을 고려하여 수준별 수업을 운영할 수 있다**: 학습능력에 적합한 수준의 교육 내용을 제공하기 위한 수준별 수업 운영 유형으로는 학급 간 이동 수업, 학급 내 수업, 학급 간 이동 수업과 학급 내 수업을 병행할 수 있을 것이다. 학급 간 수준별 이동 수업을 위한 분반 형태는 학급 수나 학생들의 성적 분포 등 학교 실정에 따라, 전체 학년을 두 수준으로 분리하여 심화반과 보충반으로 구성하거나, 세 수준으로 분리하여 심화반, 기본반, 보충반으로 편성하기도 하며, 네 수준으로 분리하여 심화반, 기본반, 보충반, 기초반으로 세분화할 수도 있다.

타. **학습자의 능력, 흥미, 인지 수준에 맞추어 다양한 동기 유발 방법과 학습 활동을 구안하여 학생 중심의 수업이 이루어지도록 한다**: 오늘날 교육의 중요한 원리 중의 하나로서 제시될 수 있는 것이 개인차를 고려한 개별화 학습이다. Rubin(1987)은 성공적인 언어 학습에 이르는 길은 학습자의 다양한 학습 양식에 따라 여러갈래의 통로가 있다고 하면서 학습 목표를 달성하기 위한 방법에서 학습자의 개인차를 인정하는 교수 접근이 필요하다고 주장하였다.

파. **개인차에 따라 수준에 맞는 학습 활동이나 과업을 수행할 수 있도록 학년별로 기본 교과서나 보조 교재를 다양한 수준으로 개발할 수 있다**: 학습자 개개인의 다양성을 모두 고려한 완전한 의미의 수준별 교육과정 운영은 불가능하더라도 개개인의 능력, 적성, 흥미, 요구 등 다양한 개인차를 반영한 교재를 개발하여 수준별 수업을 실시한다면, 학습자에게 더 많은 선택의 기회를 제공함으로써 학습 활동의 적극적인 주체로서의 역할을 하도록 할 수 있다.

하. **교수-학습 자료를 개발할 때는 성취 기준의 내용을 바탕으로 언어 기능, 어휘, 언어 형식 등을 학생 수준에 맞추어 재구성하여 사용하고, 이에 맞추어 교수방법을 다양화한다**: 언어 교육의 궁극적인 목표는 의사소통능력 신장, 즉 실제 언어 사용 능력의 향상이므로, 교실수업을 통해 학생들이 수준에 따라 다양한 학습 단계를 거쳐 실제 언어 사용 단계에 이르도록 하는 것 중요하다. 목표 성취 기준에 이르지 못한 학생들에게는 보충 자료를 통해 정확성에 중점을 둔 다양한 연습 활동을 추가적으로 부여하는 것이 필요하다. 한편, 성취 기준을 달성한 학생들에게는 심화 자료를 통해 유창성에 중점을 둔 다양한 언어 사용 활동을 추가적으로 부과함으로써 유창성을 보다 심화할 수 있도록 해야 한다.

CHAPTER 02 Grammar Translation Method

> **단원 길라잡이**
> - 가장 기본적인 문법 번역식 교수법의 원리를 이해하고 교실 활동을 활용할 수 있다.
> - 교실활동에서 학생과 교사, 교재의 역할을 이해한다.

Introduction

외국어를 배우는 최초의 언어교수법은 14세기 초반에 라틴어를 배우는 문법번역식 방법에서 시작되었다. 어려운 문헌을 읽고, 어휘를 외우고, 문법규칙을 습득하는 방법이 그 기초가 되었다. 그래서 이 방법은 communication보다는 reading과 writing을 강조하는 학습법이 되었다. 그리고, 19세기에 와서 French와 German, English를 배우는 방법으로 발전되어서 오늘날에까지 이어져왔다.

(1) Features

- Classes are taught in the mother tongue, with little active use of the target language.
- Much vocabulary is taught in the form of lists of isolated words.
- Long elaborate explanations of the intricacies of grammar are given.
- Grammar provides the rules for putting words together, and instruction often focuses on the form and inflection of words.
- Reading of difficult classical texts is begun early.
- Little attention is paid to the content of texts, which are treated as exercises in grammatical analysis.
- Often the only drills are exercises in translating disconnected sentences from the target language into the mother tongue.
- Little or no attention is given to pronunciation.

(2) Advantages

① Reduced Teacher Stress

Resources for GTMs are easier to come by than other approaches and generally require less teacher involvement. Class activities or learning games are rarely necessary, as students are translating text to another language directly. Teachers who are not fluent in English can teach English as the emphasis is not on the spoken word but on translations. Communication between student and teacher is reduced with this method, which avoids misunderstandings and prevents language barriers that may occur in a method that focuses on teacher-student communication or verbal language learning.

② Focus on Grammar, Sentence Structure and Word Meanings

Unlike a verbal approach to language learning, GTM focuses on the application of grammar and correct sentence structure. This is especially helpful in teaching students how to write and read in another language, allowing them to explore interchangeable words and phrases (i.e. different words for different tenses) more effectively than a verbal teaching method. The approach is also easily applied and can be less stressful on students; verbal teaching methods do not describe the application of grammar and sentence structure as effectively as GTM does. Word meanings are also easily learned through direct translation. A foreign word can be compared to the native language quickly. The method of comparing/translation of the learned language with a native language provides reference for students.

(3) Disadvantages

① Learner Motivation and Participation

The GTM approach involves no learner participation and little teacher-student relationship. Students are required to learn from a textbook and use the same method throughout their learning. Because lessons using GTM are not interactive and engaging for students, they become more likely to lose interest in their subject and less motivated to learn. Furthermore, the method does not require students to participate in any activities or communicate with each other, so they will not learn how to use the language in a real-life conversation or situation and will only know how to translate one language to another.

② Unnatural and Inaccurate Pronunciation

As children, people generally learn how to speak before they learn how to write and read. In the GTM approach, this natural learning method is reversed. Students are only taught how to read and write the language. This can affect how they learn to speak the learned language. The mere application of grammar and sentence structure cannot adequately prepare them for realistic conversations or verbal communication, as no emphasis is given to spoken language in the GTM approach. Translations may also be inaccurate, as it is not always possible to simply translate one word or phrase accurately to another language.

(4) Classroom Activities

Translation of a Literary Passage	Translating target language to native language
Reading Comprehension Questions	Finding information in a passage, making inferences and relating to personal experience
Antonyms / Synonyms	Finding antonyms and synonyms for words or sets of words
Deductive Application of Rule	Understanding grammar rules and their exceptions, then applying them to new examples
Fill-in-the-blanks	Filling in gaps in sentences with new words or items of a particular grammar type
Memorization	Memorizing vocabulary lists, grammatical rules and grammatical paradigms
Use Words in Sentences	Students create sentences to illustrate they know the meaning and use of new words
Composition	Students write about a topic using the target language

CHAPTER 03 The Direct Method

> **단원 길라잡이**
> - 문법 번역식 교수법에 반대하여 출현한 직접식 교수법의 장점과 단점을 이해하고 그 적용점을 살펴본다.
> - 직접식 교수법을 이용하여 현재 적용될 수 있는 교수방법을 이해한다.

Introduction

　Direct Method는 Gouin이라는 학자가 3년 동안의 독일유학시절 고전교수법(문법 번역식 교수법)을 바탕으로 성공적 독일어학습을 위해 다양한 노력을 기울였지만 결국 독일어 학습에 실패하고 만다. 고국 프랑스로 돌아온 뒤 그는 한 가지 놀라운 사실을 발견하게 된다. 3년 전 Gouin이 독일유학을 떠나던 때, 아무 말도 못했던 3살짜리 조카가 프랑스어를 능란하게 구사하는 것이었다. 이에 힌트를 얻어, 아동의 모국어 학습 관찰에 상당시간을 보낸 후, Gouin은 다음과 같은 결론을 얻게 된다. 언어 학습이란 결국 perception을 conception으로 전환하는 활동이다. 아동은 자신의 개념을 표현하기 위해 언어를 사용한다. 언어는 사고의 수단이며, 세상을 자기 자신에게 표현하기 위한 수단이다. Gouin의 naturalistic approach —아동의 모국어 습득과 같이 자연스런 방법으로 외국어를 가르친다는 입장— 은 즉각적인 호응을 얻지 못했고, 한 세기가 지난 다음에야, 응용 언어학자들이 그러한 접근법의 신빙성을 입증하게 된다. 즉, the Direct Method란 이름으로 널리 알려지고 실제 교수-학습장에서 활용된 것은 20세기 전환기에 이르러서였다.

> **핵심플러스** **The Direct Method의 기본 원리**
> - 2언어 학습은 모국어 학습과 유사한 방식으로 이뤄져야 한다.
> - 많은 구어적 상호작용(oral interaction)이 요구된다.
> - 언어의 즉각적 사용을 중시한다.
> - 모국어와 2언어 사이에서 번역을 하지 않는다.

01 Teaching and Learning

(1) Principles

The Direct Method was an answer to the dissatisfaction with the older Grammar Translation Method, which teaches students grammar and vocabulary through direct translations and thus focuses on the written language. There was an attempt to set up conditions that imitate mother tongue acquisition, which is why the beginnings of these attempts were called the natural method. At the turn of the 18th and 19th centuries, Sauveur and Franke proposed that language teaching should be undertaken within the target-language system, which was the first stimulus for the rise of the direct method. The Audiolingual Method was developed in an attempt to address some of the perceived weaknesses of the Direct method. The Direct Method of teaching, sometimes called the Natural Method. Not limited to but often used in teaching foreign languages, the method refrains from using the learners' native language and uses only the target language. It was established in Germany and France around 1900. Characteristic features of the direct method are:

- teaching concepts and vocabulary through pantomiming, real-life objects, realia and other visual materials
- teaching grammar by using an inductive approach (i.e. having learners find out rules through the presentation of adequate linguistic forms in the target language)
- centrality of spoken language (including a native-like pronunciation)
- focus on question-answer patterns

(2) Language Classroom

- Classroom instructions are conducted exclusively in the target language.
- Only everyday vocabulary and sentences are taught during the initial phase; grammar, reading and writing are introduced in intermediate phase.
- Oral communication skills are built up in a carefully graded progression organized around question-and-answer exchanges between teachers and students in small, intensive classes.
- Grammar is taught inductively.
- New teaching points are introduced orally.
- Concrete vocabulary is taught through demonstration, objects, and pictures; abstract vocabulary is taught by association of ideas.
- Both speech and listening comprehensions are taught.
- Correct pronunciation and grammar are emphasized.

- Students should be speaking approximately 80% of the time during the lesson.
- Students are taught from inception to ask questions as well as answer them.

02 Classroom Techniques

(1) Objectives

The basic premise of the Direct Method is that students will learn to communicate in the target language, partly by learning how to think in that language and by not involving L1 in the language learning process whatsoever. Objectives include teaching the students how to use the language spontaneously and orally, linking meaning with the target language through the use of realia, pictures or pantomime (Larsen-Freeman 1986:24). There is to be a direct connection between concepts and the language to be learned.

(2) Classroom Techniques

Techniques	Activity
Reading Aloud	Reading sections of passages, plays or dialogs out loud
Question and Answer Exercise	Asking questions in the target language and having students answer in full sentences
Student Self-Correction	Teacher facilitates opportunities for students to self correct using follow-up questions, tone, etc.
Conversation Practice	Teacher asks students and students ask students questions using the target language.
Fill-in-the-blank Exercise	Items use target language only and inductive rather than explicit grammar rules.
Dictation	Teacher reads passage aloud various amount of times at various tempos, students writing down what they hear.
Paragraph Writing	Students write paragraphs in their own words using the target language and various models.

Towards the end of the late 1800s, a revolution in language teaching philosophy took place that is seen by many as the dawn of modern foreign language teaching. Teachers, frustrated by the limits of the Grammar Translation Method in terms of its inability to create communicative competence in students, began to experiment with new ways of teaching language. Basically, teachers began attempting to teach foreign languages in a way that was more similar to first language acquisition. It incorporated techniques designed to address all the areas that the Grammar Translation did not – namely oral communication, more spontaneous use of the language, and developing the ability to think in the target language. Perhaps in an almost reflexive action, the method also moved as far away as possible from various techniques typical of the Grammar Translation Method – for instance using L1 as the language of instruction, memorizing grammatical rules and lots of translation between L1 and the target language.

The appearance of the Direct Method thus coincided with a new school of thinking that dictated that all foreign language teaching should occur in the target language only, with no translation and an emphasis on linking meaning to the language being learned. The method became very popular during the first quarter of the 20th century, especially in private language schools in Europe where highly motivated students could study new languages and not need to travel far in order to try them out and apply them communicatively. One of the most famous advocates of the Direct Method was the German Charles Berlitz, whose schools and Berlitz Method are now world-renowned.

Still, the Direct Method was not without its problems. As Brown (1994:56) points out, (it) did not take well in public education where the constraints of budget, classroom size, time, and teacher background made such a method difficult to use. By the late 1920s, the method was starting to go into decline and there was even a return to the Grammar Translation Method, which guaranteed more in the way of scholastic language learning orientated around reading and grammar skills. But the Direct Method continues to enjoy a popular following in private language school circles, and it was one of the foundations upon which the well-known Audiolingual Method expanded from starting half way through the 20th century.

CHAPTER 04 Audiolingual Method

단원 길라잡이
- 언어연습에 가장 많이 활용되고 있는 ALM의 특징과 교실 활동을 적용해 본다.
- ALM이 가지고 있는 수업방법의 장점과 한계점을 살펴본다.

Introduction

1950년대 이전 Direct Method는 여러 가지 이유로 유럽에서 만큼의 호응을 미국에서 얻지 못했다. 원어민 교사를 구하기가 힘들었고 학습한 외국어 말하기 기술을 실제 상황에서 사용해 보기 위해선 너무나 먼 여행을 떠나야 했다. 미국 교육당국은 외국어 학습에 있어 oral approach보다는 reading approach가 훨씬 유용하다는 입장을 고수했다. 왜냐면, 다양한 언어를 사용하는 국가들이 인접해 있어 서로 잦은 대화, 즉 말하기가 필요했던 유럽과 달리 미국은 말하기 능력이 그다지 필요 없었기 때문이다. 1929년 Coleman 보고서는 말하기 기술의 비실용성과 읽기의 중요성을 강조했다. 그래서 1930-40년대 미국의 교육기관들은 소위 읽기지도의 기본인 문법 번역식 교수법을 다시 채택했다. 제2차 세계대전이 발발하게 되고, 미국은 동맹국과 적대국 언어의 능숙한 구두능력이 절실히 필요하게 되었다. 이에, 미군은 army specialized training program (ASTP) 또는 Army Method라고 불렸던 집중적인 듣기와 말하기 언어코스를 만들게 된다. 이 언어 학습 프로그램이 1950년대에 이르러 Audiolingual Method로 알려지게 되었다.

Charles Fries는 University of Michigan에서 English Language Institute의 director로 일하면서 learning structure나 grammar를 언어학습의 시작점으로 보고 있다. 즉, 학습자가 해야 하는 일은 기본 sentence patterns와 grammatical structures를 구두로 recite하는 것으로 보고 있으며, 교사는 이러한 drills들을 가능하게 하기 위하여 충분한 vocabulary가 제공해야 된다고 믿었다.

01 Teaching and Learning

(1) Principles

The Audiolingual Method, Army Method, or New Key, is a style of teaching used in teaching foreign languages. It is based on behaviorist theory, which professes that certain traits of living things, and in this case humans, could be trained through a system of reinforcement — correct use of a trait would receive positive feedback while incorrect use of that trait would receive negative feedback. This approach to language learning was similar to another, earlier method called the Direct Method. Like the Direct Method, the Audiolingual Method advised that students be taught a language directly, without using the students' native language to explain new words or grammar in the target language. However, unlike the Direct Method, the Audiolingual Method didn't focus on teaching vocabulary. Rather, the teacher drilled students in the use of grammar.

Applied to language instruction, and often within the context of the language lab, this means that the instructor would present the correct model of a sentence and the students would have to repeat it. The teacher would then continue by presenting new words for the students to sample in the same structure. In audiolingualism, there is no explicit grammar instruction — everything is simply memorized in form. The idea is for the students to practice the particular construct until they can use it spontaneously. In this manner, the lessons are built on static drills in which the students have little or no control on their own output; the teacher is expecting a particular response and not providing that will result in a student receiving negative feedback. This type of activity, for the foundation of language learning, is in direct opposition with communicative language teaching.

(2) Disadvantages

① In the late 1950s, the theoretical underpinnings of the method were questioned by linguists such as Noam Chomsky, who pointed out the limitations of structural linguistics. The relevance of behaviorist psychology to language learning was also questioned, most famously by Chomsky's review of B.F. Skinner's Verbal Behavior in 1959. The Audiolingual Method was thus deprived of its scientific credibility and it was only a matter of time before the effectiveness of the method itself was questioned.

② In 1964, Wilga Rivers released a critique of the method in her book, The Psychologist and the Foreign Language Teacher. It produced results which showed explicit grammatical instruction in the mother language to be more productive. These developments, coupled with the emergence of humanist pedagogy led to a rapid decline in the popularity of audiolingualism. Philip Smith's study from 1965-1969 provided significant proof that Audiolingual Methods were less effective than a more traditional cognitive approach involving the learner's first language.

02 Selection of Materials

(1) Major advocates in contrastive analysis

① Transfer: Individuals tend to transfer the forms and meanings, and the distribution of forms and meanings of their native language and culture to the foreign language and culture — both productively when attempting to speak the language and to act in the culture, and receptively when attempting to grasp and understand the language and the culture as practiced by natives.

② Difficulty: We assume that the student who comes in contact with a foreign language will find some features of it quite easy and others extremely difficult. Those elements that are similar to his native language will be simple for him, and those elements that are different will be difficult. (Lado, 1957).

(2) Methods for contrastive analysis

- Description: a formal description of the two languages involved
- Selection: certain areas or items of the two languages were chosen
- Comparison: the identification of areas of difference and similarity
- Prediction: determining which areas where likely to cause errors

(3) Presentation - Practice - Application (Production)

- Presentation: oral, dialogue, little explanation, L1 discouraged, errors corrected, accuracy emphasized, accurate repetition and memorization of the dialogue as goal of this stage
- Practice: pattern drills, mastery of the structure, fluency emphasized
- Application: use of the structure in different contexts

03 Language in Audiolingual Method

(1) Features

Features	• Oral-based approach based on behavioral psychology • Drills in the use of grammatical sentence patterns • Conditioning: helping learners to respond correctly to stimuli through shaping and reinforcement • Habit-formation
Goals	• Able to use the target language communicatively • Overlearning: automatically without stopping to think • Forming new habits through overcoming the old habit
Teacher Roles	• Like an orchestra leader. • Providing students with a good model for imitation.
Interaction	• Interaction is teacher-directed. • Student-student interaction → chain drills and dialogues
Teaching/ Learning process	• New vocabulary and structural patterns are presented through dialogs. • Dialogs - learning through imitation and repetition • Positively reinforced • Grammar is induced from the examples.
Views of language	• The view of language is influenced by descriptive linguists. • Each level (phonological, morphological) has its own distinctive patterns. • Everyday speech is emphasized. • The level of complexity of the speech is graded.
Language Skills	• Vocabulary is kept to a minimum while the students are mastering the sound system and grammatical patterns. • The natural order of skills is adhered to listening, speaking, reading, and writing. • The oral/ aural skills receive most of the attention.
Role of L1	• The habits of the students' native language are thought to interfere with the students' attempts to master the target language. • The target language is mostly used in the classroom instead of the native language.
Evaluation	• Discrete-point tests • Each question on the test would focus on only one point of the language at a time. 예 Students are asked to distinguish word meanings in a minimal pair.
Errors	• Students errors are to be avoided if at all possible.

(2) Characteristics of Language

- New material is presented in dialog form.
- There is dependence on mimicry, memorization of set phrases, and over-learning.
- Structures are sequenced by means of contrastive analysis and taught one at a time.
- Structural patterns are taught using repetitive drills.
- There is little or no grammatical explanation. Grammar is taught by inductive analogy rather than deductive explanation.
- Vocabulary is strictly limited and learned in context.
- There is much use of tapes, language labs, and visual aids.
- Great importance is attached to pronunciation.
- Very little use of the mother tongue by teachers is permitted.
- Successful responses are immediately reinforced.
- There is great effort to get students to produce error-free utterances.
- There is a tendency to manipulate language and disregard content.

(3) Techniques

Techniques	Activity
Dialog Memorization	Students memorize an opening dialog using mimicry and applied role-playing.
Repetition Drill	Students repeat teacher's model as quickly and accurately as possible.
Chain Drill	Students ask and answer each other one-by-one in a circular chain around the classroom.
Substitution Drill	Teacher states a line from the dialog, then uses a word or a phrase as a cue that students, when repeating the line, must substitute into the sentence in the correct place.
Transformation Drill	Teacher provides a sentence that must be turned into something else, 예) A question to be turned into a statement, an active sentence to be turned into a negative statement, etc.
Use of Minimal Pairs	Using contrastive analysis, teacher selects a pair of words that sound identical except for a single sound that typically poses difficulty for the learners - students are to pronounce and differentiate the two words.
Complete the Dialog	Selected words are erased from a line in the dialog - students must find and insert.
Grammar Games	Various games designed to practice a grammar point in context, using lots of repetition.

(4) Types of Drill Practice

① Repetition : The student repeats an utterance aloud as soon as he has heard it. He does this without looking at a printed text.

T : This is the seventh month.
S : This is the seventh month.
T : I used to know him years ago.
S : I used to know him years ago.

② Inflection : One word in an utterance appears in another form when repeated.

T : I bought the ticket.
S : I bought the tickets.
T : He bought the candy.
S : She bought the candy.

③ Restatement : The student rephrases an utterance and addresses it to someone else, according to instructions.

T : Tell him to wait for you.
S : Wait for me.
T : Ask her how old she is.
S : How old are you?

④ Completion : The student hears an utterance that is complete except for one word, then repeats the utterance in completed form.

T : I'll go my way and you go...
S : I'll go my way and you go yours.
T : We all have our troubles and they have ....
S : They have theirs.

⑤ Transposition : A change in word order is necessary when a word is added.

T : I'm hungry. (so)
S : So am I.
T : I'll never do it again. (neither)
S : Neither will I ...

⑥ Expansion : When a word is added it takes a certain place in the sequence.

T : I know him. (hardly)
S : I hardly know him.
T : I know him. (well)
S : I know him well ...

⑦ Contraction : A single word stands for a phrase or clause.

    T : I'll go my way and you go …
    S : I'll go my way and you go yours.
    T : We all have … own troubles.
    S : We all have our own troubles, …

⑧ Transformation : A sentence is transformed by being made negative or interrogative or through changes in tense, mood, voice, aspect, or modality.

    T : He knows my address.
    S : He doesn't know my address.
    T : He used to know my address.
    S : If he had known my address.

⑨ Integration : Two separate utterances are integrated into one.

    T : They must be honest. This is important.
    S : It is important that they be honest.
    T : I know that man. He is looking for you.
    S : I know the man who is looking for you.

⑩ Rejoinder : The student makes an appropriate rejoinder to a given utterance.

    T : Thank you.
    S : You're welcome.
    T : May I take one?
    S : Certainly.

⑪ Restoration : The student is given a sequence of words that have been culled from a sentence but still bear its basic meaning. He uses these words with a minimum of changes and additions to restore the sentence to its original form. He may be told whether the time is present, past, or future.

    T : students/ waiting/ bus
    S : The students are waiting for the bus.
    T : boys/ build/ house/ tree
    S : The boys built a house in a tree.

Audiolingual Method

The next revolution in terms of language teaching methodology coincided with World War II, when America became aware that it needed people to learn foreign languages very quickly as part of its overall military operations. The Army Method was suddenly developed to build communicative competence in translators through very intensive language courses focusing on aural/ oral skills. This in combination with some new ideas about language learning coming from the disciplines of descriptive linguistics and behavioral psychology went on to become what is known as the Audiolingual Method (ALM).

This new method incorporated many of the features typical of the earlier Direct Method, but the disciplines mentioned above added the concepts of teaching linguistic patterns in combination with something generally referred to as habit-forming. This method was one of the first to have its roots firmly grounded in linguistic and psychological theory (Brown 1994:57), which apparently added to its credibility and probably had some influence in the popularity it enjoyed over a long period of time. It also had a major influence on the language teaching methods that were to follow, and can still be seen in major or minor manifestations of language teaching methodology even to this day.

Another factor that accounted for the method's popularity was the quick success it achieved in leading learners towards communicative competence. Through extensive mimicry, memorization and over-learning of language patterns and forms, students and teachers were often able to see immediate results. This was both its strength and its failure in the long run, as critics began to point out that the method did not deliver in terms of producing *long-term* communicative ability. The study of linguistics itself was to change, and the area of second language learning became a discipline in its own right. Cognitive psychologists developed new views on learning in general, arguing that mimicry and rote learning could not account for the fact that language learning involved affective and interpersonal factors, that learners were able to produce language forms and patterns that they had never heard before. The idea that thinking processes themselves led to the discovery of independent language rule formation (rather than habit formation), and a belief that affective factors influenced their application, paved the way toward the new methods that were to follow the Audiolingual Method.

Just as with the Direct Method, the Audiolingual Method represents a major step in language teaching methodology that was still aimed squarely at communicative competence. A teacher that can use the method well will generally be able to create what appear to be very productive students. The extensive and elaborate drills designed to facilitate over-learning and good language habit forming were an innovative addition to the techniques used to practice language, and many of them are featured as essential parts of communicative methods that followed the Audiolingual Method.

The method's original appearance under the name The Army Method is apt, and from it one ought not to be surprised that the method is all about highly controlled practice involving extensive repetition aimed at habit forming. If you can imagine a squad of new military recruits doing marching drills in the exercise yard, listening to the terse commands and repeating the movements in various combinations until they become second nature and do not need to be thought about, then you have yourself an effective picture of how the Audiolingual Method essentially works and creates the desired result. The experts representing descriptive linguistics at that time can be seen as disseminating the patterns required to perform the various marching drills piece by piece, and the behavioral psychologists dictated the various ways for the drills to be repeated in order to create an effective habit-forming process.

The (however slightly simplified) picture presented above ought to also indicate to the modern, enlightened and eclectic language teacher the obvious ways in which the Audiolingual Method falls far short of the overall goal of creating sustainable long-term communicative competence in language learners. The linguistic principles upon which the theory was based emphasized surface forms of language and not the deep structure. Cognitive principles aimed at explaining how learners learn and develop independent concepts were to change considerably in the period following the Audiolingual Method.

Still, there are reasons why the method is still popular, and perhaps even appropriate in certain educational contexts. In countries where one of the prime objectives of learning English is to take and achieve successful results in a variety of tests, and where many learners are not intrinsically motivated to learn English but do so because they feel they have to, the method is not without merits. The term practice makes perfect was coined at a time when the concept of practice was synonymous with repetition, and if English is seen as just another subject to be learned, then the philosophy of repeating the required patterns until you get them right without needing to think about them does have a lot of supporters.

One of the key responsibilities of the modern day teacher of any discipline, however, is to actively create and build intrinsic motivation in their learners, to empower them with the ability and confidence to learn how to learn, to develop a sense of responsibility for their own development, and to regard peers as possible sources of learning as well. They should also be encouraged to experiment with and formulate their own ongoing set of language rules, and to deduct through active independent application where and how the rules need to be adapted. The idea that errors are a natural and even necessary part of the learning process needs to be encouraged and supported. The Audiolingual Method does nothing to address those issues, and as a whole is little more than a very effective way of running highly teacher-orientated classrooms designed to produce language users whose proficiency stems from some kind of auto pilot mentality.

CHAPTER 05 Community Language Learning

단원 길라잡이
- 인본주의적 학습을 중시한 최초의 교수법인 Community Language Learning의 특성과 교실 활동을 살펴본다.
- 학습자를 중심으로 한 교수법이 가질 수 있는 장점과 한계점을 이해한다.

Introduction

1970년대의 Chomsky의 언어적 혁명덕분에 언어학자와 언어교사들이 surface structure와 rote practice에 집중했던 Audiolingual method로부터 벗어나서 deep structure로 돌아서게 되면서 다양한 교수법이 나오게 되었다. 그 중 하나인 Community Language Learning (CLL)은 학습자가 새로운 언어를 배우면서 가질 수 있는 걱정, 위협이나 개인적이고 언어적인 문제들을 덜어주는 데 초점을 맞추는 counseling technique이다. 그리고 이 방법은 Carl Rogers의 심리학적 견해에 영향을 받아 Charles Curran이 창시하게 된 언어교수법이다. 이 교육적인 상담-학습 유형은 교실에서의 학습자를 어떤 상담 치료가 필요한 그룹 안에서 보려고 하고 있다. 아래 그림에서와 같이 상담을 하는 형태로 앉아 수업을 진행하게 된다.

01 Principles

(1) Conditions

The social dynamics occurring in the group are very important and a number of conditions are needed for learning to take place.

① Members should interact in an interpersonal relationship. Students and teachers work together to facilitate learning by:
- valuing each other
- lowering the defense that prevent interpersonal interaction
- reducing anxiety
- constituting a supportive community

② Teachers role is that of a true counselor.
- They are not perceived as a threat.
- They don't impose boundaries and limits.
- They concentrate on the learners needs.

(2) Stages

Learners go through five stages in their learning process.

① Birth stage: Feeling of security and belonging is established. Dependence on the knower as learners have little or no idea of the target language.

② Self stage: As the learner's ability improves and starts to get an idea of how language works, they achieve a measure of independence from the parent although they still seek help from the knower.

③ Separate existence: Learners can speak independently.

④ Adolescence: The learners are independent although they are aware of gaps in their knowledge and feel secure enough to take criticism and being corrected.

⑤ Independence: Complete independence from the knower. The child becomes an adult and becomes the knower.

(3) Advantages of CLL

- CLL is an attempt to overcome the threatening affective factors in EFL and ESL.
- The counselor allows the learners to determine type of conversation and to analyze the language inductively.
- The student centered nature of the method can provide extrincic motivation and capitalize on intrinsic motivation.

(4) Disadvantages of CLL

- The counselor/ teacher can become too non-directive even when students often need directions.
- The method relies completely on inductive learning. It is worthwhile noting that deductive learning is also a viable strategy of learning.
- Translation is an intricate and difficult task. The success of the method relies largely on the translation expertise of the counselor.

02 Lesson Design

(1) Objectives

Since linguistic or communicative competence is specified only in social terms, explicit linguistic or communicative objectives are not defined in the literature on Community Language Learning. Most of what has been written about CLL describes its use in introductory conversation courses in a foreign language. The assumption seems to be that through the method, the teacher can successfully transfer his or her knowledge and proficiency in the target language to the learners, which implies that attaining near-native like mastery of the target language is set as a goal. Specific objectives are not addressed.

(2) Syllabus

Community Language Learning is most often used in the teaching of oral proficiency, but with some modifications it may be used in the teaching of writing, as Tranel (1968) has demonstrated. CLL does not use a conventional language syllabus, which sets out in advance the grammar, vocabulary, and other language items to be taught and the order in which they will be covered.

① If a course is based on Curran's recommended procedures, the course progression is topic based, with learners nominating things they wish to talk about and messages they wish to communicate to other learners.

② The teacher's responsibility is to provide a conveyance for these meanings in a way appropriate to the learners' proficiency level. Although CLL is not explicit about this, skilled CLL teachers seem to sift the learners' intentions through the teacher's implicit syllabus, providing translations that match what learners can be expected to do and say at that level.

③ A CLL syllabus emerges from the interaction between the learner's expressed communicative intentions and the teacher's reformulations of these into suitable target language utterances.

④ Specific grammatical points, lexical patterns, and generalizations will sometimes be isolated by the teacher for more detailed, study and analysis, and subsequent specification of these as a retrospective account of what the course covered could be a way of deriving a CLL language syllabus. Each CLL course would evolve its own syllabus, however, since what develops out of teacher-learner interactions in one course will be different from what happens in another.

(3) Learning Procedure

1. Informal greetings and self-introductions were made.
2. The teacher made a statement of the goals and guidelines for the course.
3. A conversation in English took place.
   - A circle was formed so that everyone had visual contact with each other.
   - One student initiated conversation with another student by giving a message in Korean.
   - The instructor, standing behind the student, whispered a close equivalent of the message in English.
   - The student then repeated the English message to its addressee and into the tape recorder as well.
   - Each student had a chance to compose and record a few messages.
   - The tape recorder was rewound and replayed at intervals.
   - Each student repeated the meaning in Korean of what he or she had said in English and helped to refresh the memory of others.
4. Students then participated in a reflection period, in which they were asked to express their feelings about the previous experience with total frankness.
5. From the materials just recorded the instructor chose sentences to write on the blackboard that highlighted elements of grammar, spelling, and peculiarities of capitalization in English.
6. Students were encouraged to ask questions about any of the items above.
7. Students were encouraged to copy sentences from the board with notes on meaning and usage. This became their "textbook" for home study.

(4) Classroom Techniques

Techniques	Activity
Tape Recording Student Conversation	Students choose what they want to say, and their target language production is recorded for later listening/dissemination.
Transcription	Teacher produces a transcription of the tape-recorded conversation with translations in the mother language – this is then used for follow up activities or analysis.
Reflection on Experience	Teacher takes time during or after various activities to allow students to express how they feel about the language and the learning experience, and the teacher indicates empathy/understanding.
Reflective Listening	Students listen to their own voices on the tape in a relaxed and reflective environment.
Human Computer	Teacher is a "human computer" for the students to control – the teacher stating anything in the target language the student wants to practice, giving them the opportunity to self correct.
Small Group Tasks	Students work in small groups to create new sentences using the transcript, afterwards sharing them with the rest of the class.

03 Instructional Roles

(1) Learner roles

In Community Language Learning, learners become members of a community – their fellow learners and the teacher – and learn through interacting with members of the community. Learning is not viewed as an individual accomplishment but as something that is achieved collaboratively. Learners are expected to listen attentively to the knower, to freely provide meanings they wish to express, to repeat target utterances without hesitation, to support fellow members of the community, to report deep inner feelings and frustrations as well as joy and pleasure, and to become counselors to other learners. CLL learners are typically grouped in a circle of six to twelve learners, with the number of knowers varying from one per group to one per student. CLL has also been used in larger schools classes where special grouping arrangements are necessary, such as organizing learners in temporary pairs in facing parallel lines.

Learning is a "whole person" process, and the learner at each stage is involved not just in the accomplishment of cognitive (language learning) tasks but in the solution of affective conflicts and the respect for the enactment of values as well (La Forge 1983: 55). CLL compares language learning to the stages of human growth. In stage 1 the learner is like an infant, completely dependent on the knower for linguistic content. A new self of the learner is generated or born in the target language (La Forge 1983:45). The learner repeats utterances made by the teacher in the target language and overhears the interchanges between other learners and knowers.

(2) Teacher roles

At the deepest level, the teacher's function derives from the functions of the counselor in Rogerian psychological counseling. A counselor's clients are people with problems, who in a typical counseling session will often use emotional language to communicate their difficulties to the counselor. The counselor's role is to respond calmly and non-judgmentally, in a supportive manner, and help the client try to understand his or her problems better by applying order and analysis to them. The counselor is not responsible for paraphrasing the client's problem element for element but rather for capturing the essence of the client's concern, such that the client might say, "Yes, that's exactly what I meant."

(3) Instructional materials

Since a CLL course evolves out of the interactions of the community, a textbook is not considered a necessary component. A textbook would impose a particular body of language content on the learners, thereby impeding their growth and interaction. Materials may be developed by the teacher as the course develops, although these generally consist of little more than summaries on the blackboard or overhead projector of some of the linguistic features of conversations generated by students. Conversations may also be transcribed and distributed for study and analysis, and learners may work in groups to produce their own materials, such as scripts for dialogues and mini-dramas.

In early accounts of CLL the use of teaching machines is recommended for necessary rote-drill and practice in language learning. The design and use of machines now appear to make possible the freeing of the teacher to do what only a human person can do... become a learning counselor (Curran 976: 6). In more recent CLL descriptions, teaching machines and their accompanying materials are not mentioned, and we assume that contemporary CLL classes do not use teaching machines at all.

CHAPTER 06 The Silent Way

> **단원 길라잡이**
> - 학습자의 참여를 최대화시킨 발견 학습으로서의 침묵식 교수법의 의의와 다양한 교실 도구를 살펴본다.
> - cognitive approach에서의 중요성을 인식할 수 있다.

Introduction

Silent Way는 혁신적인 교수법이라 할 수 있으며 1970년대 초반에 Caleb Gattegno에 의해 창시되었다. 이 approach의 기본적인 원리는 다음과 같다:

- 학습은 기억이나 반복하는 것보다 발견해낼 때 촉진된다.
- 학습은 구체적 물체에 의해 도움된다.
- 문제해결은 학습의 중심이 된다.

Silent Way에서 교사는 학습자가 가능한 한 많은 말을 할 수 있도록 침묵해야한 한다는 전제에서 나오는 것이 때문에 silence의 의미는 중요하다. 이 개념은 이제까지 교사는 설명하고 학생은 듣는다는 기본전제와는 상반되는 원리에서 그 시작을 하고 있다. 이 교수법은 building-block approach라고도 설명되고 문법적 복합성에 근거하여 일관된 sequence에 따라 sentences를 통해 언어를 가르치도록 하는 structural approach라고 할 수 있다.

01 Principles

(1) Learning Acquisition
① Learning is facilitated if the learner discovers or creates rather than remembers and repeats what is to be learned.
② Learning is facilitated by accompanying (mediating) physical objects.
③ Learning is facilitated by problem solving involving the material to be learned.

(2) Principles
① Teachers should concentrate on how students learn, not on how to teach.
② Imitation and drill are not the primary means by which students learn.
③ Learning consists of trial and error, deliberate experimentation, suspending judgement, and revising conclusions.
④ In learning, learners draw on everything that they already know, especially their native language.
⑤ The teacher must not interfere with the learning process.

(3) Objectives
Teachers using the Silent Way want their students to become highly independent and experimental learners. Making errors is a natural part of the process and a key learning device, as it is a sign that students are testing out their hypotheses and arriving at various conclusions about the language through a trial and error style approach. The teacher tries to facilitate activities whereby the students discover for themselves the conceptual rules governing the language, rather than imitating or memorizing them – Brown(1994:63) expresses this as being a process whereby "students construct conceptual hierarchies of their *own* which are a product of the time they have invested." In addition to the idea that students become more autonomous learners and "develop their own inner criteria for correctness" (Larsen Freeman, 1986:62), another key objective was to encourage students to work as a group—to try and solve problems in the target language together. Based on these principles and using the techniques described below, it was hoped that students would eventually be able to actively use the language for self-expression, relating their thoughts, feelings and perceptions.

(4) Syllabus
The Silent Way uses a structural syllabus, and structures are constantly reviewed and recycled. The choice of vocabulary is important, with functional and versatile words seen as the best. Translation and rote repetition are avoided and the language is usually practiced in meaningful contexts. Evaluation is carried out by observation, and the teacher may never set a formal test.

02 Learning and Teaching

1. Lesson Procedure

① The teacher has introduced the idea of pronouns as in "Give me a green rod".

② The class will then use this structure until it is clearly assimilated, using, in addition, all the other colours.

③ One member of the class would now like to ask another to pass a rod to a third student but she does not know the word "her", only that it cannot be "me".

④ At this point the teacher would intervene and supply the new item: "Give her the green rod" and the learners will continue until the next new item is needed (probably "him"). This minimalist role of the teacher has led some critics to describe Silent Way teachers as "aloof" and, indeed, this apparently excessive degree of self-restraint can be seen as such.

2. Teaching Materials

(1) Color charts

A fidel chart for English is used to teach spelling. The sound-color chart consists of blocks of color, with one color representing one sound in the language being learned. The teacher uses this chart to help teach pronunciation; as well as pointing to colors to help students with the different sounds, she can also tap particular colors very hard to help students learn word stress. Later in the learning process, students can point to the chart themselves. The chart can help students perceive sounds that may not occur in their first language, and it also allows students to practice making these sounds without relying on mechanical repetition. It also provides an easily verifiable record of which sounds the students and which they have not, which can help their autonomy.

The word charts contain the functional vocabulary of the target language, and use the same color scheme as the sound-color chart. Each letter is colored in a way that indicates its pronunciation. The teacher can point to the chart to highlight the pronunciation of different words in sentences that the students are learning. There are twelve word charts in English, containing a total of around five hundred words. The Fidel charts also use the same color-coding, and list the various ways that sounds can be spelled. 예 In English, the entry for the sound /ey/ contains the spellings ay, ea, ei, eigh, etc., all written in the same color. These can be used to help students associate sounds with their spelling.

(2) Cuisenaire rods

The Cuisenaire rods are wooden, and come in ten different lengths, but identical cross-section; each length has its own assigned color. The rods are used in a wide variety of situations in the classroom. At the beginning stages they can be used to practice colors and numbers, and later they can be used in more complex grammar. 예 To teach prepositions the teacher could use the statement 'The blue rod is between the green one and the yellow one'. They can also be used more abstractly, perhaps to represent a clock or the floor plan of a house.

3. Classroom Techniques

Techniques	Activity
Sound-Color Chart	The teacher refers students to a color-coded wall chart depicting individual sounds in the target language—students use this to point out and build words with correct pronunciation.
Teacher's Silence	Teacher is generally silent, only giving help when it is absolutely necessary.
Peer Correction	Students are encouraged to help each other in a cooperative and not competitive spirit.
Rods	Rods are used to trigger meaning, and to introduce or actively practice language. They can symbolize whatever words are being taught and be manipulated directly or abstractly to create sentences.
Self-correction Gestures	Teacher uses hands to indicate that something is incorrect or needs changing, using fingers as words then touching the finger / word that is in need of correction.
Word Chart	Words are depicted on charts, the sounds in each word corresponding in color to the Sound-Color Chart described above—students use this to build sentences.
Fidel Chart	A chart that is color-coded according to the sound-color chart but includes the various English spellings so that they can be directly related to actual sounds.
Structured Feedback	Students are invited to make observations about the day's lesson and what they have learned.

CHAPTER 07 Suggestopedia

> **단원 길라잡이**
> - 학습자의 잠재능력을 인정하여 학습의 극대화를 추구할 수 있다.
> - Suggestopedia의 cognitive적인 특성과 활동을 이해한다.

Introduction

Suggestopedic course은 학습자들이 가능한 최대의 안정감을 느끼는 교실에서 진행될 수 있도록 한다. 이상적인 환경으로, 안락한 의자, 은은한 불빛, 음악 모두 학습자에게 편안함을 조성하는 데 이용된다. 학습자의 주변 환경 학습(peripheral learning)을 이용하기 위해선 새로운 언어에 관한 문법정보를 예시하는 포스터가 교실 주변에 걸려 있다. 교실의 포스터는 매 주 바뀐다. 이러한 교실 환경을 상상해 보자!

미정이는 수업을 위해 영어 이름, Claire로 바꾸고 직업도 journalist를 선택한다. 이 과정에서 미정이는 새로운 신분에 어울리는 전반적인 전기를 쓰게 된다. 미정이 공부하는 텍스트는 영어로 된 매우 긴 대화가 들어있는 자료이다. 대화 옆에는 미정이의 모국어, 한국어로 된 번역문이 있다. 대화에는 어휘와 문법에 대한 주석이 있다. 교사는 두 협주곡이 나오는 동안에 대화를 제시한다. 이 협주곡들은 첫 번째 단계인 수용적 단계(receptive phase)를 대표한다. 첫 번째 협주곡에서 교사는 목소리를 음악의 리듬과 높낮이에 맞추어 대화를 낭독한다. 이런 식으로, 미정이의 뇌 전체가 활성화된다. 교사가 목표언어의 대화를 큰 소리로 낭독할 때 미정이와 반 친구들은 따라서 한다. 미정이는 번역문을 점검하기도 한다. 두 번째 협주곡이 나오는 동안 미정이는 편안히 앉아 있기도 하고 교사는 정상속도로 대화를 낭독한다. 과제로서 미정이는 잠자리에 들기 전에 그리고 다음날 아침에 잠자리에서 일어났을 때 이 대화를 읽어본다. 이어서 두 번째 주요 단계인 활성화단계(activation phase)가 오는데, 이 단계에서 미정이는 새로운 자료를 쉽게 사용하는 데 도움을 주도록 고안된 여러 가지 활동을 수행한다. 이 활동에는 role play, game, song, qna 등이 포함된다.

01 Principles

Suggestopedia is a teaching method developed by the Bulgarian psychotherapist Georgi Lozanov. It is used in different fields, but mostly in the field of foreign language learning. Lozanov has claimed that by using this method a teacher's students can learn a language approximately three to five times as quickly as through conventional teaching methods. Suggestopedia has been called a pseudoscience. It strongly depends on the trust that students develop towards the method by simply believing that it works. The theory applied positive suggestion in teaching when it was developed in the 1970s. However, as the method improved, it has focused more on desuggestive learning and now is often called desuggestopedia. Suggestopedia is a portmanteau of the words suggestion and pedagogy. A common misconception is to link suggestion to hypnosis. However, Lozanov intended it in the sense of offering or proposing, emphasising student choice.

(1) Theory

The intended purpose was to enhance learning by tapping into the power of suggestion. Suggestopedia is a system for liberation; liberation from the preliminary negative concept regarding the difficulties in the process of learning that is established throughout their life in the society. Desuggestopedia focuses more on liberation as Lozanov describes 'desuggestive learning' as free, without a mildest pressure, liberation of previously suggested programs to restrict intelligence and spontaneous acquisition of knowledge, skills and habits. The method implements this by working not only on the conscious level of human mind but also on the subconscious level, the mind's reserves.

(2) Objectives

The prime objective of Suggestopedia is to tap into more of students' mental potential to learn, in order to accelerate the process by which they learn to understand and use the target language for communication. Four factors considered essential in this process were the provision of a relaxed and comfortable learning environment, the use of soft Baroque music to help increase alpha brain waves and decrease blood pressure and heart rate, desuggestion in terms of the psychological barriers learners place on their own learning potential, and suggestibility through the encouragement of learners assuming child-like and/or new roles and names in the target language.

(3) Features

① Learning is facilitated in an environment that is as comfortable as possible, featuring soft cushioned seating and dim lighting. Peripheral learning is encouraged through the presence in the learning environment of posters and decorations featuring the target language and various grammatical information.

② The teacher assumes a role of complete authority and control in the classroom. Self-perceived and psychological barriers to learners' potential to learn are desuggested.

③ Students are encouraged to be child-like, take mental trips with the teacher and assume new roles and names in the target language in order to become more suggestible. Students work from lengthy dialogs in the target language, with an accompanying translation into the students' native language.

④ Baroque music is played softly in the background to increase mental relaxation and potential to take in and retain new material during the lesson. Music, drama and the Arts are integrated into the learning process as often as possible.

⑤ Homework is limited to students re-reading the dialog they are studying – once before they go to sleep at night and once in the morning before they get up. Errors are tolerated, the emphasis being on content and not structure. Grammar and vocabulary are presented and given treatment from the teacher, but not dwelt on.

02 Procedure

(1) Classroom Techniques

Techniques	Activity
Classroom Set-up	Emphasis is placed on creating a physical environment that does not feel like a normal classroom, and makes the students feel as relaxed and comfortable as possible.
Peripheral Learning	Students can absorb information effortlessly when it is perceived as part of the environment, rather than the material to be attended to.
Positive Suggestion	Teachers appeal to students' consciousness and subconscious in order to better orchestrate the suggestive factors involved in the learning situation.
Visualization	Students are asked to close their eyes and visualize scenes and events, to help them relax, facilitate positive suggestion and encourage creativity from the students.
Choose a New Identity	Students select a target language name and / or occupation that places them inside the language they are learning.
Role-play	Students pretend temporarily that they are someone else and perform a role using the target language.
First Concert	Teacher does a slow, dramatic reading of the dialog synchronized in intonation with classical music.

Techniques	Activity
Second Concert	Students put aside their scripts and the teacher reads at normal speed according to the content, not the accompanying pre-Classical or Baroque music—this typically ends the class for the day.
Primary Activation	Students playfully reread the target language out loud, as individuals or in groups.
Secondary Activation	Students engage in various activities designed to help the students learn the material and use it more spontaneously—activities include singing, dancing, dramatizations and games – communicative intent and not form being the focus.

(2) Teacher Roles

Teachers should not act in a directive way, although this method is teacher-controlled and not student-controlled. 예 They should act as a real partner to the students, participating in the activities such as games and songs naturally and genuinely. In the concert session, they should fully include classical art in their behaviors. Although there are many techniques that the teachers use, factors such as communication in the spirit of love, respect for man as a human being, the specific humanitarian way of applying their 'techniques' are crucial. The teachers not only need to know the techniques and to acquire the practical methodology completely, but also to fully understand the theory, because, if they implement those techniques without complete understanding, they will not be able lead their learners to successful results, or they could even cause a negative impact on their learning. Therefore, the teacher has to be trained in a course taught by certified trainers.

- Covering a huge bulk of learning material.
- Structuring the material in the suggestopaedic way: global-partial partial-global, and global in the part – part in the global, related to the golden proportion.
- As a professional, on one hand, and a personality, on the other hand, the teacher should be a highly-regarded professional, reliable and credible.
- The teacher should love his students (of course, not sentimentally but as human beings) and teach them with personal participation through games, songs, classical arts, and pleasure.

CHAPTER 08 Total Physical Response

> **단원 길라잡이**
> - comprehension-based 교수법의 중심이 된 TPR 교수법의 배경이론과 활동의 특성을 파악한다.
> - 교사와 학생의 역할을 통해 TPR의 장점을 이해한다.

Introduction

　TPR교수법은 가장 기본적으로 2언어도 모국어 어린이들의 언어습득과 다르지 않다는 기본전제 하에서 발생되었다. 많은 입력이 들어가고 그것이 right brain을 자극하는 행동과 함께 이루어지면 언어가 습득된다는 교수이론이다. 그래서 현재 우리나라에서는 초등학교 어린이들에게 많이 이용되고 있는 활동이라고 할 수 있다. 다음과 같이 간단한 활동들을 듣고 바로 행할 수 있도록 하는데 목표를 두고 있다. 아래 그림과 같이 교실안에서 교사의 commands에 따라 학생들이 "learn and perform these actions" 하는 것을 볼 수 있다.

01 Principles

(1) Theory

- Total Physical Response (TPR) is a language-teaching method developed by James Asher, a professor emeritus of psychology at San Jose State University. It is based on the coordination of language and physical movement. In TPR, instructors give commands to students in the target language, and students respond with whole-body actions.
- The teacher directs and students act in response – "The instructor is the director of a stage play in which the students are the actors (Asher, 1977:43)."
- Listening and physical response skills are emphasized over oral production.
- The imperative mood is the most common language function employed, even well into advanced levels. Interrogatives are also heavily used.
- Whenever possible, humor is injected into the lessons to make them more enjoyable for learners.
- Students are not required to speak until they feel naturally ready or confident enough to do so.
- Grammar and vocabulary are emphasized over other language areas. Spoken language is emphasized over written language.

(2) Reception

TPR is often criticized as being only suitable for beginning students. However, the encyclopedia notes that there are several publications available about how to use TPR with intermediate and advanced students. According to its proponents, Total Physical Response has a number of advantages:

① Students enjoy getting out of their chairs and moving around. Simple TPR activities do not require a great deal of preparation on the part of the teacher. TPR is aptitude-free, working well with a mixed ability class, and with students having various disabilities. It is good for kinesthetic learners who need to be active in the class. Class size need not be a problem, and it works effectively for children and adults.

② It is recognized that TPR is most useful for beginners, though it can be used at higher levels where preparation becomes an issue for the teacher. It does not give students the opportunity to express their own thoughts in a creative way. Further, it is easy to overuse TPR – "Any novelty, if carried on too long, will trigger adaptation." It can be a challenge for shy students. Additionally, the nature of TPR places an unnaturally heavy emphasis on the use of the imperative mood, that is to say commands such as sit down and stand up. These features are of limited utility to the learner, and can lead to a learner appearing rude when attempting to use his new language. As a TPR class progresses, group activities and descriptions can extend basic TPR concepts into full communication situations.

③ Because of its participatory approach, TPR may also be a useful alternative teaching strategy for students with dyslexia or related learning disabilities, who typically experience difficulty learning foreign languages with traditional classroom instruction.

(3) Teaching Materials

Total physical response lessons typically use a wide variety of realia, posters, and props. Teaching materials are not compulsory, and for the very first lessons they may not be used. As students progress in ability the teacher may begin to use objects found in the classroom such as furniture or books, and later may use word charts, pictures, and realia. There are a number of specialized TPR teaching products available, including student kits developed by Asher and an interactive CD-ROM for students to practice with privately.

(4) Procedures

The majority of class time in TPR lessons is spent doing drills in which the instructor gives commands using the imperative mood. Students respond to these commands with physical actions.

① Initially, students learn the meaning of the commands they hear by direct observation. After they learn the meaning of the words in these commands, the teacher issues commands that use novel combinations of the words the students have learned.

② Instructors limit the number of new vocabulary items at any one time. This is to help students differentiate the new words from those previously learned, and to facilitate integration with their existing language knowledge. Students can learn between 12 and 36 words for every hour of instruction, depending on their language level and class size.

③ While drills using the imperative are the mainstay of total physical response classes, teachers can use other activities as well. Some typical other activities are role plays and slide presentations. However, beginners are not made to learn conversational dialogs until 120 hours into their course.

④ There is little error correction. Teachers should treat learners' mistakes the same way a parent would treat their children's. Errors made by beginning-level students are usually overlooked, but as students become more advanced teachers may correct more of their errors, as children get older parents tend to correct their grammatical mistakes more often.

⑤ TPR lesson plans should contain the detailed commands. The teacher says, "*It is wise to write out the exact utterances you will be using and especially the novel commands because the action is so fast-moving there is usually no time for you to create spontaneously.*"

(5) Classroom Techniques

Techniques	Activity
Using Commands to Direct Behavior	The use of commands requiring physical actions from the students in response is the major teaching technique
Role Reversal	Students direct the teacher and fellow learners
Action Sequence	Teacher gives interconnected directions which create a sequence of actions— as students progress in proficiency, more and more commands are added to the action sequence. Most everyday activities can be broken down into a sequence of actions

02 Teaching Principles

Total physical response is an example of the comprehension approach to language teaching. Methods in the comprehension approach emphasize the importance of listening on language development, and do not require spoken output in the early stages of learning. In total physical response, students are not forced to speak. Instead, teachers wait until students acquire enough language through listening that they start to speak spontaneously. At the beginning stages of instruction students can respond to the instructor in their native language.

- While the majority of class time is spent on listening comprehension, the ultimate goal of the method is to develop oral fluency. J. Asher sees developing listening comprehension skills as the most efficient way of developing spoken language skills. Lessons in TPR are organized around grammar, and in particular around the verb. Instructors issue commands based on the verbs and vocabulary to be learned in that lesson.

- Total Physical Response is both a teaching technique and a philosophy of language teaching. Teachers do not have to limit themselves to TPR techniques to teach according to the principles of the total physical response method. Because the students are only expected to listen and not to speak, the teacher has the sole responsibility for deciding what input students hear.

- The primary focus in lessons is on meaning, which distinguishes TPR from other grammar-based methods such as grammar-translation. Grammar is not explicitly taught, but is learned by induction. Students are expected to subconsciously acquire the grammatical structure of the language through exposure to spoken language input, in addition to decoding the messages in the input to find their meaning.

문헌읽기

Already in the late 1800s, a French teacher of Latin by the name of Francois Gouin was hard at work devising a method of language teaching that capitalized on the way children naturally learn their first language, through the transformation of perceptions into conceptions and then the expression of those conceptions using language. His approach became known as the *Series Method*, involving direct conceptual teaching of language using series of inter-connected sentences that are simple and easy to perceive, because the language being used can be directly related to whatever the speaker is doing at the immediate time of utterance (ie, one's actions and language match each other). His thinking was well ahead of his time, and the Series Method became swamped in the enthusiasm surrounding the other new approach at the time in the form of the Direct Method.

Some 80 years later, in the 1960s, James Asher began experimenting with a method he called Total Physical Response, and its basic premise had a lot in common with Gouin's. The method was to become well known in the 70s, and it drew on several other insights in addition to the trace theory that memory is stimulated and increased when it is closely associated with motor activity. The method owes a lot to some basic principles of language acquisition in young learners, most notably that the process involves a substantial amount of listening and comprehension in combination with various physical responses (smiling, reaching, grabbing, looking, etc) — well before learners begin to use the language orally. It also focused on the ideas that learning should be as fun and stress-free as possible, and that it should be dynamic through the use of accompanying physical activity.

Asher (1977) also had a lot to say about right-brained learning (the part of the brain that deals with motor activity), believing it should precede the language processing element covered by the left-brain. TPR is now a household name among teachers of foreign languages. It is widely acclaimed as a highly effective method at beginning levels, and almost a standard requirement in the instruction of young learners. It is also admired as a method due to its inherent simplicity, making it accessible to a wide range of teachers and learning environments.

CHAPTER 09 The Natural Approach

단원 길라잡이
- TPR과 함께 comprehension-based approach의 대표인 natural approach의 발생이론과 수업활동을 파악한다.
- natural approach가 교실안에서 가질 수 있는 장점을 이해한다.

01 Principles

(1) Background

The Natural Approach is a method of language teaching developed by Stephen Krashen and Tracy Terrell in the late 1970s and early 1980s. It aims to foster naturalistic language acquisition in a classroom setting, and to this end it emphasizes communication, and places decreased importance on conscious grammar study and explicit correction of student errors. Efforts are also made to make the learning environment as stress-free as possible. In the Natural Approach, language output is not forced, but allowed to emerge spontaneously after students have attended to large amounts of comprehensible language input.

The Natural Approach has become closely associated with Krashen's monitor model, and it is often seen as an application of the theory to language teaching. Despite this perception, there are some differences, particularly Terrell's view that some degree of conscious grammar study can be beneficial. The syllabus focuses on activities which Terrell sees as promoting subconscious language acquisition. He divides these activities into four main areas: content activities, such as learning a new subject in the target language; activities which focus on personalizing language, such as students sharing their favorite music, games, and problem-solving activities.

(2) Objectives

The aim of the Natural Approach is to develop communicative skills, and it is primarily intended to be used with beginning learners. It is presented as a set of principles that can apply to a wide range of learners and teaching situations, and concrete objectives depend on the specific context in which it is used. Terrell outlines three basic principles of the approach:

- Focus of instruction is on communication rather than its form.
- Speech production comes slowly and is never forced.
- Early speech goes through natural stages (yes or no response, one-word answers, lists of words, short phrases, complete sentences.)

These principles result in classrooms where the teacher emphasizes interesting, comprehensible input and low-anxiety situations. Lessons in the Natural Approach focus on understanding messages in the foreign language, and place little or no importance on error correction, drilling or on conscious learning of grammar rules. They also emphasize learning of a wide vocabulary base over learning new grammatical structures. In addition, teachers using the Natural Approach aim to create situations in the classroom that are intrinsically motivating for students.

Terrell sees learners going through three stages in their acquisition of speech: comprehension, early speech, and speech emergence. In the comprehension stage Terrell focuses on students' vocabulary knowledge. His aim is to make the vocabulary stick in students' long term memory, a process which he calls binding. Terrell sees some techniques as more binding than others; for example, the use of gestures or actions, such as in Total Physical Response, is seen to be more binding than the use of translation.

According to Terrell, students' speech will only emerge after enough language has been bound through communicative input. When this occurs, the learners enter the early speech stage. In this stage, students answer simple questions, use single words and set phrases, and fill in simple charts in the foreign language. In the speech emergence stage, students take part in activities requiring more advanced language, such as role-plays and problem-solving activities.

(3) Theory

Although Terrell originally created the Natural Approach without relying on a particular theoretical model, his subsequent collaboration with Krashen has meant that the method is often seen as an application to language teaching of Krashen's monitor model. Krashen outlined five hypotheses in his model:

① *The acquisition-learning hypothesis.* This states that there is a strict separation between conscious learning of language and subconscious acquisition of language, and that only acquisition can lead to fluent language use.

② *The monitor hypothesis.* This states that language knowledge that is consciously learned can only be used to monitor output, not to generate new language. Monitoring output requires learners to be focused on the rule and to have time to apply it.

③ *The input hypothesis.* This states that language is acquired by exposure to comprehensible input at a level a little higher than that the learner can already understand. Krashen names this kind of input 'i+1'.

④ *The natural order hypothesis.* This states that learners acquire the grammatical features of a language in a fixed order, and that this is not affected by instruction.

⑤ *The affective filter hypothesis.* This states that learners must be relaxed and open to learning in order for language to be acquired. Learners who are nervous or distressed may not learn features in the input that more relaxed learners would pick up with little effort.

Despite its basis in Krashen's theory, the Natural Approach does not adhere to the theory strictly. In particular, Terrell perceives a greater role for the conscious learning of grammar than Krashen. Krashen's monitor hypothesis contends that conscious learning has no effect on learners' ability to generate novel language, whereas Terrell is of the opinion that some conscious learning of grammar rules can be beneficial.

02 Learning Procedure

(1) Stages

① Preproduction stage: Students participate in the language activity without having to respond in the target language. For example, students can act out physical commands, identify student colleagues from teacher description, point to pictures, and so forth.

② Early production stage: Students respond to either-or questions, use single words and short phrases, fill in charts and use fixed conversational patterns, 예 How are you? What's your name?

③ Speech emergent phase: Students involve themselves in role play and games, contribute personal information and opinions, and participate in group problem solving.

(2) Teacher Roles

- Teacher is the primary source of comprehensible input in the target language. Class time is devoted primarily to providing input for acquisition.
- Teacher creates a classroom atmosphere that is interesting, friendly, and in which there is a low affective filter for learning. The technique does not demand speech from the students before they are ready for it, not correcting student errors and providing subject matter of high interest to students.
- Teacher must choose and orchestrate a rich mix of classroom activities, involving a variety of group sizes, content, and contexts. Teacher is seen as responsible for collecting materials and designing not just on teacher perceptions but on elicited student needs and interests.

문헌읽기

Stephen Krashen and Tracy Terrell developed the Natural Approach in the early eighties (Krashen and Terrell, 1983), based on Krashen's theories about second language acquisition. The approach shared a lot in common with Asher's Total Physical Response method in terms of advocating the need for a silent phase, waiting for spoken production to emerge of its own accord, and emphasizing the need to make learners as relaxed as possible during the learning process. Some important underlying principles are that there should be a lot of language acquisition as opposed to language processing, and there needs to be a considerable amount of *comprehensible input* from the teacher. Meaning is considered as the essence of language and vocabulary (not grammar) is the heart of language.

As part of the Natural Approach, students listen to the teacher using the target language communicatively from the very beginning. It has certain similarities with the much earlier Direct Method, with the important exception that students are allowed to use their native language alongside the target language as part of the language learning process. In early stages, students are not corrected during oral production, as the teacher is focusing on meaning rather than form (unless the error is so drastic that it actually hinders meaning).

Communicative activities prevail throughout a language course employing the Natural Approach, focusing on a wide range of activities including games, role-plays, dialogs, group work and discussions. There are three generic stages identified in the approach: (a) Preproduction – developing listening skills; (b) Early Production – students struggle with the language and make many errors which are corrected based on content and not structure ; (c) Extending Production – promoting fluency through a variety of more challenging activities.

Krashen's theories and the Natural approach have received plenty of criticism, particularly orientated around the recommendation of a silent period that is terminated when students feel ready to emerge into oral production, and the idea of comprehensible input. Critics point out that students will emerge at different times (or perhaps not at all!) and it is hard to determine which forms of language input will be comprehensible to the students. These factors can create a classroom that is essentially very difficult to manage unless the teacher is highly skilled. Still, this was the first attempt at creating an expansive and overall approach rather than a specific method, and the Natural Approach led naturally into the generally accepted norm for effective language teaching: Communicative Language Teaching.

CHAPTER 10 Communicative Language Teaching

> **단원 길라잡이**
> - communicative language teaching의 배경과 주요원리를 이해한다.
> - communicative language teaching의 종류와 특성들을 이해 적용한다.

Introduction

지금까지 초기 traditional 영어교수법과 소수그룹의 목적으로 만들어진 designer methods에 대하여 살펴보았다. 이제 현대 영어교수법의 가장 중요한 영역인 communicative language teaching (CLT)의 역사와 방법에 대해서 알아보기로 하자. 1970년 초에 이제까지의 language를 중심으로 한 교수법의 반대로 function을 언어습득의 중심으로 하는 notional-functional syllabus가 영국에서 시작되어 지금까지 이어지고 있다. 물론 지금의 CLT은 초기 시대의 내용이나 형식과는 많이 달라져 있지만 의사소통이 가능한 학습을 목적으로 하는 기본정신은 같이 한다고 할 수 있겠다.

조금 더 세부적으로 들어가 보자. CLT의 교수법 중에서 task-based language teaching이 가장 대표적인 교수법이다. task-based language teaching는 현재 교실현장에서 가장 많이 쓰이고 있고, 모든 언어능력을 가르칠 수 있는 교수법으로 설명될 수 있다. 의사소통능력을 위해서 필요한 4가지 요소, grammatical, discourse, sociolinguistic과 strategic competence 모두를 발달 시킬 수 있는 수업 형식을 갖추고 있다. 또 다른 종류의 CLT에는 content-based language teaching으로, content, 즉 subject matter를 가르치는 데 초점을 두는 교수법이 있다. 그 외에 theme-based, experiential-based, strategy-based language teaching등이 학습자들의 의사소통능력을 발달시키는데 그 목적을 두고 있다. 각각의 교수법에 대한 자세한 내용은 본문 안에서 살펴보기로 한다.

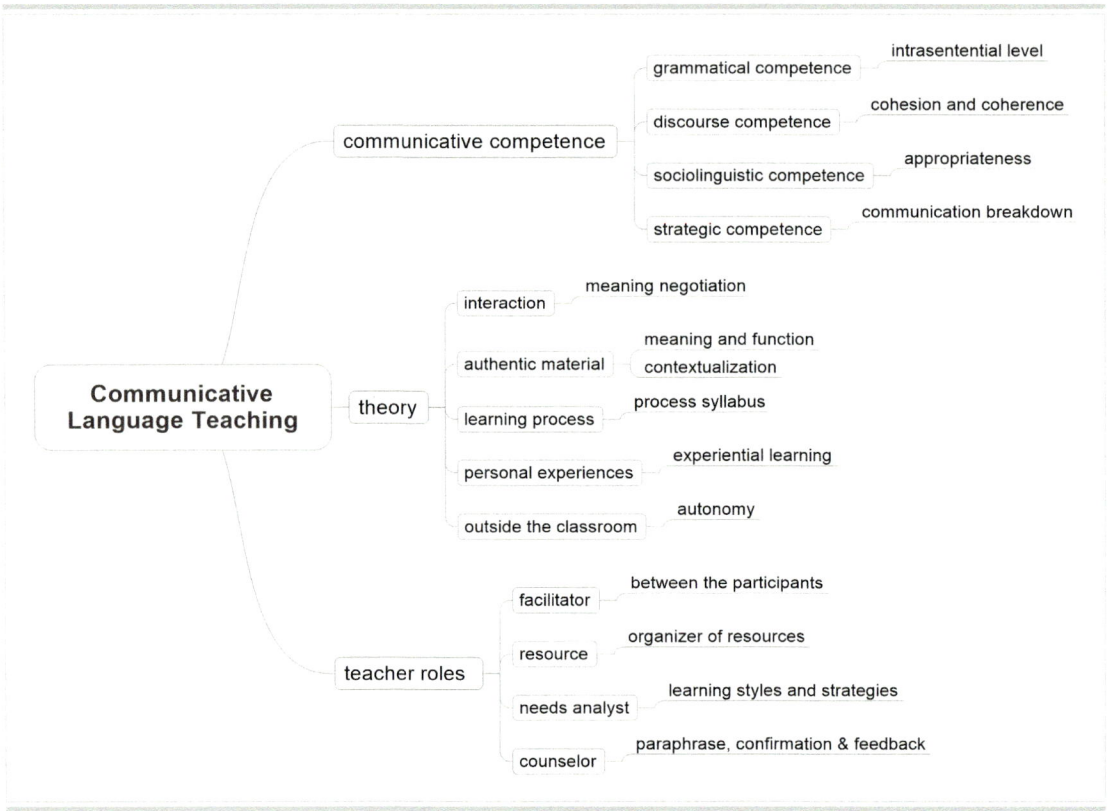

핵심플러스 Enlightened Eclectics

In the move away from teachers following one specific methodology, the eclectic approach is the label given to a teacher's use of techniques and activities from a range of language teaching approaches and methodologies. The teacher decides what methodology or approach to use depending on the aims of the lesson and the learners in the group. Almost all modern course books have a mixture of approaches and methodologies. For example, the class starts with an inductive activity with learners identifying the different uses of synonyms of movement using a reading text. They then practise these using TPR. In another class the input is recycled through a task-based lesson, with learners producing the instructions for an exercise manual. In the classroom, a typical lesson might combine elements from various sources such as TPR and TBL (the examples); the communicative approach, 예 in communication gap activities; the lexical approach, 예 focusing on lexical chunks in reading; and the structural-situational approach, 예 establishing a clear context for the presentation of new structures.

> Every language teaching method has its foundation, certain theoretical underpinnings. And these foundations almost always combine more than one discipline, for language teaching is not just linguistics or psychology, but involves both, along with pedagogical, sociological and other interdisciplinary considerations.

01 Communicative Language Teaching

Introduction

과거의 교수법은 언어학분야의 언어기술과 해당 언어기술의 교육적 적용 측면에 관심의 초점이 주어졌다. Chomsky의 생성문법을 교육 현장에 적용시키는 방법을 고민했고, 대조분석 가설로부터의 탈피를 꺼려했다. 2언어 교수-학습분야는 거의 전적으로 언어학 분야의 연구에 의존했다. 단지, 반복연습과 기억을 통한 과잉학습을 주창하는 교수법에 대한 의문이 제기되기 시작했으며, 아동의 자연스러운 모국어 습득 방법으로부터 얻어진 통찰이 연구되기 시작했다. 오늘날 교수-학습 방법에 관한 논의는 예전보다 훨씬 복잡하고 이질적이다. 의사소통의 문법적, 담화적 요소뿐만 아니라 언어의 사회적, 문화적, 화용론적 특징들에 대한 연구가 이뤄지고 있다. 그리고 실제 상황과 같은 의사소통을 교실 내에서 구현하기 위한 교육적 방법이 모색되고 있으며 정확성뿐만 아니라 유창성 향상을 위한 노력도 경주되고 있다. 학습자가 교실 밖의 실제 상황에서도 즉각적인 의사소통을 수행할 수 있는 능력을 갖추도록 하고 있으며, 교실 내에서의 즉각적 학습과제(tasks) 뿐만 아니라, 2언어에 대한 평생학습을 촉진시킬 수 있는 방안에 대해 고민하고 있다. 학습자는 언어 학습이라는 여정의 동반자로 간주되며, 자신의 잠재능력을 최대한 발휘할 수 있도록 학습자의 내적 동기를 불러일으키는 제반 요소들을 2언어 교수-학습 활동 속에 포함시키려는 노력이 이뤄지고 있다.

1. Backgrounds

The origins of Communicative Language Teaching (CLT) are to be found in the changes in the British language teaching tradition dating from the late 1960s. Until then, Situational Language represented the major British approach to teaching English as a foreign language. In Situational Language Teaching, language was taught by practicing basic structures in meaningful situation-based activities. British applied linguists emphasized another fundamental dimension of language that was inadequately addressed in current approaches to language teaching at that time – the functional and communicative potential of language. They saw the need to focus in language teaching on communicative proficiency rather than on mere mastery of structures.

Another impetus for different approaches to foreign language teaching came from changing educational realities in Europe. With the increasing interdependence of European countries came the need for greater efforts to teach adults the major languages of the European Common Market and the Council of Europe, a regional organization for cultural and educational cooperation. Education was one of the Council of Europe's major areas of activity. It sponsored international conferences on language teaching, published monographs and books about language teaching. The need to articulate and develop alternative methods of language teaching was considered a high priority.

In 1971 a group of experts began to investigate the possibility of developing language courses on a unit-credit system, a system in which learning tasks are broken down into portions or units, each of which corresponds to a component of a learner's needs and is systematically related to all the other portions (van Ek and Alexander 1980: 6). The group used studies of the needs of European language learners, and in particular a preliminary document prepared by a British linguist, D. Wilkins (1972), which proposed a functional or communicative definition of language that could serve as a basis for developing communicative syllabuses for language teaching. Wilkins's contribution was an analysis of the communicative meanings that a language learner needs to understand and express. Rather than describe the core of language through traditional concepts of grammar and vocabulary, Wilkins attempted to demonstrate the systems of meanings that lay behind the communicative uses of language.

The work of the Council of Europe; the writings of Wilkins, Widdowson, Candlin, Christopher Brumfit, Keith Johnson, and other British applied linguists on the theoretical basis for a communicative or functional approach to language teaching; the rapid application of these ideas by textbook writers; and the equally rapid acceptance of these new principles by British language teaching specialists, curriculum development centers, and even governments gave prominence nationally and internationally to what came to be referred to as the Communicative Approach, or simply Communicative Language Teaching. (The terms notional-functional approach and functional approach are also sometimes used.) Although the movement began as a largely British innovation, focusing on alternative conceptions of a syllabus, since the mid-1970s the scope of Communicative Language Teaching has expanded. Both American and British proponents now see it as an approach (and not a method) that aims to (a) make communicative competence the goal of language teaching and (b) develop procedures for the teaching of the four language skills that acknowledge the interdependence of language and communication. Characteristics of CLT are:

- Language is a system for the expression of meaning.
- The primary function of language is for interaction and communication.
- The structure of language reflects its functional and communicative uses.
- The primary units of language are not merely its grammatical and structural features, but categories of functional and communicative meaning as exemplified in discourse.

2. Audiolingual Method vs Communicative Language Teaching

Finocchiaro and Brumfit (1983) contrast the major distinctive features of the Audiolingual Method and the Communicative Approach, according to their interpretation.

Audiolingual Method	Communicative Language Teaching
• 1940's	• Late 1960's ~ 1970's
• Origins and forerunners: Behavioural psychology (Skinner), structural linguistics (Bloomfield, Fries, Lado), ASTP (Army Specialized Training Programs)	• Forerunners: C. Candlin, H. Widdowson, Hymes. European Common Market. 1980: Van Ek and Alexander (the threshold level), Wilkins, Brumfit (functional-notional categories)
• Attends to structure and form, more than meaning	• Need to focus in language teaching on communicative proficiency
• Demands memorization of structure-based dialogs	• Meaning is paramount. Dialogs, if used, centre around communicative functions and are not normally memorized.
• Language items are not necessarily contextualised.	• Contextualization is a basic premise.
• Language learning is structures, sounds, or words.	• Language learning is learning to communicate.
• Drilling is a central technique.	• Communicative activities from the very beginning
• Native-speaker-like pronunciation.	• Comprehensible pronunciation: Native language accepted where feasible.
• Language is habit, so errors must be prevented at all costs.	• Language is created by the individual often through trial and error.
• Accuracy	• Fluency
• Linguistic competence	• Competence and performance

3. Approach

The communicative approach in language teaching starts from a theory of language as communication. The goal of language teaching is to develop what D. Hymes (1972) referred to as communicative competence. Hymes coined this term in order to contrast a communicative view of language and Chomsky's theory of competence. Chomsky held that linguistic theory is concerned primarily with an ideal speaker-listener in a completely homogeneous speech community, who knows its language perfectly and is unaffected by such grammatically irrelevant conditions as memory limitation, distractions, shifts of attention and interest, and errors (random or characteristic) in applying his knowledge of the language in actual performance. (Chomsky 1965: 3)

For Chomsky, the focus of linguistic theory was to characterize the abstract abilities speakers possess that enable them to produce grammatically correct sentences in a language. Hymes held that such a view of linguistic theory was sterile, that linguistic theory needed to be seen as part of a more general theory incorporating communication and culture. Hymes's theory of communicative competence was a definition of what a speaker needs to know in order to be communicatively competent in a speech community. In Hymes's view, a person who acquires communicative competence acquires both knowledge and ability for language use with respect to:

- whether something is formally possible;
- whether something is feasible in virtue of the means of implementation available;
- whether something is appropriate (adequate, happy, successful) in relation to a context in which it is used and evaluated;
- whether something is in fact done, actually performed, and what its doing entails.

This theory of what knowing a language entails offers a much more comprehensive view than Chomsky's view of competence, which deals primarily with abstract grammatical knowledge. Another linguistic theory of communication favored in CLT is Halliday's functional account of language use. Linguistics is concerned with the description of speech acts or texts, since only through the study of language in use are all the functions of language, and therefore all components of meaning, brought into focus (Halliday 1970: 145). In a number of influential books and papers, Halliday has elaborated a powerful theory of the functions of language, which complements Hymes' view of communicative competence for many writers on CLT.

4. Theory of Learning

In contrast to the amount that has been written in Communicative Language Teaching literature about communicative dimensions of language, little has been written about learning theory. Neither Brumfit and Johnson (1979) nor Littlewood (1981), for example, offers any discussion of learning theory. Elements of an underlying learning theory can be discerned in some CLT practices, however. One such element might be described as the communication principle: Activities that involve real communication promote learning. A second element is the task principle: Activities in which language is used for carrying out meaningful tasks promote learning (Johnson 1982). A third element is the meaningfulness principle: Language that is meaningful to the learner supports the learning process. Learning activities are consequently selected according to how well they engage the learner in meaningful and authentic language use, rather than merely mechanical practice of language patterns. These principles, we suggest, can be inferred from CLT practices (Little-wood 1981; Johnson 1982). They address the conditions needed to promote second language learning, rather than the processes of language acquisition.

More recent accounts of Communicative Language Teaching, however, have attempted to describe theories of language learning processes that are compatible with the communicative approach. Savignon (1983) surveys second language acquisition research as a source for learning theories and considers the role of linguistic, social, cognitive, and individual variables in language acquisition. Other theorists (Stephen Krashen, who is not directly associated with Communicative Language Teaching) have developed theories cited as compatible with the principles of CLT. Krashen sees acquisition as the basic process involved in developing language proficiency and distinguishes this process from learning. Acquisition refers to the unconscious development of the target language system as a result of using the language for real communication. Learning is the conscious representation of grammatical knowledge that has resulted from instruction, and it cannot lead to acquisition. It is the acquired system that we call upon to create utterances during spontaneous language use. The learned system can serve only as a monitor of the output of the acquired system. Krashen and other second language acquisition theorists typically stress that language learning comes about through using language communicatively, rather than through practicing language skills.

5. Design

(1) Objectives

Piepho (1981) discusses the following levels of objectives in a communicative approach. These are proposed as general objectives, applicable to any teaching situation:

- An integrative and content level (language as a means of expression)
- A linguistic and instrumental level (language as a semiotic system and an object of learning)
- An affective level of interpersonal relationships and conduct (language as a means of expressing values and judgments about oneself and others)
- A level of individual learning needs (remedial learning based on error analysis)
- A general educational level of extralinguistic goals (language learning within the school curriculum)

 KEY NOTE

Action Research

Action research is a development tool for a teacher that involves observing or gathering other data about a class through interviews, case studies, and questionnaires. A teacher can establish a cycle of identifying problems, planning changes in response, implementing changes and gathering and analysing data to evaluate the implementation.

Action research can be used to help general development or to resolve specific problems with teaching or learners. For example, a teacher has problems with giving feedback to learners on speaking problems and decides to record their classes. They then analyse the recordings to identify more effective ways of correction. They implement changes based on this, and collect data to analyse whether feedback is now more useful to learners. In the classroom, peer observations, learner and teacher diaries, audio and video recordings, case studies, questionnaires and interviews with learners are all methods that can be used to gather data for action research.

(2) Teacher roles

① Traditional Role of English teachers

The traditional method is largely teacher-centered, with the teachers hogging the limelight always. They lecture at length on particular topics and students listen to them with rapt attention - this has been the methodology for teaching English for decades now. Using this methodology, teachers have been teaching discrete points of grammar or phonology in separate lessons, focusing mainly on the formal features of the language at the expense of encouraging students to use the language. (예 repetitive practice, mechanical drills and memorization of grammar rules) This approach could be regarded as what Wilkins (1976) calls a "synthetic" approach in which "different parts of the language are taught separately and step by step so that acquisition is a process of gradual accumulation of parts until the whole structure of language has been built up."

This linear approach to language learning is explained well by Nunan (1996). Nunan likens it to the construction of a wall in the following manner: "The language wall is erected one linguistic brick at a time. The easy grammatical bricks are laid at the bottom of the wall, and they provide a foundation for the more difficult ones. The task for the learner is to get the linguistic bricks in the right order: first the word bricks, and then the sentence bricks. If the bricks are not in the correct order, the wall will collapse under its own ungrammaticality." Freire (1982) calls this the "banking" system of education in which the learners are considered to be similar to bank accounts into which regular deposits are made to be drawn later for specific purposes like examination. Obviously, the onus here lies on the individuals making the deposits for it is they who are responsible for earning the money and it is only they who can make the bank accounts swell. Using this analogy for the traditional language classroom would inevitably mean that the teacher is almost like the Titan, Atlas, of Greek mythology.

② Focus on the Learner

As we have already seen, the traditional method of teaching English makes the teacher the all-powerful authority in the classroom, almost obliterating the existence of the learner sometimes. Dewey (1938) objected to this kind of spoon-feeding of knowledge, and pointed out the importance of the role of the learner as an active agent in his or her learning. Dewey laid the foundation of what we now call learner-centeredness, a term which has now gained tremendous currency in English language teaching. It reflects, as Tudor (1996) points out, a widespread desire in the language teaching community to develop means of allowing learners to play a fuller, more active and participatory role in their language study. However, learner-centeredness in ELT is not a product of a single school of thought, but a result of the confluence of several innovative perspectives on language teaching. Among them, mention must be made of;

- Humanistic approaches to language teaching which developed during the later half of the twentieth century and which talked about giving equal attention to both the intellectual and the emotional development of the learner
- Communicative language teaching, which developed in the 1960s and 1970s and which was both a reaction against the prevalent structure-oriented drill methods of language teaching popular during the time and a result of the desire to make language teaching more flexible and more responsive to students, real world communicative needs.

(3) Innovative role of the teacher in task-based language teaching

In the current paradigm of Task-based Language Teaching (TBLT), which is basically an offshoot of communicative language teaching, learner-centerdness has found a new expression. The main conceptual basis for TBLT is, as Nunan(2004) points out, "experiential learning" or "learning by doing". In this way, TBLT goes a long way in breaking down the hierarchies of the traditional classroom because the very act of trying to complete a communicative task involves planning and using strategies on the part of the learner. A communicative task has been defined by Nunan(2004) as a piece of classroom work that involves learners in comprehending, manipulating, producing, or interacting in the target language while their attention is focused on mobilizing their grammatical knowledge in order to express meaning, and in which the intention is to convey meaning rather than to manipulate form.

In a learner-centered approach to language teaching, like TBLT, for instance, the role of the learner is significantly altered, as the learner is in the thick of all classroom activities getting a hands-on practical experience of using the language for communicative purposes. But does it mean that the role of the teacher in such a case is diminished? The answer is a firm "NO" because though the teacher is not really the focus here, the teacher performs an important mediational role which encompasses a wide range of responsibilities, albeit qualitatively different from the traditional role of the teacher as the disseminator of information. In teaching through mediation, the teacher becomes a true facilitator of learning for the language learners, guiding them through dialogic communication (Vygotsky, 1978) as they co-construct knowledge with the teacher. Hence, teachers should facilitate this process by creating diverse communicative activities, especially intended for pair-work and group-work, that are interesting and challenging to the learners, as they progress in the path of acquiring and using the target language beyond the textbook and the classroom.

(4) Instructional materials

A wide variety of materials have been used to support communicative approaches to language teaching. Unlike some contemporary methodologies, such as Community

Language Learning, practitioners of Communicative Language Teaching view materials as a way of influencing the quality of classroom interaction and language use. Materials thus have the primary role of promoting communicative language use. We will consider three kinds of materials currently used in CLT and label these text-based, task-based, and realia.

① Text-Based Materials: Morrow and Johnson's Communicate (1979), for example, has none of the usual dialogues, drills, or sentence patterns and uses visual cues, taped cues, pictures, and sentence fragments to initiate conversation. Watcyn-Jones's Pair Work (1981) consists of two different texts for pair work, each containing different information needed to enact role plays and carry out other pair activities.

② Task-Based Materials: A variety of games, role plays, simulations, and task-based communication activities have been prepared to support Communicative Language Teaching classes. These typically are in the form of one-of-a-kind items: exercise handbooks, cue cards, activity cards, pair-communication practice materials, and student-interaction practice booklets. In pair-communication materials, there are typically two sets of material for a pair of students, each set containing different kinds of information. Sometimes the information is complementary, and partners must fit their respective parts of the jigsaw into a composite whole. Others assume different role relationships for the partners (예 an interviewer and an interviewee). Still others provide drills and practice material in interactional formats.

③ Realia : Many proponents of Communicative Language Teaching have advocated the use of authentic, real-life materials in the classroom. These might include language-based realia, such as signs, magazines, advertisements, and newspapers, or graphic and visual sources around which communicative activities can be built, such as maps, pictures, symbols, graphs, and charts. Different kinds of objects can be used to support communicative exercises, such as a plastic model to assemble from directions.

핵심플러스 Key note Basic Features of CLT (D. Nunan, 1991)

- An emphasis on learning to communicate through interaction in the target language.
- The introduction of authentic texts into the learning situation.
- The provision of opportunities for learners to focus, not only on the language but also on the learning process itself.
- An enhancement of the learner's own personal experiences as important contributing elements to classroom learning.
- An attempt to link classroom language learning with language activation outside the classroom.

02 Task-Based Instruction

Introduction

이제는 communicative teaching approach 중에서 현재 교실현장에 가장 많이 활용되고 있는 task-based instruction에 대해 알아보려고 한다. 우선 task을 활용하여 영어를 가르치려고 할 때, task의 유형을 살펴보고 어떤 것이 효과적인지 또 그것을 어떤 방법으로 적용하는 것이 효과적인지를 숙고할 필요가 있다. task의 유형을 분류하는 것은 교사가 일정 task을 수업에 도입하고자 할 때, 학생에게 제공하는 task의 특성과 학생의 proficiency level이나 needs등을 고려하여 적용해야하기 때문이다. 교사가 task의 여러 유형을 검토하여 학생의 수준과 학습내용에 가장 적합한 유형의 task을 선택하여 제공하는 것이 중요하다. 특히 우리나라와 같이 일상생활에서 영어를 전혀 사용하지 않는 EFL상황에서는 실생활에 가까운 target task을 고려하여 계획하는 것이 더욱 중요하다 하겠다. task의 유형을 분류하는 것은 기준에 따라 여러 가지 방법이 있다. 영어 사용을 촉진시키기 위한 task의 유형을 target과 pedagogical로 나누어 전체적으로 살펴보고 자세히 들어가기로 하자.

(1) Target Tasks

Prabhu (1987)에서는 task을 활동의 내용을 두고 포괄적으로 분류하여 크게 information-gap, reasoning-gap, opinion-gap의 세 가지 유형으로 분류한다. information-gap은 주어진 정보를 한사람에게서 다른 사람 또는 한 장소에서 다른 장소로 또는 하나의 형태에서 또 다른 형태로 전달하는 것을 포함하는 것이다. reasoning-gap은 주어진 정보로부터 연역적 또는 귀납적 관계에 있는 유형의 인지 과정을 통하여 새로운 정보를 이끌어내는 활동으로, information-gap과 다른 점은 전달된 정보가 처음 주어진 정보와 동일하지 않다는 점이다. 즉 학생의 추론(reasoning)이 서로 다른 두 개의 정보를 연결해준다. opinion-gap은 개인적인 선호나 주어진 상황에 대한 태도의 표현 또는 확인의 과정을 포함한다. 이 활동은 언어 수준이 상당히 높은 단계에서 사용할 수 있다. 언어수준이 낮은 단계에서는 주로 information-gap을 많이 하며, information-gap은 reasoning-gap의 예비단계로서 사용할 수 있고 상호작용에 있어서 발전적인 협의보다는 반복적인 협의를 의미한다. 구체적인 유형으로는 도표와 형식, 그리기, 모형시계, 달력, 지도, 학교 시간표, 프로그램 및 여행, 기차 시간표, 나이와 생일, 돈, 거리 규칙, 우편체제, 전보, 이야기와 대화 분류, 개인적 목록 등이 있다.

(2) Pedagogical Tasks

Willis and Willis(1996)는 task 종류를 listing, ordering & categorizing, comparing, problem solving, anecdote telling, creative task 등으로 분류하고 있다. 교육적인 과업의 성격을 띠고 있는 이들 task은 교실 내에서 가능한 유형들을 다양하게 제시하고 있다. 유형별 특성에 따라 pre-task단계 활동에서 task cycle단계, post-task단계 활동으로 단계적으로 이어지도록 제시되었으며, 학습자가 가지고 있는 지식을 최대한 활용하여 활동을 하면서 그 지식을 새로운 지식으로 확장시키도록 하고 있다. Willis는 이러한 task을 시작하기 위한 출발점으로 여러 가지 유형의 과업을 배합하는 것을 권장했으며, 개인적인 지식과 경험을 관련시키는 것이 학습자의 흥미를 이끌 수 있다고 한다. 모든 task은 기본적으로 학습자의 개인적이고 전문적인 지식과 경험을 바탕으로 이루어져야 한다고 보며, 또한 task 은 그림, 사진, 표와 도표를 바탕으로 이루어져야 하며 특히 초보자의 경우는 시각적인 자극이 더욱 필요하다고 하였다. 이제 본격적으로 task-based instruction에 대하여 공부해보자.

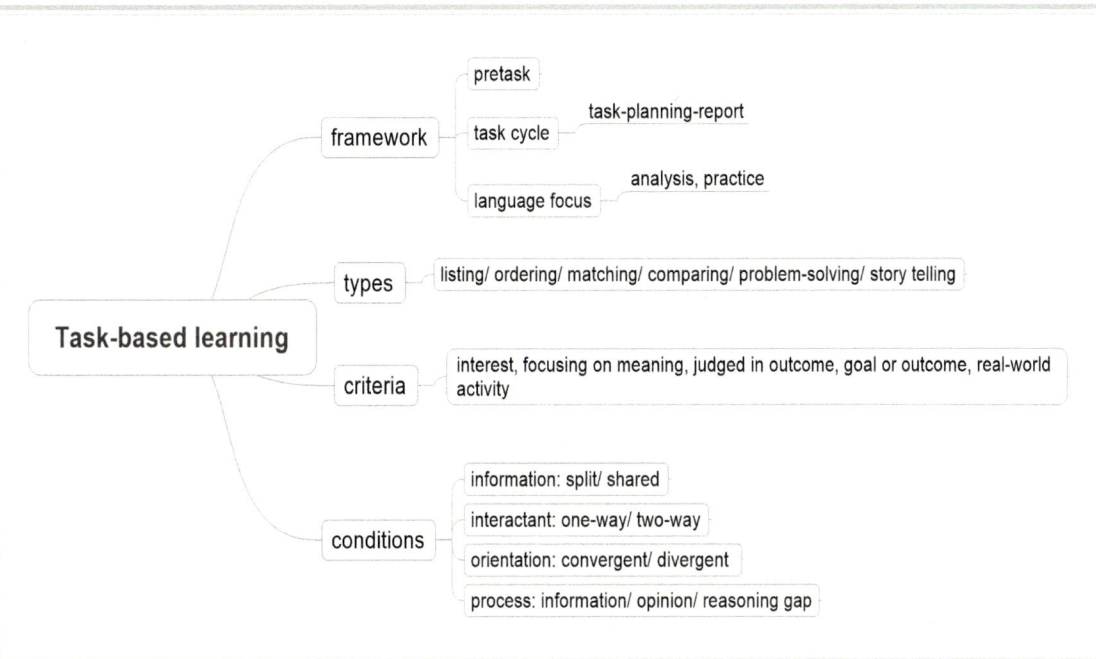

1. Present-Practice-Produce vs Task-based approach

(1) Present-Practice-Produce

1) procedure

① First, the teacher presents an item of language in a clear context to get across its meaning. This could be done in a variety of ways: through a text, a situation build, a dialogue etc.

② Students are then asked to complete a controlled practice stage, where they may have to repeat target items through choral and individual drilling, fill gaps or match halves of sentences. All of this practice demands that the student uses the language correctly and helps them to become more comfortable with it.

③ Finally, they move on to the production stage, sometimes called the 'free practice' stage. Students are given a communication task such as a role play and are expected to produce the target language and use any other language that has already been learnt and is suitable for completing it.

2) problems

- Students can give the impression that they are comfortable with the new language as they are producing it accurately in the class. Often though a few lessons later, students will either not be able to produce the language correctly or even won't produce it at all.
- Students will often produce the language but overuse the target structure so that it sounds completely unnatural.
- Students may not produce the target language during the free practice stage because they find they are able to use existing language resources to complete the task.

(2) Task-based approach

1) procedure

Task-based learning offers an alternative for language teachers. In a task-based lesson the teacher doesn't predetermine what language will be studied, the lesson is based around the completion of a central task and the language studied is determined by what happens as the students complete it. The lesson follows certain stages.

① Pre-task: The teacher introduces the topic and gives the students clear instructions on what they will have to do at the task stage and might help the students to recall some language that may be useful for the task. The pre-task stage can also often include playing a recording of people doing the task. This gives the students a clear model of what will be expected of them. The students can take notes and spend time preparing for the task.

② Task: The students complete a task in pairs or groups using the language resources that they have as the teacher monitors and offers encouragement.

③ Planning: Students prepare a short oral or written report to tell the class what happened during their task. They then practise what they are going to say in their groups. Meanwhile the teacher is available for the students to ask for advice to clear up any language questions they may have.

④ Report: Students then report back to the class orally or read the written report. The teacher chooses the order of when students will present their reports and may give the students some quick feedback on the content. At this stage the teacher may also play a recording of others doing the same task for the students to compare.

⑤ Analysis: The teacher then highlights relevant parts from the text of the recording for the students to analyse. They may ask students to notice interesting features within this text. The teacher can also highlight the language that the students used during the report phase for analysis.

⑥ Practice: Finally, the teacher selects language areas to practise based upon the needs of the students and what emerged from the task and report phases. The students then do practice activities to increase their confidence and make a note of useful language.

2) advantages

① Unlike a PPP approach, the students are free of language control. In all three stages they must use all their language resources rather than just practising one preselected item.

② A natural context is developed from the students' experiences with the language that is personalised and relevant to them. With PPP it is necessary to create contexts in which to present the language and sometimes they can be very unnatural.

③ The students will have a much more varied exposure to language with TBL. They will be exposed to a whole range of lexical phrases, collocations and patterns as well as language forms.

④ The language explored arises from the students' needs. This need dictates what will be covered in the lesson rather than a decision made by the teacher or the coursebook.

⑤ It is a strong communicative approach where students spend a lot of time communicating. PPP lessons seem very teacher-centered by comparison. Just watch how much time the students spend communicating during a task-based lesson. It is enjoyable and motivating.

PPP offers a very simplified approach to language learning. It is based upon the idea that you can present language in neat little blocks, adding from one lesson to the next. However, research shows us that we cannot predict or guarantee what the students will learn and that ultimately a wide exposure to language is the best way of ensuring that students will acquire it effectively. Restricting their experience to single pieces of target language is unnatural.

2. Task Procedure

Pre-Task

Teacher explores the topic with the class, highlights useful words and phrases, and helps learners understand task instructions and prepare. Learners may hear a recording of others doing a similar task, or read part of a text as a lead in to a task.

Task Cycle

Task	Planning	Report
Students do the task, in pairs or small groups. Teacher monitors from a distance, encouraging all attempts at communication, not correcting. Since this situation has a "private" feel, students feel free to experiment. Mistakes don't matter.	Students prepare to report to the whole class (orally or in writing) how they did the task, what they decided or discovered. Since the report stage is public, students will naturally want to be accurate, so the teacher stands by to give language advice.	Some groups present their reports to the class, or exchange written reports, and compare results. Teacher acts as a chairperson, and then comments on the content of the reports.

Language Focus

Analysis	Practice
Students examine and then discuss specific features of the text or transcript of the recording. They can enter new words, phrases and patterns in vocabulary books.	Teacher conducts practice of new words, phrases, and patterns occurring in the data, either during or after the Analysis.

---

(1) Pre-task (Priming phase)

The aim of this stage is to prepare learners for doing the main target task. For this they will need vocabulary to express the meanings they may wish to express when doing the target task. Any of the suggestions above for teacher-led tasks could be used at this stage. Most textbook units start with some vocabulary building activities to introduce the words and phrases that are useful for the new theme or topic. These can often be made into mini-tasks that are more engaging than just listen and repeat. If there are pictures, use them for *Correct the teacher / True or False games* (teacher-led or with learners in pairs or groups) or memory challenge tasks.

> With your partner, look at the picture of the house for one minute and try to remember the names of the furniture in each room. Close your books. You now have two minutes to draw/ write a list of things in each room. How many things have you got in each room? Now say/ read your list to another pair and see who got the most... Finally ask your teacher if she/he can remember what furniture is where.

(2) Task Cycle: Task - Planning - Report

The final instructions were "Now tell another pair your story/ what you have done/ Tell the class who you chose and say your reasons". This is what is often called the Report stage. At this stage, because they are going public and talking to a wider audience, learners naturally want to use their best language – they will feel the need to plan well, use the right words, speak as fluently as they can and avoid mistakes. But most learners will need help to prepare for this.

If you incorporate a Planning stage between the task and the report back stage, learners will have a chance to focus on the language they want to use and improve it. They can check out words in a dictionary, and ask you to help them say what they want to mean. They can even rehearse their report in pairs. So you as teacher will be acting as language advisor, and learners will each be working at their own level, building on, improving and extending the language they already have. Thus we achieve a learner-centered focus on language in the context of the task. During the final Report phase, there is a simultaneous focus on fluency and accuracy, and the Planning stage helps them to prepare for this.

(3) Language Focus (Focus on Form)

Now is the time to turn to the grammar sections in your textbook. Learners will now have experienced quite a lot of this language in use, and the grammar exercises can often be done quickly as consolidation exercises. To save time, start each exercise off in class and let them finish them at home working at their own pace. Some books have grammar reference and/or review pages – use these as a basis for a grammar quiz prepared by learners at home.

3. Task Criteria

(1) Activity

The activities are primarily form-focused activities, designed to practise language items. In contrast, learners doing tasks, focusing on meanings, will be making free use of whatever English they can recall to express the things that they really want to say or write in the process of achieving the task goal. Activities have differences from the tasks as below;

- speaking to practise a new structure 예 doing a drill or enacting a dialogue or asking and answering questions using the new patterns
- writing to display their control of certain language items

(2) Task

Willis and Willis (2007:12-14) offer the following criteria in the form of questions. The more confidently you can answer yes to each of these questions, the more task-like the activity.

> a) Will the activity engage learners' interest?
> b) Is there a primary focus on meaning?
> c) Is there a goal or an outcome?
> d) Is success judged in terms of outcome?
> e) Is completion a priority?
> f) Does the activity relate to real world activities?'

Let us consider the task 'Planning a class night out' in the light of these criteria. I think the lesson would certainly engage my learners' interest, especially if they knew they would actually be going on the chosen night out, so a) is Yes. Learners have strong preferences about nights out and would definitely be meaning what they say, so Yes to b). The first outcome for each pair is their finished plan for the night out, (which must be complete before they tell the class about it so the class can vote on the best plan) and a second outcome might be the real-world night out, so a confident Yes to c), d), e) and f). Next is an example of an activity designed for an adult class. Which of the questions a) to f) might you answer with a fairly confident Yes? How task-like do you think it would be, and why?

> - Think of the busiest day you have had recently. Work in pairs.
> - Tell your partner all the things you did.
> - Decide which of you had the busiest day, then tell the class about it.
> - Decide who in the whole class had the most hectic day (and say why.)
> - Finally, from memory, write a list of the things one person did on their busiest day, and, without revealing their name, read it out to the class (or display it on the wall) to see how many people can remember whose day it was.

Generally adults enjoy talking about (even bragging about) how busy they are/have been, so this would score a Yes for a), b) and f). The first goal is to compare their busiest days. The natural completion point for each learner is the end of their day – and the final outcome – the selection of the busiest person is also clear, so we can answer Yes quite confidently to the other questions. The final writing activity sets up an engaging memory challenge game with a clear outcome – to identify the person written about. Both the above activities, then, would count as tasks, and both generate several kinds of genuine meaning-focused interaction amongst learners and teacher.

How can you upgrade a less task-like activity? This activity comes at the end of a unit focusing on the language of past time:

> - Work in pairs. Talk about your grandparents.
> - Tell each other what you know about their past lives.
> - Use the phrases and patterns: *have been ....., used to ...., a long time ago ......*

You might answer Yes to a) and f) with some degree of confidence. We do, in real life, occasionally talk about our grandparents and our memories of them. If the topic 'Grandparents' does not engage all learners, let them choose instead an elderly person they knew well. For b), the answer would probably be No, because the final instruction (Use the phrases and patterns from the box above) shows that this activity is intended largely to practise these particular ways of expressing past time presented earlier in the unit. Co-operative learners will be trying to make sentences about their grandparents not simply to give information but primarily to show mastery of the new forms. This is unlike natural language use. To make it more task-like, we could delete the final instruction, and do this activity early on in the unit, so learners are focusing more on meanings i.e. sharing their memories of their grandparents in a natural way rather than trying to incorporate particular language forms. Then the answer to b) would be Yes. For c), d) and e) the answers are also likely to be No; there is no goal or purpose given for talking about grandparents and learners have no way of knowing when they have said enough to complete the activity, or whether indeed they have succeeded or not. Some learners might end up saying very little.

> Adding a goal or outcome to make a task: For the 'Grandparents' activity we need to add a goal to give the activity a purpose and make the outcome more specific so that learners know when they have completed the task. Some sample outcomes follow here and you could add one of these sets of instructions, depending on which outcome you think would best engage the learners in your class.

- Try to find out three things that your grandparents' and your partner's grandparents' lives had in common. What was the biggest difference between them?

- Decide which one of your partner's grandparents was / is the most interesting person and give two reasons why you think so. Then tell the class about him/her and vote to decide on the three most interesting grandparents in the class.
- Describe two early memories you have of one particular grandparent. Tell your group. Take notes when listening to each other.
- Compare your memories – whose were the most interesting, most vivid, most amusing, saddest or strangest?
- Compare your groups' memories and try to find ways to classify them (예 to do with food or meal-times? games? outings? being ill? negative/ positive things?) Then report your categories to the class, with examples. Did you all have similar ways of classifying?
- So there are several potential outcomes (and you might well think of others) that could be created out of this activity to make it more task-like. In fact each of these would make a different task. If learners are clear what the outcome should be, and know the number of things to list or describe, they are more likely to engage with the task, speak with more confidence and know when they have completed it. Successful task achievement will greatly increase their satisfaction and motivation. When, after completing the task cycle, they look more closely at language forms used by others doing similar tasks, they will already be familiar with the contexts and have experienced the need for some of those forms.

4. Six types of Task

Listing and Brainstorming	You can list people, places, things, actions, reasons, everyday problems, things to do in various circumstances etc. 例 In pairs, agree on a list of four or five people who were famous in the 20th century and give at least one reason for including each person; Can you remember your partner's busiest day?
Ordering and Sorting	例 Look at your list of famous people. Which people are most likely to remain popular and become 20th century icons? Rank them from most popular to least popular, and justify your order to another pair.
Matching	例 Read the texts — each is about a famous person but the person is not named — and look at the photos. Match each text to a photo. Then talk to your partner, and say how you were able to match them. Prepare to tell the class how you did it.
Comparing	例 Compare your list of possible 20th century icons with your partner's list. Did you have any people in common? Tell each other why you chose them. How many reasons did you both think of? Finally, combine your two lists, but keep it to five people.
Problem-solving	Problem-solving tasks are over too quickly – learners agree on the first solution that comes to mind, using minimal language, 例 'Noisy neighbours? OK – so call police'. The instructions for the town centre traffic problem in the example below incorporate six or seven ways of generating richer interaction. 例 Think of a town centre where there is too much traffic. In twos, think of three alternative solutions to this problem. List the advantages and disadvantages of each alternative. Then decide which alternative would be the cheapest one, the most innovative one, the most environmentally friendly one. Report your decisions to another group and discuss which solution would be the best one to put forward to the local government.
Sharing personal experiences & story telling	Activities where learners are asked to recount their personal experiences and tell stories are valuable because they give learners a chance to speak for longer and in a more sustained way in real-life. In order to encourage richer interaction, we usually need to add a clear goal, make instructions more precise, and give clear completion points.

5. Methodology

(1) A general task framework

Design feature	Key dimensions
Input (the nature of the input provided in the task)	1. Medium a. pictorial b. oral c. written 2. Organization a. tight structure b. loose structure
Conditions (the way in which the information is presented to the learners and the way in which it is to be used)	1. Information configuration a. split b. shared 2. Interactant relationship a. one-way b. two-way 3. Interaction requirement a. required b. optional 4. Orientation a. convergent b. divergent
Processes (the nature of the cognitive operations and the discourse the task requires)	1. Cognitive a. exchanging information b. exchanging opinions c. explaining / reasoning 2. Discourse mode a. monologic b. dialogic
Outcomes (the nature of the product that results from the task)	1. Medium a. pictorial b. oral c. written 2. Discourse domain / genre 예 description, argument, political speeches 3. Scope a. closed b. open

(2) A psycholinguistic typology of tasks

Task Type	Interactant relationship	Interaction relationship	Outcome options	Goal orientation
Jigsaw	two-way	required	closed	convergent
Information gap		required	closed	convergent
Problem solving	one-way or two-way		closed	convergent
Decision making	one-way or two-way	optional	open	
Opinion exchange		optional	open	divergent

(3) Task design features affecting learner production

Design Variable	Fluency	Accuracy	Complexity
A. Input variables			
1. Contextual support	Tasks with contextual support	Tasks with no contextual support	
2. Number of elements	Tasks with few elements	–	Tasks with many elements
3. Topic	Tasks that are familiar		Tasks that generate conflict
B. Task conditions			
1. Shared vs. split information		Split information	Shared information
2. Tasks demands	Tasks that pose a single demand		Tasks that pose multiple demands
C. Task outcomes			
1. Closed vs. open tasks	Closed tasks	Open tasks	Open tasks with divergent goals
2. Inherent structure of the outcome	A clear inherent structure	A clear inherent structure together with opportunity for planning	
3. Discourse mode	Narrative 〉 descriptive task Argument 〉 discussion		

(4) Criteria for grading tasks

Criterion	Easy	Difficult
A. Input		
1. Medium	pictorial → written	oral
2. Code complexity	high frequency vocabulary: short and simple sentences	low frequency vocabulary: complex sentence structure
3. Cognitive complexity 　a. information type 　b. amount of information 　c. degree of structure 　d. context dependency	static → dynamic few elements relationships well-defined structure here-and-now orientation	abstract many elements relationships little structure there-and-then orientation
4. Familiarity of information	familiar	unfamiliar
B. Conditions		
1. Interactant relationship (negotiation of meaning)	two-way	one-way
2. Task demands	single task	dual-task
3. Discourse mode required to perform the task	dialogic	monologic
C. Processes		
1. Cognitive operations: 　a. type 　b. reasoning need	exchanging information & reasoning few steps involved	exchanging opinions many steps involved
D. Outcomes		
1. Medium	pictorial	written → oral
2. Scope	closed (예 information gap)	open (예 opinion gap)
3. Discourse mode of task outcome	lists, descriptions, narratives, classifications	instructions, arguments

03 Content-Based Instruction

1. Introduction

Content-Based Instruction (CBI) is a significant approach in language education (Brinton, Snow, & Wesche, 1989). CBI is designed to provide second-language learners instruction in content and language. Historically, the word content has changed its meaning in language teaching. Content used to refer to the methods of Grammar-translation, Audiolingual methodology and vocabulary or sound patterns in dialog form. Recently, content is interpreted as the use of subject matter as a vehicle for second or foreign language teaching/ learning.

(1) Advantages

- Learning language becomes automatic: Learners are exposed to a considerable amount of language through stimulating content. Learners explore interesting content and are engaged in appropriate language-dependant activities.
- CBI supports contextualized learning: Learners are taught useful language that is embedded within relevant discourse contexts rather than as isolated language fragments. Hence students make greater connections with the language and what they already know. Complex information is delivered through real life context for the students to grasp well and leads to intrinsic motivation.
- Greater flexibility and adaptability in the curriculum can be deployed as per the students interest: In CBI information is reiterated by strategically delivering information at right time and situation compelling the students to learn out of passion.

(2) Student Involvement

Because it falls under the more general rubric of communicative language teaching (CLT), the CBI classroom is learner rather than teacher centered (Littlewood, 1981). In such classrooms, students learn through doing and are actively engaged in the learning process. They do not depend on the teacher to direct all learning or to be the source of all information. Central to CBI is the belief that learning occurs not only through exposure to the teacher's input, but also through peer input and interactions. Accordingly, students assume active, social roles in the classroom that involve interactive learning, negotiation, information gathering and the co-construction of meaning (Lee and VanPatten, 1995). William Glasser's "control theory" exemplifies his attempts to empower students and give them voice by focusing on their basic, human needs: Unless students are given power, they may exert what little power they have to thwart learning and achievement through inappropriate behavior and mediocrity. Thus, it is important for teachers to give students voice, especially in the current educational climate, which is dominated by standardization and testing (Simmons and Page, 2010).

(3) Motivation

Keeping students motivated and interested are two important factors underlying content-based instruction. Motivation and interest are crucial in supporting student success with challenging, informative activities that support success and which help the student learn complex skills (Grabe & Stoller, 1997). When students are motivated and interested in the material they are learning, they make greater connections between topics, elaborations with learning material and can recall information better. In short, when a student is intrinsically motivated the student achieves more. This in turn leads to a perception of success, of gaining positive attributes which will continue a circular learning pattern of success and interest. Krapp, Hidi and Renninger (1992) state that, "situational interest, triggered by environmental factors, may evoke or contribute to the development of long-lasting individual interests." Because CBI is student centered, one of its goals is to keep students interested and motivation high by generating stimulating content instruction and materials.

2. Types of Content-based Instruction

(1) A Continuum of Content and Language Integration

Content-Driven	Language-Driven
• Content is taught in L2. • Content learning is priority. • Language learning is secondary. • Teachers must select language objectives. • Students evaluated on content mastery.	• Content is used to learn L2. • Language learning is priority. • Content learning is incidental. • Students evaluated on content to be integrated. • Students evaluated on skills/ proficiency.

Total Immersion	Partial Immersion	Sheltered Courses	Adjunct Model	Theme-Based Courses	Language classes with content for language practice

(2) Sheltered Instruction

Sheltered instruction is an approach to teaching English language learners which integrates language and content instruction. The dual goals of sheltered instruction are: (a) to provide access to mainstream, grade-level content, and (b) to promote the development of English language proficiency.

- Increase wait time, be patient: Give your students time to think and process the information before you provide answers. A student may know the answers but need more processing time in order to say it in English.
- Respond to the student's message, don't correct errors (Expansion). If a student has the correct answer and it is understandable, don't correct his or her grammar. The exact word and correct grammatical response will develop with time. Instead, repeat his or her answer, putting it into standard English, and use positive reinforcement techniques.
- Simplify teacher language: Speak directly to the student, emphasizing important nouns and verbs, using as few extra words as possible. Repetition and speaking louder don't help; rephrasing, and body language do.
- Don't force oral production: Instead, give the student an opportunity to demonstrate his or her comprehension and knowledge through body actions, drawing pictures, manipulating objects, or pointing. Then speech will emerge.
- Demonstrate and use visuals and manipulatives: Whenever possible, accompany your message with gestures, pictures, and objects that help get the meaning across. Use a variety of different pictures or objects for the same idea. Give an immediate context for new words. Understanding input is the key to language acquisition.
- Adapt the materials to student's language level, maintain content integrity: Make the concepts more accessible and comprehensible by adding pictures, charts, maps, time-lines, and diagrams, in addition to simplifying the language.
- Increase your knowledge: Learn as much as you can about the language and culture of your students. Go to movies, read books, look at pictures of the countries. Keep the similarities and differences in mind and then check your knowledge by asking your students whether they agree with your impressions. Learn as much of the student's language as you can; even a few words help.
- Build on the student's prior knowledge: Find out as much as you can about how and ideas and concepts you are teaching and the student's previous knowledge or previous way of being taught. Encourage the students to point out differences and connect similarities.

(3) Adjunct Model

Adjunct classes are usually taught by ESL teachers. The aim of these classes is to prepare students for "mainstream" classes where they will join English L1 learners. Adjunct classes may resemble EAP or ESP classes where emphasis is placed on acquiring specific target vocabulary. They may also feature study skills sessions to familiarize the students with listening, note taking and skimming and scanning texts. Some adjunct classes are taught during the summer months before regular college classes begin, while others run concurrently with regular lessons.

(4) Theme Based Model

Theme based CBI is usually found in EFL contexts. Theme based CBI can be taught by an EFL teacher or team taught with a content specialist. The teacher(s) can create a course of study designed to unlock and build on their own students' interests and the content can be chosen from an enormous number of diverse topics.

04 Whole Language Approach

(1) Introduction

A teaching methodology or instructional philosophy focusing on language learning as a natural, holistic process. It prioritizes meaningful use of language in authentic contexts, integrating reading, writing, speaking, and listening rather than teaching these as separate skills.

(2) Key Concepts

Ken Goodman is one of the educators most often associated with the term "whole language" and one of the earliest principle advocates of the whole language approach as we know it today. Goodman (1986) described whole language as a "top-to-bottom" rather than a "bottom-up" view of language learning, a view that does not break language into bits and pieces. Language is taught in real and natural contexts, and thus, language learning is easier and more interesting and relevant to the learner. Rather than depend on basal readers, textbooks, and workbooks that often stress decontextualized language exercises, whole language teachers build on learners' existing knowledge and work with learners on authentic reading and writing activities, such as reading trade books, writing letters, or developing and working on extended writing projects. Learners, therefore, develop control over the mechanics of language through real reading and real writing. Whole language, however, cannot be reduced to a set of activities or strategies, but instead involves basic assumptions about how students learn. Whole language practitioners believe that language is a social process that is learned as we interact within a given context; that students bring knowledge to the classroom that should be valued, respected, and built upon; that language learning involves risk, and students should be encouraged to try and try again if they fail; and that form follows function in language development and not vice versa.

(3) Teacher Roles

One of the first steps a whole language teacher should take is to share with learners his or her views on how language is learned. The notion that literacy is functional and contextual should be emphasized, as many adults come to the classroom with the notion that literacy is an academic hurdle to overcome rather than a tool for larger goals or everyday needs. Learners should be encouraged to take risks and develop their literacy in ways that are relevant to their personal situations. This elaboration of assumptions about whole language opens the way for the teacher to introduce activities such as journal and letter writing, the language experience approach (see Taylor, 1992), and story writing and publishing, rather than focusing on drills and grammar exercises. Some educators have learners write personal stories reflecting their experiences – sorrows, joys, problems, and memories – and publish them to use as a basis for additional reading, writing, and discussion activities (see Peyton, 1991, for examples).

(4) Material & Assessment

Authentic reading that is meaningful and of interest to learners is also part of the whole language approach. As Smith (1983) points out, "The only way to make learning to read easy is to make reading easy". By this he means that students learn to read only by reading and focusing on meaning and not primarily focusing on words, pronunciation, speed, or accuracy.

Because standardized tests are not a major part of the whole language classroom, teachers in whole language literacy programs use alternative measures of evaluation that are integrated into the daily classroom activities and thus reflect the use of language in real contexts. Such measures include, for example, the holistic examination of learner stories, learner self-observation forms, and journals.

(5) Teach Reading and Writing

① Part-Centered Methods; Code-emphasis; Bottom-up

Phonics	• Match individual letters of the alphabet with their specific English pronunciations • Children can sound out or decode new words. • Children are explicitly taught sound-symbol patterns, and the conscious learning of rules. • First learn individual sounds, and later put them together into combinations, and then into words. • Sound-letter relationships with the knowledge of phonemic awareness

Linguistic Approaches	• With a scientific knowledge of language • It contains regular spelling patterns so that they can infer the letter−sound relationships in words take−bake−lake−cake / went−cent−tent−bent.
Sight word/ Look−say method	• Recognizing whole words, using flash cards or other techniques to help children quickly identify such common words as 'of', 'and', and 'the' • Knowing the most frequent words will help students learn to read more efficiently. • Once children can recognize words, comprehension takes care of itself.
Basal reader	• Children should be taught to read through careful control and sequencing of the language and the sounds that they are exposed to. • Graded, sequenced, controlled

② Socio−Psycholinguistic Approaches; Meaning−emphasis; Top−down

Language Experience Approach	• If children are given material to read that they are already familiar with, it will help them learn to read. • If the actual language and content of the stories are familiar to readers, they should be able to learn to read it even more easily. • Having students generate their own stories. • Transcripts of the stories become reading material. • Allowing children to see a direct link between oral and written language.
Literature − based Approach	• Using students' literature with the intention of focusing on meaning, interests, and enjoyment • Holding an individual conference about their reading • Individual skills should not be taught. • Students' interests and individual needs are respected to facilitate their success and skill development.
Whole Language Approach	• Language serves personal, social, and academic aspects of children's lives. • Children become literate as they grapple with the meaning and uses of print in their environments. • Storybook reading, writing their own texts • LEA and Literature−based approach belong within Whole Language Approach. • It incorporates all of the language skills, not only one discrete skill. • Uses of authentic texts from various genres is vital.

05 Participatory Approach

1. Introduction

　The participatory approach was popularized by the work of Paulo Freire, an educator who developed the approach while working with peasant groups in Brazil (Spener, 1990). Freire stressed in his writings that the prior experiences, knowledge, strengths, and community concerns of the learners must be the starting point for literacy instruction. Freire also stressed the use of literacy development for personal transformation and social action. A participatory approach not only develops words and themes meaningful to learners, but also extends those themes and activities into action that will better the learners' lives.

2. Key Concepts

① The term "participatory" is often used interchangeably with "learner-centered." Indeed, the participatory approach is also a learner-centered approach in that the content and learning objectives are determined through ongoing dialogue between teacher and learners.

② The participatory approach, however, goes beyond a learner-centered approach because it advocates literacy as a vehicle for personal transformation and social change. Learners discuss issues in class that are significant to them and determine ways of dealing with these issues in real life. Learners are seen as agents for change, for bettering their lives and the lives of those close to them. The participatory approach extends the themes discussed in class to action outside the classroom.

③ Educators have elaborated extensively on the participatory approach to literacy. Auerbach (1992), for example, writes about the importance of social context as a resource that informs literacy development. She notes that if educators define literacy broadly, to include a range of activities and practices that are integrated into the fabric of daily life, the social context becomes a rich resource that can inform rather than impede learning.

④ Fingeret (1989) defines participatory literacy education as a philosophy and a set of practices "based on the belief that learners – their characteristics, aspirations, backgrounds, and needs – should be at the center of literacy instruction....[Learners] help to define, create, and maintain the program". For example, a teacher may learn from a Hispanic family that their children have been raised to value cooperative, rather than individual, work. Thus, rather than viewing the child's hesitancy to engage in competitive behavior in the class in a negative light, the teacher appreciates this cultural difference and provides more opportunities for this child to engage in group work within the class.

⑤ An example of the application of a participatory approach to curriculum development in a family literacy program can be seen in Auerbach (1992), who describes a program in Boston. The process, which she stresses is cyclical and not linear, includes listening activities to find student themes; exploration of themes through a variety of activities such as photo stories, oral histories, and language experience stories; extending literacy to action inside and outside of the classroom; and an evaluation process that includes learners reflecting on their own progress.

06 Lexical Approach

(1) Principles

The principles of the Lexical Approach have been around since Michael Lewis published 'The Lexical Approach' 10 years ago. It seems, however, that many teachers and researchers do not have a clear idea of what the Lexical Approach actually looks like in practice. According to Lewis (1997, 2000) native speakers carry a pool of hundreds of thousands, and possibly millions, of lexical chunks in their heads ready to draw upon in order to produce fluent, accurate and meaningful language. Too many items for teachers and materials to present to learners, ask learners to practise and then produce even if you believed that a PPP methodology — which has been denigrated in recent years — would lead to the acquisition of these language items. One of the criticisms levelled at the Lexical Approach is its lack of a detailed learning theory. It is worth noting, however, that Lewis (1993) argues the Lexical Approach is not a break with the Communicative Approach, but a development of it.

① Principle 1 — Grammaticalised lexis

In recent years it has been recognised both that native speakers have a vast stock of these lexical chunks and that these lexical chunks are vital for fluent production. Fluency does not depend so much on having a set of generative grammar rules and a separate stock of words — the 'slot and filler' or open choice principle — as on having rapid access to a stock of chunks. The basic principle of the lexical approach, then, is: "Language is grammaticalised lexis, not lexicalised grammar" (Lewis 1993). In other words, lexis is central in creating meaning, grammar plays a subservient managerial role. If you accept this principle then the logical implication is that we should spend more time helping learners develop their stock of phrases, and less time on grammatical structures.

② Principle 2 – Collocation in action

In an application form a candidate referred to a 'large theme' in his thesis. This sounded ugly, but there is nothing intrinsically ugly about either word, it's just a strange combination to a native-speaker ear. In the Lexical Approach, sensitising students to acceptable collocations is very important, so you might find this kind of task: Underline the word which does not collocate with 'theme':

main theme / large theme / important theme / central theme / major theme

(2) Language Acquisition

He makes a helpful summary of the findings from first language acquisition research which he thinks are relevant to second language acquisition:

- Language is not learnt by learning individual sounds and structures and then combining them, but by an increasing ability to break down wholes into parts.
- Grammar is acquired by a process of observation, hypothesis and experiment.
- We can use whole phrases without understanding their constituent parts.
- Acquisition is accelerated by contact with a sympathetic interlocutor with a higher level of competence in the target language.

Schmitt (2000) makes a significant contribution to a learning theory for the Lexical Approach by adding that 'the mind stores and processes these [lexical] chunks as individual wholes.' The mind is able to store large amounts of information in long-term memory but its short-term capacity is much more limited, when producing language in speech for example, so it is much more efficient for the brain to recall a chunk of language as if it were one piece of information.

In our view it is not possible, or even desirable, to attempt to 'teach' an unlimited number of lexical chunks. But, it is beneficial for language learners to gain exposure to lexical chunks and to gain experience in analyzing those chunks in order to begin the process of internalisation. We believe, like Lewis, that encouraging learners to notice language, specifically lexical chunks and collocations, is central to any methodology connected to a lexical view of language.

(3) Key Concepts

① 'Lexical chunk' is an umbrella term which includes all the other terms. We define a lexical chunk as any pair or group of words which are commonly found together, or in close proximity.

② 'Collocation' is also included in the term 'lexical chunk', but we refer to it separately from time to time, so we define it as a pair of lexical content words commonly found together. Following this definition, 'basic'+'principles' is a collocation, but 'look'+'at' is not because it combines a lexical content word and a grammar function word. Identifying chunks and collocations is often a question of intuition, unless you have access to a corpus.

Lexical Chunks (that are not collocations)	Lexical Chunks (that are collocations)
• by the way	• totally convinced
• up to now	• strong accent
• upside down	• terrible accident
• If I were you	• sense of humour
• a long way off	• sounds exciting
• out of my mind	• brings good luck

07 Multiple Intelligences

1. Theoretical Background

The theory of multiple intelligences is a model of intelligence that differentiates it into specific (primarily sensory) "modalities", rather than seeing intelligence as dominated by a single general ability. This model was proposed by Howard Gardner in his 1983 book Frames of Mind: The Theory of Multiple Intelligences. Gardner articulated seven criteria for a behavior to be considered an intelligence. These were that the intelligences showed: potential for brain isolation by brain damage, place in evolutionary history, presence of core operations, susceptibility to encoding (symbolic expression), a distinct developmental progression, the existence of savants, prodigies and other exceptional people, and support from experimental psychology and psychometric findings.

Gardner chose eight abilities that he held to meet these criteria: musical-rhythmic, visual-spatial, verbal-linguistic, logical-mathematical, bodily-kinesthetic, interpersonal, intrapersonal, and naturalistic. He later suggested that existential and moral intelligence may also be worthy of inclusion. Although the distinction between intelligences has been set out in great detail, Gardner opposes the idea of labelling learners to a specific intelligence. Each individual possesses a unique blend of all the intelligences. Gardner firmly maintains that his theory of multiple intelligences should "empower learners", not restrict them to one modality of learning.

2. Learning Types

Types	Advantages	Methods	Activities
linguistic (word player)	Reading and writing stories	Saying, hearing and seeing words	Memory games Trivia quizzes/ Stories
logical / mathematical (questioner)	Solving puzzles Exploring patterns Reasoning and Logic	Asking questions, categorising and working with patterns	Puzzles Problem solving.
visual / spatial (visualiser)	Drawing and building arts and crafts	Visualising, using the mind's eye	Flashcards Colours / Pictures / Drawing Project work.
musical (music lover)	Singing and listening to music Playing instruments	Using rhythm with music on	Using songs Chants Drilling.
kinesthetic (mover)	Moving around Touching things Body language	Moving Touching and doing	TPR activities Action songs Running dictations Miming/ Realia
interpersonal (socialiser)	Mixing with others Leading groups, understanding others and mediating	Co-operating Working in groups and sharing	Mingle activities Group work Debates Discussions.
intrapersonal (loner)	Working alone Pursuing own interests	Working alone	Working individually on personalised projects
naturalistic (natural lover)	Nature	Working outside Observing nature	Environmental projects.

3. Lesson Procedure

① Stage 1 : Awaken the Intelligence. The teacher brings many different objects to class. Students experience feeling things that are soft, rough, cold, smooth, and so on. Experiences like this help activate and make learners aware of the sensory bases of experience.

② Stage 2 : Amplify the Intelligence. Students are asked to bring objects to class or to use something in their possession. Teams of students describe each object attending to the five physical senses.

③ Stage 3 : Teach for the Intelligence. At this stage, the teacher structures larger sections of lesson so as to reenforce and emphasize sensory experiences and the language that accompanies these experiences.

④ Stage 4 : Transfer of the Intelligence. This stage is concerned with application of the intelligence to daily living. Students are asked to reflect on both the content of the lesson and its operational procedures.

4

Teaching Language Skills

01. Integrated Skills
02. Teaching Listening
03. Teaching Speaking and Pronunciation
04. Teaching Reading
05. Teaching Writing
06. Form-focused Instruction
07. Teaching Vocabulary

CHAPTER 01 Integrated Skills

> **단원 길라잡이**
> - 듣기, 말하기, 읽기, 쓰기, 문법, 단어학습에 관련한 영어교수법의 특징과 개념을 이해할 수 있게 될 것이다.
> - 교수 원리를 바탕으로 각 영역을 위한 수업 계획을 만들 수 있을 것이다.
> - 각 영역에서의 어려운 점과 특성, 효과적인 교수 방안들을 파악할 수 있을 것이다.

Introduction

지금까지 2언어 습득 원리, 영어 교수법과 교재론 등 영어교육론의 기초가 되는 이론적인 내용을 다루어 보았다. 이제 부터는 학습자들의 실제적인 4기능의 습득을 위한 언어적인 측면에 대하여 살펴 보도록 하겠다. 우리가 영어선생님으로서 가장 중요한 부분은 이러한 언어영역을 '어떻게 가르칠 것인가'에 있다. 4기능 학습방법에 들어가기 전에 잠시 이전에 했던 이론을 간단히 살펴보고 가자.

2언어 습득을 위해서 만들어진 이론은 크게 3가지로 볼 수 있는데 Behaviorism, Cognitivism과 Constructivism이 그에 속한다. 각각의 중심 개념은 pattern practice, consciousness raising과 social context로 설명될 수 있으며 이 중심개념들을 이용하여 학습할 때 2언어습득이 가장 효과적으로 이루어질 수 있다고 설명하고 있다. 영어교수법 초기에는 Grammar translation method가 있었다. 이 교수법은 어떤 이론적인 근거를 가지고 시작했다기 보다는 어려운 라틴어를 배우기 위해 문법과 어휘를 번역하고 암기하는 방식의 교수법으로 존재했다. 우리나라에서도 중고등학교에서 오랫동안 이 방법으로 영어를 가르쳐왔다. 그 후에 말하고 듣기를 위한 교수법으로서 Direct method와 Audiolingual method가 만들어졌다. 특히 Audiolingual method는 Behavioral psychology와 Structural linguistics에 기초한 교수법으로 우리나라 중고등학교에서 많은 사랑을 받아왔다.

이제 4기능 listening, speaking, reading, writing과 함께 grammar & vocabulary을 가르치기 위해서 가장 먼저 integrated skill의 의미를 알고 시작해야겠다. 언어는 production과 reception을 따로 생각할 수 없으므로 integrated skill은 authenticity로 대표될 수 있다. 또 하나 중요한 개념은 communication이 이루어지는 interaction속에서 언어가 reinforcement될 수 있다는 데 있다. 우리가 들은 것을 modelling로 하여 말할 수도 있으며 읽은 것을 토대로 하여 쓰는 방법을 터득하게 되는 것이다. 예 reading수업에서 listening, speaking과 writing skills이 서로 연관되어 통합되는 과정을 보여준다.

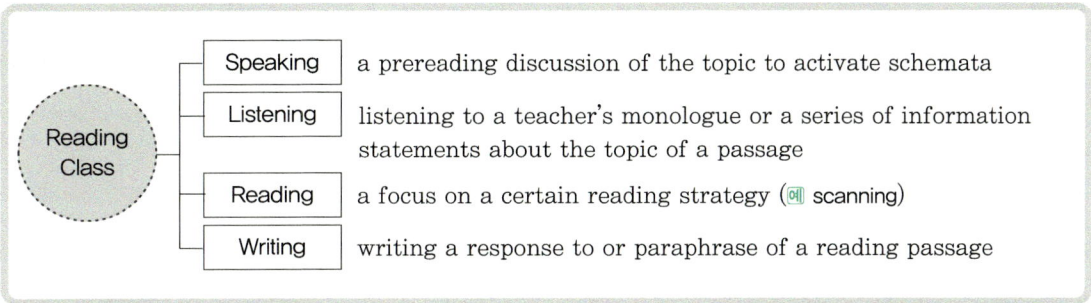

01 Integrated Lesson

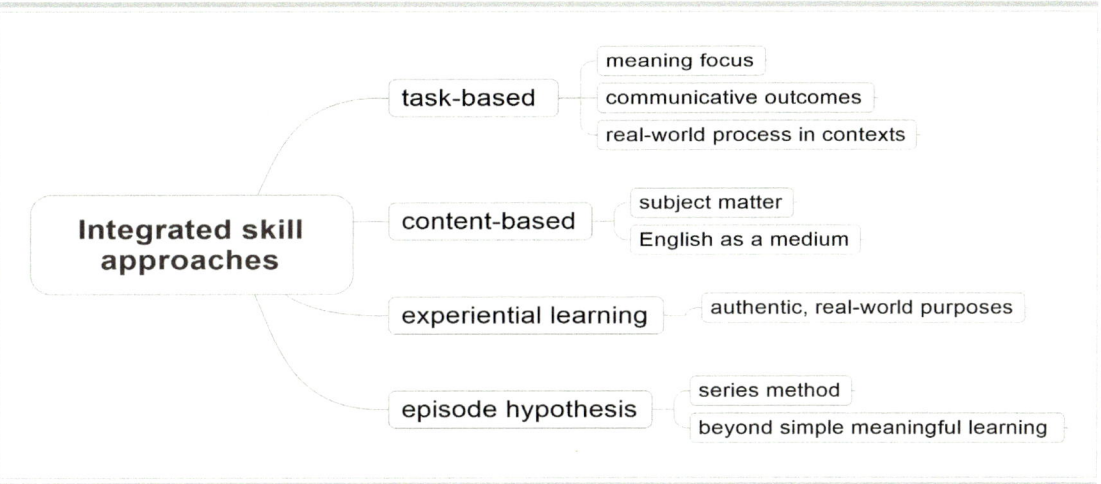

1. Task-based Teaching

A school in Korea has long used a communication-oriented syllabus but many teachers, despite their high proficiency in English, teach more grammar and test-taking skills due to the pressure of raising students' test scores. The school is now looking into ways to help students learn English through well-sequenced activities focusing primarily on meaning and clearly defined communicative outcomes. They believe this change will enhance students' ability to engage in real-world processes of language use in communicative contexts.

speeches	directions	telephone directories
conversations	invitations	menus
narratives	textbooks	labels
public announcements	interviews	games and puzzles
cartoon strips	oral descriptions	diaries
letters (e-mails)	media extracts	songs
poems	photos	

2. Content-Based Instruction

A primary school in a special economic zone, where English is used as a main medium of communication, wants to ensure that their students attain grade-appropriate language and academic achievements in their second language, English. They maintain that though these students are placed in the program where all courses are taught in English, they can be on par with their native English speaking peers and, eventually, become functional bilinguals.

> In an international studies program, Korean students are enrolled concurrently in linked courses: a content course alongside native English speaking students and a separate English course without native English speaking students. In order to meet Korean students' academic and language needs, the English courses and content courses provide the same content base and share mutually coordinated objectives and assignments.

3. Theme-based Teaching

[Sample Lesson] : Environmental awareness and action

1. Use environmental statistics and facts for classroom reading, writing, discussion, and debate.

(1) Intermediate to Advanced students

    (R) scan [reading selections] for particular information

    (W) do compare-and-contrast exercises

    (R) look for biases in statistics

    (L, S) use statistics in argument

    (W) use the discourse features of persuasive writing

    (W) write personal opinion essays

    (L, S) discuss issues

    (L, S) engage in formal debates

(2) Beginning students
- (S, W) use imperatives (*Don't buy aerosol spray cans.*)
- (S) practice verb tenses (*The ozone layer is vanishing.*)
- (L, S, R, W) develop new vocabulary
- (S, W) use cardinal and ordinal numbers
- (L, S) practice simple conversations/ dialogues like:

2. **Carry out research and writing projects.**
syllabus에 연구프로젝트가 들어가게 될 때 환경에 관한 주제를 연구하는 활동은 내재적으로 동기부여가 될 수 있는 과제물이 된다.

3. **Have students create their own environmental awareness material.**
학습자들은 나이나 수준에 관련 없이 *지구를 구하자* 라는 주제에서 할 수 있는 실제적인 것들을 정리할 수 있는 포스터, 벽보, 신문 기사, 팸플릿 등을 만들어 낼 수 있는 Language Experience Approach (LEA)으로부터 많은 양의 언어나 내용자료를 얻을 수 있다.

4. **Arrange Field Trips.**
- pre-trip module of reading, researching and other fact finding
- post-trip module of summary and conclusion들이 포함

5. **Conduct simulation games.**
환경의 위기를 주제로 이용하는 많은 시뮬레이션 게임들이 만들어져서 수업에 이용된다.

4. Experiential Learning

① Principles
- to engage both left-brain and right-brain processing
- to integrate skills
- to point toward authentic, real-world purposes

② Features
- to give students concrete experiences through which they discover language principles by trial and error, by processing feedback, by building hypotheses about language, and by revising these assumptions in order to become fluent.
- to give students opportunities to use language as they grapple with the problem-solving complexities of a variety of concrete experiences.

③ Activities

Learner-centered	Teacher-centered
• hands-on projects 예 nature projects • computer activities in small groups • research projects • cross-cultural experiences 예 camps, dinner groups, etc • field trips and other on-site visits 예 to a grocery store • role plays and simulations	• using props, realia, visuals, show-and-tell sessions • playing games (strategy) and singing • utilizing media 예 television, radio, and movies

5. Episode Hypothesis

① Theoretical Backgrounds

Series method (Gouin) → Episode Hypothesis (John Oller): Text (discourse in any form) will be easier to reproduce, understand, and recall, to the extent that it is structured episodically. The episode hypothesis goes well beyond simple meaningful learning. Most of our communicative textbooks may illustrate certain grammatical or discourse features, but they don't grip the learner with suspense.

② Ways of contributing integrated-skills teaching
- to present interesting, natural language
- to require reading and writing skills
- to provide stimulus for spoken or written questions and respond to by speaking or writing
- to be encouraged to write their own episodes

6. Integrated Lesson

4기능을 개별로 들어가기 전에 integrated lesson이 실제로 어떻게 우리나라 교실에서 이용되는지 살펴보기로 하자. 이 수업은 이제까지 설명된 approach를 이용하여 4기능을 통합하고 있는 모습을 보여주고 있다. 첫째, 'likes'와 'dislikes'를 표현하기 위해서 tasks를 이용하고 있다. 둘째, 이 수업은 전체적으로 occupations, 즉 jobs이라는 theme을 중심으로 이루어지고 있다. 셋째, Jacques가 이야기 하고 있는 narrative안에는 episode hypothesis의 개념이 포함되어 있다. 마지막으로 학습자들이 employment광고에서 jobs을 찾아보거나, 여러 다른 jobs의 종류를 교실에서 이야기하거나, 자신들이 좋아하는 것과 싫어하는 것을 발표하는 등의 experiential learning이 포함된다는 것이 다음과 같이 정리될 수 있다.

- Tasks of expressing likes and dislikes
- Theme of occupations and jobs
- Episode involved in the Jacque's narrative
- Experiential learning of finding jobs in ads and reporting of their likes

---

- context: English Language school in Korea
- level: High Intermediate
- course focus: Multiple skills, emphasis on oral skills
- students: 12 young adults, wishing to improve English skills
- lesson: Unit 7, Lesson 2, New Vistas, Book 3 (Brown, 2000)
- class hour: 60 minutes
- focus: [situational] occupations, work, employment opportunities
                   [functional] Expressing likes and dislikes
                   [formal] ing gerunds; vocabulary for types of workers

Warm-up (L) — 5 min.

　　T : asks Ss to name careers, jobs, occupations and writes them on the board.
　　T : briefly tells about a job she had as a waitress in a restaurant — how she found the job, the interview, and what the job was like

A. Presentation (L, R, S) — 10 min.

　　T : directs Ss to the opening page of Lesson 2, a full-page advertisement for summer employment at a "water park" in Clear Lake, Texas.
　　T : tells Ss to skim the page individually and decide if they would like to work at Clear Lake Water Park.
　　T : asks Ss to pair up and tell their partner what they like or don't like, and why they feel that way.
　　T : engages the whole class in a brief whole-class discussion of what Ss liked and didn't like, and puts a few key phrases on the board (good pay, benefits, discounts on rides in the park, flexible hours, etc).

B. Listening Focus (L, R, W, S) — 10 min.

　　T : directs Ss to the second page, and plays a CD recording of a conversation in which a man named Jacques describes why he doesn't like his job. T plays the conversation once for general listening…
　　　… and a second time for Ss to look at and complete the written exercise in the book that requires using the -ing form of verbs like work, write, apply, etc.
　　T : asks Ss to compare their responses with their partner and make any corrections.

C. Grammar Focus (L, R, W, S) — 15 min.

In the next exercise, Ss are asked to make one list of job-related activities you like and another list of those you dislike.

T : then calls attention to the expressions in the book: I can't stand/ I don't mind/ I enjoy/ I hate/ I prefer + V-ing (-ing form of verb)

T : puts Ss into groups of four and directs them to share their likes and dislikes, using the expressions + gerund. T offers some suggestions as prompts.

D. Focus on types of workers (R, S, L, W) — 10 min.

On the next page, six types of workers are described and pictured: realistic, investigative, artistic, social, enterprising, and conventional.

T : directs Ss to the page and calls on six Ss to each read aloud one of the short descriptions; T makes a few pronunciation corrections.

T : directs Ss to reread the descriptions and write a short paragraph describing themselves. Ss can use the gerunds used in the descriptions.

Wind down (L, S) — 5 min.

T : asks Ss to look over their paragraph descriptions, and to revise them if they want to for homework.

T : calls on selected Ss and asks them about what type of worker they are, and if they like or dislike a job they have had.

CHAPTER 02 Teaching Listening

단원 길라잡이
- 듣기지도의 중요성을 교수법의 이론을 통해 이해한다.
- 실제 듣기가 일어나는 Top-down과 Bottom-up의 과정을 이해한다.

Introduction

듣기는 언어 학습에서 가장 기본이 되는 skill이라고 할 수 있다. 1970년대 이전에는 2언어습득에서 듣기가 무시되는 영역이었지만 그 이후에 중요성을 인정받아 comprehension-based approach에서 이론적인 바탕을 쌓아가기 시작하였다. comprehension-based approach는 의사소통식 교수법에서 강조하는 말하기의 표현력보다 이해도에 중요성을 두는 모든 수업이론을 대표하고 있다. 대표적인 영어교수법에는 Total physical response approach와 Natural approach가 해당된다. Krashen의 2언어습득 원리에 기초하고 있으며 어린이가 모국어를 배우는 자연스러운 과정을 기초로 하여 학습법이 나왔다고 볼 수 있다. 그래서 어린이가 처음에는 거의 말하지 않고 어른이 하는 말을 들으면서 배우는 침묵기간을 인정하고 이 학습법의 중요한 핵심으로 놓고 있다. 그래서 학습자의 침묵기간에는 표현하지 않고 받아들이는 입력을 중시하고 학습자의 레벨에서 한단계 높은 영역으로 발전할 수 있도록 교수하는데 그 목적을 두고 있다.

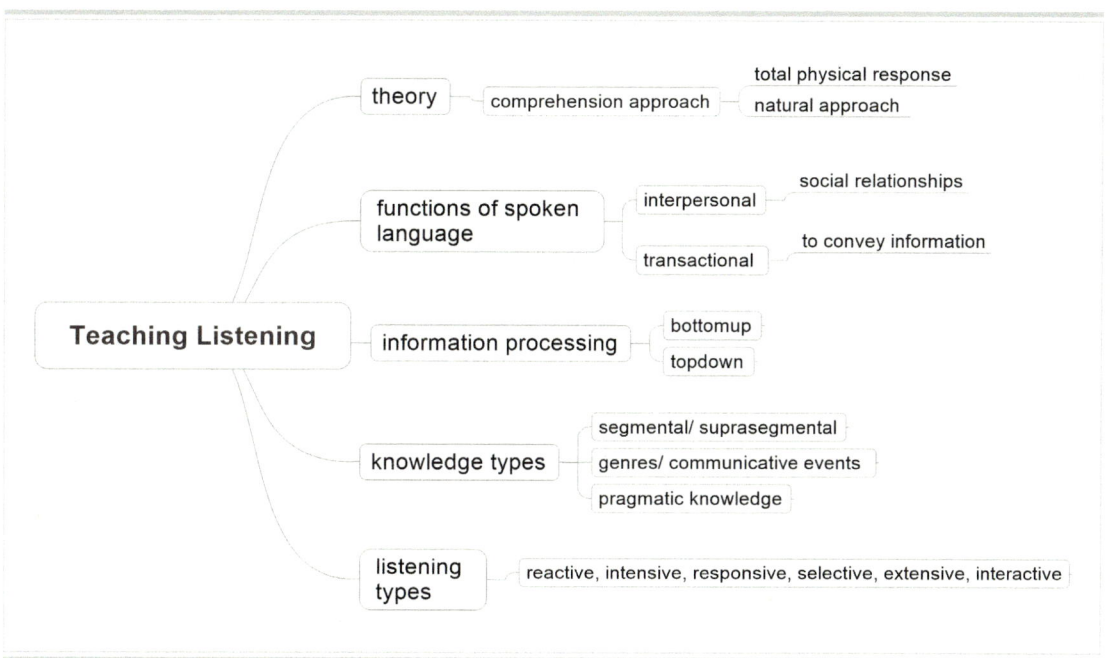

교육과정 - 이해력 (Reception) 중학교 성취 기준

  2022 개정 영어과 교육과정에서는 지금까지 듣기, 말하기, 읽기, 쓰기의 네 가지 언어 기능 관점으로 교육 내용의 영역을 분류하던 기존 방식에서 탈피하여 언어의 사회적 목적 관점에 따라 '이해(reception)'와 '표현(production)'의 두 가지 영역을 설정하였다. 이해 영역에서는 담화와 글뿐만 아니라 이미지, 동영상 등이 다양하게 결합된 방식으로 제공되는 영어 지식 정보를 처리하고 사용하는 능력을 기른다. 표현 영역에서는 다양한 매체를 통해 말, 글, 시청각 이미지 등을 활용하여 자신의 느낌, 생각, 의견 등을 전달하는 능력을 기른다. 이해 영역과 표현 영역은 독자적인 영역으로 기능하는 한편, 두 영역의 결합된 형태로 영어 사용자 간 상호 작용도 가능하게 한다. 상호 작용은 대화, 토론, 문자 교환 등 참여자 간의 다양한 소통 방식으로 이루어질 수 있다.

> [9영01-01] 단어, 어구, 문장을 듣고 연음이나 축약된 소리를 식별한다.
> [9영01-02] 친숙한 주제에 관한 담화나 글에서 세부 정보를 파악한다.
> [9영01-03] 친숙한 주제에 관한 담화나 글의 중심 내용을 파악한다.
> [9영01-04] 친숙한 주제에 관한 담화나 글에서 일이나 사건의 논리적 관계를 파악한다.
> [9영01-05] 친숙한 주제에 관한 담화나 글에서 인물의 기분이나 감정을 추론한다.
> [9영01-06] 친숙한 주제에 관한 담화나 글에서 화자나 필자의 의도나 목적을 추론한다.
> [9영01-07] 단어, 어구, 문장의 함축적 의미를 추론한다.
> [9영01-08] 적절한 전략을 활용하여 다양한 매체로 표현된 담화나 글을 듣거나 읽는다.
> [9영01-09] 다양한 관점을 존중하는 태도로 듣거나 읽는다.
> [9영01-10] 자신의 관심사에 관한 다양한 담화나 글을 선택하여 적극적으로 듣거나 읽는다.

(가) 성취기준 해설

- [9영01-01] 이 성취기준은 자주 사용되는 단어나 어구 또는 다양한 언어 형식의 문장을 듣고 영어의 리듬, 강세, 억양뿐만 아니라 연음이나 축약된 소리를 식별하여 자연스럽게 영어로 말하는 것을 듣고 이해할 수 있는 것을 의미한다.
- [9영01-02] 이 성취기준은 학습자가 개인 생활, 학교생활, 사회생활 등에서 흔히 접할 수 있는 친숙한 주제에 관하여, 말이나 대화를 듣거나 글을 읽고 그 속에서 숫자, 위치, 사건 등의 세부 정보를 파악할 수 있으며, 그림, 사진, 도표 등의 시각적 정보를 포함한 말, 대화, 글에서 세부 정보를 파악할 수 있는 것을 의미한다.
- [9영01-03] 이 성취기준은 학습자가 개인 생활, 학교생활, 사회생활 등에서 흔히 접할 수 있는 친숙한 주제에 관하여, 말이나 대화를 듣거나 글을 읽고, 줄거리, 주제, 요지 등의 중심 내용을 파악할 수 있는 것을 의미한다.
- [9영01-04] 이 성취기준은 학습자가 개인 생활, 학교생활, 사회생활 등에서 흔히 접할 수 있는 친숙한 주제에 관하여, 말이나 대화를 듣거나 글을 읽고 일이나 사건의 순서, 전후 관계, 원인과 결과 등의 논리적 관계를 파악할 수 있는 것을 의미한다.

- [9영01-08] 이 성취기준은 학습자가 방송, 영상, 인터넷 등 다양한 매체로 표현된 친숙한 주제에 관한 말, 대화 또는 글을 듣거나 읽을 때, '다음에 나올 내용을 추측하며 듣거나 읽기'와 '훑어보기'와 같은 다양한 전략을 적절하게 활용할 수 있는 것을 의미한다.
- [9영01-10] 이 성취기준은 학습자가 자신의 관심 분야와 관련된 말, 대화 또는 글을 스스로 선택하여 계획성 있고 적극적인 태도로 듣거나 읽을 수 있는 것을 의미한다.

(나) 성취기준 적용 시 고려사항

- 학습자의 듣기와 읽기 능력을 균형적으로 향상하는 데 중점을 두어 지도한다. 또한 이해 영역의 듣기와 읽기를 연계한 활동뿐만 아니라 이해한 내용을 말하거나 쓰기, 질문하며 답하기 등의 활동을 활용하여 이해 영역 활동이 자연스럽게 표현 영역 활동에 연결되도록 통합적으로 지도한다.
- 학교생활, 음식, 스포츠, 봉사 활동, 지속가능한 사회를 위한 노력 등 학습자에게 친숙한 주제의 다양한 자료를 활용하여 지도한다. 또한 흥미를 유발하고 학습 효과를 높일 수 있도록 실생활에서 접하는 다양한 매체의 자료, 즉 오프라인 매체뿐만 아니라 온라인 매체의 자료를 활용하여 지도한다.
- 듣기와 읽기 활동은 전·중·후 활동으로 구성하여 단계별로 지도하며, 상향식 과정, 하향식 과정, 상호 작용식 과정을 적절히 활용하여 지도한다.
- 교수·학습 활동과 평가를 연계하여 학습의 과정에서 형성평가를 통해 성취기준 도달 정도를 점검하고 학습자에게 적절한 피드백을 제공하여 성취기준에 도달할 수 있도록 지도한다.
- 평가의 내용과 수준은 성취기준을 근거로 선정하며 성취기준에 따라 적절한 평가 방법을 활용한다. 지필평가, 수행평가, 자기 평가, 동료 평가 등 다양한 평가 방법을 적용하여 성취수준이 어느 정도인지 다각도로 점검한다.
- 평가의 목적과 학습자의 수준에 따라 사실적 이해 능력과 추론적 이해 능력을 측정하는 문항의 비중을 적절히 조절하며 평가한다.
- 학습자의 관심과 흥미가 진로와 자연스럽게 연계될 수 있도록 듣기와 읽기 자료를 제공하며 학습자가 자신의 진로를 탐색하고 계획하는 데 도움이 되는 수업과 평가 활동을 제공한다.
- 이해 영역의 [9영01-08], [9영01-09], [9영01-10] 성취기준의 경우 지필평가보다는 수행평가, 학생의 자기 평가, 동료 평가 등의 방법을 활용하여 평가하며, 각 성취기준에 어느 정도 도달하였는지를 독립적으로 평가하기보다는 다른 성취기준과 연계하여 평가한다.

01 Features of Listening

1. Types of Spoken Language

(1) Monologue

① planned: to manifest little redundancy and therefore relatively difficult to comprehend; 예 speeches, lectures, readings, news broadcasts

② unplanned: to exhibit more redundancy, which makes for ease in comprehension, but the presence of more performance variables and other hesitations can either help or hinder comprehension; 예 impromptu lectures and long stories in conversations

(2) Dialogue

① Interpersonal Dialogue : to promote social relationships

② Transactional Dialogue : to convey propositional or factual information

2. Features of Language

Listening and reading are skills which are categorized as receptive skills as they involve responding to language rather than producing it. Spoken language is different from written language. Look at the comparison between written and spoken language below:

Written Language	Spoken Language
Stays on page and doesn't disappear.	Disappears as soon as it is spoken. Sometimes it is spoken fast and sometime slowly, with or without pauses.
Uses punctuation and capital letters to show sentences.	Shows sentences and meaningful groups of words through stress and intonation.
Consists of letters, words, sentences and punctuation joined together into text.	Consists of connected speech, sentences, incomplete sentences or single words.
Has no visual support-except photos or pictures sometimes.	The speaker uses body language to support his/her communication; 예 gestures (movements of hands or arms to help people understand us), and facial expressions (the looks on our face).

① Clustering: In spoken language, due to memory limitations and our predisposition for chunking or clustering, we break down speech into smaller groups of words.

② Redundancy: Spoken language has a good deal of redundancy, rephrasings, repetitions, elaborations and little insertions of *I mean* and *You know*.

③ Reduced forms: These reductions pose significant difficulties, especially for classroom learners who may have initially been exposed to the full forms of the English language.
- Phonological (예 *Djeetyet? – Did you eat yet?*)
- Morphological (예 *I'll – I will*)
- Syntactic (예 *When will you be back? – Tomorrow, maybe.*)
- Pragmatic (예 *Mum! Phone!*)

④ Performance Variables: In spoken language, except for planned discourse (speeches, lectures, etc) hesitations, false starts, pauses and corrections are common.

> But, uh –I also –to go with this of course if you're playing well– if you're playing well then you get uptight about your game. You get keyed up and it's easy to concentrate. You know you're playing well and you know… in with a chance then it's easier, much easier to – to you know get in there and – and start to … you don't have to think about it. I mean it's gotta be automatic.

⑤ Colloquial language: Idioms, slang, reduced forms, and shared cultural knowledge are all manifested at some point in conversations.

⑥ Rate of Delivery: In listening the hearer may not always have the opportunity to stop the speaker. Instead, the stream of speech will continue to flow.

⑦ Stress, rhythm, intonation: Because English is a stress-timed language, English sentence, "The PREsident is INTerested in eLIMinating the emBARgo," with 4 stressed syllables out of 18, theoretically takes about the same amount of time to utter as "Dead men wear plaid." Intonation patterns are very significant not just for interpreting straightforward elements such as questions, statements, and emphasis but for understanding more subtle messages like sarcasm, endearment, insult, solicitation, praise, etc.

⑧ Interaction: Conversation is especially subject to all the rules of interaction: negotiation, clarification; attending signals; turn-taking; and topic nomination, maintenance, and termination.

02. Procedures of Listening

1. Information Processing

① Top-down processing: to describe the way meaning is inferred and constructed from the application of prior knowledge about language and the world
② Bottom-up processing: to describe the way meaning is built up from the decoded sounds

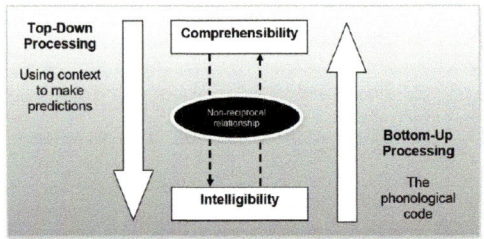

In psycholinguistics, cognitive psychology, and information processing, a contrast is made between two different ways in which humans analyze and process language as part of comprehension and learning. One way, known as top-down processing, makes use of higher level, non-sensory information to predict or interpret lower level information that is present in the data. The other way, bottom-up processing, makes use of the information present in the input to achieve higher level meaning. The meanings of these terms varies depending on the unit of analysis. For example, in word recognition, the higher level information is knowledge of permissible words as well as actual words of a language, while the lower level information is the actual phonetic input (or orthographic input in the case of written word recognition). In sentence comprehension or the interpretation of an utterance, the lower level information is words, while the higher level information includes knowledge of grammar, semantics, and pragmatics. As applied to the full understanding of a novel, lower level information consists of words and sentences, while higher level information includes the readers previously existing knowledge of the world, including cultural and moral values, scripts, schemas and literary genres.

Bottom-up processes	Top-down processes
• Retain input while it is being processed • Recognize word divisions • Recognize key words in utterances • Use knowledge of word-order patterns to identify constituents in utterances • Recognize grammatical relations between key elements in sentences • Recognize the functions of word stress in sentences • Recognize the functions of intonation in sentences	• Use key words to construct the schema of a discourse • Construct plans and schema from elements of a discourse • Infer the role of the participants in a situation • Infer the topic of an event • Infer the cause or effect of an event • Infer unstated details of a situation • Infer the sequence of a series of events • Infer comparisons • Distinguish between literal and figurative meanings • Distinguish between facts and opinions

▶ **Example of Top-down processing**

> A : And what other subjects did you take?
> B : I got Maths, Physics and Engineering Drawing. And English too. But I only just passed that. I took French but I failed it. I'm not much good at languages. But you can take the National Certificate if you've got four O levels so I was all right.
> A : And where are you working?
> B : In a local firm. They make parts for the motor industry, you know,… crankshafts, crankrods, connecting rods and so on … Reynolds Supply Company. They're very good. They started me off in the model shop…

2. Knowledge of Language

① Sounds
- segmental level: discrete sound elements, learners need to know how vowel and consonants combine to produce words
- suprasegmental level: beyond individual sounds, learners need to know that words in English have different stress patterns

② Spoken grammar: ellipsis, question tags, hesitations, repeats, false starts, incompletion syntactic blends

③ Vocabulary knowledge: formulaic expressions, prefabricated lexical chunks

④ Discourse and language use
- adjacency pairs: one speaker asks a question or makes a comment and the listener responds
- discourse markers: signalling the way

⑤ Genres or communicative events

⑥ Pragmatic knowledge
- to enable to go beyond the literal meaning of decoding and parsing of the input
- to draw conclusions about the speakers' intention

3. Classroom Applications

(1) Listening Skills and Strategies

Listening Skills	Listening Strategies
Listen for details	Planning
Listen selectively	Focusing attention
Listen for global understanding	Monitoring
Listen for main ideas	Evaluation
Listen and infer	Inferencing
Listen and predict	Elaboration
	Prediction
	Contextualization
	Reorganizing
	Using linguistic and learning resources
	Cooperation

(2) Process-oriented Listening

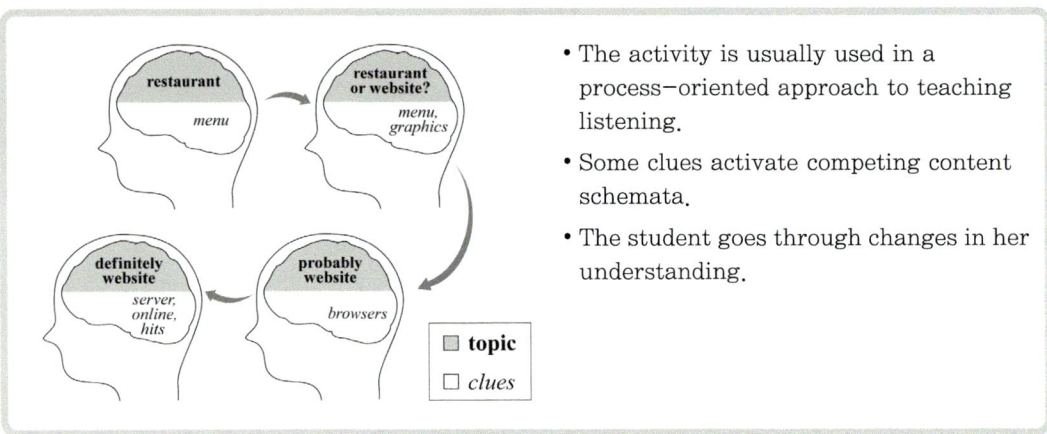

- The activity is usually used in a process-oriented approach to teaching listening.
- Some clues activate competing content schemata.
- The student goes through changes in her understanding.

① Students' knowledge of language, discourse and language use is to enable to decode speech signals & to make predictions or inferences, to construct interpretations.

② Teacher's guidance and scaffolding can help the students to process learning to listen.

③ Task-based metacognitive instruction can develop the students' metacognitive awareness about listening while offering plenty of listening practice.

4. Types of Listening Activities

There are a number of techniques of teaching listening available for the teachers. D. Brown (2008) categories types of classroom listening performance into: reactive, intensive, responsive, selective, extensive, and interactive.

① Reactive : The learner only listens to the surface structure of an utterance for the single purpose of repeating it. In this case, Nunan (1991, 18) associates listeners role as 'tape recorder.' This kind of performance does not require high meaningful processing. 예 brief individual or choral pronunciation drill

② Intensive : This technique focuses on components of discourse such as phonemes, words, intonation, discourse marker, etc. 예 The teacher asks the students to listen to the stress pattern of some words or intonation of a sentence.

③ Responsive : This technique requires students to quickly process the teacher talk and make/ fashion appropriate reply. 예 The teacher greets students, *good morning*, or giving command, *Would you please repeat your answer*?

④ Selective : The purpose of this technique is to look for the important information (such as dates, location, main idea, etc.) in a long discourse such as speeches, stories, and media broadcast.

⑤ Extensive : The purpose of this performance is to develop a top down, global understanding of spoken language. 예 The students are asked to take notes or discuss after listening to a lengthy lectures.

⑥ Interactive : This performance includes all five of the above types. This may include other skills and conduct in the authentic communicative exchange. 예 The learners are asked to participate in a debate, conversation, role play and other group work.

문헌읽기 Top-down and Bottom-up Listening

> Imagine the following situations : Over lunch, your friend tells you a story about a recent holiday, which was a disaster. You listen with interest and interject at appropriate moments, maybe to express surprise or sympathy. That evening, another friend calls to invite you to a party at her house the following Saturday. As you've never been to her house before, she gives you directions. You listen carefully and make notes.

With the holiday anecdote, your main concern was probably understanding the general idea and knowing when some response was expected. In contrast, when listening to the directions to a party, understanding the exact words is likely to be more important - if you want to get there without incident, that is! The way you listened to the holiday anecdote could be characterised as top-down listening. This refers to the use of background knowledge in understanding the meaning of the message. Background knowledge consists of context, that is, the situation and topic, and co-text, in other words, what came before and after. The context of chatting to a friend in a casual environment itself narrows down the range of possible topics. Once the topic of a holiday has been established, our knowledge of the kind of things that can happen on holiday comes into play and helps us to 'match' the incoming sound signal against our expectations of what we might hear and to fill out specific details. In contrast, when listening to directions to a friend's house, comprehension is achieved by dividing and decoding the sound signal bit by bit. The ability to separate the stream of speech into individual words becomes more important here, if we are to recognise, for example, the name of a street or an instruction to take a particular bus. In reality, fluent listening normally depends on the use of both processes operating simultaneously. Think about talking to your friends (in your first language) in a noisy bar. It is likely that you 'guess' the content of large sections of the conversation, based on your knowledge of the topic and what has already been said.

In this way, you rely more on top-down processing to make up for unreliability in the sound signal, which forms an obstacle to bottom-up processing. Similarly, second-language listeners often revert to their knowledge of the topic and situation when faced with unfamiliar vocabulary or structures, so using top-down processing to compensate for difficulties in bottom-up processing. On the other hand, if a listener is unable to understand anything of what she hears, she will not even be able to establish the topic of conversation, so top-down processing will also be very limited.

① Top-down Listening Activities

Do you ever get your students to predict the content of a listening beforehand, maybe using information about the topic or situation, pictures, or key words? If so, you are already helping them to develop their top-down processing skills, by encouraging them to use their knowledge of the topic to help them understand the content. This is an essential skill given that, in a real-life listening situation, even advanced learners are likely to come across some unknown vocabulary. By using their knowledge of context and co-text, they should either be able to guess the meaning of the unknown word, or understand the general idea without getting distracted by it. Other examples of common Top-down listening activities include putting a series of pictures or sequence of events in order, listening to conversations and identifying where they take place, reading information about a topic then listening to find whether or not the same points are mentioned, or inferring the relationships between the people involved.

② **Bottom-up Listening Activities**

The emphasis in EFL listening materials in recent years has been on developing top-down listening processes. There are good reasons for this given that learners need to be able to listen effectively even when faced with unfamiliar vocabulary or structures. However, if the learner understands very few words from the incoming signal, even knowledge about the context may not be sufficient for her to understand what is happening, and she can easily get lost. Of course, low level learners may simply not have enough vocabulary or knowledge of the language yet, but most teachers will be familiar with the situation in which higher-level students fail to recognise known words in the stream of fast connected speech. Bottom-up listening activities can help learners to understand enough linguistic elements of what they hear to then be able to use their top-down skills to fill in the gaps. The following procedure for developing bottom-up listening skills draws on dictogloss, and is designed to help learners recognise the divisions between words, an important bottom-up listening skill. The teacher reads out a number of sentences, and asks learners to write down how many words there would be in the written form. While the task might sound easy, for learners the weak forms in normal connected speech can make it problematic, so it is very important for the teacher to say the sentences in a very natural way, rather than dictating them word-by-word. Some suitable sentences are:

> Do you want some chocolate?   Let's have a party!
> What have you got?   There isn't any coffee.
> What are you doing?   I'm going to the shop.
> I'd better go soon.   He doesn't like it.
> You shouldn't have told him.

Learners can be asked to compare their answers in pairs, before listening again to check. While listening a third time, they could write what they hear, before reconstructing the complete sentences in pairs or groups. By comparing their version with the correct sentences, learners will become more aware of the sounds of normal spoken English, and how this is different from the written or carefully-spoken form. This will help them to develop the skill of recognising known words and identifying word divisions in fast connected speech. Successful listening depends on the ability to combine these two types of processing. Activities which work on each strategy separately should help students to combine Top-down and bottom-up processes to become more effective listeners in real-life situations or longer classroom listenings.

CHAPTER 03 Teaching Speaking and Pronunciation

단원 길라잡이
- 말하기 교실 활동의 종류를 알고 특성과 차이점을 이해한다.
- 담화 분석의 규칙과 문체를 이해한다.
- 발음 교수의 주요 핵심 사항을 분석한다.

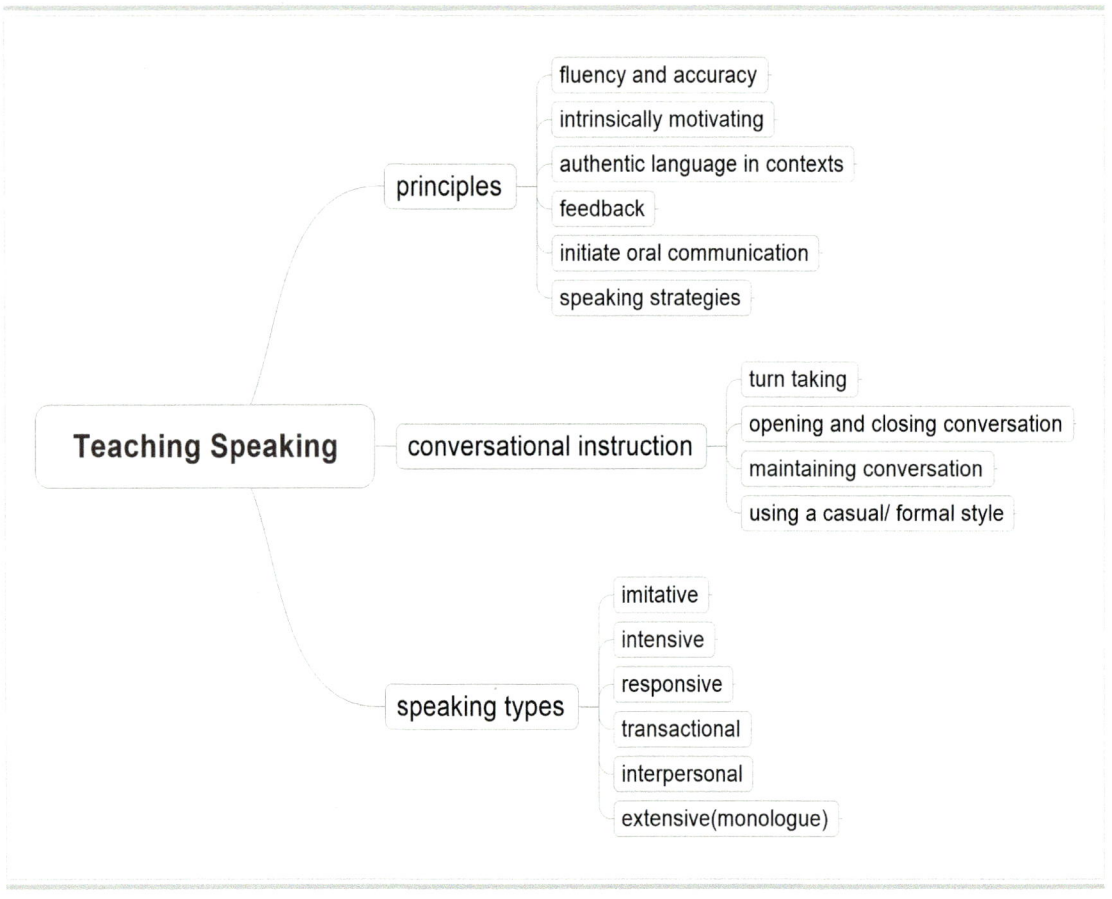

교육과정 - 표현력 (Production) 중학교 성취 기준

[9영02-01] 연음이나 축약된 소리를 활용하여 단어, 어구, 문장을 말한다.
[9영02-02] 대상이나 인물의 감정을 묘사한다.
[9영02-03] 친숙한 주제에 관해 사실적 정보를 설명한다.
[9영02-04] 친숙한 주제에 관해 경험이나 계획을 설명한다.
[9영02-05] 친숙한 주제에 관해 일이나 사건의 논리적 관계를 설명한다.
[9영02-06] 친숙한 주제에 관해 자신의 의견을 주장한다.
[9영02-07] 친숙한 주제에 관해 듣거나 읽고 내용을 요약한다.
[9영02-08] 간단한 일기, 편지, 이메일 등의 글을 쓴다.
[9영02-09] 적절한 매체를 활용하여 정보 윤리를 준수하며 말하거나 쓴다.
[9영02-10] 적절한 전략을 활용하여 상황이나 목적에 맞게 말하거나 쓴다.
[9영02-11] 상대방을 배려하는 태도로 말하거나 쓴다.

(가) 성취기준 해설

- [9영02-01] 이 성취기준은 학습자가 영어의 리듬, 강세, 억양뿐만 아니라 연음이나 축약된 소리를 적절히 활용하여 실제 상황에서 단어, 어구, 문장을 이해할 수 있는 발음으로 자연스럽게 말할 수 있는 것을 의미한다.

- [9영02-02] 이 성취기준은 학습자가 개인 생활, 학교생활, 사회생활 등에서 흔히 접할 수 있는 친숙한 주제에 관해, 자신이나 상대방이 느끼는 기분이나 감정을 묘사하는 말이나 대화를 하거나 문장 또는 문단으로 쓸 수 있는 것을 의미한다. 또한 주변 사람이나 사물 등에 대해 적절하게 묘사하는 말이나 대화를 하거나 문장 또는 문단으로 쓸 수 있는 것을 의미한다.

- [9영02-03] 이 성취기준은 학습자가 개인 생활, 학교생활, 사회생활 등에서 흔히 접할 수 있는 친숙한 주제에 관해 사람, 사물, 위치나 장소, 방법이나 절차 등을 적절하게 설명하는 말이나 대화를 하거나 문장이나 문단으로 쓸 수 있는 것을 의미한다. 또한 그림, 사진, 도표 등 시각적 정보와 관련하여 특정 정보를 설명하는 말이나 대화를 하거나 문장이나 문단으로 쓸 수 있는 것을 의미한다.

- [9영02-05] 이 성취기준은 학습자가 개인 생활, 학교생활, 사회생활 등에서 흔히 접할 수 있는 친숙한 주제에 관한 일이나 사건의 상황에 대해 분석적으로 생각해 보고 이를 통해 일이나 사건의 순서, 전후 관계, 원인과 결과 등의 논리적 관계에 대해 말이나 대화를 하거나 문장이나 문단으로 쓸 수 있는 것을 의미한다.

- [9영02-06] 이 성취기준은 학습자가 개인 생활, 학교생활, 사회생활 등에서 흔히 접할 수 있는 친숙한 주제에 관해 자신의 의견을 주장하는 말이나 대화를 하거나 문장이나 문단으로 쓸수 있는 것을 의미한다. 이는 또한 학습자의 주장이 설득력을 갖추기 위해 의견을 뒷받침할 만한 근거를 함께 제시할 수 있도록 하는 것이다.

(나) 성취기준 적용 시 고려사항

- 말하기와 쓰기 능력을 균형 있게 향상하는 데 중점을 두어 지도한다. 또한 표현 영역의 말하기와 쓰기를 연계한 활동뿐만 아니라 듣고 말하기, 읽고 쓰기 등의 활동을 활용하여 이해 영역 활동과 표현 영역 활동이 자연스럽게 연결되도록 통합적으로 지도한다.
- 말하기와 쓰기 활동은 전·중·후 활동으로 나누어 단계별로 지도하며, 학습자의 흥미와 수준에 맞는 다양한 말하기 및 쓰기 과업을 활용하여 지도한다.
- 학습자의 흥미를 유발하고 학습 효과를 높일 수 있도록 실생활에서 접하는 다양한 매체, 즉 오프라인 매체와 온라인 매체를 함께 활용하여 지도한다.
- 교수·학습 활동과 평가를 연계하여 학습의 과정에서 형성평가를 통해 성취기준에 어느 정도 도달하였는지를 점검하고, 학습자에게 적절한 피드백을 제공하여 성취기준에 도달할 수 있도록 지도한다.
- 말하기·쓰기 활동의 과정 중에는 의미 전달에 지장을 주지 않는 한 교사의 즉각적인 오류 수정을 자제하여 유창성을 높이도록 지도하며, 최종 결과물에 대해서는 유창성뿐만 아니라 정확성에도 중점을 두어 지도한다.
- 평가의 내용과 수준은 성취기준을 근거로 선정하며 성취기준에 따라 적절한 평가 방법을 활용하고 지필평가, 수행평가, 자기 평가, 동료 평가 등 다양한 평가 방법을 적용하여 성취수준을 다각도로 점검한다. 말하기·쓰기 평가기준은 학습자 수준과 평가 과업에 따라 분석적 채점과 총괄적 채점을 적절히 사용하여 평가한다.
- 표현 영역의 [9영02-09], [9영02-10], [9영02-11] 성취기준의 경우 지필평가뿐만 아니라, 수행평가, 자기 평가, 동료 평가 등의 방법을 활용하여 평가할 수 있으며, 각 성취기준에 대한 도달 정도를 독립적으로 평가하기보다는 다른 성취기준과 연계하여 평가한다.

01 Integration of Listening and Speaking

From a communicative pragmatic view of the language classroom, listening and speaking skills are closely intertwined. The important issues for teaching speakings are as followings;

(1) Conversational discourse

The benchmark of successful language acquisition is almost always the demonstration of an ability to accomplish pragmatic goals through interactive discourse with other speakers of the language. Teaching conversation should include the followings;

- transactional and interactional conversation
- techniques for teaching students conversation rules for topic nomination, maintaining a conversation, turn-taking, interruption, and termination
- sociolinguistic appropriateness, styles of speech, nonverbal communication, and conversational routines
- phonological, lexical, and syntactic properties of language

(2) Accuracy and Fluency

While fluency may in many communicative language courses be an initial goal in language teaching, accuracy is achieved to some extent by allowing students to focus on the elements of phonology, grammar, and discourse in their spoken output. Current approaches to language teaching lean strongly toward message orientation with language usage offering a supporting role.

(3) Affective factors

One of the major obstacles learners have to overcome in learning to speak is the anxiety generated over the risks of blurting things out that are wrong, stupid, or incomprehensible. Because of the language ego that informs others that "you are what you speak," learners are reluctant to be judged by hearers. Our job as teachers is to provide the kind of warm, embracing climate that encourages students to speak, however halting or broken their attempts may be.

(4) The interaction effect

Conversations are collaborative as participants engage in a process of negotiation of meaning. David Nunan (1991) noted that interlocutor effect, or the difficulty of a speaking task as gauged by the skills of one's interlocutor in interactive discourse. In other words, one learners' performance is always colored by that of the person he or she is talking with.

(5) Intelligibility

Materials, technology, and teacher education programs are being challenged to grapple with the issue of intelligibility, and to adopt new standards of correctness and new attitudes toward accent in order to meet current global realities.

(6) Spoken Corpora

The intelligibility issue is now being informed by what McCarthy and O'Keefe (2004) describe as a rapid growth of readily available corpora of spoken language – one of the key developments in research on teaching oral production. Therefore, our notions of what is correct, acceptable, or appropriate, both phonologically and grammatically, are being forced to change.

(7) Genres of spoken language

Research on spoken language has recently attended to a specification of differences among various genres of oral interaction, and how to teach those variations. What is judged to be acceptable and correct varies by contexts, or genres, such as small talk, discussion, and narrative, among others. As research more accurately describe the constraints of such genres on spoken language, we will be better able to pinpoint models of appropriateness for students' specific purposes in learning English.

▶ **Differences between Spoken and Written Grammar**

Spoken Grammar	Written Grammar
clause is the basic unit of construction	sentence is the basic unit of construction
clauses are usually added (coordination)	clauses are often embedded (subordination)
head + body + tail construction	subject + verb + object construction
direct speech favoured	reported speech favoured
vagueness tolerated	precision favoured
a lot of ellipsis	little ellipsis
many question tags	no question tags
performance effects: hesitations, repeats, false starts, incompletion syntactic blends	no performance effects

02 Principles of Speaking

1. Features of Speaking

① Clustering: Fluent speech is phrasal, not word by word. Learners can organize their output both cognitively and physically through such clustering.

② Redundancy: The speaker has an opportunity to make meaning clearer through the redundancy of language. Learners can capitalize on this feature of spoken language.

③ Reduced forms: Contractions, elisions, reduced vowel, etc., all form special problems in teaching spoken English. Students who don't learn colloquial contractions can sometimes develop a stilted, bookish quality of speaking that in turn stigmatizes them.

④ Performance variables: Learners can actually be taught how to pause and hesitate. For example, in English our thinking time is not silent; we insert certain fillers such as *uh, um, well, you know, I mean, like,* etc. One of the most salient differences between native and nonnative speakers of a language is in their hesitation phenomena.

⑤ Colloquial language: Make sure your students are reasonably well acquainted with the words, idioms, and phrases of colloquial language that they get practice in producing these forms.

⑥ Rate of Delivery: Another salient characteristic of fluency is rate of delivery. One of your tasks in teaching spoken English is to help learners achieve an acceptable speed along with other attributes of fluency.

⑦ Stress, Rhythm, Intonation: This is the most important characteristic of English pronunciation. The stress-timed rhythm of spoken English and its intonation patterns convey important messages.

⑧ Interaction: Learning to produce language without interlocutors would rob speaking skill of its richest component: the creativity of conversational negotiation.

2. Teaching Speaking

① Focus on both fluency and accuracy, depending on your objective.

We need to bear in mind a spectrum of learner needs from language-based focus on accuracy to message-based focus on interaction, meaning, and fluency.

② Provide intrinsically motivating techniques.

Try to appeal to students' ultimate goals and interests, to their need for knowledge, for status, for achieving competence and autonomy, and for being all that they can be.

③ Encourage the use of authentic language in meaningful contexts.

It takes energy and creativity to devise authentic contexts and meaningful interaction, but with the help of a storehouse of teacher resource material it can be done. Even drills can be structured to provide a sense of authenticity.

④ Provide appropriate feedback and correction.

It is important that you take advantage of your knowledge of English to inject the kinds of corrective feedback that are appropriate for the moment.

⑤ Capitalize on the natural link between speaking and listening.

As you are focusing on speaking goals, listening goals may naturally coincide, and the two skills can reinforce each other. Skills in producing language are often initiated through comprehension.

⑥ Give students opportunities to initiate oral communication.

Part of oral communication competence is the ability to initiate conversations, to nominate topics, to ask questions, to control conversations, and to change the subject.

⑦ Develop speaking strategies.

Language students should be aware of strategic competence. The classroom can be one in which students become aware of, and have a chance to practice, such strategies as;

- asking for clarification: *What?*
- asking someone to repeat something: *Huh? Excuse me?*
- using fillers in order to gain time to process: *Uh, I mean, Well*
- getting someone's attention: *Hey Say, So*
- using formulaic expressions at the survival stage: *How much does it cost?*
- using paraphrases for structures one can't produce
- appealing for assistance from the interlocutor to get a word or phrase
- using mime and nonverbal expressions to convey meaning

3. Transactional and Interpersonal Functions

A distinction that is sometimes made between uses of language where the primary focus is on social interaction between the speakers and the need to communicate such things as rapport, empathy, interest and social harmony (interactional function), and those where the primary focus is on communicating information and completing different kinds of real world transactions (transactional function). Interactional communication is primarily person-orientated, whereas transactional communication is primarily message focused. Interactional and transactional language may differ in terms of such things as conventions for turn-taking, topics, and discourse management.

Text Type	Purpose	Participation	Planning
airport announcements	transactional	non-interactive	planned
sports commentary	transactional	non-interactive	unplanned
job interview	transactional	interactive	(partly) planned
service encounter	transactional	interactive	unplanned
joke telling	interpersonal	(partly) interactive	(partly) planned
voice-mail message	transactional or interpersonal	non-interactive	unplanned
casual conversation	interpersonal	interactive	unplanned

핵심플러스 Features of Communicative Activity

- The motivation of the activity is to achieve some outcome using language.
- The activity takes place in real time.
- Achieving the outcome requires the participants to interact, i.e. to listen as well as speak.
- The outcome is not 100% predictable because of the spontaneous and jointly constructed nature of the interaction.
- There is no restriction on the language used.

03. Conversational Analysis

1. Teaching conversation

(1) Teaching Approaches

① Indirect Approach: Learners are more or less set loose to engage in interaction. Teacher does not actually teach conversation, but rather that students acquire conversational competence peripherally by engaging in meaningful tasks.

② Direct Approach: It involves planning a conversation program around the specific microskills, strategies, and processes that are involved in fluent conversation. It explicitly calls students' attention to conversational rules, conventions, and strategies.

(2) Conversation in task-based instructions

The prevailing approach to teaching conversation includes the learner's inductive involvement in meaningful tasks as well as consciousness-raising elements of focus on form.

- transactional and interactional purposes
- short and long turns in conversation
- strategies for managing turn-taking
- strategies for opening and closing conversations
- how to initiate and respond to talk and how to develop and maintain talk
- how to use a casual style of speaking and a neutral or more formal style
- how to use conversation in different social settings
- strategies for repairing
- how to maintain fluency
- how to use conversational fillers and conversational routines

2. Types of Speaking Performance

① Imitative: This technique focuses on some particular elements of language form. The example of this is drilling. To some extent, drilling is good as it helps learners to establish psychomotor pattern (to loosen the tongue).

② Intensive: This performance is intended to attempt some phonological or grammatical aspects of language.

③ Responsive: The example is short reply to teacher or student-initiated question.

> T : How are you today?
> S : Pretty good, thanks, and you?
> T : What is the main idea in this essay?
> S : The United Nations should have more authority.
> S1 : So, what did you write for question number one?
> S2 : Well, I wasn't sure, so I left it blank.

④ Transactional Dialogue: The purpose of transactional dialogue is to convey or exchange specific information.

> A : Good afternoon. Enquiries.
> B : Hello, I'm making a journey from Ealing Broadway to Leamington Spa tomorrow morning and I don't have the new timetable. Please could you confirm that there's still a 7.25 from Ealing Broadway and an Intercity from Reading at 8.46?
> A : Just a minute, please... Yes, that's right. Departing Ealing Broadway 7.25, arriving Reading 8.10. Then departing Reading 8.46 arriving Leamington 9.59.
> B : Thanks very much.

⑤ Interpersonal Dialogue: The purpose of this performance is to maintain social relationship. This type of dialogue is rather tricky as it may convey aspects such as casual register, colloquial language, slang, ellipsis, sarcasm, etc.

> A : Hey, Stef, how's it going?
> B : Not bad, and yourself?
> A : I'm good.
> B : Cool. Okay, gotta go.

⑥ Extensive (monologue): Monologue can be planned or impromptu. Teacher may ask students to perform monologue in the form of oral reports, summaries or short speeches.

04. Discourse Analysis

1. Definitions of Discourse Analysis

Discourse analysis is the study of how sentences in spoken and written language form larger meaningful units such as paragraphs, conversations, interviews, etc. For example, discourse analysis deals with: (a) how the choice of articles, pronouns, and tenses affects the structure of the discourse (b) the relationship between utterances in a discourse (c) the moves made by speakers to introduce a new topic, change the topic, or assert a higher role relationship to the other participants. Analysis of spoken discourse is sometimes called conversational analysis. Some linguists use the term text linguistics for the study of written discourse. Another focus of discourse analysis is the discourse used in the classroom. Such analyses can be useful in finding out about the effectiveness of teaching methods and the types of teacher-student interactions.

핵심플러스 Types of References

(1) Cataphoric reference means that a word in a text refers to another later in the text and you need to look forward to understand. It can be compared with anaphoric reference, which means a word refers back to another word for its meaning. For example, 'When he arrived, John noticed that the door was open'. In the classroom, matching parts of sentences can help learners understand how cataphoric reference works, for example:
   a) As she entered the building 1) Jim fell over
   b) When he was running upstairs 2) the woman saw a huge crowd

(2) Anaphoric reference means that a word in a text refers back to other ideas in the text for its meaning. It can be compared with cataphoric reference, which means a word refers to ideas later in the text. For example, 'I went out with Jo on Sunday. She looked awful.' 'She' clearly refers to Jo, there is no need to repeat her name. In the classroom, asking learners to identify what or who the pronouns in a text refer to is one way to raise awareness. They can then practise this by using pronouns to replace words themselves. Comparing texts with well managed referencing to ones with poorly managed referencing can help students develop an idea of effective referencing even at low levels.

(3) Hedges are an important part of polite conversation. We use hedges to soften what we say or write to make what we say less direct. The most common forms of hedging involve tense and aspect, modal expressions including modal verbs and adverbs, vague language such as 'sort of' and 'kind of', and some verbs. In academic writing, it is prudent to be cautious in one's statements so as to distinguish between facts and claims. This is commonly known as hedging. Hedging is the use of linguistic devices to express hesitation or uncertainty as well as to demonstrate politeness and indirectness.

(4) Backchanneling is a strategy that provides students with the opportunity to converse about content informally, both during class and outside of the traditional class period. Benefits of backchanneling are as follows:
- By leveraging student communication preferences for chatting and texting, as well as encouraging communication and collaboration, backchanneling keeps students engaged and involved.
- Every student has a voice: When using a backchannel, students don't have to wait for their turn to speak by raising their hands. In addition, a backchannel's nonthreatening environment allows both shy and more confident students to contribute to the conversation equally.
- Teachers can get real time feedback on whether or not students understand concepts being discussed so they can make a shift to address student needs if necessary.

2. Applications of Registers

Register use is one of the most important aspects of correct English usage for advanced users of the language. In other languages (French, German, Italian, etc.), formality can be signalled through the formal/ informal "you" (du – Sie, tu – Vous, tu – Lei, etc.). In English, register is a key element in expressing degrees of formality. Here is an overview of registers with specific examples for specific occasions.
- Register – Type of language used when speaking to others
- Vertical Register – Language used varying in degrees of formality
- Horizontal Register – jargon, slang, etc. used in communicating with your friends, colleagues

One of the more interesting parts of the discussion centered around this hierarchy of vertical registers proposed by Cheryl Carter.
① Frozen – Language that does not change – prayers and pledges, set speech which is often scripted
   예 Welcome to the Hugh Brothers Industrial Center. Where tomorrow's world meets today's. Please remember that no flash photography is allowed during this tour...
② Formal – Complete sentences and specific word usage. – Formal English often used to show respect used in places such as work, school and public offices
   예 I hope you don't mind my stating that the service is unsatisfactory. I would like a refund.
③ Consultative – Formal register used in conversation – colleagues, peers, etc
   예 Excuse me Ms. Anderson. As I understand the task, we need to focus on improving our delivery times rather than blaming our suppliers.

④ Casual – Language used in conversation with friends. – idiomatic and often full of slang, used to signal belonging to a given group

> 예 Oh, Bob. Just a moment! Listen, you know... well... what was with that off-key comment last night?

⑤ Intimate – Language between lovers (and twins) – private language full of codewords only known to the two

> 예 I'm sick and tired of your crap!

05 Teaching Pronunciation

1. Techniques and Activities

(1) Receptive Skills

Students need to learn to hear the difference between phonemes. For example, particularly where such a contrast does not exist in their L1. Drills are useful in the development of both kinds of skills, while noticing tasks used with listening texts will be most effective in the development of receptive skills.

(2) Productive skills

- Drilling aims to help students achieve between pronunciation of language items, and to help them remember new items. It is fundamental to the teaching of word stress, sentence stress and intonation.
- Chaining can be used for sentences which prove difficult for student to pronounce, either because they are long or because they include difficult words and sounds.

Back Chain	Front Chain
The sentence is drilled and built up from the end, gradually adding to its length. Each part of the sentence is modelled by the teacher, and the students repeat.	The sentence is drilled and built up from the start, gradually adding to its length. Certain parts may be drilled separately, if they present problems. Each part of the sentence is modelled by the teacher, and the students repeat.
... told him. ... would've told him. ... I would've told him. ... seen him, I would've told him. If I'd seen him, I would've told him.	If I'd seen ... If I'd seen him ... If I'd seen him, I would've ... If I'd seen him, I would've told ... If I'd seen him, I would've told him.

2. Pronunciation in Listening and Reading activities

(1) Listening Comprehension Exercises

They are designed to sound as realistic as possible, with the participants talking at a normal speed and using natural language. These can play a key role in helping students to notice the existence of a pronunciation feature. For example, prior to doing a listening task, students can have the meaning and the pronunciation of a particular aspect of language brought to their attention, and practise it in very controlled ways. An extended listening stage can precede an eliciting and drilling stage. Indeed it can be argued that putting the listening exercise first might even make the pronunciation elements of the lesson more of an issue with regard to comprehension, and more likely to be noticed by the students. Students would initially have to listen out for and interpret the use of the language and related pronunciation areas selected for study, in order to complete a set of tasks; work on the pronunciation and use of the language area in question could then follow on from the listening exercise. The concept of **noticing** is important in pronunciation work. A language item needs to be relevant to the student at a particular time in order for there to be conscious **intake** and before the student can use it consistently. The same applies to features of pronunciation.

(2) Reading Activities

Many teachers stage reading activities either by having an initial exercise to allow students to get the gist of the text they are reading, or by establishing the type of text being used, followed by some more detailed work to focus on specific details when the text is read again. At some stage, when a text is read aloud either by the teacher or the students, pronunciation work can be integrated. Such texts as poems, rhymes, extracts from plays, song lyrics etc. can be used creatively in the classroom and can offer plenty of scope for pronunciation work.

3. Key Terms in Pronunciation

(1) Segmental phonemes and Suprasegmental

Sometimes a distinction is made between the segmental phonemes (i.e. the vowels and consonants of a language) and the suprasegmentals, i.e. such sound phenomena as accent and intonation, which may stretch over more than one segment. In phonetics and phonology, a unit which extends over more than one sound in an utterance, 예 stress and tone. The term suprasegmental is used particularly by American linguists.

(2) Stress

The pronunciation of a syllable or word with more respiratory energy or muscular force than other syllables or words in the same utterance: A listener often hears a stressed word or syllable as being louder, higher in pitch, and longer than the surrounding words or syllables. Different types of stress can be distinguished:

① Word stress refers to the pattern of stressed and unstressed syllables in a word. A distinction used to be made in long words between stressed syllables of varying degree, i.e. it was said that the syllable with the greatest prominence had the primary stress and the next stressed syllable the secondary stress. Now it is felt that while such distinctions are relevant for citation forms, in an utterance the overall intonation tends to neutralize the degree of stress within the individual word. Word stress may distinguish between two words that are otherwise alike. 예 *IMport* as a noun is stressed on the first syllable, and *imPORT* as a verb is stressed on the second.

② Sentence stress refers to the pattern of stressed and unstressed words in a sentence or utterance. English sentence stress most commonly falls on content words that contain new information. 예 *He was going to LONdon*, where the strongest stress falls on the first syllable of the word *London*.

③ In emphatic stress, a speaker can emphasize any syllable or word that he or she wishes to highlight. Emphatic stress is considered to be contrastive stress when the highlighted word is explicitly or implicitly contrasted with another word. 예 *SHE was getting ON the plane* while *HE was getting OFF*.

(3) Accent

Greater emphasis on a syllable so that it stands out from the other syllables in a word: For example, in English the noun *'import (This car is a foreign import)* has the accent on the first syllable *im-* while the verb *im'port* has the accent on the second syllable *-port (We import all our coffee)*.

(4) Prominence

In discourse, greater stress on the words or syllables which the speaker wishes to emphasize. Prominence may be given to different words according to what has been said before by another speaker. 예 *He may come toMORRow.* (as a reply to "When is Mr Jones coming?") *He MAY come tomorrow.* (as a reply to "Is Mr Jones likely to come tomorrow?") Prominence may be accompanied by pitch movement on the prominent syllable.

4. Sample lessons

(1) Find a partner: stress patterns

Lesson type: practice

Materials: sentence and word cards

　The teacher gives half of the students a card each with a word on, and the other half a card with a sentence on. Each word card has a sentence card match, the word and sentence both having the same stress pattern. Students mingle, saying their words or sentences out loud, and, through listening, trying to find their partner. When they think they have found a partner, they check with the teacher, and if they are indeed a pair, they can sit down. Once all of the students are paired up, the pairs read out their word and sentence to the other students, who write down the stress pattern, using a small circle to represent unstressed syllables, and a large one to represent a stressed syllable;

- (Policitian) ooOo
- (It's important) ooOo

　No meaning relationship is implied through the pairs having the same pattern; it is simply an exercise to help students to notice the difference between stressed and unstressed syllables;

Politician	It's important
Policeman	He's English
Electrician	Can I help you?
Photographer	You idiot!
Interior designer	I want to go to London

(2) Misunderstanding dialogues

Lesson type: practice

Materials: scripted dialogues (contrastive stress)

　In this activity, a dialogue is used which involves a series of misunderstandings. The dialogue itself may seem rather artificial, but the exercise helps underline the idea of contrastive stress, and how moving a tonic syllable can change the emphasis of what the speaker is saying. The teacher gives student B some lines to say, and student A is given a line which they will need to say in various ways, depending on what the misunderstood point is. The activity works better if there is no preparation, and students are put on the spot; they may not always get the point straight away, but it's worth perservering.

Student A	Student B
I'd like a big, red cotton shirt.	Here you are. A big, red cotton skirt.
No, I said a big, red cotton shirt.	Here you are. A big, red nylon shirt.
No, I said a big, red cotton shirt.	Here you are. A big, blue cotton shirt.
No, I said a big, red cotton shirt.	Sorry, I haven't got one.

To make the task slightly easier, the relevant stresses can be indicated on the students' role cards. A similar exercise is seen below.

Student A	Student B
It's a pity you weren't at the party.	I WAS at the party.
Did you say your were at the barbecue?	I was at the PARty.
Did you say Enrico was at the party?	I was at the party.

(3) Elision and other features of connected speech

Lesson type: Practice

Materials: Sound or video recording of natural speech

The teacher uses a cassette or video recording where one or two people are talking. The source of the recording is not very important; the teacher could even use a coursebook tape recording which has previously been used for another classroom purpose. However, the more relevant and interesting the tape is to the students, the more useful it will be in helping them to work on the features the teacher wants to investigate. Practice lesson like this can be invaluable in helping students to decode rapid, connected speech. While we may not realistically expect all students to incorporate such features consistently into their own language, they are at least becoming aware of these features.

CHAPTER 04 Teaching Reading

단원 길라잡이
- 입력되는 자료의 정보처리과정을 이해한다.
- 효과적인 읽기 수업을 위한 전략을 정리한다.

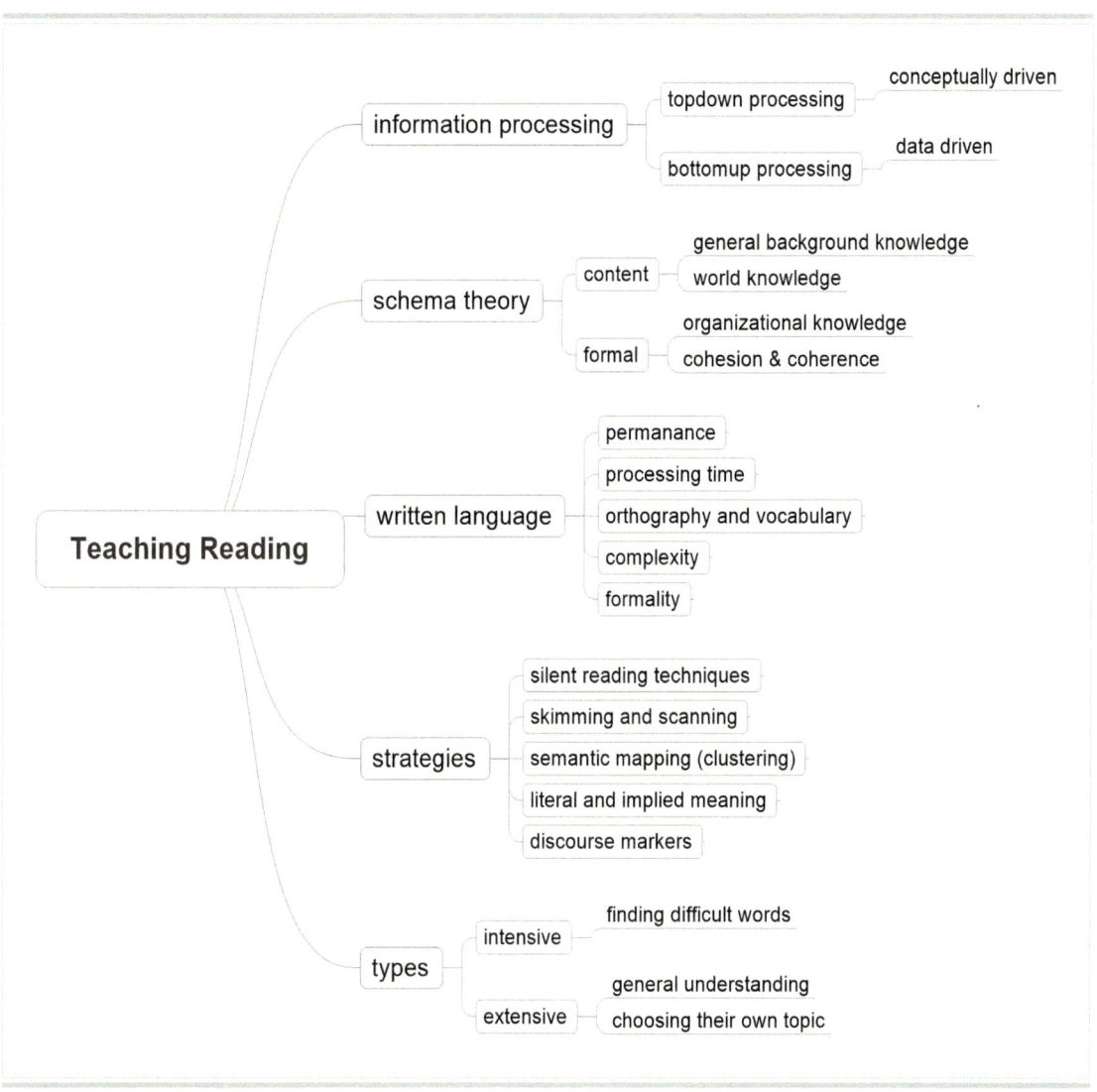

01 Principles for Reading

1. Top down processing and Bottom up processing

(1) Top down processing

Top-down processing of language happens when someone uses background information to predict the meaning of language they are going to listen to or read. Rather than relying first on the actual words or sounds (bottom up), they develop expectations about what they will hear or read, and confirm or reject these as they listen or read. Top-down processing is thought to be an effective way of processing language; it makes the most of what the person brings to the situation.

For example, asking learners to predict what a newspaper article might be about from the headline or first sentence will encourage them to use top-down processing on the article. In the classroom, learners can be encouraged to use both bottom-up and top-down strategies to help them understand a text. In a reading comprehension learners use their knowledge of the genre to predict what will be in the text (top down), and their understanding of affixation to guess meaning (bottom up).

(2) Bottom up processing

Bottom-up processing happens when someone tries to understand language by looking at individual meanings or grammatical characteristics of the most basic units of the text, (예 sounds for a listening or words for a reading), and moves from these to trying to understand the whole text. Bottom-up processing is not thought to be a very efficient way to approach a text initially, and is often contrasted with top-down processing, which is thought to be more efficient. For example, asking learners to read aloud may encourage bottom-up processing because they focus on word forms, not meaning.

2. Schema Theory

The theory that in comprehending language people activate relevant schemata allowing them to process and interpret new experiences quickly and efficiently; Schemata serve as a reference store from which a person can retrieve relevant existing knowledge and into which new information is assimilated. When encountering a topic in reading or listening, the reader activates the schema for that topic and makes use of it to anticipate, infer, and make different kinds of judgements and decisions about it. Schema theory plays an important role in theories of second language reading and listening comprehension.

A difference is sometimes made between content schemata and formal schemata. Content schemata deal with general background knowledge related to the topic such as might be associated with the topic of an earthquake. Formal schemata deal with the rhetorical structure of language and a person's knowledge of the structure of a particular genre, such as news reports or journal articles.

(1) **content schema**: In theories of reading comprehension, a distinction is sometimes made between two kinds of schema that people make use of in understanding texts. Content schema refers to background knowledge about the content of a text, i.e. depending on whether it is a text about an earthquake, the economy, French art or cooking.

(2) **formal schema**: This type of schematic knowledge is contrasted with formal schema, i.e. knowledge about the formal, rhetorical, organizational structure of different kinds of texts, such as whether the text is a simple story, a scientific text, a news report, etc. Knowledge of both types of schemata influence how a reader understands a text.

① Coherence means the connection of ideas at the idea level, and cohesion means the connection of ideas at the sentence level. Basically, coherence refers to the "rhetorical" aspects of your writing, which include developing and supporting your argument (예 thesis statement development), synthesizing and integrating readings, organizing and clarifying ideas. The cohesion of writing focuses on the "grammatical" aspects of writing.

② Cohesion is also a very important aspect of academic writing, because it immediately affects the tone of your writing. Although some instructors may say that you will not lose points because of grammatical errors in your paper, you may lose points if the tone of your writing is sloppy or too casual (예 a diary-type of writing or choppy sentences will make the tone of your writing too casual for academic writing). But cohesive writing does not mean just "grammatically correct" sentences; cohesive writing refers to the connection of your ideas both at the sentence level and at the paragraph level.

3. Characteristics of written language

① Permanence: Written language is permanent and therefore the reader has an opportunity to return again and again, if necessary, to a word or phrase or sentence, or even a whole text.

② Processing time: Most reading contexts allow readers to read at their own rate.

③ Distance: The task of the reader is to interpret language that was written in some other place at some other time with only the written words themselves as contextual clues.

④ Orthography: In spoken language, we have phonemes that correspond to writing's graphemes. But we also have stress, rhythm, juncture, intonation, pauses, volume, voice quality, settings, and nonverbal cue, all of which enhance the message. In writing we have graphemes. Punctuation, pictures or charts lend a helping hand.

⑤ Complexity: Spoken language tends to have shorter clauses and connected by more coordinate conjunctions, while writing has longer clauses and more subordination as shown in the following examples.

Written version	Spoken version
"Because of the frequent ambiguity that therefore is present in a good deal of writing, readers must do their best to infer, to interpret, and to read between the lines."	"There's frequent ambiguity in a lot of writing. And so, readers have to infer a lot. They also have to interpret what they read. And sometimes they have to read between the lines."

⑥ Vocabulary: Written English typically utilizes a greater variety of lexical items than spoken conversational English. Because writing allows the writer more processing time, because of a desire to be precise in writing, and simply because of the formal conventions of writing, lower-frequency words often appear.

⑦ Formality: Writing is quite frequently more formal than speech. Formality refers to prescribed forms that certain written messages must adhere to. We have rhetorical, or organizational formality in essay writing that demands a writer's conformity to conventions like paragraph topics.

02 Teaching Reading

1. Reading Strategies

(1) Identify the purpose in reading.

Efficient reading consists of clearly identifying the purpose in reading something. By doing so, you know what you're looking for and can weed out potential distracting information.

(2) Use graphemic rules and patterns to aid in bottom-up decoding.

At the beginning levels of learning English, one of the difficulties students encounter in learning to read is making the correspondences between spoken and written English. These phonics approaches to reading can prove useful for learners at the beginning level and especially useful for teaching children and nonliterate adults.

- short vowel sound in VC patterns: bat, him, leg, wish
- long vowel sound in VCe (final silent 'e') patterns: late, time, bite
- long vowel sound in VV patterns: seat, coat
- distinguishing hard 'c' and 'g' from soft 'c' and 'g': cat vs. city, game vs gem

(3) Use efficient silent reading techniques for improving fluency.

Your intermediate-to-advanced level students need not be speed readers, but you can help them increase reading rate and comprehension efficiency by teaching a few silent reading rules.

(4) Skim the text for main ideas.

Skimming consists of quickly running one's eyes across a whole text for its gist. Skimming gives readers the advantage of being able to predict the purpose of the passage, the main topic, or message, and possibly some of the developing or supporting ideas.

(5) Scan the text for specific information.

The purpose of scanning is to extract specific information without reading through the whole text. For academic English, scanning is absolutely essential. In vocational or general English, scanning is important in dealing with genres like schedules, manuals, forms, etc.

(6) Use semantic-mapping or clustering.

The strategy of semantic mapping, or grouping ideas into meaningful clusters, helps the reader to provide some order to the chaos. Making such semantic maps can be done individually, but they make for a productive group work technique as students collectively induce order and hierarchy to a passage.

(7) Guess when you aren't certain.

Learners should utilize all their skills and put forth as much effort as possible to be on target with their hypotheses. The point here is that reading is, after all, a guessing game of sorts, and the sooner learners understand this game, the better off they are. The key to successful guessing is to make it reasonably accurate.

(8) Analyze vocabulary.

- Look for prefixes (co-, inter-, un-, etc.) that may give clues.
- Look for suffixes (-tion, -tive, -ally, etc.) that may indicate what part of speech it is.
- Look for roots that are familiar.
- Look for grammatical contexts that may signal information.
- Look at the semantic context (topic) for clues.

(9) Distinguish between literal and implied meanings.

This requires the application of sophisticated top-down processing skills. Implied meaning usually has to be derived from processing pragmatic information; The request in (a) is obvious only if the reader recognizes the nature of many indirect requests in which we ask people to do things without ever forming a question. We can't be sure in (b) if the policeman literally stopped the car with his hand, but the assumption is that this is a traffic policeman whose hand signal was obeyed by a driver.

(a) Bill walked into the frigid classroom and immediately noticed Bob, sitting by the open window, with a heavy sweatshirt on. "It's sure cold in here, Bob." Bob glanced up from his book and growled, "Oh, all right, I'll close the window."

(b) The policeman held up his hand and stopped the car.

(10) Capitalize on discourse markers to process relationships.

Many discourse markers in English signal relationships among ideas as expressed through phrases, clauses, and sentences. A clear comprehension of such markers can greatly enhance learners' reading efficiency.

2. Intensive and Extensive Reading

Reading is an activity that can add someone's knowledge about important news and also some new vocabulary items. Realizing the importance of reading, some collages make it as one of subject. There are two kinds of teaching reading; extensive and intensive. Extensive and intensive are different in some cases. There are three differences between extensive reading and intensive reading; therefore extensive reading has more important purpose compared to intensive reading in broadening students' knowledge.

The first difference is that extensive reading covers large area, while intensive reading covers narrower area. According to Graham Stanley, extensive reading involves students reading long texts or large quantities for general understanding, with the intention of enjoying the texts. It means that students are given freedom to choose their own topic which they think are interested to be discussed. In this case, the students also have to find supported articles related to the topic in order to give them background knowledge, so that they know more about the topic they have chosen. It is different from intensive reading that does not allow the students to find a topic they like. The topic is given by the teacher. The students also do not necessary to look for supported articles because the topic which is chosen by the teacher is usually short and easy to understand.

The second difference is about students' activity in class. In extensive reading the students' activity is more complex than in intensive reading. The students, in extensive reading class, usually are asked to write a summary after reading an article/ passage. As we know, writing summary is not an easy thing to do. It allows learners to assert full control, both of the main factual or fictional content of an article/ book, and of the grammar and vocabulary used to express it (Bell, 1998). Besides, the students also will do a short presentation on what they have read. By doing short presentation, the students will have knowledge of the right preparation, self-independence and autonomy (Bell, 1998). While in intensive reading, instead of writing summary and having presentation, the students are asked to answer some questions related to the topic which is given by the teacher. Usually, all of the answers are available on the text, so that the students only rewrite it.

Extensive reading will discourage the over use of dictionary (Bell, 1998); on the contrary dictionary is a must in intensive reading. It is true that dictionary have an important place in reading activity, but as stated by Bell (1998) that the students will focus only on the language if they always consult the dictionary every time they find an unfamiliar word. They will not pay attention to the message conveyed. Bell also said that this habit will cause inefficient reading and destroy the pleasure that reading is intended to provide. Graham Stanley from British Council, Barcelona said that by avoiding dictionary, the students are expected to be encouraged to jot down the words they come across in a vocabulary notebook and they can look them up after they have finished reading. It will make the students guess the meaning based on the context. By doing this, the students are able to always remember the meaning of a word because they find it by themselves. Meanwhile in intensive reading, students have to find difficult words while they are reading. The frequency of using dictionary is often because in intensive reading, a text will be used to answer some questions, so the students have to know the meaning of all words in the text in order to make them easy to answer the questions.

In conclusion, through doing complex activities, extensive reading can broaden students' knowledge more than intensive reading. In extensive reading, students write summary and do presentation which lead them to minimize the use of dictionary. In opposition, the students' activities in intensive reading are more limited. The activities depend on the teacher's guidance only. This kind of activities will not encourage students to explore their abilities; they cannot broaden knowledge by themselves as well as in extensive reading.

(1) Extensive Reading

- Reading as much as possible, perhaps in and out of the classroom
- Being a variety of materials on a wide range of topics available
- Selecting what they want to read
- Relating the purposes of reading to pleasure, information, and general understanding
- Reading on its own reward.
- Reading materials well within the linguistic vocabulary and grammar
- Reading individually and silently at the students' own pace

(2) Intensive Reading

- Looking at different levels of comprehension (main idea vs. details)
- Understanding what is implied vs. what is stated
- Discussing what inferences a reader can reasonably make
- Determining the order in which information is presented and its effect on the message
- Identifying words that connect one idea to another
- Identifying words that signal movement from one section to another
- Noting which words indicate authors' certainty about the information presented

(3) Literature Reading

- Improving language proficiency
- Providing optimal input for language acquisition
- Providing contexts for language learning in which the language itself (syntax, semantics, and pragmatics) becomes more memorable
- Providing useful contexts for developing linguistic knowledge both on a usage and use level

- Providing authentic materials to read
- Giving students experience with various text types
- Providing lively, enjoyable, high-interest readings
- Increasing students' motivation to interact with a text and thus increase their reading proficiency
- Promoting students' cultural understanding and perhaps spur their own creation of imaginative works
- Personalizing the classroom by focusing on human experiences and needs
- Providing an opportunity for reflection and personal growth

3. Reading Curriculum

(1) Principles of Reading Curriculum

① Students build reading abilities through practice and exposure.
② Students engage in reading when texts are interesting, varied, abundant, accessible.
③ Students' choice for reading material leads engagement, motivation, autonomy.
④ Students call up background knowledge for comprehension.
⑤ Lessons should be around a pre-, during-, and post-reading framework.
⑥ Students need to experience success.
⑦ Actual texts should be included in class.
⑧ Curricular should integrate the instructional goals;
  - promote word recognition efficiency
  - assist students in building a large recognition vocabulary
  - create for comprehension skills practice
  - build students' discourse-structure awareness
  - develop strategic reader
  - build students' reading fluency
  - provide extensive reading
  - motivate students to read
  - integrate content- & language-learning goals

(2) Motivation for Reading

- Teachers identify students' interests to find related readings; teachers share their reading interests; teachers devise attention-catching introductions.

- Students share what they are reading; teachers grant students' choice in reading materials; teachers promote group cohesiveness; teachers help students discover what they learn from reading.
- Teachers build relevance into the curriculum; teachers guide students in building real levels of expertise (content-based instruction); teachers increase students' expectancy of success with texts within their ability levels.

4. Classroom Activities

When designing tasks for students, one of the most recommended routines is to design tasks that follow the format of pre-reading activities, while-reading activities and post-reading activities.

(1) Pre-reading Activities

These tasks are intended to construct background knowledge. The teacher becomes a bridge builder between what students already know about a concept – schemata – and what they need to know in order to understand a particular text, that is, the interaction between those schemata and the input coming from the text. Pre-reading tasks are intended to prepare the learners for a reading selection, or to give them the first steps in order to develop skills in anticipation and prediction for the reading, activating background knowledge so they could later interact with the text. With these tasks, teachers give students meaningful pieces of information that they would encounter in the reading.

(2) While-reading Activities

The aims of this stage are to help students to understand the specific content and to perceive the rhetorical structure of the text (Celce-Murcia, 1991). With these tasks teachers take the learners through the reading and they interact in the text.

(3) Post-Reading Activities

Post-reading tasks are intended to verify and expand the knowledge acquired in the reading. These last tasks also lead the learners to discuss and analyze issues presented in the reading. Post-activities are tasks in which learners, after interacting with the reading, reflect, argue and give their points of view.

(4) Authentic Material

Although textbooks reading materials may be appropriate for language readers, it is also good for learners to be challenged with authentic materials. Authentic materials are materials written by native writers for native readers.

5. Lesson Plan

Reading and listening should be treated somewhat differently from speaking and writing when planning a lesson. This is because they are receptive language skills while speaking and writing are productive language skills. The goal of all lesson plans should be for the students to produce the language, of course, but different skills focuses require a slightly different path, if you will. While productive lessons typically follow the PPP format, receptive lessons have a language focus and pre-, post-, and during reading activities, also called PDP (pre-, during, post-) format.

Lead In	As with a PPP lesson, you will want to begin the class by activating the students' background knowledge (what they already know about a topic or concept) and reduce their affective barriers (basically, make them feel comfortable using English.) For example, if you were reading Old Yeller, you could begin by asking the students if anyone had ever had a pet and then spend a few minutes talking about what it is like to own a pet. This will subtly get the students thinking about animals and pets before you introduce the book.
Language Focus	The language focus can occur at various points during a reading lesson. Some experts have very strong opinions about whether it should be a pre- or post-listening task. I like to introduce any language likely to prevent the students from easily understanding the story before they begin reading. If the story is at or below the students' level, then it can be left until after they have read, more as a reinforcement activity. Assuming you are introducing new language to the students, you should try to use as many methods as necessary to help them understand clearly: mime, gestures, flashcards, etc. You should also show them the words in writing. This is very important. Many students need to see something in writing to understand it clearly. Furthermore, there are generally so many ways in which a word could be spelled in English that many students are unlikely to guess the correct one on their own. Even if a word only has one acceptable spelling, your students can't be expected to guess what it is. To make it more visually appealing for my students, which will hopefully keep their attention a bit longer,
Pre-Reading	Before the students begin the text, they should be given a purpose for reading. Let them know there is a task waiting for them. Ask them some questions to get them to make predictions about what they are about to read. This will engage them in the text, because they will want to know if they were right. To create a prediction task, simply ask the students a few questions after showing them the cover, picture(s) from the story, or even just the title. If you want to get a little fancier, you can create a true/false handout with several statements about the story. After reading, they can go back and check their answers against what actually happened, but more about that in the post-reading section.

	If you are reading non-fiction, have the students fill out a KWL chart about what they already Know and what they Want to know. As a post-reading task, they can fill in what they Learned. They can use their KWL charts as a springboard for any number of activities, but let's save that for another time.
During Reading	There are two ways to have students read a text: for gist or for details. If you just want the students to focus on understanding the main idea, you will want to give them one (or more) gist tasks. On the other hand, if you want them to find specific information in the story, you will want to use detail tasks. If you want them to do both, you can have them read the text once quickly for the main idea, and again more slowly for a detail task. Some examples of detail tasks include: finding a phone number, price, TV show listing, train time on a schedule, a date, etc. Basically, any task which requires the students to listen for a name, number, or other specific information is a detail task. You could even pull out the true/ false questions and have students change the false questions to be true, according to the text.
Post-Reading	Once the students have read the text, they need to use it as a means to develop their language skills. There are any number of post-reading activities which can help students use the text and the terms introduced in the language focus. If they have filled out a KWL chart for a given text, have them discuss their answers with a partner. Since each student presumably knows at least slightly different things, they can compare and contrast what they knew before reading, what they were curious to learn (or predicted would be answered by they text), and what they actually learned. Alternatively, they could make posters to present to the class or write a response to the text. Other post-reading activities include creating a role play from the text. Students could discuss the text in groups to develop characters and write dialogue. They could then present the role play to their class. If they haven't done so already, they should go back to any predictions they made (written or not) and discuss how close they were to the actual story. This can be done as a class or in small groups, but in general, quieter students will be more likely to speak up in a crowd.
Wrap up	All good things must come to an end. You could end the lesson in a variety of ways: asking their favorite part, anything they didn't understand, etc. But, you should always provide feedback to the students, offering gentle corrections of errors overheard during the productive tasks. 예 "I heard X, but it is usually said Y in English."

03 Classroom Applications

1. Vocabulary activities

(1) Word recognition efficiency

　　word-recognition practice (eg. oral paired rereading, word matching, word recognition exercises, flashcards)

① Word- and phrase-recognition exercises
   - "Beat the clock" (timed recognition) : rapid word recognition play in reading

② Timed semantic-connection exercises
   - select the one word that (a) has something in common with the key word (b) is similar in meaning (c) is a common collocate of the key word

③ Lexical access fluency exercise
   - for more advanced students
   - advanced form of semantic-connection exercise
   - finding definitions in each set

(2) Large recognition vocabulary

① Procedures for selecting words for explicit instruction
   - a systematic way to decide which words to focus on; (+ +) (- -)

② Concept-of-definition map for introducing vocabulary
   - Students view a key word from four points.

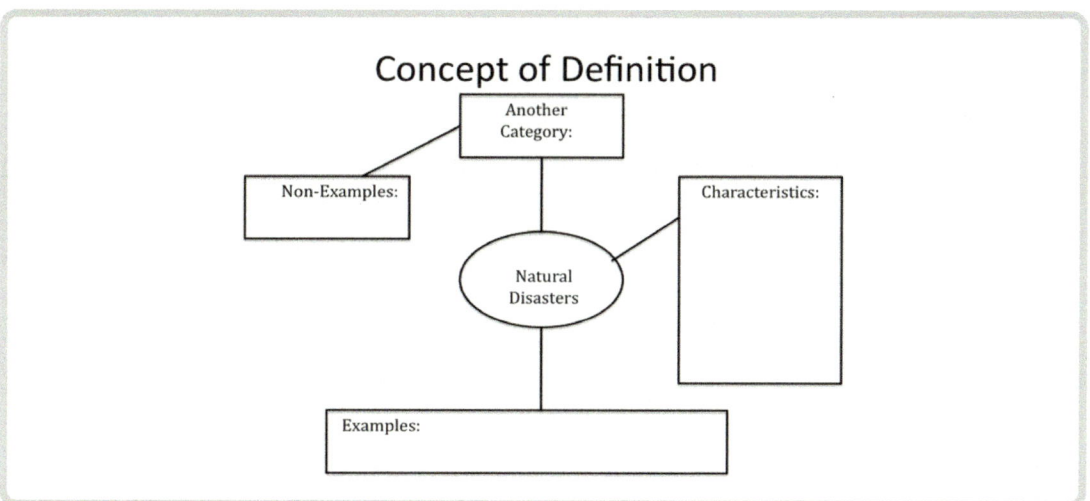

2. Reading Comprehension

(1) Skilled reading abilities

Automatic word-recognition & fluent phrase & clause-recognition	Decoding graphic forms
	Accessing the meanings of a large number of words
	Drawing meaning from phrase- and clause-level
Main idea comprehension using discourse structure	Combining clause meanings into text comprehension
	Recognizing discourse structures
Strategic processing for comprehension of difficult texts	Using reading strategies for academic reading tasks
	Setting goals for reading
	Using inferences
	Drawing on prior knowledge
	Evaluating, integrating, synthesizing information for critical reading comprehension
Reading fluency development & motivation	Maintaining these processes fluently
	Sustaining motivation

(2) Comprehension skills practice

① Comprehension: grammar knowledge, ability to identify main ideas, awareness of discourse structure and strategic processing

② Main-idea comprehension : Teacher assesses comprehension rather than teaches it.

③ Class conversation comprehension questions at post-reading
- Explain why an answer is appropriate.
- Point out where the text supports their answer.
- Discuss how to understand better, building reading strategies.
- Elaborative interrogation: 'why' questions with comprehension to reread and explain answers; exploration of main ideas, text recalling, inferencing, coherence building
- Comprehension monitoring: a reading strategy to improve main-idea comprehension and modeling the strategies, discussing them, guiding students in using them

(3) Discourse-structure awareness

Good readers recognize (a) how textual information is organized and (b) how discourse structure is signaled.

① Building discourse-structure awareness at pre-reading stage
- Students examine text headings and subheadings.
- Students hypothesize what each section is about.

② Raising Students' awareness of discourse-structure at during-reading stage
- Complete an outline of the text
- Fill in a graphic organizer
- Underline lexical clues
- Highlight transition words and phrases
- Assign a brief main-idea label to each paragraph

③ Building discourse-structure awareness at post-reading stage
- Students reread to match main ideas and supporting information.
- Students reorganize the scrambled paragraphs/ sentences.
- Students remove inappropriate parts in a teacher-generated summary.

3. Strategy Reading

(1) Strategic reader and promote strategic reading

① Directed Reading-Thinking Activity (DRTA)
- thinking like good readers: anticipating, predicting, confirming, modifying, summarizing
- prediction cycle: make predictions – confirm or refute predictions – discuss and reformulate predictions – summarize what they have read

② Know-Want-How-Learned chart (KWHL)
- for strategic reading and motivating
- pre-reading (KWH) and post-reading segment (L)

③ Identification of challenging parts of a text
- Students benefited from working through difficult texts as a class.
- Students discuss the process of comprehension and develop strategies to carry over to other reading contexts.

(2) Reading fluency

① Rereading
- rereading function: building reading fluency and consolidating content learning
- rereading tasks: fluency practice (skimming, scanning, inferencing) and vocabulary recycling

② Repeated reading
- unassisted repeated reading: reading short passages aloud alone until a set reading rate
- assisted repeated reading: reading passages; silently with audio, aloud with audio, or with a teacher.

③ Oral paired reading
- Fluency building: The goal is to advance further in the text in the second round.
- Students work in pairs with passages that already read for other purposes.

(3) Extensive reading: scaffolded silent reading (ScSR)

- Teacher schedules ScSR sessions regularly; students read student-selected materials and can change them.
- Teacher teaches strategies; teacher models fluent reading or comprehension strategy in short lesson.
- Teacher monitors students engagement and text comprehension; teacher holds students accountable for time spent reading silently.

(4) Concept-Oriented Reading Instruction (CORI)

instructional principles for stimulating students' interest and motivation to read

4 stages	Activities
• immersion in a main theme through students' personal engagement • wide reading & information • reading-strategy instruction • project work with outcome	• strategy training • vocabulary development • fluency practice • extensive reading

(5) Collaborative Strategic Reading (CSR)

- Reading comprehension-strategy instruction + Cooperative Learning principles
- Reciprocal teaching aims to promote content learning, language mastery, reading comprehension.

문헌읽기　**Learners' Reading Comprehension of Expository Texts**

1. **What Skillful Readers Can Do**

   There are three characteristics skillful readers have when they read expository texts: activation of their background knowledge, making inferences, and possession of rich experience.

   a. Activation of Background Knowledge

   When skillful readers happen upon information or words they have not learned, they activate their background knowledge to relate the new information or words to previously acquired information or word knowledge. Even when they simply read passages, they can bring out connected information as much as possible from their prior knowledge. For example, while reading a text about fish, they tap their schemata to gather information regarding fish, such as types of fish, places they live, and their characteristics. Making associations with the text information helps them understand the text. On the other hand, struggling readers do not connect new information or words to old by making use of their background knowledge. This isolates struggling readers and causes increased difficulty.

   b. Making Inferences

   Readers have to read between the lines and relate the text information that has a less explicit explanation to their existing knowledge for better comprehension. The use of background knowledge assists readers to grasp the content of expository texts, as they can refer to their prior knowledge in order to fill in gaps between old and new information. On the other hand, struggling readers have no idea what to do when they read a text because their critical thinking does not get involved in their reading process. They either keep reading without understanding much of what is written, or stop reading when they think they cannot understand any further.

   c. Possession of Rich Experience

   Another aspect of skillful readers is that they have rich experience; whereas, struggling readers generally lack experience and fail to establish their vocabulary knowledge or reading understanding. For example, if readers have a variety of experience with animals, it is less complicated for them to categorize animals, understand their characteristics, and learn new vocabulary related to animals. Reading can be more concrete to them because they know, or at least can guess, what a text is talking about. However, struggling readers who have less experience with animals may have a hard time understanding the content and making inferences from unfamiliar information in texts, for they do not have prior knowledge with which to make any connections.

2. **Suggested Strategies**

   There are some strategies that are recommended to develop a reader's vocabulary base and activate background knowledge for better understanding of expository texts.

   a. Use of Transition Words

   It is beneficial for readers to learn and practice recognizing key and clue words. If a text contains transition words such as "first," "second," and "third," readers know this text structure is listing some concepts or events in order. When readers know contradictory key words including "however," "but," and "on the other hand," they know they are going to read something opposed to the information they have just read. Additional clue words like "moreover," "in addition," and "also," assist readers in expecting that they will gain extra facts or concepts related to the information they have read so far, or in understanding that the sentences they are about to read will describe events, concepts, or facts before these particular transition words. In sum, learning to spot major and clue words aids readers to read the text clearly.

b. Organizing Text Information

Awareness of text pattern is indispensable for readers (Peregoy, & Boyle, 2001). Since expository texts contain specific text structure, it is useful for readers to know each text frame. If readers know they are reading passages that compare and contrast two things, events, or concepts, they can categorize information into appropriate groups. Koda (2005) points out the effectiveness of teaching how texts are organized by using first language experiences or knowledge. Reading a text with the understanding of its text framework helps readers organize information. This facilitates their reading comprehension.

c. Establishing Vocabulary Knowledge

Because expository texts tend to have complicated vocabularies, it is essential for readers to develop their vocabulary knowledge. Understanding new vocabulary should be meaningful to them. Memorizing new words without connecting them to readers' schemata may work in their short term memory. However, if readers learn unfamiliar vocabulary by associating it with something they already know, it is more effective for them to capture its meaning and store its information in their long term memory.

d. Use of Semantic Mapping

Semantic mapping is a graphic display that shows clusters of related words. Readers write down a key word or concept from their reading in the middle of a sheet, then add and connect linked information or terms from their prior knowledge. Relating words to their existing knowledge is important. This facilitates readers to connect their old and new information, which requires them to activate their background knowledge and cognitive processes.

e. Use of Vocabulary

Another approach for establishing vocabulary knowledge is making a "vocabulary card bank." On an index card, readers write a new word, its definition, and an original sentence using the new term (not just copying a sentence from a dictionary), as well as some pictures that can trigger them to remember the new vocabulary. This gets the readers involved in relating new vocabulary to their existing knowledge. In short, associating new terms with meaningful information is significant for readers to develop their vocabulary knowledge.

CHAPTER
05 Teaching Writing

단원 길라잡이
- 결과중심과 과정중심의 쓰기 지도법을 비교 분석한다.
- 과정중심 쓰기 지도법의 과정을 이해한다.

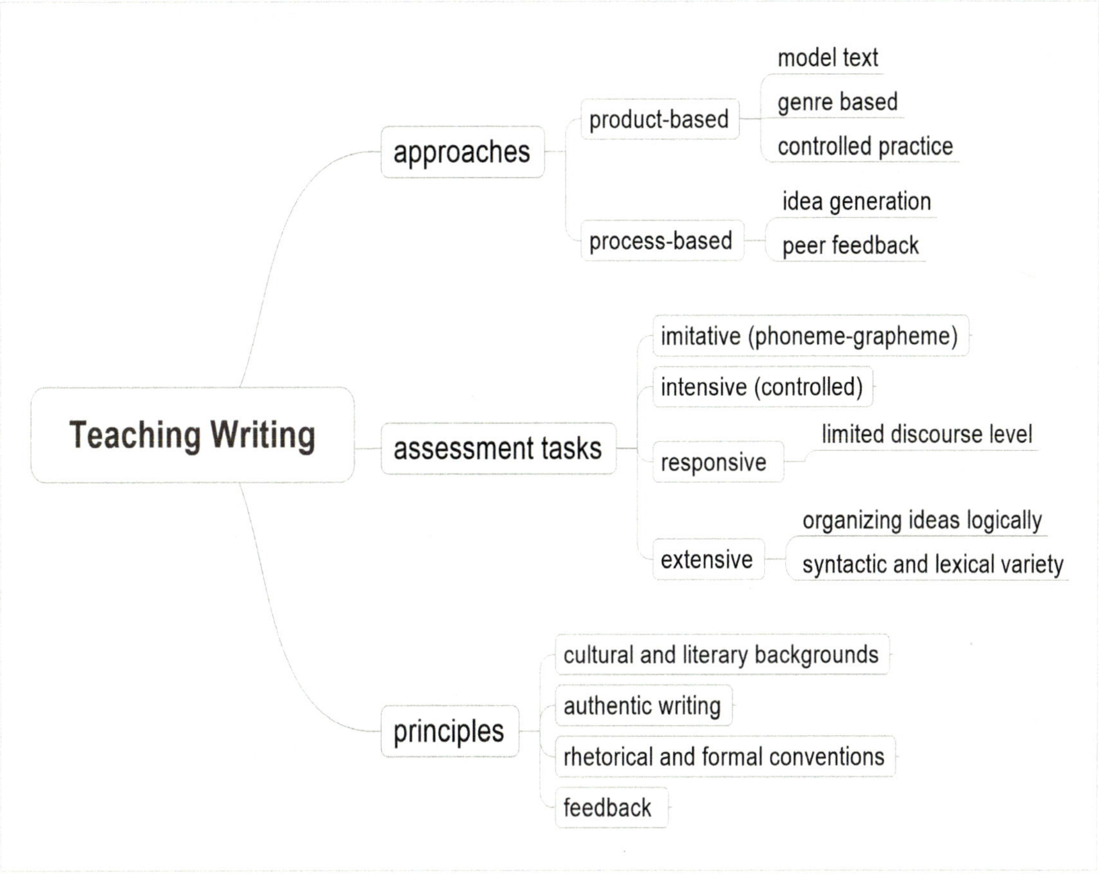

Teaching Writing

- approaches
  - product-based
    - model text
    - genre based
    - controlled practice
  - process-based
    - idea generation
    - peer feedback
- assessment tasks
  - imitative (phoneme-grapheme)
  - intensive (controlled)
  - responsive — limited discourse level
  - extensive
    - organizing ideas logically
    - syntactic and lexical variety
- principles
  - cultural and literary backgrounds
  - authentic writing
  - rhetorical and formal conventions
  - feedback

01 Writing Approaches

1. Product and Process-based approaches

(1) Differences between writing approaches

Product approach	Process approach
• Stage 1: Model texts are read, and then features of the genre are highlighted. • Stage 2: This consists of controlled practice of the highlighted features, usually in isolation. • Stage 3: Organisation of ideas. This stage is very important. • Stage 4: The end result of the learning process. Students choose from a choice of comparable writing tasks.	• Stage 1: Generating ideas by brainstorming and discussion. • Stage 2: Students extend ideas into note form, and judge quality and usefulness of ideas. • Stage 3: Students organise ideas into a mind map, spidergram, or linear form. • Stage 4: Students write the first draft. This is done in class and frequently in pairs or groups. • Stage 5: Drafts are exchanged, so that students become the readers of each other's work. • Stage 6: Drafts are returned and improvements are made based upon peer feedback. • Stage 7: A final draft is written. • Stage 8: Students once again exchange and read each other's work and perhaps even write a response or reply.
This is a traditional approach, in which students are encouraged to mimic a model text, which is usually presented and analysed at an early stage. • text as a resource for comparison • imitate model text • one draft • features highlighted including controlled practice of those features • individual • emphasis on end product	Process approaches to writing tend to focus more on the varied classroom activities which promote the development of language use: brainstorming, group discussion, re-writing. • ideas as starting point • more than one draft • more global, focus on purpose, theme, text type, i.e., reader is emphasised • collaborative • emphasis on creative process

Process-driven approaches show some similarities with task-based learning, in that students are given considerable freedom within the task. They are not curbed by preemptive teaching of lexical or grammatical items. However, process approaches do not repudiate all interest in the product, (i.e. the final draft). The aim is to achieve the best product possible. What differentiates a process-focussed approach from a product-centered one is that the outcome of the writing, the product, is not preconceived.

(2) Which approach in use

The approach that you decide to use will depend on you, the teacher, and on the students, and the genre of the text. Certain genres lend themselves more favourably to one approach than the other. Formal letters, for example, or postcards, in which the features are very fixed, would be perhaps more suited to a product-driven approach, in which focus on the layout, style, organisation and grammar could greatly help students in dealing with this type of writing task.

Other genres, such as discursive essays and narrative, may lend themselves to process-driven approaches, which focus on students' ideas. Discursive activities are suited to brainstorming and discussing ideas in groups, and the collaborative writing and exchanging of texts help the students to direct their writing to their reader, therefore making a more successful text.

The two approaches are not necessarily incompatible. I believe that process writing, i.e. re-drafting, collaboration, can be integrated with the practice of studying written models in the classroom. What I take from the process approach is the collaborative work, the discussion which is so important in generating and organising ideas. Once students have written their first drafts, model texts can be introduced as texts for comparison. Lightbown found that learning appeared to be optimal in 'those situations in which the students knew what they wanted to say and the teacher's intervention made clear to them there was a particular way to say it.' Teacher intervention through model texts could thus aid the learning process.

I also like to incorporate the exchanging of drafts, so that the students become the readers of each others work. This is an important part of the writing experience as it is by responding as readers, both during the collaborative stage of writing in groups, as well as when reading another group's work, that students develop an awareness of the fact that a writer is producing something to be read by someone else. As Lewis Carroll makes clear in Alice's adventures in Wonderland. "I haven't opened it yet," said the White Rabbit, "but it seems to be a letter, written by the prisoner to somebody." "It must have been that," said the King, "unless it was written to nobody, which isn't usual, you know."

2. Conferencing

The focus of the conference as below for the student's draft, and the extract serves to show significant aspects of the teacher's approach to writing.

① Students are actually involved in the process of writing in class.

② With the supports of colleagues and the teacher, the student is able to engage in the creation of a contextualized piece of communication, a review.

③ The main focus of this conference is on the ideas student wants to express and on ways of organizing them. Student provides her own context for learning the vocabulary 'interact', 'misuse', and 'pebble' that she needs, and because her immediate needs are supplied she is very quick to pick them up.

S: My problem here is ... I want to say ... I want to write about the characters and how they are ... how they act ... together ...

T: The way they interact ... yes ...

S: Interact ... yes, so that's the plot, isn't it? But also, it's the theme, I think. I'm not sure how I should start ...

T: Well, what's the most important thing about the play to you?

S: How he shows the middle class people ... they are just super – superficial ... and they don't care about the working class ...

S: [who is listening in] The bourgeoisie... they are hypocrites ... n'cest ce pas?

T: Yes, we can use the French word ... bourgeoisie ... Well, why not put that first and then go on to explain how he does this, by presenting a particular family...

S: So, this bit here [reads] 'The Birlings are a middle class family ...' up to here ... yes, I think so ... this can follow?

T: Let's look at it .. [reads] Priestley shows how they ...' you can say 'misuse' here... 'their power'. Yes, that's very clear. You've got a couple of wrong spellings here. I'll underline them quickly and you can look at them later. Don't bother till you've finished the writing.

S: So what about this bit...?

T: What does this say...? I can't read it...

S: [reads] 'Stone... a small stone...'

T: Ah, you mean a pebble... Oh, that's very good, we can talk about throwing a pebble into a pool.. it describes it very well.

S: You see... what happens... the story... its' how when you throw a st– pebble? ... pebble in the water... you get waves going out...

T: Yes, ripples... [demonstrates] ripples spreading...

S: So the inspector shows the family how...

Note: S=student, T=teacher

02 Writing Assessment Tasks

(1) Imitative or Writing down

This category includes the ability to spell correctly and to perceive phoneme-grapheme correspondences in the English spelling system. At this stage, form is the primary if not exclusive focus, while context and meaning are of secondary concern.

예 *assessment tasks: writing letters, words, and punctuation*

- Copying
- Listening cloze selection tasks
- Picture-cued writing exercises
- Completing forms and questionnaires

(2) Intensive or controlled

As one may think, intensive writing as described here has nothing to do with writing intensively, but controlled. Under this definition, students are supposed to copy sentences and words, rewrite texts and passages, order sentences among others.

① Dictation
- Dictation is basically copying what your hear (imitative)
- Rewrite a paragraph with their recollection from what was understood

② Grammatical transformation tasks
- combination of sentences or reduced forms
- practical, reliable
- direct to indirect and active to passive

(3) Responsive

It requires learners to perform at a limited discourse level, connecting sentences into a paragraph and creating a logically connected sequence of two or three paragraphs. The writer has already mastered the fundamentals of sentence-level grammar and is more focused on the discourse conventions that will achieve the objectives of the written text. 예 brief narratives and descriptions, a lab report, summaries and etc.

(4) Extensive

It implies successful management of all the processes and strategies of writing for all purposes. Writers work focusing on the achievement of a purpose. Organizing ideas logically, using details to support or illustrate it and demonstrating syntactic and lexical variety; 예 an essay, a term paper, a major research project report, a thesis and etc.

Both extensive and responsive writers are able to produce real writing. They are able to process ideas in a conscious way and their texts are expected to be meaningful. They become involved in the art of composing a text instead of simply displaying it.

① Common issues related to assess responsive and extensive writers:

- Authenticity : It is a trait that is given special attention. You need to check the validity of the production presented by a test-taker and it needs to be authentic in order to bring out the best in the writer. In this case the teacher becomes less of an instructor and more of a coach or facilitator.
- Scoring : These two last stages (responsive and extensive) are the hardest to be assessed. You must assess not only the form (the way the writer put words together), but also the function of the text (what the writer is trying to say).
- Time : It is the only skill in which the writer is not constrained by time. The writer is free to write as many drafts as he wants before it becomes a final product.

② Designing Assessment Tasks: Responsive and Extensive writing

- Paraphrasing
- Guided Question and Answer
- Paragraph
    - Topic Sentence writing
    - Topic Development within a paragraph
    - Development of main and supporting ideas across paragraphs

Imitative and Intensive	Responsive and Extensive
• Produce graphemes and orthographic patterns of English. • Produce writing at an efficient rate of speed to suit the purpose. • Produce an acceptable core of words and use appropriate word order patterns.	• Use the rhetorical forms and conventions of written discourse. • Appropriately accomplish the communicative functions of written texts according to form and purpose. • Distinguish between literal and implied meanings when writing.

03 Principles for teaching Writing Skills

(1) Incorporate Practices of Good Writers.

① Pre-Writing
② Drafting
③ Real Writing
④ Free-Writing
⑤ Revising

- spend some time planning to write
- focus on a goal or main idea in writing
- follow a general organizational plan as they write
- perceptively gauge their audience & purpose
- easily let their first ideas flow onto the paper
- are not wedded to certain surface structures
- revise their work willingly and efficiently
- solicit and utilize feedback on their writing

Revising의 예시: Time Expressions and Tenses

1. Use the following time expressions to express things that happen during the day.

| in the morning | in the afternoon | in the evening | at night |

They do the cleaning in the morning.
He goes to bed late at night.

2. Time Expressions to use with the Present Simple

| every day | every month, year, etc. | adverbs of frequency (usually, sometimes, often, etc.) |

She travels to Las Vegas every year.
Jack tries to exercise every day.
They sometimes play golf.
She rarely smokes.

3. Time Expressions to use with the Present Continuous

| now | today | at the moment |

Tom is watching TV now.
I'm working on the Smith project today.
Jane is doing her homework at the moment.

4. Time Expressions often used in the Past

| last | yesterday | ago | when | in |

> *They went on holiday last month.*   *I visited my best friend yesterday.*
> *We flew to Cleveland three weeks ago.*   *She graduated in 1976.*
> *I played tennis every day when I was a teenager.*
>
> 5. Time Expressions used in the Future
>
> | next | by (date) | tomorrow | by the time + time clause |
> | in X weeks, days, years time | | | |
>
> *We are going to visit our friends in Chicago next week.*
> *He'll be at the meeting tomorrow.*
> *We will be swimming in a crystal blue sea in two weeks time.*
> *I will have finished the report by April 15.*
> *She will have bought a new home by the time he arrives.*

(2) Balance process and product.

Students are carefully led through appropriate stages in the process of composing. This includes careful attention to your own role as a guide and as a responder. At the same time, don't get so caught up in the stages leading up to the final product that your lose sight of the ultimate attainment: a clear, articulate, well-organized, effective piece of writing.

(3) Account for cultural/ literary backgrounds.

If there are some apparent contrasts between students' native traditions and those that your are trying to teach, try to help students to understand what it is, exactly, that they are accustomed to and then, by degrees, bring them to the use of acceptable English rhetoric.

(4) Connect reading and writing.

Students learn to write in part by carefully observing what is already written. By reading and studying a variety of relevant types of text, students can gain important insights both about how they should write and about subject matter that may become the topic of their writing.

(5) Provide as much authentic writing as possible.

Whether writing is real writing or for display writing, it can still be authentic in that the purposes for writing are clear to the students, the audience is specified overtly, and there is at least some intent to convey meaning. Sharing writing with other students in the class is one way to add authenticity. 예 Publishing a class newsletter, writing letters to people outside of class, writing a script for a skit or dramatic presentation, writing a resume, writing advertisement.

(6) Frame your techniques in terms of prewriting, drafting, and revising stages.

① Pre-writing stage encourages the generation of ideas in numerous ways:
- reading : reading extensively, skimming & scanning a passage
- brainstorming : group work and free writing
- clustering : begin with a key word, then add other words, using free association
- listing : in writing – individually
- discussing a topic or question

② Drafting / revising stages are the core of process writing.
- getting started: adapting the freewriting technique
- optimal monitoring of one's writing: without premature editing and diverted attention to wording, grammar, etc.
- peer-reviewing for content: accepting/ using classmates' comments
- using the instructor's feedback
- editing for grammatical errors
- proofreading

(7) Strive to offer techniques that are as interactive as possible.

- interactive : Students work in pairs and groups to generate ideas and to peer-edit.
- learner centered : Students have ample opportunities to initiate activity and exchange ideas.
- focus on purposes : letters, forms, memos, directions, short reports

(8) Apply methods of responding to and correcting your students' writing.

① Guidelines for first draft
- Resist the temptation to treat minor-local grammatical errors; major-global errors within relevant paragraphs can at this stage be indicated directly or indirectly.
- Comment holistically, in terms of the clarity of the overall thesis and the general structural organization.
- Comment on the introductory paragraph.

② Guidelines for second draft
- Minor (local) grammatical and mechanical (spelling, punctuation) errors should be indicated, but not corrected for the student.
- Comment on the specific clarity and strength of all main ideas, supporting ideas, and on argument and logic.
- Check cohesive devices within and across paragraphs.
- Comment on the adequacy and strength of the conclusion.

(9) Instruct the rhetorical, formal conventions of academic writing.
- a clear statement of the thesis or topic or purpose
- use of main ideas to develop or clarify the thesis
- use of supporting ideas
- describing, giving evidence, facts, statistic, etc.
- linking cause and effect
- using comparison and contrast

04 Feedback on writing

(1) Teacher's responding

> **Dear Mihyun,**
> I really enjoyed reading your draft. You have some good expression, "… you look to the dark sky and it seems like…" Why don't you begin with that sentence? "… I looked up at the dark sky and it seemed a special.." Then you can explain what New York's Eve means in Korea, how families and friends come together and how everyone hopes for the future.

Responding to student writing by the teacher (or by peers) has a central role to play in the successful implementation of process writing. Responding intervenes between drafting and revising. It is the teacher's quick initial reaction to students' drafts. Response can be oral or in writing, after the students have produced the first draft and just before they proceed to revise. The failure of many writing programmes in schools today may be ascribed to the fact that responding is done in the final stage when the teacher simultaneously responds and evaluates, and even edits students' finished texts, thus giving students the impression that nothing more needs to be done. Text-specific responses in the form of helpful suggestions and questions rather than 'rubber-stamped' comments ('organisation is OK', 'ideas are too vague' etc.) by the teacher will help students rediscover meanings and facilitate the revision of initial drafts.

(2) Correction Symbols

This is a common tool to optimise learning opportunities from mistakes learners make in written homework and to encourage the editing stages of process writing. A teacher shows the learners where the mistakes are and what kind they are, and then they try to correct them as a second stage to the initial writing task. The codes shown here are just an example and are not meant to all be used at every level. You need to find out which ones work for the learners.

Symbol	Meaning	Example error
S	Spelling error	*The <u>naswer</u> is obvious.*
WO	Mistake in word order	*I <u>like very much it</u>.*
G	Grammar mistake	*I am going to buy some furniture<u>s</u>.*
T	Wrong verb tense	*I <u>have seen him</u> yesterday.*
C	Coordinated mistake (예 the subject verb agreement)	*People <u>is</u> angry.*
∧	Something has been left out.	*He told ∧ that he was sorry.*
WW	Wrong word	*I am interested <u>on</u> jazz music.*
{ }	Not necessary.	*He was not {too} strong enough.*
M	Meaning is unclear.	*That is a <u>very excited photograph</u>.*
P	Punctuation mistake	*Do you like <u>l</u>ondon.*
F/I	Formal or informal	*<u>Hi Mr Franklin,</u> Thank you for your letter…*

CHAPTER 06 Form-focused Instruction

> 단원 길라잡이
> - 문법 교수방법의 종류를 알고 활용방법을 이해한다.
> - Focus-on-FormS와 Focus-on-Form의 다른 교수유형을 비교분석한다.

교육과정

언어 형식은 의사소통 중심의 교육에서 언어 형식의 필요성 때문에 개정 교육과정에서 보완된 부분이다. 즉, 의사소통능력을 키우기 위해 유창성을 강조한 이면에는 정확성에 대한 배려 또한 소홀히 할 수 없기 때문이다. 그러나 영어교육의 목표로 유창성과 정확성을 함께 추구하는 것을 전제로 했을 때, 의사소통 기능과 언어 형식 양쪽을 모두 추구해야 하지만 과거의 영어교육에서처럼 언어 형식에 지나치게 집중하는 것을 우려하여 '참고 자료'의 성격으로 제시한 것이다. 따라서 문법 용어를 사용하여 지도하는 것이 권장되지는 않는다.

교육과정에서는 의사소통 기능과 언어 형식을 구분하여 제시하고 있다. 언어 형식은 6차 교육과정에서는 없던 부분으로 의사소통에 필요한 언어 형식을 의미한다. 실제 의사소통 기능과 예시문에 한정하여 영어 학습을 한 결과, 문법에 대한 정확한 지식이 부족한 채로 언어 능력을 습득하는 것에는 한계가 있었으며, 언어 형식은 이러한 배경 하에 탄생한 것이다. 또한 이것은 EFL 환경에서 영어를 학습하는 경우의 한계점을 고려하여 교육과정에 신설된 부분이다. 즉, 충분한 언어 입력에 노출된 ESL 환경일 경우, 의사소통을 통해서 유창성과 함께 언어 형식을 체득할 수 있으나 우리나라와 같은 EFL 상황에서는 불충분한 언어 입력량으로 인해 유창성과 정확성을 동시에 충족시키기는 어려운 상황이다. 언어 형식은 이러한 배경 하에 신설된 것이다. '의사소통 기능과 예시문에 제시된 형식을 우선으로 하되, 충분하지 않을 때는 의사소통에 필요한 언어 형식을 참고할 것'을 권장한다. 교육과정에 제시된 의사소통 기능, 예시문, 언어 형식이 필요한 표현을 다 포괄하는 것에는 또한 한계가 있다. 개정 교육과정에 제시된 언어 형식 항목은 총 36개로서, 시제, 진행형, 완료형, 부정문, 의문문, 조동사, 부정사, 사역동사, 동명사, 수동태, 단·복수 대명사, 유도 부사, 비인칭 주어, 비교급, 최상급, 동등 비교, 의문형용사, 부사, 접속사, 등위 접속사, 관계 대명사, 명사절, 화법, 분사 구문, 가정법, 도치 구문, 강조 구문, 생략, 동격, 한정 표현, 부가 의문문, 가주어·가목적어, 문장 형식 등이다. 제시된 언어 형식은 문법 용어를 사용하지 않고 제시된 문장을 활용하여 의사소통 활동을 하는 가운데 귀납적으로 해당 언어 형식을 인지할 수 있도록 한다.

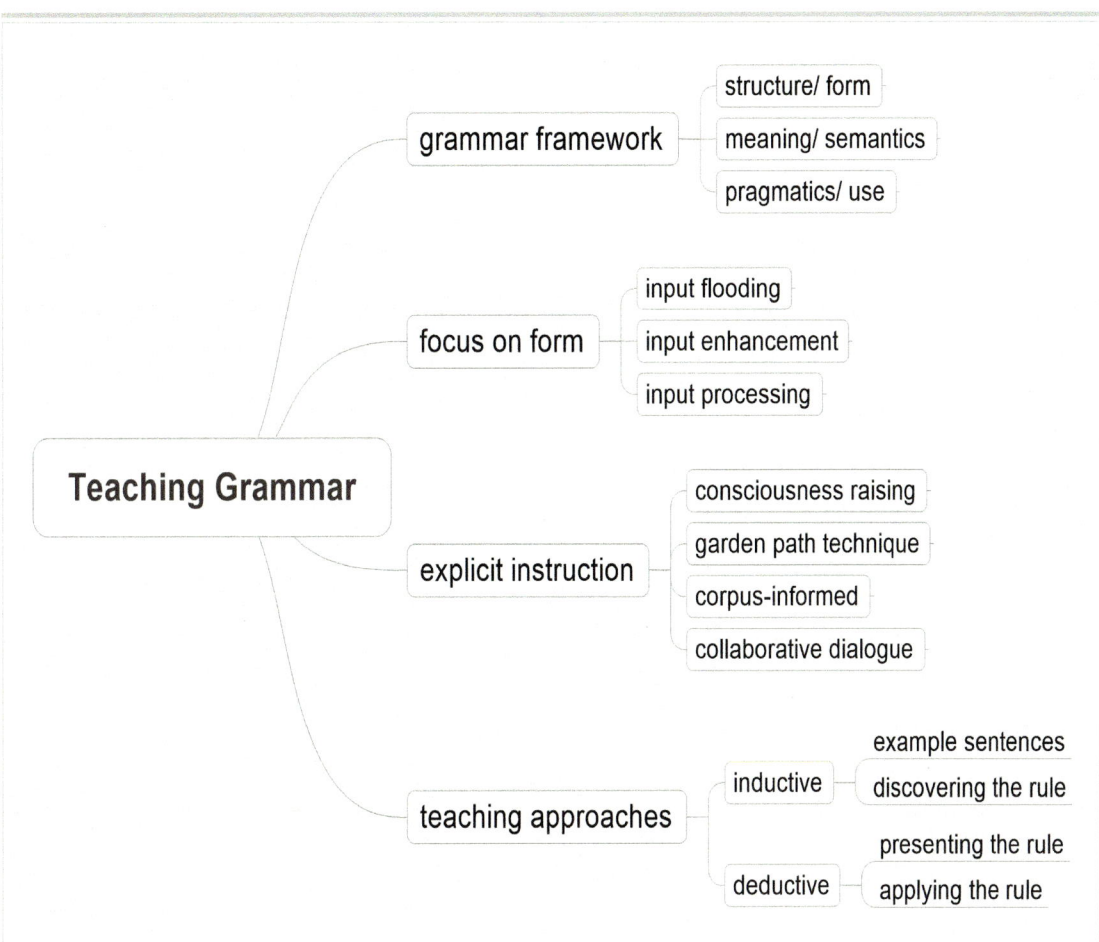

01 Classroom Applications

1. Teaching Process

(1) Grammaring

A goal of grammar instruction should be grammaring for the following reasons;

- to promote students' awareness and to engage students in meaningful production
- to move beyond semantic processing to syntactic processing
- to test their hypothesis

(2) Three-dimensional grammar framework

Form (Structure)	Meaning (Semantics)	Use (Pragmatics)
a great deal of meaningful iteration 예 language game: 'complete a family portrait'	fast mapping of form and meaning 예 'an operation': making a telephone call	difficult to select a construction for a context 예 role plays, discipline-based writing
• lexicogrammatical patterns and morphosyntactic forms • sound(phonemic), writing patterns(graphemic)	(a) lexical meaning: dictionary definition (b) grammatical meaning: 예 conditional states both a condition and an outcome	the use of language in context (a) Paradigmatic choice • 'Do you have time?' vs 'Please tell me the time.' (b) Syntagmatic choice • 'Jenny gave Hank a brand-new comb.' vs 'Jenny gave a brand-new comb to Hank.'
phrasal verbs		
• verb + particle (+preposition) • separable/ inseparable	• literal, figurative, multiple meanings • focal attention is given to meaning (no systematic way of learning)	• informal discourse • principle of dominance

2. Focus on Form

Input enhancement	Input flooding	Input processing
to receive students' attention through highlighting	to get saliency and noticing through choosing texts with frequency	to attend to language structure meaningfully

(1) Input Enhancement

To highlight it in a text in some fashion; enhancing the input might be an especially effective way to focus students' attention on grammar structures. Choosing texts in which a particular structure or structural contrast or especially frequent would enhance its saliency and thus might promote noticing. In the technique known as input enhancement, forms are highlighted with different colored inks, bold lettering, underlining, or other cues intended to raise students' awareness of a structure. Fotos (2002) describes an implicit structure-based task in which students compared two cities. Pairs of students told each other about features of familiar cities and recorded the information on task sheets. They were then instructed to write sentences comparing the cities according to the features they had described. Students were not explicitly taught comparative structures at any point during the task, but they had to use comparative forms to complete it. Afterwards, their instructor taught a lesson on comparatives, and students rewrote incorrect sentences, did more production exercises, and read stories that contained frequent instances of the comparative form.

(2) Input Processing

Rather than working on rule learning and rule application, input processing activities push learners to attend to properties of language during activities where the structure is being used meaningfully. Learners make use of this material for dual purposes, namely, comprehension and acquisition.

1) Principles

A basic understanding for SLA researchers is that, as input is converted into intake, learners make use of this material for dual purposes, namely, comprehension and acquisition. Drawing this distinction is important for both theory-making and empirical investigations (Faerch & Kasper, 1980; Krashen, 1982; Sharwood Smith, 1986; Swain, 1985; VanPatten, 1996). Learners have the natural inclination to decode linguistic input for meaning to achieve successful communication. But the type of intake derived from processing-for-meaning is not equivalent or sufficient to that which is needed for acquisition, which entails the creation of new or revised mental structures.

2) Beyond Immersion program

Swain's (1985) study of a French immersion program revealed that, based on communicative and comprehensible input alone, learners may achieve native-like proficiency in their comprehension. But their proficiency and accuracy in production lags behind that of native speakers despite years of exposure. Swain's study provides support that comprehensible input does not necessarily lead to acquisition. At the same time, it is also true that, without comprehensible input, learners would not be able to make the necessary form-meaning connection for acquisition to occur. This distinction between processing for comprehension and acquisition is another concept that is commonly accepted in the field of SLA research. The models focus on how input is processed differently for comprehension and acquisition, and they lay out additional processes that need to occur beyond comprehension to trigger acquisition.

3. Explicit Grammar Instruction

Consciousness-raising	Garden path	Corpus-informed	Collaborative dialogue
to induce grammatical generalization	to teach the exceptions to the rule from the students' overgeneralization	(data-driven approach) to learn from genuine examples	to discuss the use of language in interaction

(1) Consciousness-Raising task

1) Instructional Activity

Explicit techniques include consciousness-raising tasks, during which learners are encouraged to determine grammar rules from evidence presented, and the focused communicative task (Ellis, 2001), which is designed to bring about the production of a target form in the context of performing a communicative task. The latter task is designed in such a way that the target feature is essential to the performance of the task. For example, a task might require one student to give another student detailed instructions for the creation of an origami bird. The first student will likely feel a need to use adverbs such as *first*, *now*, *then*, and *next* to talk the second student through the sequential steps of the task.

2) Comparisons between consciousness-raising and practice

It should be clear from this list that the main purpose of consciousness-raising is to develop explicit knowledge of grammar. I want to emphasise, however, that this is not the same as metalingual knowledge. It is perfectly possible to develop an explicit understanding of how a grammatical structure works without learning much in the way of grammatical terminology. Grammar can be explained, and, therefore, understood in everyday language. It may be, however, that access to some metalanguage will facilitate the development of explicit knowledge.

The main difference is that consciousness-raising does not involve the learner in repeated production. This is because the aim of this kind of grammar teaching is not to enable the learner to perform a structure correctly but simply to help her to 'know about it'. Here is how Rutherford and Sharwood(1985) put it : CR is considered as a potential facilitator for the acquisition of linguistic competence and has nothing directly to do with the use of that competence for the achievement of specific communicative objectives, or with the achievement of 'fluency'.

Whereas practice is primarily behavioural, consciousness-raising is essentially concept-forming in orientation. The two types of grammar work are not mutually exclusive, however. Thus, grammar teaching can involve a combination of practice and consciousness-raising and, indeed, traditionally does so. Thus, many methodologists recommend that practice work be preceded by a presentation stage, to ensure that the learners have a clear idea about what the targeted structure consists of. This presentation stage may involve an inductive or deductive treatment of the structure.

(2) Garden Path strategy

This means giving students information about structure without giving them the full picture, thus making it seem easier than it is. The reason for giving students only a partial explanation is that they are more likely to learn the exception to the overgeneralization error is made than if they are given a long list of "exceptions to the rule" to memorize in advance. Error correction strategies are another way to explicitly focus on form within a primarily meaning-focused activity, in that they help learners notice differences between their production and the target.

In the example below, the student is corrected and thereby is made aware of the exception to the grammatical rule. Celce-Murcia (2007) suggests that, instead of creating grammar correction exercises using decontextualized sentences from learners' writing, teachers should create short texts that include common error types made by students in their writing. Students can work together to edit the more authentic texts, which helps them learn to correct their own work more successfully. Among these strategies, the *garden path technique* introduces a grammatical rule and then leads learners into situations in which they may overgeneralize, so they can consider the correct form. Nation & Newton (2008) give the following example of a typical garden path technique:

Teacher:	Here is a sentence using these words: *think* and *problem*. *I thought about the problem*. Now you make one using these words: *talk* and *problem*.
Learner:	We talked about the problem.
Teacher:	Good. *Argue* and *result*.
Learner:	We argued about the result.
Teacher:	Good. *Discuss* and *advantages*.
Learner:	We discussed about the advantages.
Teacher:	No. With *discuss* we do not use *about*.

(3) Collaborative dialogue

Through Collaborative dialogue learners can provide support for each other, has spurred development of learners' interlanguage. Larsen-Freeman (2003) discusses and gives examples of the following techniques. *Collaborative dialogues* are conversations in which students work together to discuss and use a new form, constructing a sentence together. The teacher coaches the student through the process of writing or saying something in English, perhaps incorporating the use of a new form. In the following example of a proleptic conversation, a teacher talks with a student who is writing a description of an important event in her past.

S:	(S writes "My baby was angry.") I pick her up, but she cry.
T:	Good. Ok, cry when? Now?
S:	No, she cried.
T:	Yes. Go ahead and write it. I'll help.
S:	(S writes "She cryed.")
T:	Right. But remember what happens to the "y"?
S:	(S erases "cryed" and writes "cried.")
T:	Right. What happened then?

In the conversation above, both teacher and student are engaged in the story. The teacher directs the student to focus also on the formation of the past tense but does not simply tell her to use the past tense form of *cry*, nor does she tell her how to spell it. In other words, the teacher defines the parameters of the problem for the student but encourages her to come to the answer on her own.

4. Providing Feedback

Options		Description
Reactive	Implicit feedback	Teacher or another student responds to a student's error without directly indicating an error has been made, e.g., by means of a recast or a clarification request.
	Explicit feedback	Teacher or another student responds to a student's error by directly indicating that an error has been made, e.g., by formally correcting the error or by using metalanguage.
Pre-emptive	Student-initiated focus on form	A student asks a question about a linguistic form.
	Teacher-initiated focus on form	Teacher gives advice about a linguistic form she thinks might be problematic or asks students a question about the form.

02. Teaching activities

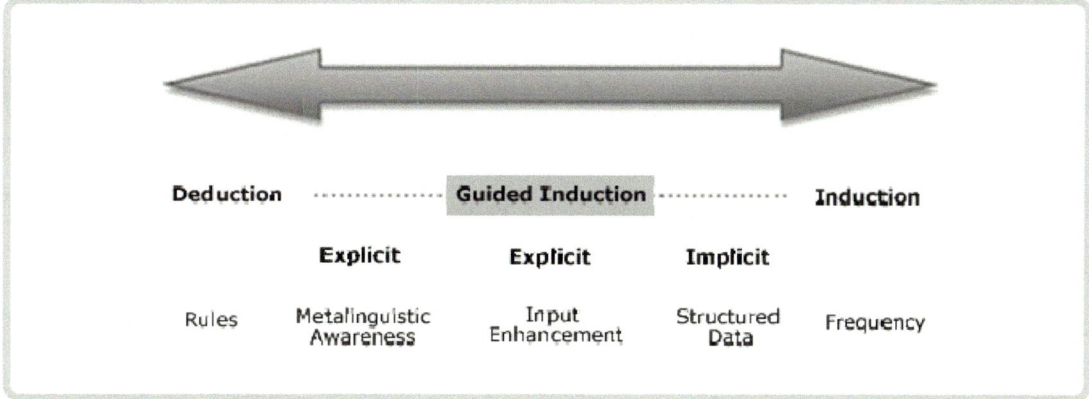

1. Inductive Activity

- An inductive approach such as using a consciousness-raising task is desirable because by using such an approach one is nurturing within the students a way of thinking.
- Teachers can assess what the students already know about a particular structure and make any necessary adjustments in their lesson plan.

▶ **Sample Lesson** Teaching the difference between past simple and present perfect through minimal sentence pairs (Pre-intermediate)

Step 1

The teacher writes the following three sets of sentences on the board:

① a. I've seen all of Jim Jarmusch's films.
   b. I saw his latest film last month.

② a. Since 1990, she's worked for three different newspapers.
   b. She worked for The Observer in 1996.

③ a. Have you ever been to Peru?
   b. When were you in Peru?

He asks the class first to identify the two verb structures in each of the sets, and establishes that each sentence a. is an example of the present perfect, while each sentence b. is an example of the past simple. If students are in any doubt about this, he quickly recaps the rules of form for each of these structures.

Step 2

He then asks the learners to consider the differences in meaning in each case, and to see if they can come up with a general rule for the difference between the present perfect and the past simple. He allows them to discuss this in pairs. In checking this task, he elicits the fact that the present perfect is used to talk about experience but without specifying when it happened. The past simple, on the other hand, is used to talk about a specific experience, often at a specified past time. To clarify this point, he draws the following timelines on the board and asks students to match them to the examples a. and b.

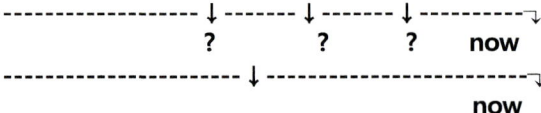

Step 3

He divides the class into pairs and sets them the following exercise which require them to choose between the two forms. Complete this job interview between an Interviewer(I) and a

Candidate(C). Put the verbs in brackets in the Present Perfect or Past Simple.

I : So, tell me a little about the things you... (do)
C : Well, I .. (study) French and German at university. Then, I .. (teach) in secondary school for a few years.
I : ... you (enjoy) teaching?
C : No, not really. I ... (not like) the discipline problems. So, I ... (start) working for a large drug company.
I : ... you (work) abroad at all?

2. Deductive Activity

- The teacher would present the generalization and then ask students to apply it to the language sample.
- If a student has particular cognitive style that is not well suited for language analysis, it may make more sense to present a grammar structure deductively.

▶ **Sample Lesson**

T : Right. The past perfect. (cueing)
T : The past perfect is formed from the past of the auxiliary 'have', plus the past participle. (rule of form)
T : For example, 'everyone had left', 'the film had started'. (examples)
T : So, what's the past perfect of 'they go'? (check)
S : 'They had gone.'
T : Good.
T : It is used when you are talking about the past, and you want to refer to an earlier point in the past. (rule of use)
T : For example, 'We were late. When we got to the cinema, the film had already started.' (example)
T : Did the film start after we arrived, at the same time as we arrived, or before we arrived? (check)
S : Before.
T : Right.
T : So, it's like this. [draws]

　　　　　------- (b) ------- (a) ------- ▶ (illustration)

T : We arrived at this point in time (a), but I need to refer to an earlier point in the past, when the film started, here (b).

03 Focus-on-form and Focus-on-formS Approaches

1. Differences

(1) Focus-on-formS

Focus-on-formS is equated with the traditional teaching of discrete points of grammar in separate lessons. It is based on the assumption that classroom foreign or second language learning derives from general cognitive processes, and thus entails the learning of a skill hence its being characterized as a 'skills-learning approach'. As such, it comprises three stages;

① providing understanding of the grammar by a variety of means (including explanation in the L1, pointing out differences between the L1 and the L2)

② exercises entailing using the grammar in both non-communicative and communicative activities for both comprehension and production

③ providing frequent opportunities for communicative use of the grammar to promote automatic, accurate use

(2) Focus-on-form

Focus-on-form refers to drawing students' attention to linguistic elements as they arise incidentally in lessons whose overriding focus is on meaning or communication (Long 1991:45-6). This derives from an assumed degree of similarity between L1 and L2 acquisition positing that the two processes are both based on an exposure to comprehensible input arising from natural interaction. However, it is also assumed that there are significant differences in the two processes;

① Exposure is insufficient to enable learners to acquire much of the second-language grammar.

② This lack needs to be compensated for by focusing learners' attention on grammatical features.

▶ **Focus-on-formS vs Focus-on-form Instructions**

	Focus-on-formS	Focus-on-form
Input-based	Any input-based option can be used: learners are directed to pay attention to the target form.	Any input-based option that centres on form-meaning mapping; learners are not told what the target form is so any attention to it is incidental.
Explicit instruction	Typically direct explicit instruction but also indirect instruction by means of consciousness-raising tasks.	No explicit instruction of any kind is provided.
Output-based	A variety of text-manipulation and text creation options. Also, both error-avoiding and error-inducing options are possible.	Only text creation options with no attempt made to either avoid or induce errors.
Corrective feedback	Typically explicit types of feedback	Typically implicit types of feedback

2. Grammar Techniques

(1) Chart

Useful devices for practicing patterns, clarifying grammatical relationships, and even for understanding sociolinguistic and discourse constraints

(Exercise) Frequency adverbs, 'never', 'seldom', etc.

Read the paragraphs on page ○○ again. Then choose the appropriate adverb of frequency.						
	never	seldom	sometimes	often	usually	always
1. Keiko works hard.						
2. She is on time for work.						
3. She is late or sick.						
4. She types letters						

(2) Dialogues

Useful exercise for introducing and practicing grammatical points

 Lesson 2 What are you doing next week?

Preparing the students	Presentation: conversation
Introduce future time expressions and the future with the present continuous tense. On the board, write the following sentence. Underline 'is' and '—ing.' • *Mark is driving to Colorado tomorrow.* Tell the students that you want them to help you continue to write a story about Mark.	Have the students look at a picture of two people. Read the conversation of A and B about a school break. Answer any questions students have about vocabulary or structures. Introduce or review the words during, break, stay, go away, and vacation. Answer the questions: • *Do A and B have a break soon?* • *Are they both staying in Dallas?* • *Where are they going?* In pairs, have the students practice the conversation to use their own ideas.

 문헌읽기 **Strategies to Teach Grammar**

1. Relate knowledge needs to learning goals : Identify the relationship of declarative knowledge and procedural knowledge to student goals for learning the language. Students who plan to use the language exclusively for reading journal articles need to focus more on the declarative knowledge of grammar and discourse structures that will help them understand those texts. Students who plan to live in-country need to focus more on the procedural knowledge that will help them manage day to day oral and written interactions.

2. Apply higher order thinking skills : Recognize that development of declarative knowledge can accelerate development of procedural knowledge. Teaching students how the language works and giving them opportunities to compare it with other languages they know allows them to draw on critical thinking and analytical skills. These processes can support the development of the innate understanding that characterizes procedural knowledge.

3. Provide plentiful, appropriate language input : Understand that students develop both procedural and declarative knowledge on the basis of the input they receive. This input includes both finely tuned input that requires students to pay attention to the relationships among form, meaning, and use for a specific grammar rule, and roughly tuned input that allows students to encounter the grammar rule in a variety of contexts.

4. Use predicting skills : Discourse analyst Douglas Biber has demonstrated that different communication types can be characterized by the clusters of linguistic features that are common to those types. Verb tense and aspect, sentence length and structure, and larger discourse patterns all may contribute to the distinctive profile of a given communication type. For example, a history textbook and a newspaper article in English both use past tense verbs almost exclusively. However, the newspaper article will use short sentences and a discourse pattern that alternates between subjects or perspectives. The history textbook will use complex sentences and will follow a timeline in its discourse structure. Awareness of these features allows students to anticipate the forms and structures they will encounter in a given communication task.

5. Limit expectations for drills
   - Mechanical drills in which students substitute pronouns for nouns or alternate the person, number, or tense of verbs can help students memorize irregular forms and challenging structures. However, students do not develop the ability to use grammar correctly in oral and written interactions by doing mechanical drills, because these drills separate form from meaning and use. The content of the prompt and the response is set in advance; the student only has to supply the correct grammatical form, and can do that without really needing to understand or communicate anything. The main lesson that students learn from doing these drills is: Grammar is boring.
   - Communicative drills encourage students to connect form, meaning, and use because multiple correct responses are possible. In communicative drills, students respond to a prompt using the grammar point under consideration, but providing their own content. For example, to practice questions and answers in the past tense in English, teacher and students can ask and answer questions about activities the previous evening. The drill is communicative because none of the content is set in advance:

CHAPTER 07 Teaching Vocabulary

> **단원 길라잡이**
> - 어휘 지도에 필수적인 내용을 이해한다.
> - 효과적인 어휘 학습 방법을 이해한다.

교육과정

교육과정에서는 좀 더 효과적인 언어 학습을 위해 학년별로 사용할 수 있는 새로운 어휘를 제한하고 있다. 각 학년 별로 '권장하는 새로운 어휘 수'는 각 학년별로 사용할 수 있는 새로운 어휘 수를 의미한다. 즉, 이전 학년에서 사용한 어휘를 제외하고 새롭게 학습자가 학습해야 하는 어휘 수를 의미한다. '~ 낱말 이내'이므로 제시된 숫자는 교과용 도서 집필의 경우 최대 사용 가능한 어휘 수이다. 3~6학년까지 사용할 수 있는 새로운 낱말 수의 누계는 500 낱말 이내이다. 3~6학년에서는 500 낱말 이내에서 학습할 것을 권장하며, 기본 어휘 목록에 제시된 초등 권장 어휘 중에서 375 낱말 이상을 학습할 것을 권장한다. 7~10학년에서는 각 학년별로 제시된 범위 내에서 학습할 것을 권장하며, 기본 어휘 목록에 제시된 낱말 중에서 75% 이상을 학습할 것을 권장한다. 우리나라 개정 교육과정에서 추구하는 어휘 및 언어형식을 가르치는 방법은 다음과 같이 정리될 수 있다.

① 어휘의 개별적 의미보다는 말이나 글의 맥락을 통하여 다양한 의미와 활용법을 익히도록 지도한다.
② 어휘는 가급적 문맥 속에서 뜻을 유추할 수 있도록 지도하되 사전 등을 이용하여 뜻을 찾는 방법도 지도한다.
③ 두 개 이상의 단어가 조합된 연어의 의미와 사용법도 지도한다.
④ 다양한 어휘자료를 활용하여 어휘에 대한 흥미를 높이고 어휘사용능력을 신장할 수 있도록 지도한다.
⑤ 언어형식은 실제적인 의사소통 기회를 통해 자연스럽게 익혀나가도록 지도한다.
⑥ 의사소통에 지장을 주지 않는 언어형식의 오류에 대해서는 즉각적인 수정을 피하고 가급적 학생 스스로 오류를 발견하고 수정할 수 있도록 도와준다.

01 Principles for Teaching Vocabulary

(1) Increase depth and breadth of vocabulary knowledge in reading.

Vocabulary knowledge plays a very important role in reading tests and reading research has consistently found a word knowledge factor on which vocabulary tests load highly. Tests of vocabulary are highly predictive of performance on tests of reading comprehension. A lot of researches show that depth of vocabulary knowledge, breadth of vocabulary knowledge and reading comprehension are highly, and positively, correlated. Depth of vocabulary knowledge made a significant, and unique, contribution to the prediction of scores on reading comprehension beyond the prediction provided by the breadth of vocabulary knowledge.

(2) Use explicit instruction of vocabulary.

All students need direct instruction of vocabulary, but it is especially imperative for second language students. They need much more exposure to new vocabulary than their native English speaking classmates (August & Shanahan, 2006). Students need to learn cognates, prefixes, suffixes, and root words to enhance their ability to make sense of new lexicon. Understanding context clues such as embedded definitions, pictures, and charts builds schema that students need in order to comprehend the text. New vocabulary needs to be explicitly taught, and each new word should be directly linked to an appropriate strategy. Students should actively engage in holistic activities to practice new vocabulary because learning words out of context is difficult for these students. Even if they memorize the meanings of the words on a list, they will not be able to use the words in their own writing or verbal production until they really understand the meanings.

(3) Introduce the most essential vocabulary before beginning.

Don't overwhelm students with too many words or concepts. Pick what is absolutely essential in each chapter. Pronounce each word for students, and have them repeat after you. Introduce the vocabulary in a familiar and meaningful context and then again in a content-specific setting. For example, in a unit on weather and tornadoes that I taught, the word front needed to be reviewed in a familiar context and then taught in the context of the unit. Provide experiences that help demonstrate the meaning of the vocabulary words. In my unit, diagrams and photographs were particularly helpful.

(4) Build background knowledge.

Explicit links to previously taught text should be emphasized to activate prior knowledge. Review relevant vocabulary that was already introduced, and highlight familiar words that have a new meaning. Access the knowledge that students bring from their native cultures.

In learning about tornadoes, for example, my students talked about some extreme weather found in their home countries and used Google in Korean and Japanese to find examples of such weather. They also watched videos of typhoons and a tsunami. Videos from your school library, Internet resources, and carefully selected educational TV programs should be used to introduce each unit. Doing so will increase vocabulary and provide students with background knowledge. Key vocabulary can also be introduced through a fictional story before it is taught from the textbook.

(5) Use visuals when introducing new words and concepts.

Elementary-aged students are usually visual or kinesthetic learners. When a teacher simply lectures, students have very little understanding of the concepts being taught. It is therefore helpful to use realia, pictures, photographs, graphic organizers, maps, and graphs. Write key words on the board, and add gestures to help students interpret meaning. Have students create their own visuals to aid their learning. In the tornado unit, each student was assigned a few content-specific vocabulary words. They had to write simple definitions and draw pictures to show what the words meant.

(6) Provide a variety of activities to practice.

Research has shown that learning is more effective when students give input into the vocabulary they need to learn (Echevarria, Vogt, & Short, 2000). To give students plenty of practice with words, I recommend providing two word walls. On one wall, I write everyday words that students need to learn and practice. These words are removed when students no longer need them. On the second wall, I write unit- or content-specific vocabulary. This wall is changed to make room for new units. I then ask students to post unfamiliar words from the text. They select key vocabulary by looking at chapter titles, headings, and bolded words. I also have students make a portable word wall which they keep in their binders so that they have their vocabulary handy when they do homework. New vocabulary should be reviewed every day. Students can work together to write a simple sentence for each word or complete a cloze activity. They can also draw pictures to illustrate vocabulary, make flashcards, or compile their own dictionaries in a notebook.

(7) Promote oral language development through cooperative learning groups.

Students need ample opportunities to speak English and authentic reasons to use academic language. Working in small groups is especially beneficial because students learn to negotiate the meanings of vocabulary words with their classmates. When students work on the previously mentioned vocabulary activities in pairs or small groups, they can better understand and discuss the key concepts of the content area unit.

02 Classroom Instruction

1. Incidental Vocabulary Instruction

> T: Okay, "clumsy." Does anyone know what that means? (*writes the word on the board*)
>
> S: (*silence*)
>
> T: No one? Okay, well, take a look at the sentence it's in. "His clumsy efforts to imitate a dancer were almost amusing." Now, was Bernard a good dancer? (*S1 raises her hand.*) Okay, Mona?
>
> S: Well, no. He was a very bad dancer, as we see in the next sentence.
>
> T: Excellent! So, what do you think "clumsy" might mean?
>
> S: Not graceful?
>
> T: Good, what else? Anyone?
>
> S: Not smooth, eh, … uncoordinated?
>
> T: Great! Okay, so "clumsy" means awkward, ungraceful, uncoordinated. (*writes synonyms on the board*) Is that clear now?

(1) Wide reading

The more you read, the more vocabulary you learn. The amount of students' reading is strongly related to their vocabulary knowledge. Students learn new words by encountering them in text, either through their own reading or by being read to. Increasing the opportunities for such encounters improves students' vocabulary knowledge, which in turn improves their ability to read more complex text. "In short, the single most important thing you can do to improve students' vocabulary is to get them to read more." (Texas Reading Initiative, 2002). Students should read different types of text at different levels, including text that is simple and enjoyable, and some that is challenging. As noted above, students will not be able to comprehend text that has too many unfamiliar words (more than 10%); on the other hand, students will not encounter many new words if they read text that is below grade level. Listening to reading aloud can be just as good a source of word meanings as reading, especially for students with learning disabilities. Stahl, Richek and Vandevier (1991) found that sixth-grade children learned word meanings from a read aloud at the same rate that children typically learned words from written context.

(2) Multiple exposure to words

The growth of word knowledge is slow and incremental, requiring multiple exposures to words (Hirsch, 2003; Stahl, 2004). This does not mean simply repeating the word and a definition or synonym, but seeing the word in different contexts. How are words learned incrementally over multiple exposures? Every time we encounter a word in context, we remember something about the word. As we encounter a word repeatedly, more and more information accumulates about that word until we have a vague notion of what it means. As we get more information we are able to define that word. "Vocabulary knowledge seems to grow gradually moving from the first meaningful exposure to a word to a full and flexible knowledge" (Stahl, 1999). It is helpful for students to understand how they gradually learn words. Teachers should encourage students to actively construct links between new information and previously known information about a word. Being active and cognizant of this process will result in better memory about new words. Dale and O'Rourke (1986) proposed a model of four levels of word knowledge. This model should be shared with students so they can be more metacognitive (thinking about thinking) and metalinguistic (thinking about the structure of words) when learning new words:

Cognitive (direct mental operation)	Metacognitive (indirect strategy)
• making associations • learning words in groups • exploring range of meaning • lexical inferencing (intralingual/ interlingual clues) • deducing from syntactic structure	• collecting words from authentic contexts • making word cards • categorizing words into lists • reactivating vocabulary in internal dialogue

(3) Multiple exposure and importance of background knowledge

Background knowledge is a student's experience and knowledge of the world. Research has established that readers' existing knowledge is critical for them to comprehend what they read. More than vocabulary is needed to understand most texts. It is possible for a student to know all the words in a passage and still not make any sense of it if he has no prior knowledge of the topic. To make constructive use of vocabulary the student also needs a threshold level of knowledge about the topic. This enables him to make sense of the word combinations and choose among multiple possible word meanings. People who know a great deal about a topic also know its vocabulary. "Word meanings are not just unrelated bits of information, but are part of larger knowledge structures." (Stahl, 1999). Reading comprehension and vocabulary are best served by spending extended time on reading to texts on the same topic and discussing the facts and ideas in them. This kind of immersion in a topic not only improves reading and develops vocabulary, it also develops writing skills (Hirsch, 2003).

2. Direct Vocabulary Instruction

(1) Promote word consciousness

Word consciousness means having an interest and awareness of words. Word consciousness involves awareness of word structure, including an understanding of word parts and word order. Students need to become aware of how written language is different from everyday conversation by drawing their attention to the distinctive structures of written language such as compound and complex sentence structures, phrasing within sentences, how punctuation is used to signal phrasing, and paragraph structure.

Word conscious students enjoy learning new words and engaging in word play (Texas Reading Initiative, 2002). One way to promote word consciousness is to point out examples of vivid descriptions, interesting metaphors, similes and other forms of figurative language, and plays on words. Ask students to select examples of exciting use of words when they read and save them in a journal or share them with other students. Teachers should take advantage of opportunities to develop student interest in words, the subtle meanings of words, how to have fun with words, and how words and concepts are related across different contexts. Students benefit from hearing language that incorporates the vocabulary and syntax (sentence structures) in high-quality written English. Literate written English uses words and grammatical structures in ways that may be new to many students, and reading good literature aloud exposes students to many genres of written English (Texas Reading Initiative, 2002).

(2) Provide intentional, explicit instruction in specific words

Although it is impossible to specifically teach all of the new words students must learn each year (between 2,000 to 3,000), it is useful to provide direct instruction in some words. This includes pre-teaching key vocabulary prior to reading a selection. It is estimated that students can be taught explicitly some 400 words per year in school (Beck, McKewon & Kucan, 2002). Teachers must remember that direct instruction of specific words is only one component of effective vocabulary instruction.

What words should the teacher choose for direct instruction? Teachers should focus on words that are important to the text, useful to know in many situations, and that are uncommon in everyday language but recurrent in books (Juel & Deffes, 2004). Direct instruction of specific words can include teaching the multiple meanings of some words, different word associations (such as antonyms and synonyms), and word concepts (such as related concept words and categories of words).

(3) Analyze word structure; word parts

When students encounter unknown words they can use knowledge of word parts (root words, suffixes and prefixes) to help determine the meaning. This is especially true when reading content textbooks because these texts often contain many words that are derived from the same word parts. 예 the Greek root 'bio' (meaning 'life, living organisms') reappears again and again in a typical middle school life science textbook (예 biology, biologist, biosphere, biodegradable, biochemical, biofuel, biohazard). Another example is the prefix 'mono' (meaning 'one, alone, single'). If students are familiar with the meaning of the prefix mono, the prefix 'poly' (meaning 'many'), and the base word 'theism' (meaning 'belief in the existence of a god or gods'), they can determine that the difference between 'monotheism' and 'polytheism' is the difference between believing in only one god or many gods.

Structural analysis of a word draws the student's attention to the individual units of meaning in the word, also known as morphemes. A free morpheme, or root word, can stand alone (예 cut), while a bound morpheme needs to be attached to another morpheme (예 -ing, un), and two free morphemes can combine to form a compound word (예 airplane).

In the beginning stages of reading, rapid and automatic word analysis is essential for developing decoding and fluency skills; at this level, the purpose of word analysis is to identify (sound out) the word. The focus of word analysis for vocabulary is on the meaningful parts of a word to help determine its overall meaning. Some students may not realize that they can use their knowledge about how to divide words into parts to figure out word meanings.

There are numerous sources for lists of common root words and affixes (suffixes and prefixes); an internet search can produce useful examples. Two publications to consult for how to teach word parts are 'Morphemes for Meaning' by Jane Greene, and 'Vocabulary Through Morphemes' by Susan Ebbers. It is important to note that struggling readers and students with learning disabilities in particular may be lacking in word analysis skills or the ability to readily learn and apply these skills.

(4) Use context to determine word meaning

Good readers often use context clues to determine the meanings of unfamiliar words, if they are available in the text. They can locate other words and phrases in a passage that give clues about what an unknown word means. Struggling readers who do not do this should be given direct instruction in how to effectively look for clues or definitions. For example, part of the 'Click and Clunk' strategy (Vaughn et al, 2001) teaches students to follow these steps when they come across a word they do not know (described as a 'clunk'):

1. Reread the sentence with the clunk. Look for key words.
2. Reread the sentence without the clunk. What word makes sense?
3. Reread the sentence before and after the clunk. Look for clues.

The clues may be any of the following types of information embedded in the text: definition, restatement, example, comparison or contrast, description, synonym or antonym. Expository, non-fiction text (예 school textbooks) tends to offer more context clues than narrative story text. One suggestion to help students become more aware of using context is to provide them with the terms rich context (has a lot of clues to figure out a word) and lean context (not much there to help figure out a word).

(5) Teach how to effectively use a dictionary

For many years, the practice of having students look up words, write down definitions, and memorize those definitions was the main strategy teachers used to teach vocabulary. We now know that having students follow this practice is one of the least effective strategies. In fact, there is a great deal of research showing that children cannot use conventional definitions to learn words (Scott & Nagy, 1997). That does not mean that students should not use dictionaries; however, their use should be limited and students must be taught how to use a dictionary and choose the right definition.

Students need explicit instruction in how to use what they find in a dictionary entry so they are able to transfer that information into something useful. Students may be confused by different meanings for the same word, or the wording in a dictionary entry may be too difficult to read or understand. The following suggestions were adapted from the Texas Center for Reading and Language Arts (2002): To choose the right definition, the student must:

- Use background knowledge about the content in the text
- Have a sense of the grammatical use in the text
- Read and understand each definition

As noted earlier, to remember the meaning of a new word, it is better for students to reword the definition in their own words, to identify synonyms and antonyms for the word, to use the word in their own meaningful sentence, and to recognize that the word may be used differently in other contexts.

(6) Activities for learning vocabulary

Encouraging students to memorize random vocabulary lists is not very helpful. The more associations you can make between different parts of the language the better. Methods that are likely to help the student:

- Group words in contexts (foods, occupations, animals) or by meaning (boiling, hot, warm, cool, cold) or opposites (open, closed)
- Ask the students to say the word out loud, or read a story aloud that contains the new word; have them write words down; ask them to draw a picture of the word
- Have them listen to new words in context on a tape; ask them to tell you about other words sounds like

3. Vocabulary Lesson

(1) Types of Vocabulary

① Content Words versus Function Words

In linguistics, function words are words that have little lexical meaning or have ambiguous meaning and express grammatical relationships among other words within a sentence, or specify the attitude or mood of the speaker. They signal the structural relationships that words have to one another and are the glue that holds sentences together. Thus, they serve as important elements to the structures of sentences. Words that are not function words are called content words (or open class words or lexical words or autosemantic words): these include nouns, verbs, adjectives, and most adverbs. Dictionaries define the specific meanings of content words, but can only describe the general usages of function words. By contrast, grammars describe the use of function words in detail, but treat lexical words in general terms only.

② Different Modality or Register

The vocabulary used by skilled speakers and writers changes according to modality and register. For some languages such as Arabic, modality differences may be highly marked since the vocabulary of the local spoken variety and the vocabulary of the more classical written variety can be very different. This makes learning the literate skills (reading and writing) more of a challenge than in a language like English where there is significant overlap between the vocabulary of the spoken and the written variety - but where the vocabulary of the written language is nonetheless much more extensive.

③ Euphemism as Sociocultural Variation

The selection of a euphemism (a word that is considered less direct and less distasteful or offensive) often reflects one or more of these factors. 예 when asking where the 'toilet' is, there are many possible lexical items one can use as euphemisms in English: *the bathroom, the powder room, the ladies room, the men's room* and etc.

(2) Functional Language Vocabulary

Copy and complete the chart with the phrases.		
I'd love to.	I'd love to but...	I'd rather not.
I'm not really sure.	No, thanks.	Perhaps
That would be great.	What a fantastic idea!	Why not?
Saying yes	Not sure	Saying no

The students say the phrases correctly, paying special attention to the intonation they use. The teacher helps them to think of ways of completing the phrase *I'd love to but...* (I'm working this evening). The teacher can now get them to practice simple invitation — reply exchanges by cueing them with words like dinner (How about coming to dinner? That would be great). In pairs they can now write longer dialogues. While they are doing this, the teacher can go round the class monitoring their progress and helping where necessary. Finally, the students read out (or act out) their dialogues and the teacher gives them feedback. It is worth noticing that the level of the original dialogue is somewhat higher than the language the students are being asked to produce. That is because students can cope with more language when they read and listen than they can when they have to come out with it themselves. When functional language like this is taught, the teacher almost always end up getting students to use phrases rather than individual words, precisely because certain common exchanges (like inviting) tend to use these pre-fabricated chunks (I'd love to, I'd rather not, Would you like to…) as a matter of course.

(3) Compound Noun

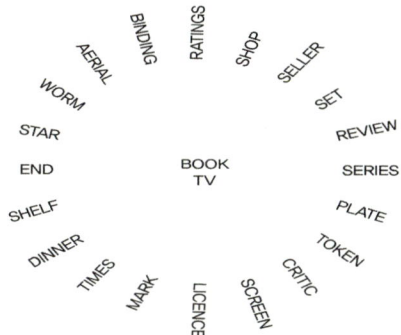

In this word circle activity, students look at a wheel of words and try to say which words combine with 'book' and 'TV' to make compound words. The teacher starts by showing students the wheel and then make sure that they realize that while 'book' + 'case' can make 'bookcase', *TV case doesn't work in the same way. Students are put into pairs or groups and told to come up with the combinations as quickly as possible.

03 Lexical Approach

Communicative language teaching안에서 나타난 교수법으로 words에 중심을 두고 있다는 점에서 lexical approach는 새로운 주목을 받고 있다. 기본 정신은 comprehension-based에 두고 있으며 어휘를 lexical phrases, unanalyzed wholes이나 chunks로 보며 이 내용이 학습자들이 받아야 할 input으로 보고 있는 것이다. 그래서 이 교수법의 창시자인 Lewis (1993)는 언어의 중심에는 syntax가 아니라 lexis가 있어야 한다고 주장하고 있다. 몇 가지 예를 보면 훨씬 더 쉽게 이해가 될 것이다. 'I'm sorry', 'I didn't mean to make you jump', 'That will never happen to me' 등은 언어 사용자가 새롭게 창조한 말이 아니라 이미 존재하는, fixed expressions을 암기해서 쓰는 것이라고 주장하는 것이다. 그러므로 수업의 중심에는 이러한 내용을 많이 배울 수 있도록 하는데 주력해야 한다는 것이다.

(1) What is Lexis

- Lexis is the basis of language.
- Lexis is misunderstood in language teaching because of the assumption that grammar is the basis of language and that mastery of the grammatical system is a prerequisite for effective communication.
- The key principle of a lexical approach is that "language consists of grammaticalized lexis, not lexicalized grammar."
- One of the central organizing principles of any meaning-centered syllabus should be lexis.

(2) Types of Lexical Units

① Collocation is the readily observable phenomenon whereby certain words co-occur in natural text with greater than random frequency (Lewis, 1997a). Furthermore, collocation is not determined by logic or frequency, but is arbitrary, decided only by linguistic convention. Some collocations are fully fixed, such as 'to catch a cold,' 'rancid butter,' and 'drug addict,' while others are more or less fixed and can be completed in a relatively small number of ways, as in the following examples:

- blood/ close/ distant/ near(est) relative
- learn by doing/ by heart/ by observation/ by rote/ from experience
- badly/ bitterly/ deeply/ seriously/ severely hurt

② Lexical approach advocates argue that language consists of meaningful chunks that, when combined, produce continuous coherent text, and only a minority of spoken sentences are entirely novel creations. The role of formulaic, many-word lexical units have been stressed in both first and second language acquisition research. (See Richards & Rodgers, 2001, for further discussion.) They have been referred to by many different labels, including 'gambits' (Keller, 1979), 'speech formulae' (Peters, 1983), 'lexicalized stems' (Pawley & Syder, 1983), and 'lexical phrases' (Nattinger & DeCarrico, 1992). Lewis (1997b) suggests the following taxonomy of lexical items:

- words (book, pen)
- polywords (by the way, upside down)
- collocations, or word partnerships (community service, absolutely convinced)
- institutionalized utterances (I'll get it; We'll see; That'll do; If I were you …; Would you like a cup of coffee?)
- sentence frames and heads (That is not as … as you think; The fact/ suggestion/ problem/ danger was …) and even text frames (In this paper we explore …; Firstly …; Secondly …; Finally …)

(3) Lexis In Language Teaching and Learning

In the lexical approach, lexis in its various types is thought to play a central role in language teaching and learning. Nattinger (1980) suggests that teaching should be based on the idea that language production is the piecing together of ready-made units appropriate for a particular situation. Comprehension of such units is dependent on knowing the patterns to predict in different situations. Instruction, therefore, should center on these patterns and the ways they can be pieced together, along with the ways they vary and the situations in which they occur. Activities used to develop learners' knowledge of lexical chains include the following:

- Intensive and extensive listening and reading in the target language
- First and second language comparisons and translation-carried out chunk-for-chunk, rather than word-for-word aimed at raising language awareness
- Repetition and recycling of activities, such as summarizing a text orally one day and again a few days later to keep words and expressions that have been learned active
- Guessing the meaning of vocabulary items from context
- Noticing and recording language patterns and collocations
- Working with dictionaries and other reference tools
- Working with language corpus created by the teacher for use in the classroom or accessible on the Internet

(4) Theory into Practice

Advances in computer-based studies of language, such as corpus linguistics, have provided huge databases of language corpora. In particular, the Cobuild project at Birmingham University in England has examined patterns of phrase and clause sequences as they appear in various texts as well as in spoken language. It has aimed at producing an accurate description of the English language in order to form the basis for design of a lexical syllabus (Sinclair, 1987). Such a syllabus was perceived by Cobuild researchers as independent and unrelated to any existing language teaching methodology. As a result, the Collins Cobuild English Course (Willis & Willis, 1989) was the most ambitious attempt to develop a syllabus based on lexical rather than grammatical principles.

Willis (1990) has attempted to provide a rationale and design for lexically based language teaching and suggests that a lexical syllabus should be matched with an instructional methodology that puts particular emphasis on language use. Such a syllabus specifies words, their meanings, and the common phrases in which they are used and identifies the most common words and patterns in their most natural environments. Thus, the lexical syllabus not only subsumes a structural syllabus, it also describes how the structures that make up the syllabus are used in natural language.

Lewis' (1993) lexical syllabus is specifically not word based, because it explicitly recognizes word patterns for (relatively) de-lexical words, collocation power for (relatively) semantically powerful words, and longer multi-word items, particularly institutionalized sentences, as requiring different, and parallel pedagogical treatment (Lewis, 1993). In his own teaching design, Lewis proposes a model that comprises the steps, Observe-Hypothesize-Experiment, as opposed to the traditional Present-Practice-Produce paradigm. Unfortunately, Lewis does not lay out any instructional sequences exemplifying how he thinks this procedure might operate in actual language classrooms.

5

Language Curriculum

01. Curriculum Design
02. Lesson Planning
03. Syllabus
04. Material Development
05. Classroom Activities
06. ICT 지도

CHAPTER 01 Curriculum Design

> **단원 길라잡이**
> - 커리큘럼 계획의 복잡성과 체계적인 과정의 중요성을 이해할 것이다: situation & needs 분석, 목표 설정, 실러버스 만들기, 교재 자료 선택, 평가
> - 커리큘럼의 전체 목표에서 수업의 효율성을 평가할 수 있을 것이다.
> - 교실 내의 상호작용의 원리를 레슨의 계획과 관찰에 적용할 수 있을 것이다.
> - 상호 작용적 방법과 과제를 적용하고 가이드라인을 따라서 활용할 수 있을 것이다.

교육과정

교육과정에서는 개인차에 따라 수준에 맞는 학습 활동이나 과업을 수행할 수 있도록 학년별로 기본 교과서나 보조 교재를 다양한 수준으로 개발할 수 있다. 학습자 개개인의 다양성을 모두 고려한 완전한 의미의 수준별 교육과정 운영은 불가능하더라도 개개인의 능력, 적성, 흥미, 요구 등 다양한 개인차를 반영한 교재를 개발하여 수준별 수업을 실시한다면, 학습자에게 더 많은 선택의 기회를 제공함으로써 학습 활동의 적극적인 주체로서의 역할을 하도록 할 수 있다. 학업 성취 수준 및 능력에 따라 난이도가 다른 과제를 부과하는 수직적 수준 구현과 함께 학생의 다양한 인지적, 정의적, 사회적 개인차를 활용하는 수평적 수준 구현을 고려한 교재 개발이 필요하다. 예를 들어 상, 중, 하 각 수준에서도 학습자의 스타일이나 다중지능 이론이 반영된 다양한 과제를 개발하여 학습자 중심의 자기 주도적 학습이 가능하도록 해야 한다.

수준별 수업에서 가장 중요한 요소가 수준에 적합한 교수-학습 자료이므로 수준에 따라 기본적인 교과서를 각기 달리 개발하는 것이 바람직하겠지만, 학급 내 수준별 수업을 실시하거나 학습자가 수준을 이동하는 경우, 그리고 정기고사에서 동일한 평가를 실시해야 하는 점 등을 감안한다면 기본적인 교과서는 통일하는 것이 현실적이다. 따라서 수준별로 차별화된 학습 활동이나 과업을 포함하는 자료를 개발하는 것이 가장 합리적인 대안이 될 수 있다. 수준별 보조 교재의 경우 교과서를 위주로 공통적인 학습 내용이 반드시 포함되도록 해야 하고, 특히 수준 간의 연계성이 유지되도록 제작되어야 한다.

(a) 심화반 (상위집단)의 교재는 개인 혹인 조별로 창의력을 요하는 다소 어려운 수준의 과업을 스스로 해결하도록 유도하고, 학습 내용을 더 자연스럽고 자신 있게 사용할 수 있도록 하는 유창성 증대를 위한 활동에 중점을 둔다.

(b) 기본반 (중위집단)은 교과서를 약간 응용하거나 변형한 수준의 과제를 제시하여 성공적으로 해결하는 경험을 통해 부족했던 자신감을 갖게 하고 개인별, 조별 경쟁을 통해 보상함으로써 적극적인 수업 참여를 유도하는 내용이 바람직하다.

(c) 보충반 (하위집단)은 교과서를 읽고 이해하는 수준의 과제를 반복적으로 설명해 주고 다양한 학습 매체를 통해 학생들의 흥미를 북돋아 줌으로써 학습 동기 유발에 도움이 되는 교재를 개발하는 것이 필요하다.

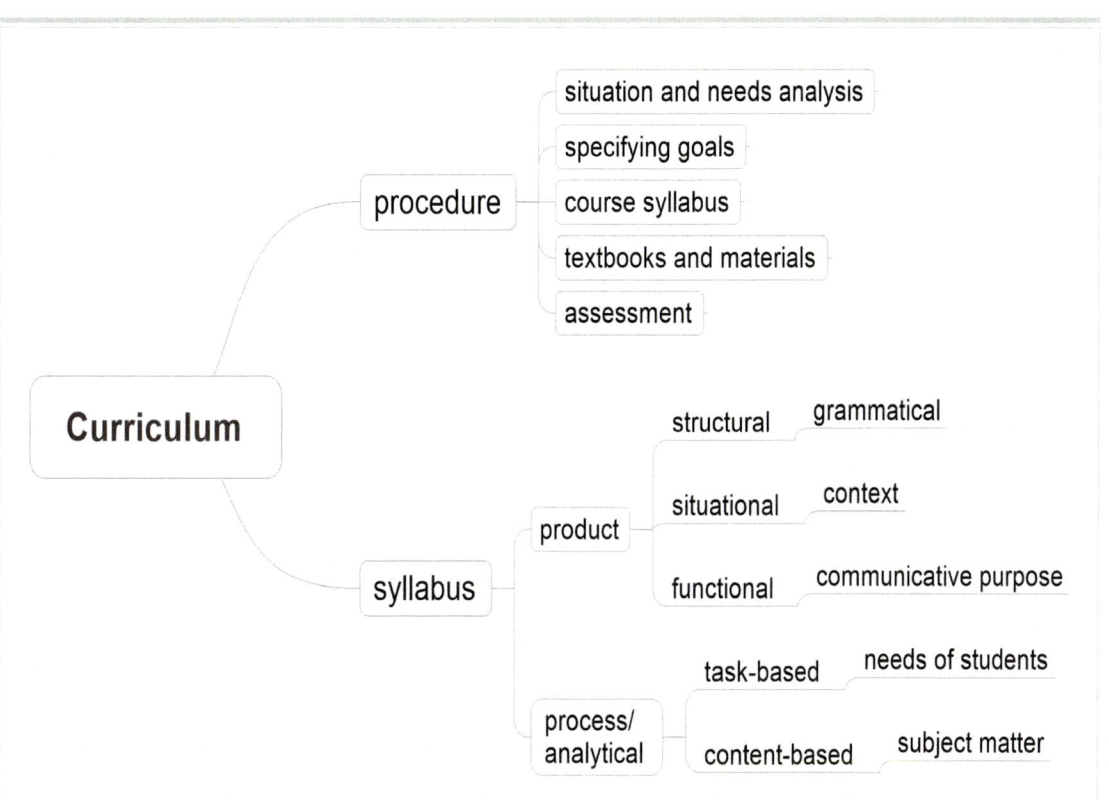

01 Concepts of Curriculum

이제까지 언어습득을 위한 이론과 언어기능을 가르치는 방법에 대하여 살펴보았다. 이 장에서는 수업을 효율적으로 하기 위하여 학교 현장에서 사용되는 실제 내용에 대하여 살펴보기로 하자. 그 시작의 첫 걸음에는 curriculum이 있다. curriculum은 학교에서 실시되는 모든 것을 포괄하는 표현이 될 것이다. 그래서 그 안에는 전체적인 계획, 코스의 디자인, 내용과 수업과 교수 계획이 다 포함된다. 이 모든 것은 학습의 결과가 효과적으로 성취되도록 하는 데 그 목적을 두고 있다. 그리고 syllabus의 내용이 효율적인 교수학습을 결정해 줄 수 있으며 topics, facts, skills 등이 input이 되며, 학습자의 performance가 되는 output을 성취할 수 있도록 한다. curriculum에는 다음의 내용들이 포함될 것이다:

- decisions about the objectives or goals of the programme
- decisions about the content – from these decisions the syllabus will be derived
- decisions about the method of instruction
- decisions about how the programme is evaluated

▶ Three approaches of curriculum

	Focus on FormS	Focus on Meaning	Focus on Form
Syllabus	• Language-centered • Sequenced from simple to complex • Pre-determined prior to a course • Linear progression	• Activity-based • Content negotiated with learners • Evolves during the course • Reflects the process of learning	• Needs-based • Objectives or competency-based
Methodology	• Transmissive and teacher-directed • Practice and control of elements • Imitation of models • Explicit presentation of rules	• Learner-centered • Experiential learning • Active engagement in interaction and communication • Meaning prioritized over accuracy	• Practice of real-life situations • Accuracy emphasized • Learning and practice of expressions and formulaic language
Role of teacher	• Teacher as instructor, model and explainer • Transmitter of knowledge • Reinforcer of correct language use	• Teacher as facilitator • Negotiator of content and process • Encourager of learner self-expression and autonomy	• Organizer of learning experiences • Model of target language performance • Planner of learning experiences

	Focus on FormS	Focus on Meaning	Focus on Form
Role of learner	• Accurate mastery of language forms • Application of learned material to new contexts • Understanding of language rules	• Negotiator of learning content and modes of learning • Development of learning strategies	• Awareness of correct usage • Development of fluency
Assessment	• Norm-referenced, summative end-of-semester or end-of-course test • Cumulative mastery of taught forms	• Negotiated assessment • Assessment for learning • Formative assessment • Self-assessment	• Criterion-referenced • Performance based • Improvement oriented

02 Procedure of Curriculum

1. Curriculum Development

(1) Situation/ Environment Analysis

The first steps in course design is an analysis of the setting, the audience, and needs of the students, otherwise known as a situation analysis.

① Educational Setting: Within what societal and cultural norms is the course situated? What is the institutional framework into which the course must be integrated? What are the broad instructional goals of the program? In general, what is the structure of the program? What are the physical conditions and resources? Who are the learners, in very general terms?

② Class characteristics: How would you describe the class in terms of the homogeneity of learners, the size of the class?

③ Faculty characteristics: What are the qualifications of teachers (예 training, experience, methodological biases)? What are the working conditions of faculty? To what extent is there collaboration among teachers?

④ Governance of course content: Who determines course content? To what extent can teachers choose content as they perceive the need to do so?

⑤ Assessment and evaluation requirements: What stipulations are in force for assessing students for placement, diagnostic or achievement purposes? How are courses evaluated and revised?

(2) Needs Analysis

A second step centers on the needs that the course presumes to address. Depending on whom you ask, they are wants, desires, demands, expectations, motivations, lacks, constraints, and requirements. A needs assessment is an important precursor to designing the goals of a course in that it can identify the overall purposes of the course, 'gaps' that the course is intended to fill, and the opinions of both course designers and learners about their reasons for designing/ taking the course. Types of needs are as below;

① Objective needs are relatively easily measured, quantified, or specified with agreement by administrators.
- demographic data on learners, including language ability, interests, etc.
- needs expressed in terms of proficiency levels
- language skills
- what learners need to do in English (target contexts)

② Subjective needs are to focus on needs as seen through the eyes of the learners themselves. Sometimes learners' perceived needs do not match their actual needs.
- learners' attitudes toward the target language and culture
- expectations that students have of themselves and of the course
- purposes that students perceive for studying English
- specific language skills that students wish to focus on
- preferences that students have about their learning

(3) Specifying goals

① Goals are rather broadly based aims and purposes in an educational context, and are therefore more appropriately associated with whole programs, courses, or perhaps sizable modules within a course.

② Objectives are much more specific than goals, both in their conception and in their context. Objectives usually refer to aims and purposes within the narrow context of a lesson or an activity within a lesson.

③ Once a situation analysis and needs analysis have confirmed some of the general parameters of a course, goals need to be carefully stated in order to be certain about what the course will accomplish and what it will not.
　예 By the end of the course, students will be able to;

- Participate in social conversations in English
- Speak with few hesitations and with only minor errors
- Successfully apply some form-focused instruction to their speech
- Self-monitor their speech for potential errors
- Participate in pair, group and whole-class discussions
- Give a simple oral presentation on a familiar topic

(4) Conceptualizing a course syllabus

As you put together what most institutions call a syllabus, it is often helpful to carry out a review of options in materials that are already available.

예 A communicative syllabus should minimally consist of;

- Goals for the course
- Suggested objectives for units and lessons
- A sequential list of functions, following from the goals, that the curriculum will fulfill
- A sequential list of topics and situations to functions
- A sequential list of grammatical, lexical and phonological forms to the above sequences
- A sequential list of skills to the above sequences
- Matched references throughout to textbook units, lessons, pages and additional resources
- Possible suggestions of assessment alternatives, including criteria and genres of assessment

(5) Selecting textbooks, materials, and resources

The process of reviewing potential textbooks, materials, and resources, beyond those that you might design yourself, is one that ideally takes place in concert with conceptualizing the syllabus:

① They should correspond to learners' needs. They should match the aims and objectives of the language program.

② They should reflect the uses that learners will make of the language. Textbooks should be chosen that will help equip students to use language effectively for their own purposes.

③ They should take account of students' needs as learners and should facilitate their learning processes.

④ They should have a clear role as a support for learning. Like teachers, they should mediate between the target language and the learner.

(6) Assessment

① Traditional periodic tests: quizzes, multiple-choice tests, fill-in-the-blank tests

② Midterm and final examinations: short essays, oral production, open-ended questions

③ Alternatives: journals, portfolios, conferences, observations, interviews, self and peer-evaluation

(7) Program Evaluation

① Everyone related to course design, students, teachers, course developers, administrators need to be consulted.

② Consider the audience of the evaluation

③ Consider various aspects of the program:
- appropriateness of the course goals
- adequacy of the syllabus to meet those goals
- textbooks and materials used to support the curriculum
- classroom methodology, activities, procedures
- the teacher's training, background and expertise
- appropriate orientation of teachers and students before the course
- the students' motivation and attitudes
- the students' perceptions of the course
- the students' actual performance as measured by assessments
- means for monitoring students' progress through assessment
- institutional support, including resources, classrooms, and environment
- staff collaboration and development before and during the course

CHAPTER 02 Syllabus

> **단원 길라잡이**
> - 여러 학습법과 교수법을 통합하는 기저에 깔린 교육적 원리를 이해할 수 있다.
> - 각 원리들에 있는 여러 측면을 교실수업에 적용시킬 수 있다.
> - 내적 동기와 외적 동기를 이해하고 내적 동기가 수업 내에서 어떻게 구현되는지 이해할 수 있을 것이다.

01 교수 과정의 발달

1. 제1차 교육과정의 시기(1954~1963)

'교육과정 시간 배당 기준령(1954.4.20)'이 공포되면서 교과 분과주의가 지양되고 통합 원리에 의한 새로운 교육과정의 틀이 잡혔다. 이에 따라 생활 경험을 중시하는 경험 중심 교육과정의 일반 목표를 설정하고, 이를 달성하기 위한 각 교과 활동의 목표와 내용이 세분화되었다. 교과 내용의 상세화라기 보다는 영어교육의 목적과 가치에 대한 장황한 진술에 그친 감이 있고, 잡다한 영어 교수법 이론의 개진으로 인하여 이론의 일관성이 결여되고 상호 모순점이 노출되어 있었다고 할 수 있다.

2. 제2차 교육과정의 시기(1963~1973)

이 시기는 자주적이고 능률적인 새 인간상 정립을 위하여 합리적 사고가 강조되고 생산성, 유용성이 높이 평가되는 시기였다. 영어과 교육과정은 간결한 표현과 논리적 체계를 특징으로 하며 Ⅰ) 목표, Ⅱ) 지도 내용, Ⅲ) 지도상의 유의점으로 조직되었다. 목표는 2개 항의 기능적 목표와 1개 항의 정의적 목표로 구성되었고, 지도 내용은 1) 듣기와 말하기, 2) 읽기, 3) 쓰기의 형태를 갖추었다.

3. 제3차 교육과정의 시기(1973~1981)

교과의 핵심적인 지식 체계를 구조화하고 탐구 학습을 강조하는 학문 중심 교육과정인 제3차 교육 과정기에서, 새로이 제시된 문형, 문법상의 제약 조건 때문에 학교 수업을 문법 설명 위주로 일관되게 하는 계기가 되었다는 비판을 받게 된다.

4. 제4차 교육과정의 시기(1981~1987)

복합적인 인간 중심 교육과정을 표방한 제4차 교육과정에서는 국제화·개방화의 국정 지표에 맞추어 영어과 교육과정을 '살아 있는 생활 영어 구사력'을 최대한 신장시키는 방향으로 개편하였다. 듣기, 말하기, 읽기, 쓰기의 기초 능력을 신장시키되, 대화 능력을 기반으로 하여 심화 발전시킬 수 있는 바탕을 강조하였다. 인쇄된 발음기호를 통한 발음지도보다 영·미인의 정확한 청각자료에 의한 발음지도를 강조하고 문자와 소리의 관계를 익혀 발음할 수 있는 음절법(phonics)의 지도를 권장하고 있다.

5. 제5차 교육과정의 시기(1987~1992)

영어 교과의 목표는 영어로 의사소통할 수 있는 능력을 길러 외국 문화를 수용하고 우리 문화를 소개할 수 있는 바탕을 마련하는 데에 두고 있다. 영어 교과목표의 특징을 의사소통능력을 기르는 것과 외국 문화를 수용하고 우리 문화를 소개하는 두 가지 기능을 대등하게 두지 않고 전자를 후자에 종속되는 관계로 설정한 것이 특색이라 할 수 있다. 교육과정의 체계는 교과 목표, 학년 목표 및 내용, 지도 및 평가상의 유의점으로 되어 있다.

6. 제6차 교육과정의 시기(1992~1997)

영어 교과의 목표는 의사소통능력을 기르는 것과 외국 문화를 수용하여 우리 문화를 발전시키고 이를 외국에 소개할 수 있는 바탕을 마련하는 데 두고 있다. 교육과정의 체계는 성격, 목표, 내용, 방법 및 평가로 되어 있으며, 제5차 교육과정과의 큰 차이점은 '성격' 항목이 추가된 것이다. 특징은 문법 중심 교수요목에서 탈피하여 개념·기능 교수요목을 과감하게 도입하고, 개념과 기능을 중심으로 교과서의 내용과 수준을 정하였다는 것이다. 그리고 또 다른 특징은, 언어 기능을 듣기와 말하기, 읽기, 쓰기로 나누지 않고 이해 기능(듣기, 읽기)과 표현 기능(말하기, 쓰기)으로 나눈 것이다. 그래서 이해 기능을 학습한 다음에 표현 기능을 학습하도록 하였다. 그리고 평가에서 평가 목표를 설정한 것이 제5차 교육과정과의 차이라고 할 수 있다.

7. 제7차 교육과정의 시기(1997~2007)

제7차 교육과정에서는 개인차를 고려한 학생 중심의 영어교육, 의사소통능력을 중시하는 영어 교육, 활동과 과업 중심의 영어교육, 논리적 사고력과 창의력을 기를 수 있는 영어교육, 국가 발전과 세계화에 기여하는 영어교육이 특징이다. 제7차 교육과정의 가장 큰 특징 중 하나는 수준별 교육 과정'으로 전환하였다는 것이다. 또한 제7차 영어과 교육과정에서는 학생들의 의사소통능력을 기르기 위해서 개념, 기능 중심 교수요목과 문법 중심 교수요목을 적절히 절충할 수 있도록 자료를 제공함과 동시에 자연스런 상황에서 의사소통능력을 기를 수 있도록 소재를 다양화했다.

8. 2022년 개정 교육과정의 시기(2008~)

① 학생 중심 교육과정 구현을 위하여 현실 적합성을 제고한 수준별 수업 운영 지원 방안을 제시하고, 선택 과목 간 수준별 차별화로 학습자의 진로와 특성 (능력, 적성, 소질)을 고려한 다양한 학습 기회를 제공하며 학습자의 요구를 반영한 교과목 및 교육 내용 설계를 강조하였다.
② 학습 내용의 연계성 강화를 위하여 학교 급 및 학년 간 교육 내용의 연계성을 강화하고 선택 과목 간에 진로별 특성을 반영한 계열성을 강화하였다.
③ 의사소통능력 향상을 위하여 교육과정의 '의사소통 기능' 및 '문화' 관련 교육 내용을 구체화 및 강화하고 '교수-학습 방법' 및 '평가' 관련 내용을 개선하였다.

▶ **교육과정의 내용 체계와 성취기준의 비교**

구분	2015 개정 교육과정	2022 개정 교육과정
내용 체계	'영역', '핵심 개념', '일반화된 지식', '내용 요소' '기능'을 표로 전 교과 공통으로 동일하게 제시	교과별로 본질과 얼개를 드러내는 핵심 아이디어(빅 아이디어)를 선정하고, **내용 체계표를 '지식·이해', '과정·기능', '가치·태도'로 구성하되** 교과별로 구현 방식을 다양화할 수 있음
	내용 요소는 일반화된 지식과 관련된 구체적인 학습 요소를 단어로 나열	**지식·이해:** 빅 아이디어를 해당 학년의 학습 내용과 결부된 일반화 형태로 구체화하는 것을 원칙으로 하되 교과별로 제시 방식 다양화
	기능을 영역별로 학교급 공통으로 나열식으로 제시	**과정·기능:** 교과 고유의 탐구 및 사고 과정과 기능을 명료화하고 학교급이 올라갈수록 심화되는 방식
		가치·태도: 교과 활동을 통해서 학생들이 갖추기 기대하는 가치와 태도를 제시
성취 기준	영역을 대표하는 핵심 개념별로 학년(군)별 내용과 기능을 정합한 문장 형태로 진술	• **지식·이해, 과정·기능, 가치 및 태도를 의미 있게 통합하여 진술**하지만, 각 차원별 진술 혹은 두 차원 이상을 통합 하여 진술하는 것도 가능 • 영역의 층위에서 학년(군)별로 교과 학습 결과로써 학생이 할 수 있어야 할 진술문 으로 제시

이상의 내용 체계에 사용된 용어 중 '이해', '과정'은 개념기반 교육과정에서 사용되는 특별한 의미를 갖는 전문 용어에 가깝다. '**이해**'는 '**깊은 이해**'나 '**개념적 이해**'를 의미하고 '**과정**'(process)은 언어 과목이라면 '독해'를, 미술 과목이라면 '그리기'를, 음악 과목에서는 '음악 공연'을, **외국어 과목**에서는 '**구두 및 문자에 의한 의사소통**'을 말한다 (Erickson et al., 2017). 또한 2022 개정 교육과정 총론 주요사항에 따르면 '역량 함양 교과 교육과정 개발'의 설명에서 '**깊이 있는 학습**'과 '**교과 간 연계와 통합**', '**삶과 연계한 학습**', '**학습과정에 대한 성찰**'을 강조하고 있다.

02 Types of Syllabus

A syllabus is an expression of opinion on the nature of language and learning; it acts as a guide for both teacher and learner by providing some goals to be attained. Hutchinson and Waters (1987:80) define syllabus as follows: At its simplest level a syllabus can be described as a statement of what is to be learnt. It reflects of language and linguistic performance. This is a rather traditional interpretation of syllabus focusing as it does on outcomes rather than process. However, a syllabus can also be seen as a "summary of the content to which learners will be exposed" (Yalden.1987: 87). It is seen as an approximation of what will be taught and that it cannot accurately predict what will be learnt.

1. Product-Oriented Syllabuses

Also known as the synthetic approach, these kinds of syllabuses emphasize the product of language learning and are prone to intervention from an authority.

(1) Structural (Grammatical) Syllabus

Historically, the most prevalent of syllabus type is perhaps the grammatical syllabus in which the selection and grading of the content is based on the complexity and simplicity of grammatical items. The learner is expected to master each structural step and add it to her grammar collection. As such the focus is on the outcomes or the product. One problem facing the syllabus designer pursuing a grammatical order to sequencing input is that the ties connecting the structural items maybe rather feeble. A more fundamental criticism is that the grammatical syllabus focuses on only one aspect of language, namely grammar, whereas in truth there exist many more aspects to language. Finally, recent corpus based research suggests there is a divergence between the grammar of the spoken and of the written language; raising implications for the grading of content in grammar based syllabuses.

> **핵심플러스** **Materials and Techniques for Communicative Language Teaching**
>
> The content of language teaching is a collection of the forms and structures, usually grammatical, of the language being taught. 예 nouns, verbs, adjectives, statements, questions, subordinate clauses, and so on

▶ **content of a grammatical syllabus**

lesson 1.	drilling copula and adjective combinations 예 She is happy.
lesson 2.	introducing -ing form 예 She is driving a car.
lesson 3.	distinguishing between mass and count nouns 예 There are some oranges and some cheese on the table.
lesson 4.	introducing verbs with stative meaning 예 I don't come from Newcastle.

(2) Situational Syllabus

These limitations led to an alternative approach where the point of departure became situational needs rather than grammatical units. Here, the principal organizing characteristic is a list of situations which reflects the way language and behavior are used everyday outside the classroom. Thus, by linking structural theory to situations the learner is able to induce the meaning from a relevant context. One advantage of the situational approach is that motivation will be heightened since it is 'learner-centered' rather than 'subject-centered'. However, a situational syllabus will be limited for students whose needs were not encompassed by the situations in the syllabus. This dissatisfaction led Wilkins to describe notional and communicative categories which had a significant impact on syllabus design.

> **핵심플러스** **Materials and Techniques for Communicative Language Teaching**
>
> The content of language teaching is a collection of real or imaginary situations in which language occurs or is used. A situation usually involves several participants who are engaged in some activity in a specific setting. The language occurring in the situation involves a number of functions, combined into a plausible segment of discourse. The primary purpose of a situational language teaching syllabus is to teach the language that occurs in the situations; 예 *seeing the dentist, complaining to the landlord, buying a book at the book store, meeting a new student, and so on*

2. Process-Oriented Syllabuses

Process-oriented syllabuses, or the analytical approach, developed as a result of a sense of failure in product-oriented courses to enhance communicative language skills. It is a process rather than a product. That is, focus is not on what the student will have accomplished on completion of the program, but on the specification of learning tasks and activities that s/he will undertake during the course.

(1) Task-Based Approaches

Prabhu's (1979) 'Bangalore Project' is a classic example of a procedural syllabus. Here, the question concerning 'what' becomes subordinate to the question concerning 'how'. The focus shifts from the linguistic element to the pedagogical, with an emphasis on learning or learner. Within such a framework the selection, ordering and grading of content is no longer wholly significant for the syllabus designer. Arranging the program around tasks such as information-gap and opinion-gap activities, it was hoped that the learner would perceive the language subconsciously whilst consciously concentrating on solving the meaning behind the tasks. There appears to be an indistinct boundary between this approach and that of language teaching methodology, and evaluating the merits of the former remain complicated.

A task-based approach assumes that speaking a language is a skill best perfected through practice and interaction, and uses tasks and activities to encourage learners to use the language communicatively in order to achieve a purpose. Tasks must be relevant to the real world language needs of the student. That is, the underlying learning theory of task based and communicative language teaching seems to suggest that activities in which language is employed to complete meaningful tasks, enhances learning.

핵심플러스 ─ Materials and Techniques for Communicative Language Teaching

The content of the teaching is a series of complex and purposeful tasks that the students want or need to perform with the language they are learning. The tasks are defined as activities with a purpose other than language learning, but, as in a content-based syllabus, the performance of the tasks is approached in a way that is intended to develop second language ability. Language learning is subordinate to task performance, and language teaching occurs only as the need arises during the performance of a given task. Tasks integrate language (and other) skills in specific settings of language use. Task-based teaching differs from situation-based teaching in that while situational teaching has the goal of teaching the specific language content that occurs in the situation (a predefined product), task-based teaching has the goal of teaching students to draw on resources to complete some piece of work (a process). The students draw on a variety of language forms, functions, and skills, often in an individual and unpredictable way, in completing the tasks. Tasks that can be used for language learning are, generally, tasks that the learners actually have to perform in any case. 예 applying for a job, talking with a social worker, getting housing information over the telephone, and so on.

(2) Content-based Syllabus

The primary purpose of instruction is to teach some content or information using the language that the students are also learning. The students are simultaneously language students and students of whatever content is being taught. The subject matter is primary, and language learning occurs incidentally to the content learning. The content teaching is not organized around the language teaching, but vice-versa. Content-based language teaching is concerned with information, while task-based language teaching is concerned with communicative and cognitive processes. 예 science class taught in the language the students need or want to learn, possibly with linguistic adjustment to make the science more comprehensible

CHAPTER 03 Lesson Planning

> **단원 길라잡이**
> - 수업계획에 필요한 내용을 파악하고 적용해본다.
> - 성공적인 수업계획의 상호의존적인 구성요소를 이해한다.

01 Guidelines for Lesson Planning

1. How to Plan

Writing a complete script for a whole hour of teaching is probably too laborious and unreasonable, but more practical and instructive as partial scripts that cover;

① Introductions to activities

② Directions for a task

③ Statements of rules or generalizations

④ Anticipated interchanges that could easily bog down or go astray

⑤ Oral testing techniques

⑥ Conclusions to activities and to the class hour

(1) Variety, Sequencing, Pacing and Timing

- Sufficient variety in techniques to keep the lesson lively and interesting
- Techniques or activities sequenced logically
- Lesson as a whole paced adequately
- Lesson appropriately timed

(2) Gauging difficulty

It takes a good deal of cognitive empathy to put yourself in your students' shoes and anticipate their problem areas. Some difficulty is caused by tasks themselves; therefore, make your directions crystal clear by writing them out in advance. Another source of difficulty is linguistic. If you can follow the $i+1$ principle of providing material that is just a little above, but not too far above, students' ability, the linguistic difficulty should be optimal.

(3) Individual differences

- Design techniques that have easy and difficult aspects or items.
- Solicit responses to easier items from students who are below the norm and to harder items from those above the norm.
- Try to design techniques that will involve all students actively.
- Each group has either a heterogeneous range of ability or a homogeneous range.
- Use small-group and pair work time to circulate and give extra attention to those below or above the norm.

(4) Student talk and teacher talk

Our natural inclination as teachers is to talk too much. As you plan your lesson, and as you perhaps script out some aspects of it, see to it that students have a chance to talk, to produce language, and even to initiate their own topics and ideas.

(5) Adapting to an established curriculum

You can keep your course focused on attainable, practical ends. To do so, consider the factors outlined as following;

① situation analysis
② needs analysis
③ materials and resources
④ assessment requirements

(6) Classroom lesson notes

A final consideration in your lesson planning process is a very practical one: What sort of lesson notes will you actually carry into the classroom with you?

	Lesson Phase
Perspective (opening)	The teacher asks the students the following question: What concepts have they learned?
	<table><tr><th>Teacher</th><th>Students</th></tr><tr><td>• Asks what students have learned in previous lesson. • Previews new lesson.</td><td>• Tell what they've learned previously. • Respond to preview.</td></tr></table>
Stimulation	The teacher poses a question to get the students thinking about the coming activity or helps the students to relate the activity to their lives.
	<table><tr><th>Teacher</th><th>Students</th></tr><tr><td>• Prepares students for new activity. • Presents attention grabber.</td><td>• Relate activity to their lives. • Respond to attention grabber.</td></tr></table>
Instruction/ Participation	The teacher can get students to interact by the use of pair work or group work.
	<table><tr><th>Teacher</th><th>Students</th></tr><tr><td>• Presents activity. • Checks for understanding. • Encourages involvement.</td><td>• Do activity. • Show understanding. • Interact with others.</td></tr></table>
Closure	The teacher checks what the students have learned by asking question such as "How did you feel about these activities?"
	<table><tr><th>Teacher</th><th>Students</th></tr><tr><td>• Asks what students have learned. • Previews future lessons.</td><td>• Tell what they have learned. • Give input on future lessons.</td></tr></table>
Follow-up	The last phase of the lesson that the teacher use to reinforce some concepts and even to introduce some new ones.
	<table><tr><th>Teacher</th><th>Students</th></tr><tr><td>• Presents other activities to reinforce same concepts. • Presents opportunities for interaction.</td><td>• Do new activities. • Interact with others.</td></tr></table>

02. Sample Lesson Planning

1. 듣기활동

Unit	Lesson 5. Time and Me	
Period 1/8	Warm Up, Listening	
Aims	1. Students can play '20 Questions Game' about precious people, things, or memories. 2. Students can understand dialogs about asking abilities and expressing inabilities. 3. Students can understand dialogs about telling opinions.	
Procedure	Activities	Teaching Aids
Introduction (5')	• T & Ss greet each other and introduce the lesson. • T review the last lesson.	
Development — Warm-up (5')	• T tells Ss teacher's own No.1 treasure like favorite people, things, or events in life. • T has Ss think of their No.1 treasure and play '20 question game' in pairs.	CD-ROM
Development — Listen on Target (7')	• T tells what the two people do in four pictures. • Ss listen to a short dialog and check what they will do next. • Ss listen to a short dialog and fill in the blanks.	
Development — Listen in Context (8')	• T checks the food names one by one. • Ss listen to a dialog and check in the foods two people will eat. • Ss listen to a dialog one more time if students want to.	CD-ROM Worksheet
Development — Listening Activities	**S** Ss listen to the dialogs and number the pictures. Ss listen to the dialogs again and check T or F. Ss listen to the CD and repeat the dialog.	CD-ROM Worksheet
	B Ss listen to the dialogs and choose the correct pictures. Ss listen to the dialogs again and fill in the blanks. Ss listen to the CD and number the sentences in the correct order.	
	A Ss listen to the dialogs and number the correct pictures. Ss listen to the dialogs again and answer the questions. Ss listen to the CD and fill in the blanks. Ss practice the dialog with partners.	
Closing (5')	• T reviews the lesson. • T gives an assignment.	

S: Supplementary level, B: Basic level, A: Advanced level

2. Video in Action

Unit	Lesson 5. Time and Me	
Period 2/8	Video In Action	
Aims	1. Students can listen and understand the dialog. 2. Students can answer the questions about the dialog. 3. Students can practice the dialog with their partners. 4. Students can summarize the dialog.	
Procedure	Activities	Teaching Aids
Introduction	• T & Ss greet each other and introduce the lesson. • T review the last lesson. • T checks the assignment.	(5')
Development — Before Watching	T talks about the picture in the textbook. T talks about the title and guess what the dialog is about.	picture (3')
Development — Watching	Ss watch the video. Ss watch the video once more. Ss answer the questions.	CD-ROM (10')
Development — After Watching	Ss practice the dialog with partners (line by line). Ss learn about listening tips (listening tips).	(12')
Development — Video Activities — S	Ss watch the video and fill in the blanks with the given words. Ss read the sentences and check T or F. Ss practice the dialog with partners.	
Development — Video Activities — B	Ss watch the video and write in words starting with the given alphabets. Ss fill in the blanks to complete the summary. Ss role-play the dialog.	
Development — Video Activities — A	Ss watch the video and fill in the blanks. T corrects the errors in the summary of the dialog. Ss make their own dialogs and talk with partners.	
Closing	T reviews the lesson. T gives an assignment; to read aloud the dialog script in the worksheet 10 times and write down the script in the notebook once.	

3. 말하기 활동

Unit	Lesson 5. Time and Me	
Period 3/8	Speaking	
Aims	1. Students can ask someone's abilities using the expression "Do you know how to ~?" 2. Students can express their inabilities using the expression "I don't know anything about ~." 3. Students can tell their opinions using the expression "I think ~."	
Procedure	Activities	Aids
Introduction (5')	T & Ss exchange greetings. T reviews the last lesson. T checks the assignment.	
Development — Talk Like This	• Ss understand the example dialog. • Ss practice the dialog with partners using the given pictures and expressions. • Ss make more dialogs about what they know how to do.	CD-ROM (7')
Development — Talk in Context	• Ss understand the example dialog. • Ss understand the verb phrase under the each picture. • Ss practice more dialogs with partners.	(8')
Development — Pronunciation Tips	• Ss practice the sounds of [e] and [iː].	(5')
Development — Speaking Activities (17') — S	• Ss understand the example dialog. • Ss practice dialogs of "what they know how to do" and "do not know anything about". • Ss play a game of telling opinions about others' likes using the expression "I think~".	
Development — Speaking Activities (17') — B	• Ss understand the example dialog. • Ss practice dialogs of "what they know how to do" and "do not know anything about". • Ss play a game of telling opinions about group members using the expression "I think~".	
Development — Speaking Activities (17') — A	• Ss understand the example dialog. • Ss talk with partners using the given expressions. • Ss play a game of telling opinions about group members and expressing agreement on the opinions.	
Closing (5')	• T reviews the lesson. • T gives an assignment ; Ss make and write down a dialog using the expressions students learned in this lesson.	

4. 읽기 활동

Unit	Lesson 5. Time and Me	
Period 5/8	Reading(1) What's your No 1 Treasure?	
Aims	1. Students can read and understand the replies on the Internet bulletin board on teenagers' No 1 treasures. 2. Students can talk or write about their own No. 1 treasures.	
Procedure	Activities	Aids
Introduction	• Ss & T exchange greetings. • T checks the assignment and review the previous lesson.	(5')
Development — Before Reading (5')	• Ss talk about the most important things in life. • T checkz the answers of the pre-reading activity. • Ss look at the pictures on the book and guess what they are going to read about.	CD-ROM
Development — Reading (30')	• T introduces the text briefly. • Ss read the passages on pages 70-73 quickly. • Ss listen to the CD. • Ss listen and repeat after the CD and read the text individually. • Ss read the text aloud together or in groups. • Ss summarize each passage. • Ss learn new words and expressions in the text. • Ss study the text in detail. • Ss answer some comprehension questions.	CD-ROM Worksheet
Closing (5')	• Ss read the text aloud together one more time. • Ss find out each person's No. 1 treasure and underline the reasons. • T gives an assignment; to write about the students' No. 1 treasures in 5-6 sentences.	

5. 쓰기 활동

Unit	Lesson 5. Time and Me	
Period 7/8	Forms in Action, Writing	
Aims	1. Students can understand the usage of subjective relative pronouns and use them. 2. Students can understand the usage of objective relative pronouns and use them. 3. Students can modify nouns with the definite article and superlative adjectives.	
Procedure	Activities	Teaching Aids
Introduction (5')	• Ss & T exchange greetings. • T checks the assignment and review the previous lesson.	
Development — Forms in Action (15')	• Ss study the kinds and usage of subjective relative pronouns: 'who' and 'which'. • Ss study the kinds and usage of objective relative pronouns and make relative pronoun clauses. • Ss study the forms of superlative adjectives. • Ss study how to modify nouns with the definite article and superlative adjectives.	CD-ROM PPT Worksheet
Development — Write	• Ss look at the people and talk about their jobs. • Ss complete the sentences using relative pronouns.	CD-ROM (5')
Development — Write in Context	• Ss look at picture and complete the sentences. • Ss describe the classmates with the definite article and superlative adjectives.	(7')
Development — Writing Activities (10') — S	• Ss write about a person who students want to marry and a house where they want to live with the given expressions. • Ss explain favorites using the given adjectives.	CD-ROM Worksheet
Development — Writing Activities (10') — B	• Ss write about a person who students want to marry and a house where they want to live with relative pronouns and the given expressions. • Ss explain favorites using the given adjectives.	
Development — Writing Activities (10') — A	• Ss write about a person who students want to marry and a house where they want to live with relative pronouns and the given expressions. • Ss complete the dialog of one's favorite food, sport, and teacher.	
Closing (3')	• T sums up the lesson. • T gives an assignment; to write about what kind of people the students want to be in the future.	

CHAPTER 04 Material Development

> **단원 길라잡이**
> - 수업자료 필수내용의 구성요소들을 파악한다.
> - 수업자료 개정을 위한 목표와 방법을 적용한다.

교육과정

　교육과정에서는 일상생활과 일반적인 화제, 학생들의 흥미, 필요, 인지적 수준 등을 고려하여 학습 의욕을 유발할 수 있는 내용, 의사소통능력, 탐구 능력, 문제해결 능력을 기르는 데 도움이 되는 내용, 교육과정에 제시된 성취 기준을 달성하는 데 적합한 내용, 상호작용에 적합한 내용, 문화 이해에 적합한 내용을 제시하여 소재 선정의 방향을 제시하고 있다. 개정 교육과정에서는 문화 요소를 소재에 통합하여 제시하였으므로 언어활동에 문화 요소가 좀 더 자연스럽게 포함되어야 한다. 또한 세계 각국과 활발히 교류가 이루어지는 상황을 반영하여 다양한 문화 이해를 강조함으로써 문화에 관한 내용을 영어권에 국한하지 않고 세계의 다양한 문화로 확대하도록 한다. 즉, 영어를 국제어 또는 글로벌 언어(English as an International or Global Language)로 설정하여 상호 문화 간 이해와 의사소통을 강조하도록 권장한다. 이와 같이 다양해진 내용을 바탕으로 수업에서 자연스럽게 문화를 소재와 연결하여 학습할 수 있도록 한다.

01 Classroom materials

1. Textbooks

(1) Advantages of Textbooks

① Textbooks are especially helpful for beginning teachers. The material to be covered and the design of each lesson are carefully spelled out in detail.

② Textbooks provide organized units of work. A textbook gives you all the plans and lessons you need to cover a topic in some detail.

③ A textbook series provides you with a balanced, chronological presentation of information.

④ Textbooks are a detailed sequence of teaching procedures that tell you what to do and when to do it. There are no surprises — everything is carefully spelled out.

⑤ Textbooks provide administrators and teachers with a complete program. The series is typically based on the latest research and teaching strategies.

⑥ Good textbooks are excellent teaching aids. They're a resource for both teachers and students.

(2) Disadvantages

① Some textbooks may fail to arouse student interest. It is not unusual for students to reject textbooks simply because of what they are – compendiums of large masses of data for large masses of students.

② Students may find it difficult to understand the relevance of so much data to their personal lives.

2. Effective Methods for Materials

(1) Guidelines for Using Textbooks

- Use the textbook as a resource for students, but not the only resource.
- Use the textbook as a guide, not a mandate, for instruction.
- Be free to modify, change, eliminate, or add to the material in the textbook.
- Supplement the textbook with lots of outside readings.
- Supplement teacher information in the textbook with teacher resource books; attendance at local, regional, or national conferences; articles in professional periodicals; and conversations with experienced teachers.

Weakness	Solutions
The textbook is designed as a the sole source of information. Students only see one perspective on a concept or issue.	Provide students with lots of information sources 예 trade books, CD-ROMS, web-sites, encyclopedias, etc.
Textbook is old or outdated. Information shared is not current or relevant.	Use textbook sparingly or supplement with other materials.
Textbook questions tend to be low level or fact-based. Students assume that learning is simply a collection of facts and figures.	Ask higher-level questions and provide creative thinking and problem-solving activities.
Textbook doesn't take students' background knowledge into account or tailor lessons to the specific attributes and interests of students.	Discover what students know about a topic prior to teaching. Design the lesson based on that knowledge.
Reading level of the textbook is too difficult. Students cannot read or understand important concepts.	Use lots of supplemental materials 예 library books, Internet, CD-ROMs, etc.
Textbook has all the answer to all the questions. Students tend to see learning as an accumulation of correct answers.	Involve students in problem-solving activities, higher-level thinking questions, and extending activities.

(2) Reviewing Exercises and Activities in the Textbook

When evaluating the quality of a textbook's exercises or activities, four key questions should be answered:

① Do the exercises and activities in the textbook contribute to learners' language acquisition?

Many exercises included in textbooks are convenient for teachers but don't necessarily contribute to students' language development. Textbooks should include exercises that give students opportunities to practice and extend their language skills. For example, activities that require students to negotiate for meaning in English (예 information gaps, jigsaw activities, role plays) may support the development of speaking skills and help students negotiate for meaning in real-life contexts.

② Are the exercises balanced in their format, containing both controlled and free practice?

Controlled exercises refer to those that guide students to a single correct answer such as a fill-in-the-blank grammar activity, whereas free practice involves exercises in which the answers are limited only by the students' creativity and knowledge. This would include open-ended discussion questions. At times, students will require more guidance with an activity, especially when practicing a structure or function for the first time. For this purpose, controlled exercises are effective. However, students should also be given the chance to extend their experience with the language, and free exercises allow this opportunity.

③ Are the exercises progressive as the students move through the textbook?

　　Exercises should build on and reinforce what students have already learned and should progress from simple, both linguistically and cognitively, to more complex and demanding. A textbook should require more from students as their language skills develop so they are continually stimulated and challenged.

④ Are the exercises varied and challenging?

　　Keeping students motivated and interested as they work through a textbook is much easier if the students see something new in each chapter. Familiarity and routine can be comforting, but too much familiarity can lead to disinterest and boredom. The textbook should fulfill its role as a stimulus for communication and not be simply an organizational tool for the teacher.

3. Checklist for Coursebooks

What does the book offer the teacher?	What does the book offer the students?
• Do the book's priorities match with your priorities? • Does the book seem to do what it claims to do? • Is it clear how to use the book? • Is the book clearly sequenced and structured? • Does it provide integrated revision of key items? • Are there any useful, additional materials? • Does it offer lots of practical ideas? • How does the book develop a balance of all 4 skills? Does this meet your needs? • Does it provide plenty of varied practice of any one set of language items? • Does it help you to set tests? • Does the book manage to avoid sexual, racial and cultural stereotypes?	• Does the book look interesting and fun? • Can the children easily see what they have to do? • Does the book provide much for them to do independently? • Does it give them activities and tasks which are interesting and worthwhile in themselves not just language exercises? • Does it provide plenty for those children who cannot read and write with confidence?

02 Authentic Materials in Classrooms

1. Authentic Materials

(1) Authentic vs Non-authentic Materials

Authentic Materials	Non-authentic Materials
• Language data produced for real life communication purposes. • They may contain false starts, and incomplete sentences. • They are useful for improving the communicative aspects of the language.	• They are specially designed for learning purposes. • They contain well formed sentences all the time. The language is artificial. • They are useful for teaching grammar.

(2) Spoken vs Written Materials

Spoken	Written
TV commercials, films, news items, weather forecasts, airport and station announcement, radio talks, interviews, debates.	recipes, articles, train timetables, advertisements, brochures, poems, application forms, instruction for use of equipment

(3) Criteria for Selecting and Using Authentic Materials

① Important factors in selecting authentic materials
- Textual authenticity
- Suitability of content
- Compatibility with course objectives
- Exploitability

② Appropriate levels

This issue has been surrounded by controversy in the field of language teaching. Some researchers such as Kilickaya (2004) and Kim (2000) claim that authentic materials can be used with intermediate and advanced level students only. On the other hand, others believe that all levels of students, even lower levels, are able to manage using authentic materials.

③ Classroom Materials

Authentic materials must be used in accordance with students' ability. (Baird, 2004). The text should be used to serve its original purpose as if it is used outside the classroom. 예 If students are working with health brochures, they must look for information they need, rather than a list of new words chosen by the teacher. In this respect, Taylor (1994) states that authenticity is not a characteristic of a text in itself: it is a feature of a text in a particular context. Therefore, a text can only be truly authentic in the context for which it was originally written.

(4) Types of Authentic Materials

Breen (1985) identifies four types of authenticity within language teaching. He indicates that these types are in continual interrelationship with one another during any language lesson.

① Authenticity of the texts which we may use as input data for our learners: This refers to the authentic qualities of a given text. Authentic texts for language learning are any sources of data which serves as a means to help the learner to develop an authentic interpretation.

② Authenticity of the learners' own interpretations of such texts: Learner authenticity means that the learner must discover the conventions of communication in the target language which will enable him or her to gradually come to interpret meaning within the text in ways which are likely to be shared with fluent users of the language.

③ Authenticity of tasks conductive to language learning: Task authenticity reflects the purpose to which language input is put. It means that the chosen tasks should involve the learners not only in authentic communication with texts and others in the classroom, but also in learning and the purpose of learning.

④ Authenticity of the actual social situation of the language classroom: The authenticity of the classroom is a special social event and environment wherein people share a primary communicative purpose that is learning. The authentic role of the language classroom is the provision of those conditions in which the participants can publicly share the problems, achievements and overall process of learning a language together as a social activity.

(5) Making Activities Authentic

Hedge (2000) indicates that speaking and writing can be authentic if they reflect the relevant criteria for task design discussed earlier, and also mirror the real world purposes and situations in which and for which language is used. 예

- A note to a neighbor apologizing for a noisy party
- A letter of complaint about a product to the manufacturer

2. Advantages and disadvantages of authentic materials

(1) Advantages of Authentic Materials
- Authentic materials have a positive effect on learner motivation.
- They provide authentic cultural information.
- They provide exposure to real language.
- They relate more closely to learners' needs and interests.
- They support a more creative approach to teaching.
- They provide a wide variety of text types, language styles not easily found in conventional teaching materials.
- Unlike traditional teaching materials, authentic materials are continuously updated.
- They have a positive effect on comprehension and learner satisfaction.

(2) Disadvantages of Authentic Materials
- Authentic materials often contain difficult language, unneeded vocabulary items and complex language structures, which causes a burden for the teacher in lower-level classes and demotivate low level students.
- Authentic materials may be too culturally biased.
- Many structures are mixed in such materials; causing lower levels have a hard time decoding the texts.
- The use of authentic materials is time consuming for the teachers.
- Authentic materials may not expose students to comprehensible input at the earliest stages of acquisition.

3. Integration with Authentic Materials

(1) Choosing Authentic Materials

There are several important points to consider when choosing authentic materials. You should make sure that you have enough copies of the materials to be used so that each student or pair of students can have a copy to use. It is best not to use material with too many pages, unless the pages are clearly numbered for easy reference. If you plan to use the same materials in more than one class, it is important that they be hardy enough to withstand a lot of handling and they should be easily refolded and put back together. Materials with multiple pieces or pages that fall out or come apart should be avoided. Also, keep in mind that some materials are more easily dated than others. 예 Last season's catalog does not have the same impact as a current one which is filled with items which the student could actually order. A menu, on the other hand, can be used as long as the prices remain contemporary. Students are generally uninterested in special events, 예 an Expo, that have already past. Remember to choose material that is appropriate for the students' level. However, a certain amount of adjustment can be made depending on the type and level of questions used in the accompanying question handout.

(2) Using Authentic Materials

When we first began using authentic materials, we handed out materials to each student and had them work individually. However, experience has shown that having students work in pairs is a better approach because they tend to be more enthusiastic and work harder. We give each pair the authentic material and a question handout. Interestingly, the student with the stronger command of English is not necessarily the one who is able to extract the most information from the material. Students of different abilities tend to complement one another and, as a result, do not get bogged down easily. Students tend to contribute individual strengths to the completion of the task. We usually tell students that question handouts will be collected since this keeps them more focused on the completion of the exercise. The teacher's personal anecdotes and other background information should be shared before the students begin concentrating on the material.

After the authentic material has been distributed, we give a brief explanation and point out, 예 the importance of the table of contents in a pamphlet or the legend in a map. We point out small print and other parts of the material that are easily missed. We have found that pointing out Japanese words and products raises the level of interest in the material. This is a good time for the teacher to explain measures, abbreviations, and difficult words and expressions. While the students are working on the assignment, we help them by answering questions and commenting on their work. This is also a good chance to give hints to those who are stuck on a particular question.

Once the allotted time is up, we collect the material along with the question handout and go over the difficult questions with the class. If the handouts are to be factored into the students' grades, it is a good idea to make sure they have a chance to work with various partners over the course of the semester.

핵심플러스 — Materials and Techniques for Communicative Language Teaching

1. **Authentic materials / Realia**
   - The high intermediate level; a real newspaper article, a live radio or television broadcast.
   - Lower level; Realia that do not contain a lot of language, but about which a lot of discussion could be generated.

2. **Scrambled sentences**

    A passage (a text) in which the sentences are in a scrambled order: Students are told to unscramble the sentence(or lines of mixed-up dialog, pictures of picture strip story) so that the sentences are restored to their original order. This type of exercise teaches students about the cohesion and coherence properties of language.

3. **Language games**
   - common with real communicative events
   - Marrow's three features of communicative activities were manifested in the card game (guessing what a student is doing next weekend!). (i) information gap (ii) unpredictability (iii) feedback

4. **Picture strip story**
   - One student in a small group was given a strip story. She showed the first picture of the story to the other members of her group and asked them to predict what the second picture would look like. Picture strip story has features: (i) information gap (ii) unpredictability (iii) feedback.
   - Picture strip story is an example of problem-solving task. Problem-solving task is communicative since students share information, or work together or arrive at a solution. This gives students practice in negotiation of meaning.

5. **Role Play**
   - to practice communicating in different social contexts and in different social roles
   - to learn language forms appropriately (i) information gap (ii) unpredictability (iii) feedback

03 Adaptation for Teaching Materials

1. Objectives and Techniques for Adaptation

① Add real choice
- In choosing the term 'real choice' we are referring to learners deciding how they want to learn rather than what they want to learn.
- Learners can decide whether they would like to follow a route that caters to their preferred cognitive learning style (style matching) or to try a cognitive style that is less comfortable (style stretching).

② Cater for all sensory learning styles

Many ESL learners have strong kinesthetic learning style preferences and their own sensory learning style, such as auditory and visual sides.

③ Provide for more learner autonomy
- Adapting material to provide for learner autonomy may mean including learner training with the objective of helping learners acquire language outside the classroom or without the guidance of the teacher.
- Activities that encourage learners to discover independently rules and conventions about the target language could also have the potential to create autonomous learners.

④ Encourage higher-level cognitive skills
- Encouraging higher-level cognitive skills means adapting materials in such a way as to require students to hypothesize, predict, infer, make connections and associations and visualize.
- This type of higher-level cognitive activity engages and motivates students as well as assists in transferring language skills already developed in their first language to the target language.

⑤ Make the language input more engaging
- One way is to rewrite or re-record text, to give it more authenticity or interest.
- Another way is to change the form of input or to change the nature of the task.

2. Techniques for Adaptation

① Adding
- Extending : When extending an activity the teacher supplies more of the same type of material, thus making a quantitative change.
- Expanding : Expanding classroom material is different from extending in that it adds something different to the materials; the change is qualitative.

② Deleting: As with the technique of adding, material can be deleted both quantitatively (subtracting) or qualitatively (abridging).

③ Simplifying: The teacher could be rewording instructions or text in order to make them more accessible to learners, or simplifying a complete activity to make it more manageable for learners and teachers.

④ Reordering: When reordering, the teacher has decided that it makes more pedagogic sense to sequence activities differently.

⑤ Modifying: The teacher can make them more relevant to students' interests and backgrounds and to restructure classroom management. In the adapted version, the original grammar exercise is adapted by using the modifying technique.

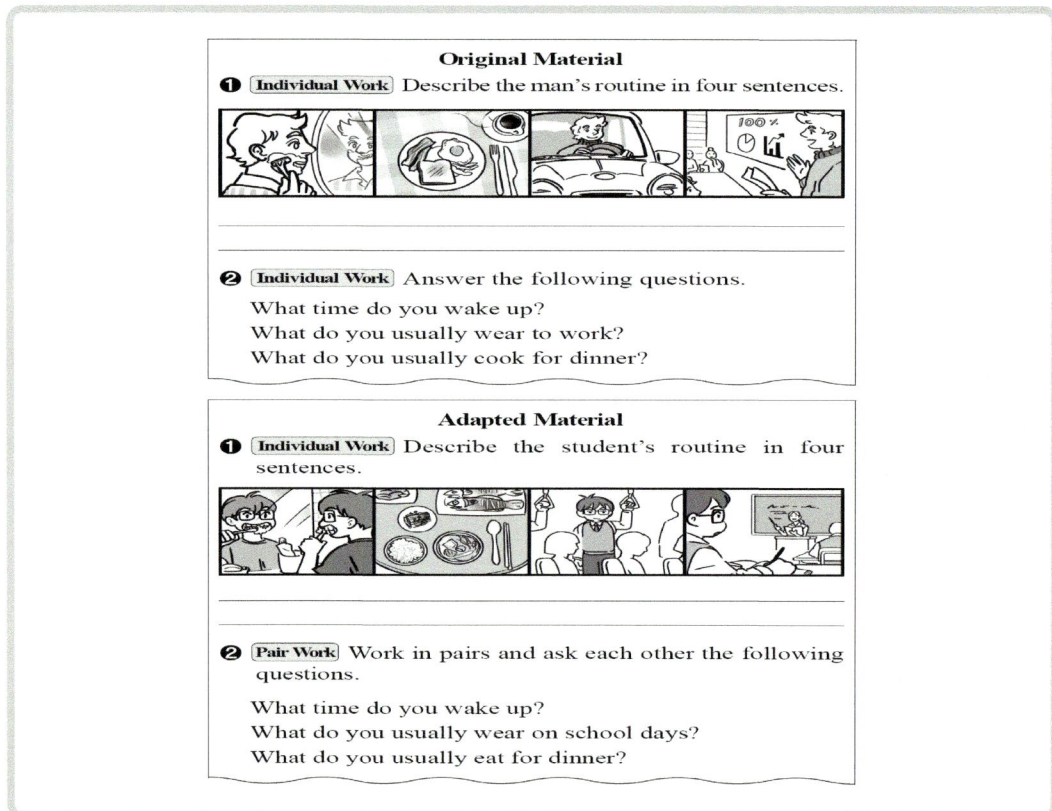

3. Material Adaptation

• 대상자 :	34명의 한국 공립중학교 학생
• 영어학습경험 :	초등학교에서 1~2년의 영어 수업경험이 있으나 간단한 구두 의사소통을 이해하는 데 어려움이 있다.
• 현재 수업 :	일주일에 5시간의 영어 수업
• 현재 자료 :	[Scenario 1, New Horizon1, p50]
• 수업 목표 :	3인칭 단수주어 동사의 현재형에 _s

UNIT 6	
vocabulary:	
sister... brother live(s) well in Australia	This is my sister Becky. She lives in Australia. She likes Korea very much. She speaks Korean well.
play-plays like-likes want-wants	I like Korea. Becky likes Korea. Emi plays tennis. Emi / play, Jun / like, Maki / want

(1) Problems for Material

- Four verbs are presented in a single context and only in writing.
- The activity lacks kinesthetic and auditory sensory input.
- The input is limited and impoverished.
- Students are not given a choice about how they learn nor are they given an opportunity to personalize the input.

(2) Methods for Adaptation

① The materials could be expanded by adding a TPR phase at the beginning to provide kinesthetic and auditory input as well as richer, more contextualized text.

② Learners have an opportunity to attend to the input globally and interpret meaning before analysing the input to understand its form.

- Teacher mimes Becky's daily routine and asks students to guess what she does each day.
- Teacher acts out Becky's daily routine while reading the script.
- Students act Becky's daily routine while teacher reads the script as below:

> Every day Becky wakes up at 6:30 in the morning. She stretches her arms and rubs her eyes and she yawns. Then she brushes her teeth and takes a shower. Sometimes she likes to sing in the shower. She puts on her clothes and eats her breakfast, usually toast and coffee. After breakfast, she speaks to her dog. At 7:30 she leaves her apartment and takes the subway to school.

(3) Procedure for Adaptation
- Extend the exercise by adding sentences about Becky.
- Students write sentences that they remember about Becky's routine.
- Students underline the verbs in the sentences about Becky.
- Students put verbs in two columns, regular and irregular verbs.

 문헌읽기

    Choosing a coursebook is one of the most important selections which teachers can make. Teachers cannot influence their working lives in many ways. You cannot choose your teaching hours, your holiday periods, the classes you teach, the learners who are in those classes, or the classrooms you use, but you can choose your coursebook. You select a coursebook for your learners and for yourself, so you first need to analyse your learners' needs and your own needs.

What do you want from a Coursebook?

    Teachers want different things from their coursebooks and they use them in different ways. Some teachers want a coursebook to provide everything. They want the teacher's book to tell us what to do, in which sequence to do each activity and how to assess the progress which our learners have made. However, some teachers do not want the coursebook to control their lives. They want to be able to plan their own lessons or even their own syllabus. They want the coursebook to be a library of materials from which they can choose to be used in the ways they choose.

What can a good Coursebook give the teacher?

A good coursebook can help a teacher by providing:

① a clearly thought out programme which is appropriately sequenced and structured to include progressive revision;
- a wider range of materials than an individual teacher may be able to collect
- security
- economy of preparation time
- a source of practical ideas

② work that the learners can do on their own so that the teacher does not need to be centre stage all the time;
- a basis for homework if this is required
- a basis for discussion and comparison with other teachers

What do your learners need from a Coursebook?

Children want a coursebook to be colourful and interesting. They hope the coursebook will contain exciting games and activities. They hope the cassettes will contain exciting stories, amusing dialogues and entertaining songs and rhymes. But what do the children need? We all know that children have short memories. They find it difficult to retain ideas and language from one lesson to the next. So the children need a coursebook which becomes an accessible and understandable record of their work. A good coursebook gives the children:

- a sense of progress, progression and purpose
- a sense of security
- scope for independent and autonomous learning
- a reference for checking and revising

The perfect Coursebook

The Perfect coursebook for every teacher and every class does not exist. When selecting a coursebook you always need to make a compromise. There will be things which you don't like about any coursebook. How important are those things? Can you create materials to substitute those aspects? Has the coursebook got something missing? Can you find or create materials to fill that gap? Remember that you work in partnership with your coursebook. Never expect the coursebook to do everything for you. You will always need to personalise your teaching with your own personality.

What can you contribute to the Coursebook?

As a teacher you have a collection of skills. There are some things which you may be very good at doing. Are you a great artist who can draw all the pictures you need? Are you a musician who can play and sing any songs you need? Do you know hundreds of simple games for your learners to play? Do you have a good competence in English? It may not be enough to be a native speaker, you also need to be able to analyse and grade the language which you teach your learners.

Sample of Level-integrated Lesson Plan

	Listening (Middle School 1)			
General Aims	<ul><li>어조나 억양으로 화자의 느낌이나 정서를 파악한다.</li><li>일상생활에 관한 말이나 대화를 듣고 요지를 파악한다.</li><li>과거, 현재, 미래에 관한 일상생활에 관련된 말이나 대화를 듣고 이해한다.</li><li>간단한 말이나 대화를 듣고 사건의 순서를 이해한다.</li><li>일상생활에 관한 말이나 대화를 듣고 상황 및 화자 간의 관계를 파악한다.</li></ul>			
Introduction (5')	Greet Present today's lesson			
	Textbook	English Activities		
		Supplementary:	Basic:	Advanced:
Development (35')	<ul><li>Get ready</li><li>Match pictures</li><li>Choose the correct answers after listening</li><li>Choose the purpose of the dialog</li><li>Check T/F</li><li>Complete the dialog</li></ul>	<ul><li>Listen and number the box</li><li>Check the correct box while listening</li><li>Choose the correct pictures after listening</li><li>Predict a dialog with given pictures and simple words</li><li>Check T or F</li><li>Distinguish a variety of accents</li><li>Listen and repeat words and sounds</li></ul>	<ul><li>Listen and match with inference</li><li>Choose the right word listening again</li><li>Number the boxes and pictures in order</li><li>Fill in the blanks and restructure in longer, more complex sentences with some clues</li></ul>	<ul><li>Write the correct words in the box while listening</li><li>Fill in the blanks for making new sentences</li><li>Predict a dialog with given some</li><li>After listening, guess what might come next in the dialog</li><li>Summarize the dialog with some words and expressions and say it</li></ul>
Consolidation (5')	<ul><li>Summarize the lesson</li><li>Give Ss homework</li></ul>			

CHAPTER 05 Classroom Activities

> **단원 길라잡이**
> - 교실활동의 의사소통적인 기능과 기계적 연습을 구별한다.
> - 그룹활동의 다양한 종류를 과업에 맞도록 적용할 줄 안다.

01 Classroom Activities

1. Types of classroom activities

(1) Manipulative and communicative sides

① Manipulative side : A technique is totally controlled by the teacher and requires a predicted response.
   예 choral repetition, cued substitution drill, dictation, reading aloud

② Communicative side : Student responses are completely open-ended and unpredictable.
   예 story-telling, brainstorming, role-plays, games

(2) Drills

① Mechanical Drills

A mechanical drill is one where there is complete control over the student's response, and where comprehension is not required in order to produce a correct response.

Teacher	Student
book	Give me the book.
ladle	Give me the ladle.

② Meaningful Drills

In language teaching and in particular audiolingualism, a distinction between different types of drills is sometimes made according to the degree of control the drill makes over the response produced by the student. A meaningful drill is one in which there is still control over the response, but understanding is required so that the student produces a correct response.

Teacher reads a sentence	Student chooses a response
I'm hot.	I'll get you something to eat.
I'm cold.	I'll turn on the air conditioning.
I'm thirsty.	I'll get you something to drink.
I'm hungry.	I'll turn on the heater.

③ Communicative Drills are one in which the type of response is controlled but the student provides his or her own content or information.

Teacher	Student completes cue
What time did you get up on Sunday?	I got up _____
What did you have for breakfast?	I had _____
What did you do after breakfast?	I _____

Drills, however, are less commonly used in language teaching today and have been replaced by more communicative teaching strategies.

02 Interactive Language Teaching

1. Principles for Interactive Language Teaching

- Automaticity: focal attention-meaning & message
- Intrinsic motivation: fulfillment & self actualization
- Strategic investment: strategies for production and comprehension
- Willingness to Communicate: "I want to reach out to others and communicate"
- Language-culture connection: cultural nuances in language
- Interlanguage: teacher feedback to the developmental process
- Communicative competence: grammatical, discourse, sociolinguistic, pragmatic, strategic

2. Group work

(1) Advantages

① Shared Ideas

One of the main benefits of group work or a team environment is the ability to share ideas among the group. Perhaps there are several possible approaches to a project, and as an individual, a staffer may be unsure of which to take. However, as a team, the members can each contribute pros and cons of approaches to tasks and methods to accomplish key goals. This kind of collaboration both benefits the project and gives team members an outlet to bounce around ideas.

② Increased Efficiency

Another key advantage of group work is that things get done faster. When a group attacks a project or task, it can be done more quickly and with greater efficiency than if just one person attempted to muddle through it. A group approach can lead to cost savings for the company, since groups accomplish more, as well as an ability to meet individual and team goals more quickly, since more people are attacking the task.

③ Accountability for Weak Areas

Working as a team not only helps to showcase people's various strengths, but can also allow for compensation of weaker areas as well. Teacher can distribute the workload so that people are playing to their strengths with their work and team up to tackle areas where they are weaker to allow for improvement.

④ Improved Relationships

When people work together as a team, they not only become more invested in the project, they become more invested in one another as well. Team members support one another, even outside of the team structure, and adapt to each other's working styles. The team relationship may result in teamwork approaches even outside of the teamwork structure, resulting in peers lending a hand on other assignments and sharing ideas or brainstorms to propel one another along to reach personal and academic goals.

(2) Types of Group Work

Types	Features
Games	In language teaching, an organized activity that usually has the following properties: (a) a particular task or objective, (b) a set of rules, (c) competition between players, (d) communication between players by spoken or written language. Games are often used as a fluency activity in communicative language teaching and humanistic methods.
Role-play	Drama-like classroom activities in which students take the roles of different participants in a situation and act out what might typically happen in that situation. 예 To practise how to express complaints and apologies in a foreign language, students might have to role-play a situation in which a customer in a shop returns a faulty article to a salesperson.
Simulation	Classroom activities which reproduce or simulate real situations and which often involve dramatization and group discussion, which does not include group discussion: In simulation activities, learners are given roles in a situation, tasks, or a problem to be solved, and are given instructions to follow (예 an employer-employee discussion over wage increases in a factory). The participants then make decisions and proposals. Consequences are "simulated" on the basis of decisions the participants take. They later discuss their actions, feelings, and what happened.
Projects	An activity which centres around the completion of a task, and which usually requires an extended amount of independent work either by an individual student or by a group of students: Much of this work takes place outside the classroom. Project work often involves three stages: ① Classroom planning: The students and teacher discuss the content and scope of the project, and their needs. ② Carrying out the project: The students move out of the classroom to complete their planned tasks (예 conducting interviews, collecting information). ③ Reviewing and monitoring: This includes discussions and feedback sessions by the teacher and participants, both during and after the project. In language teaching, project work is thought to be an activity which promotes co-operative learning, reflects the principles of student centered teaching, and promotes language learning through using the language for authentic communicative purposes.
Interview	A conversation between an investigator and an individual or a group of individuals in order to gather information. Interviews are used to gather data for linguistic analysis and may be used in needs analysis.

Types	Features
Brainstorming	In language teaching, a group activity in which learners have a free and relatively unstructured discussion on an assigned topic as a way of generating ideas: It often serves as preparation for another activity. In teaching writing, a form of prewriting in which a group of students write down as many thoughts as possible on a topic without paying attention to organization, sentence structure or spelling. It serves to gather ideas, viewpoints, or ideas related to a writing topic and is said to help the writer produce ideas. Other writing activities sometimes included under brainstorming are: • clustering: the student writes a topic or concept in the middle of a page and gathers ideas into clusters around the topic. • word bank: the student lists words that come to mind about a topic and then arranges them into categories. • mapping: the student prepares a graphic representation of key words to be used in a composition.
Information gap	In communication between two or more people, there is a situation where information is known by only some of those present. In communicative language teaching in order to promote real communication between students, there must be an information gap between them. Without such a gap the classroom activities and exercises will be mechanical and artificial.
Jigsaw task	The teacher takes a written narrative or conversation and cuts each sentence of the text into a strip, and gives one to each student. Students read their strip and report to the others what it contains. Students work together to decide where each of their sentences belongs in the whole context of the story, to stand in their position once it is determined, and to read off the reconstructed story.
Decision making	The aim is to teach students the steps involved in effective decision-making/ problem-solving. This skill is a useful skill for students to learn, as it will assist students to consider all the options that are available to them and the related consequences of each option when they are making a decision or solving a potential problem. Decision making/ problem solving can be one skill used to help students to make an informed decision if they are considering either initiating or ceasing computer game use.
Problem-solving tasks	Simple tasks, often involving word puzzles or simple drawings, used to stimulate pair work and oral discussion among small groups of second language learners: The use of such tasks is characteristic of some phases of lessons in the communicative approach.

Types	Features
Reasoning Gap	Which are the most important qualities in a small company manager? Add four more to the list, then compare your work with your partner's and justify your choice. Work in pairs. normally patient strict on deadlines sense of humor help with personal problems
Dialog journal	This offers students a way to convey real thoughts and get feedback from the teacher on both form and content in the form of written conversation.

(3) Group work vs Pair work

Both pair work and group work have a place in English language classes. Using a variety of seating arrangements and groupings of students is important as it allows learners to practice different types of things. Working with others gives students the opportunity to interact with a variety of people and learn from one another. It also encourages cooperation which will help students get along in class and could reduce the number of student outbursts too.

① Pair work

Pair work is great for practicing model dialogues, playing games such as battleship, conducting vocabulary checks, and completing worksheets. Working in pairs gives individual students a lot of speaking time. If working together, students will often have more confidence than when completing exercises individually. If students are competing with their partners, they will be more motivated.

② Group work

Students can work in groups or form teams for role plays, races, games such as board games or card games, and discussions. Groups give students the opportunity to create more complex dialogues, explore relationships between characters, pool knowledge together, and have a more social learning environment. Additionally there is a better chance for self correction or peer correction and for a discussion on a wider range of thoughts and opinions with larger group sizes. On the other hand, individual speaking time is limited when working in groups. You can increase the amount of speaking time students have by decreasing the size of groups to three or four people. If you are in a large class and want all the groups to present material at the end of the lesson, larger groups may be necessary but limit group size to about six.

③ Seating arrangement

Besides pair work and group work, students can also complete activities individually and as a class. Mixing up the structure of your activities will keep classes interesting but be sure not to waste a lot of time rearranging the classroom. If you make groups for an activity at the beginning of class, it may be best to stick with that arrangement for the duration of the lesson.

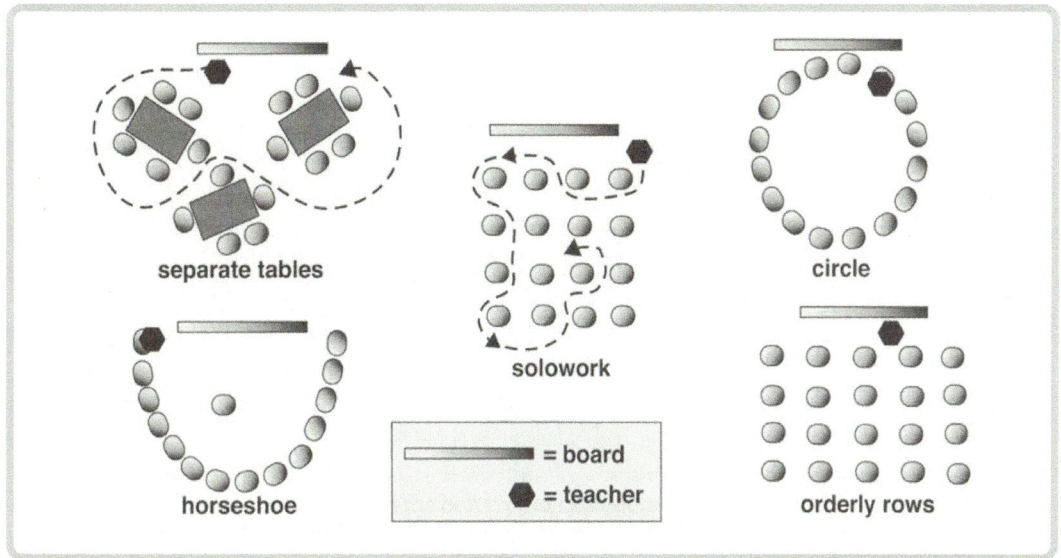

문헌읽기 **Group work vs Whole-class activities**

(1) Group work

Group work came into the standard EFL teaching repertoire with communicative methodologies in the 1970s. At that time, studies of contemporary foreign language classes revealed that as much as 80% of lesson time consisted of the teacher talking to (at) the students. In a class of, say, 30 students, it is evident that the learner hardly got a chance to practise the language. Teacher Talking Time (TTT) became taboo and ways were devised to stamp it out and train the students to actually perform in the language they were learning.

Group work was thus introduced into the EFL repertoire to come to grips with a particular problem. Group work made it possible for the teacher to devote more time to the students' oral production, which perhaps before had not been a priority of the foreign language classroom. Thanks to group work, less confident students get the chance to put their knowledge of the new language into practice in a non-threatening environment, away from the critical eye and ear of the teacher. Instead of being dependent on the teacher, students get used to helping and learning from each other. Meanwhile, the teacher is left free to discreetly monitor progress and give help, advice and encouragement where and when it is needed.

(2) Whole-class discussion

An important aspect of whole-class discussion is the welding together of the whole group and the camaraderie that comes about when a whole group works together towards a common goal. Moreover, there is diversity in numbers; the larger the group, the more variety there is in the ideas, opinions and experiences which can contribute to the learning process. This can stimulate a greater involvement in each member of the class. Furthermore, whole-class discussion is likely to be content based, rather than form based, encouraging fluency and a more memorable and meaningful exchange among the participants. It might also be more appropriate for the introverted and reflective learner. Finally, if we are talking about classes of 15 students or so, there are likely to be many opportunities of letting the whole class function as a single unit instead of dividing it into groups.

The two techniques can go hand in hand. After a session of group work, a whole-class feedback phase will give cohesion to the learning process. Ideally, the group work that has gone before will ensure that everyone has something to say, and also a reason for listening. Having "rehearsed" in a more intimate context beforehand, students may face the whole class with more confidence in their ability to handle the target language.

CHAPTER 06 ICT 지도

> **단원 길라잡이**
> - 여러 학습법과 교수법을 통합하는 기저에 깔린 교육적 원리를 이해할 수 있다.
> - 각 원리들에 있는 여러 측면을 교실수업에 적용시킬 수 있다.
> - 내적 동기와 외적 동기를 이해하고 내적 동기가 수업 내에서 어떻게 구현되는지 이해할 수 있을 것이다.

교육과정

1. 학생 중심 영어 교육

기본적인 교수방법이 과거에는 교사위주로 주입식 교육이 되어왔으나 제6차 교육과정에서부터 학생의 요구와 활동중심으로 변화되었다. 교재의 구성은 학습자의 인지발달, 학습심리, 사고력 창조 등을 고려하여 학생의 능동적 참여를 유도하도록 하였고 영어 학습에 흥미를 느낄 수 있도록 내용을 개정하였다. 또한 단일 문장에서 사용할 수 있는 어휘를 제한하여 학생들의 지적수준에 알맞은 수준의 문장을 예시문으로 선정하여 학생들의 학습 부담을 줄이도록 했다. 중학교와 고등학교에서 공통적으로 사용할 수 있는 기본어휘를 사용하여 난이도 격차를 줄이고 연계성이 있는 교육이 되도록 했다.

2. 4기능을 위한 교육과정

중학교와 고등학교는 단계형과 심화 보충형으로 구성되어 있어 수준별 학습을 지향하고 있다. 교과서는 이러한 언어의 네 가지 기능을 개발하는 데 필요한 대화연습(dialogues), 듣기연습(listening), 듣고 말하는 연습(listen and speak), 발음연습(pronunciation), 읽기학습(reading), 쓰기학습(writing), 문법(grammar), 어휘(vocabulary), 다양한 협동학습(cooperative learning activities) 등의 학습요소들로 구성되어 있다. 학습요소는 영어과 학습시 교수 대상이 되는 학습내용으로 대화는 의사소통(예 길묻기), 듣기학습(예 그림과 소리를 일치시키는 능력), 발음(예 유사한 발음듣고 차이점 인지하고 따라하기), 문법(예 그림을 보고 주어진 단어로 문법에 알맞게 변형하여 넣는 능력), 단어학습(예 그림을 보고 빈칸에 단어를 생각하여 알맞게 넣을 수 있는 능력), 작문학습(예 주어진 주제에 알맞게 글을 써보는 능력), 문화학습(예 영어 문화권에 특징적인 요소들을 그림으로 제시하여 관련소리를 들어보기) 등으로 구분하였다.

3. 멀티미디어 자료 개발의 의의

학습자들의 지속적인 학습을 위한 다양한 학습에로의 방법을 위해 멀티미디어 학습자료 개발은 학생들의 의사소통능력을 신장시키고 영어 학습이 일어날 수 있도록 추출한 학습요소에 게임형을 접목시킨 학습활동을 개발해서 영어학습이 유의적이고 흥미로운 학습이 될 수 있도록 했다. 학습자 자료들은 청각적인 자료와 시각적인 자료들을 이용하여 언어를 발표할 수 있도록 멀티미디어 요소를 통합하여 제시했다. 또한 교사들이 다양한 협동 학습을 통하여 영어를 영어로 가르칠 수 있도록 협동학습 모듈을 연구 고안하여 "영어를 영어로 (Teaching English through English)" 가르칠 수 있도록 했다.

01. ICT in the classroom

There has been much debate over the use of information and communication technology (ICT) in the ESL/EFL classroom over the past decade. Many teachers feel that ICT is useful to teaching and/or learning experience. There are many uses of the computer in the classroom. In today's feature ICT can be successfully employed not only for grammar practice and correction, but also for communicative activities. Successful communication learning is dependent on the student's desire to participate.

Most teachers are familiar with students who complain about poor speaking and communication skills, who however, when asked to communicate, are often reluctant to do so. This lack of participation is often caused by the artificial nature of the classroom. When asked to communicate about various situations, students should also be involved in the actual situation. Decision making, asking for advice, agreeing and disagreeing, and compromising with fellow students are all tasks that cry out for "authentic" settings. It is in these settings that ICT can be used to great advantage. By using the computer as a tool to create student projects, research information and provide context, teachers can employ the computer to help students become more involved in the task at hand, thereby facilitating the necessity of effective communication within a group setting.

1. Advantages using ICT

- Opportunity for learners to notice language forms
- A means for providing optimal modified input to learners
- Multimodal (visual, auditory, written) practice
- Immediate, personalized feedback
- Individualization in a large class
- Self-pacing
- Private space to make mistakes
- Convenient mode for [distance] teacher feedback
- Convenient venue for [written] practice of the L2
- Collaborative projects
- Variety in the resources available and learning styles used
- Exploratory learning with large amounts of language(corpus) data
- Real-life skill building in computer use
- The fun factor

2. Exercises using ICT

(1) Exercise 1: Focus on Passive Voice

Generally, students coming from around the world are more than happy to speak about their native country. Obviously, when speaking about a country (city, state etc.) the passive voice is required. The following activity using the computer will be of great assistance in helping students focus on the correct use of the passive voice for communication and reading and writing skills.

- Inductively review the passive structures in class (or introduce the passive structures).
- Provide a text example, focusing on a specific location, that includes many passive voice structures.
- Have students read through the text.
- As a follow up, have students separate passive voice and active voice examples.
- Using a program or any other multimedia encyclopaedia, (or the Internet) have students working in small groups find information about their own nation.
- Based on the information they have found, students then write a short report together at the computer (using a spell check, communicating about formatting etc.).
- Students then report back to the class presenting their report created at the computer.

This exercise is a perfect example of involving students in an authentic activity that focuses on communication skills while at the same time including a grammar focus, and uses the computer as a tool. Students have fun together, communicate in English and are proud of the results they achieve – all ingredients for successful inductive learning of the passive voice in a communicative manner.

(2) Exercise 2: Strategy Games

For younger learners of English, strategy games can be one of the most effective ways to get students to communicate, agree and disagree, ask for opinions and generally use their English in an authentic setting. Students are asked to focus on the successful completion of a task such as solving riddles (*Myst, Riven*) and developing strategies (SIM City). Choose a strategy game such as a SIM or mystery;

- Have students divide into teams
- Create a specific task in the game itself, such as the completion of a certain level, the creation of a certain type of environment, the solving of a specific riddle. This is important for providing a framework and specific language needs/goals for a common ground in the classroom.
- Have students complete the task.
- Have students come together in the classroom and compare strategies.

Once again, students who find it difficult to participate in a classroom setting (예 Describe your favourite holiday? Where did you go? What did you do? etc.) generally become involved. The focus is not on their completing a task which can be judged as correct or incorrect, but rather on the enjoyable atmosphere of team work which a computer strategy game provides.

02 Methods of using ICT

1. Computer Adaptive Testing (CAT)

(1) Tests

CAT successively selects questions so as to maximize the precision of the exam based on what is known about the examinee from previous questions. From the examinee's perspective, the difficulty of the exam seems to tailor itself to his or her level of ability. 예 If an examinee performs well on an item of intermediate difficulty, he will then be presented with a more difficult question. Or, if he performed poorly, he would be presented with a simpler question. Compared to static multiple choice tests that nearly everyone has experienced, with a fixed set of items administered to all examinees, computer-adaptive tests require fewer test items to arrive at equally accurate scores. (Of course, there is nothing about the CAT methodology that requires the items to be multiple-choice; but just as most exams are multiple-choice, most CAT exams also use this format.)

(2) Advantages and Disadvantages

Adaptive tests can provide uniformly precise scores for most test-takers. In contrast, standard fixed tests almost always provide the best precision for test-takers of medium ability and increasingly poorer precision for test-takers with more extreme test scores. An adaptive test can typically be shortened by 50% and still maintain a higher level of precision than a fixed version. This translates into a time savings for the test-taker. Test-takers do not waste their time attempting items that are too hard or trivially easy. Additionally, the testing organization benefits from the time savings; the cost of examinee seat time is substantially reduced. Like any computer-based test, adaptive tests may show results immediately after testing. Adaptive testing, depending on the item selection algorithm, may reduce exposure of some items because examinees typically receive different sets of items rather than the whole population being administered a single set. However, because the development of a CAT involves much more expense than a standard fixed-form test, a large population is necessary for a CAT testing program to be financially fruitful. It may increase the exposure of others (namely the medium or medium/easy items presented to most examinees at the beginning of the test).

2. Concordance

(1) Definition

A list of all the words which are used in a particular text or in the works of a particular author, together with a list of the contexts in which each word occurs (usually not including highly frequent grammatical words such as articles and prepositions): Concordances have been used in the study of word frequencies, grammar, discourse and stylistics. In recent years the preparation of concordances by computers has been used to analyze individual texts, large samples of writing by a particular author, or different genres and registers. A collection of texts for such purposes is called a corpus. Computer concordances are now often used in the preparation of dictionaries, since they enable lexicographers to study how words are used in a wide range of contexts.

(2) Uses

- Collaborative projects
- Peer-editing of compositions
- E-mail
- Blogs and Web-based bulletin board communication
- Web page design
- Videoconferencing
- Reinforcement of classroom material
- Podcasting
- Games and simulations
- Computer-adaptive testing
- Speech recognition software
- Concordancing
- Multimedia presentations

▶ Sample of ICT: Online Chatting

	Online Chatting				
평가 목표	온라인 채팅에 관한 토론을 할 수 있다.				
활동 개요	온라인 채팅에 관해 모둠별로 찬성 또는 반대의 입장을 정리하여 쓸 수 있다. 주어진 표현을 사용하여 찬성 혹은 반대의 이유를 말할 수 있다.				
소요시간	2차시	대상학년	중 2	활동 유형	모둠 활동 〈발표〉

---

1. 1차시 – 발표 준비

- 주어진 topic과 관련하여 토론을 거쳐 모둠의 입장을 결정
- 주어진 표현을 사용하여 찬성 또는 반대의 이유를 4가지 이상 작성
- 모둠의 발표문 작성 시 사전을 참조하거나 교사에게 문의
- 작성한 것은 수업 종료 전 교사에게 제출
- 〈Speaking Practice〉를 통하여 온라인 채팅과 관련한 표현을 연습

〈Speaking Practice〉

Things to remember:
- Each group should say 5 or more reasons.
- Use all the key sentences and highlight them.
- Hand in one copy per group at the end of this class. Key Expressions:

    I'm for (against) ~.   It's good for ~.
    It helps us ~.   It's (easy/hard) to spend (too) much time ~ing

Work with a classmate and take turns saying each sentence using the words given.
Online chatting:

1. It's good for *making friends*. (sharing ideas, getting information)
2. It helps us *relax*. (learn more)
3. It's *easy* to spend too much time chatting online. (bad, unhealthy)
4. It's not as *natural* as *talking face to face*. (good, easy, chatting on the phone)

2. 2차시 - 발표

- 모둠의 조장은 먼저 모둠의 입장을 밝히고 구성원은 모둠의 입장을 지지하는 이유를 한 가지씩 차례로 발표
- 발표시 동료 평가를 통해 다른 모둠의 발표를 경청하도록 유도

A. 교사 평가표

Student ID	Category										Total (10)
	Worksheet (4)				Presentation(4)				Peer Evaluation(2)		
	Sub-mission	Key Expression	Creativity	Team Work	Fluency	Delivery	Attitude	Peer response	Attitude	Sub mission	
1.											
2.											

B. 동료 평가표

Student ID	Title	Evaluation								Best Team
		Fluency				Delivery				
		S1	S2	S3	S4	S1	S2	S3	S4	

권영주 영어교육론

문헌읽기   ICT learning

ICT (Information and Communication Technology) learning in the ESL (English as a Second Language) context refers to the integration of digital tools and technology to enhance the teaching and learning of English. It leverages computers, tablets, smartphones, online platforms, and multimedia resources to create dynamic and interactive learning experiences for students.

(1) Key Features of ICT Learning in ESL

① Digital Tools for Language Practice
- Online dictionaries, grammar checkers, and thesauruses for vocabulary building.
- Pronunciation apps and software for practicing speaking and listening skills.
- Interactive whiteboards and multimedia presentations to support visual and auditory learning.

② E-Learning Platforms
- Learning Management Systems (LMS) like Moodle, Blackboard, or Google Classroom to organize resources and track progress.
- Online courses or tutorials for self-paced learning.

③ Authentic Language Exposure
- Access to real-world materials like podcasts, news articles, videos, and blogs.
- Virtual exchanges or communication with native speakers through platforms like Zoom or Skype.

④ Collaborative Learning
- Tools like Padlet, Google Docs, or Microsoft Teams to encourage group projects and peer feedback.
- Forums and discussion boards for interactive learning.

⑤ Gamification
- Apps and platforms like Duolingo, Kahoot, and Quizlet use games to motivate and engage learners in vocabulary and grammar practice.

⑥ Assessment and Feedback
- Online quizzes and tests to provide instant feedback.
- AI-powered tools for evaluating writing (e.g., Grammarly) or speaking (e.g., ELSA Speak).

(2) Advantages of ICT

- Enhanced Engagement: ICT tools make learning interactive and engaging through multimedia and gamified approaches.
- Personalized Learning: Adaptive technologies can cater to different proficiency levels, learning paces, and styles.
- Increased Accessibility: Learners can access resources anytime and anywhere, breaking geographical and temporal barriers.

- Authentic Communication: ICT allows learners to practice real-life language use through virtual interactions with native speakers or culturally relevant materials.
- Immediate Feedback: Tools like language apps and quizzes provide instant correction and guidance.

(3) Challenges of ICT in ESL
- Digital Divide: Not all students have equal access to devices or reliable internet connections.
- Teacher Training: Instructors may lack the technical skills or confidence to integrate ICT effectively.
- Overreliance on Technology: Excessive use of ICT can reduce face-to-face interaction and cultural immersion.
- Quality Control: Online resources vary widely in quality, and learners may encounter misleading or incorrect materials.

(4) Strategies for Effective ICT Integration
- Blended Learning Approach: Combine traditional teaching methods with ICT tools to balance technology use with interpersonal interaction.
- Training for Teachers: Provide professional development workshops to help teachers learn how to use ICT tools effectively.
- Promote Digital Literacy: Teach students how to use ICT responsibly and evaluate the reliability of online resources.
- Interactive and Task-Based Learning: Use ICT tools for meaningful tasks like creating digital presentations, blogging, or participating in virtual cultural exchanges.

ICT learning in ESL contexts represents a transformative approach to language acquisition. By integrating technology into the curriculum, it enriches the learning experience, making it more engaging, accessible, and aligned with the needs of 21st-century learners. However, it requires thoughtful implementation and support to overcome challenges and maximize its potential.

6

Language Assessment

01. Assessment Principles
02. Assessing Language Skills

CHAPTER 01 Assessment Principles

단원 길라잡이
- 평가의 원리와 종류를 익힌다.
- 수행 평가의 종류와 특성을 알아 수업에 활용한다.

Introduction

평가를 이야기할 때 가장 중요한 관점 중의 하나는 learning과 teaching 그리고 assessment (testing)을 따로 생각하지 말아야 한다는 것이다. 이제 평가는 학습자에게 위협을 끼치는 단순히 grading을 부여하거나 correction의 수단으로만 쓰여서는 안된다. 즉 평가는 학습과정 안에서 이용되고 다음 학습을 강화하기 위하여 만들어져야 한다. 그래서 평가내용은 authentic하고 실제생활에 있는 tasks를 이용하고 communicative competence를 목표로 하여 평가할 수 있게 됩니다. testing은 교사와 interaction을 하게 되는 기회이며, 학생들의 언어능력 향상을 도와 주도록 의도되어야 한다.

임용시험의 평가영역에서는 다섯 종류의 평가 원리, validity, reliability, practicality, authenticity, washback을 이해하는 것으로 시작되어야 할 것이다. 그리고 multiple-choice test에서의 item analysis에 대한 이해가 필요하다. 세부적으로 language skills를 평가할 때 사용하는 평가도구에 대한 분석을 통해 실제 교실에 적용할 수 있도록 발달되어야 할 것이다.

교육과정

가. 평가 계획

(1) 평가 계획의 방향
- ㈎ 영어과 평가의 원리를 반영하여 평가 계획을 세운다.
- ㈏ 평가 목적을 달성하고 그 효과를 극대화하기 위해 사전에 준비하고 계획한다.
- ㈐ 교수·학습 활동과 평가를 연계하여 학습 과정과 성취 기준 도달 여부를 평가한다.

(2) 평가 계획의 방법 : 평가계획서를 작성
- ㈎ 평가의 목적
- ㈏ 평가의 대상과 시기
- ㈐ 평가의 내용 (언어기능, 의사소통기능, 주제, 소재)
- ㈑ 평가 방법 (분리평가와 통합평가의 비율, 선택형과 서답형의 비율 등)
- ㈒ 평가 세부 사항

문항 수	언어 형태	배점 및 시간	평가 기법	수행평가 기준
	음성/문자 언어		각 언어기능 별로 구체적인 평가 기법	채점척도와 각 척도에 대한 설명

- ㈓ 평가 시행 절차와 채점 방법과 절차
- ㈔ 평가 결과 보고 방법과 절차

(3) 평가 계획상의 유의점
- ㈎ 학습의 결과와 과정을 모두 평가하여 교육의 목표 달성 여부와 정도를 효과적으로 알 수 있도록 계획한다.
- ㈏ 동일한 평가에 관한 기존의 결과분석 자료 등을 평가 계획 수립에 참고한다.

나. 평가 목표와 내용

(1) 평가 목표 수립과 내용 선정의 방향
- ㈎ 평가 목표와 내용은 교육과정에서 제시한 교육목표와 성취 기준에 바탕을 두도록 한다.
- ㈏ 언어능력을 적정하게 평가할 수 있도록 평가 목표를 수립하고 내용을 선정하여 내용타당도를 높인다.

(2) 평가 내용 선정상의 유의점
- ㈎ 적절한 과업을 통해 언어적 요소와 의사소통적 요소를 측정할수 있도록 평가내용을 선정한다.
- ㈏ 평가 내용에 포함될 언어와 과업은 진정성 있는 것을 선정하되, 학생의 수준 등을 고려하여 재구성할 수 있다.
- ㈐ 단편적인 지식보다는 학생의 언어 지식, 배경 지식, 의사소통 책략 등이 복합적으로 활발한 상호작용을 할 수 있는 평가 내용을 선정한다.
- ㈑ 영어 학습에 대한 긍정적 태도를 가지며 자기 주도적인 학습이 이루어질 수 있도록 적절한 평가 내용을 선정한다.

다. 평가 방법

(1) 평가 방법 선정의 방향
(가) 평가의 목적과 종류, 학생의 수준에 따라 적절한 평가 방법을 사용한다.
(나) 언어 및 배경지식, 의사소통 전략 등을 활용할 수 있는 평가 방법을 사용한다.
(다) 표현기능 (말하기, 쓰기) 평가는 수행 평가를 통해 가급적 직접 평가 방법을 활용한다.
(라) 학생의 통합적인 영어 능력을 신장시킬 수 있도록 듣기, 말하기, 읽기, 쓰기의 개별 기능에 대한 평가뿐 아니라 두 가지 이상의 기능을 통합한 평가도 적절히 실시한다.
(마) 평가 문항 제작, 평가의 시행과 채점에서 적정한 신뢰도를 유지하도록 한다.
(바) 학생의 의사소통능력을 효과적으로 측정하고, 영어 능력을 충분히 발휘할 수 있도록 다양한 평가방법을 사용한다.

(2) 평가 방법 및 절차
(가) 평가 방법
① 평가는 교사가 직접 하거나 (교사평가), 다른 학생이 하거나 (또래평가), 학생 스스로 할 수 있다 (자기 평가).
② 평가 대상과 관련해서는 학생 개인별로 평가하거나, 짝 단위 혹은 모둠 단위로 평가할 수 있다.
③ 영어과 평가 내용에 있어서는 영어에 대한 이해 및 영어 사용 능력을 평가할 수 있다.
④ 평가를 위한 자료와 관련해서는 지필평가나 수행평가 (관찰, 구술, 면접, 시연 등)를 통하여 얻는다.
⑤ 평가 문항 형태에 있어서는 선택형 문항이나 서답형 문항을 사용할 수 있다.

선택형	서답형
진위형, 선다형, 연결형, 배열형	단답형, 제한적 논술형, 논술형

⑥ 하나의 평가 자료에 대해 단일 채점자가 평가하거나, 복수 채점자가 평가할 수 있다.
⑦ 평가는 주관식 평가나 객관식 평가로 할 수 있다.
⑧ 관찰, 구술, 면접 등에 대한 채점과 관련해서는 수행 현장에서 실시간으로 채점하거나, 녹음 또는 녹화를 해서 추후 채점을 할 수 있다.

(나) 평가 절차
① 평가의 시행에 있어서는 평가계획서에 제시된 방법과 절차를 따른다.
② 문항 초안을 작성한 후에는 동료교사 등의 검토를 받아 수정하고 개선한다.
③ 학생이 평가의 세부 절차와 유의사항을 분명히 알 수 있도록 사전에 명확하게 안내한다.
④ 수행평가의 채점과 관련해서는 사전에 준비된 채점 기준과 척도에 근거해서 해야하고, 사전에 학생이 알 수 있도록 제시해야 한다.

(3) 평가 방법상의 유의점
(가) 교수·학습에서 사용한 과업의 형태와 방법도 활용하여 학습과 평가가 상호 연계될 수 있도록 한다.
(나) 평가의 목적과 종류, 학습자의 수준에 따라 다양한 유형의 과제와 적절한 난이도의 문항을 선정하여 평가한다.

(다) 단편적인 지식이나 능력에 대한 측정보다 언어 지식과 배경 지식, 의사소통 책략을 창의적으로 활용할 수 있는 평가 방법을 사용한다.
(라) 수행 평가를 실시할 때에는 평가의 목표, 내용, 문항 유형, 채점 기준 등을 명확히 한 후에 실시한다.
(마) 관찰, 역할극, 포트폴리오 평가, 시연 등을 실시하여 학습 과정과 결과를 함께 평가한다.
(바) 평가 문항 제작, 평가의 시행과 채점에 관한 사항을 평가 계획서에 근거하여 점검표로 만들고 각 항목을 하나씩 점검함으로써 높은 신뢰도를 유지하도록 한다.

라. 평가의 활용

(1) 평가 활용의 방향
(가) 평가의 활용은 평가의 목적과 종류에 따라 그 활용도가 다를 수 있으나, 영어과 교수·학습의 개선에 기여하는 방향으로 활용토록 한다.
(나) 평가를 하는 과정에서 학생이 자신의 성취도에 대해 인식하며 자극을 받고 학습동기가 유발될 수 있도록 한다.
(다) 평가 결과에 대해 학생에게 알려줌으로써, 부족한 부분에 대한 보충 및 심화학습이 이루어지도록 한다.

(2) 평가 활용의 방법

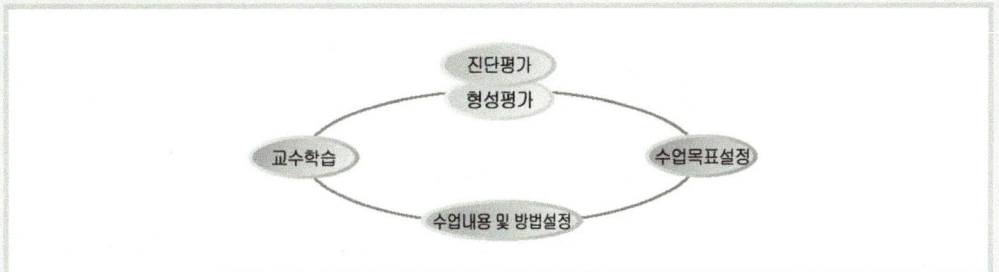

(가) 진단 평가를 통하여 학생의 수준을 진단한 후 그 결과를 활용하여 학습 내용을 재구성하거나 적합한 교수·학습 방법을 적용한다.
(나) 형성 평가를 통하여 교수·학습 방법이 적절한지 확인하고, 그 결과를 교수·학습 방법 개선 자료로 활용한다.
(다) 상시적 과정 평가와 총괄적 성취도 평가를 균형 있게 시행한다.
(라) 평가의 결과는 차후 평가계획 수립에 반영하고, 교사의 교수·학습 개선 및 학생의 개별 지도 등에 활용하도록 한다.

(3) 평가 활용상의 유의점
① 평가 결과를 해석할 때는 학생 개인의 성적 변화, 시험 및 문항 분석 결과, 학교전체의 성적 및 예년과 비교한 경향 등을 포함하여 해석할 수 있다.
② 평가 결과를 해석하고 통보할 때는 학생의 장점을 중심으로 하여, 학습동기와 의욕을 유지하도록 한다.

01 Categories in Assessment

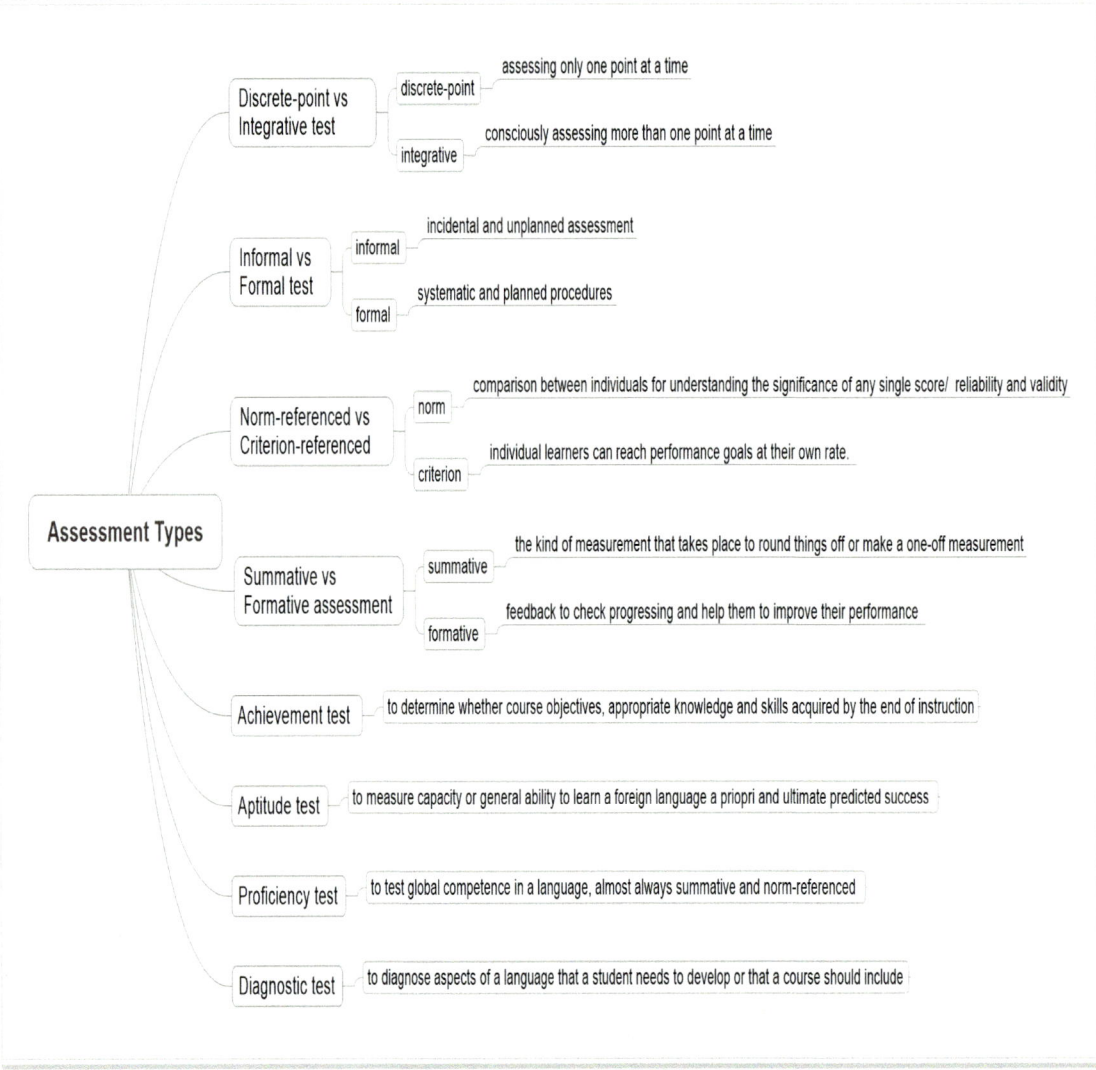

1. Informal vs Formal Assessment

Informal	• incidental, unplanned comments and responses, impromptu feedback • nonjudgmental not making ultimate decisions about the students' performance
Formal	• exercises or procedures designed to tap into a storehouse of skills and knowledge • systematic, planned sampling techniques

2. Formative vs Summative Assessment

Formative	• Primary focus is the ongoing development of the learner's language. • Conditions: delivery by the teacher, internalization of appropriate feedback on performance by the student, future continuation of learning
Summative	• Aims to measure and summarize what a student has grasped at the end of a course • Final exams in a course, general proficiency exams

3. Norm-referenced vs Criterion-referenced Assessment

Norm-referenced	• standardized tests in the form of a numerical score and a percentile rank • to place test-takers along a mathematical continuum in rank order • to concern cost and efficiency primarily
Criterion-referenced	• to give test-takers feedback in the form of grades on specific course or lesson objectives • to deliver useful, appropriate feedback to students, instructional value

4. Discrete Point vs Integrative Assessment

(1) Discrete Point Testing

- This type of test has the advantages of often being practical to mark and remain objective in terms of marking. However, they show only the child's capability to identify single objects. DPT provides evidence of the child's capacity to identify specific components of any language, but do not demonstrate how they might use those in communication.

- Designing discrete point tests is highly time and energy-consuming but it's easy to score and achieve reliable scores.
- Discrete point testing covers a wide range of language components and can share the prompt feedback on the student's attempt. Students are provided with the quantification of their responses through this test.
- From the assessment perspective, discrete point testing can be both norms referenced as well as criterion-referenced.

(2) Integrative Language Testing

- Integrative tests attempt to assess learner's ability to use multiple pieces all simultaneously. ILT can serve both purposes, it can be direct and indirect. The use of the term integrative refers to test more than one skill or item of knowledge at a time.
- Integrative tests are frequently pragmatic because they set the activities and assignments that cause the students to process sequences of components in any language that adjusts to the ordinary logical imperatives of that language. They focus on the ability to use language adequately for communication and using it includes integration of every highlight.
- ILT tests any students' ability to use many components simultaneously, and while exercising these components of grammar, and perhaps more than one traditional aspect of skills whereas discrete test attempts to test language's one component at a moment. Following are two types of Integrative Language Testing:

    A. Cloze Test: In this kind of test, each sixth/seventh word is expelled; the student is required to fit the left-out words that fit into those spaces. The consequences of this test are serious, and they easily measure overall performance and proficiency. Many theoretical constructs suggest that the capacity to flexibly suitable words in spaces requires a few capacities that lie at the core of capability in a language: grammar, vocabulary, sentence structure, punctuation, understanding aptitudes and procedures.

    B. Dictation: This is the most common technique we all have been to in our playing years. The teacher, Instructor, or and audio device is played, and learners are directed to keep a keen ear to that. At the same time what they hear they must write that in their copies using correct spellings. The listening is categorized into three stages: an oral reading without pauses; an oral reading with long pauses between every phrase; reading at a normal speed. Keen and careful listening leads towards successful results, this adds up in students writing skills and the memory to remember the new words into their vocabulary treasure.

5. Classroom Tests

(1) Diagnostic test is a test that helps the teacher and learners identify problems that they have with the language. 예 At the start of the course, the teacher gives the learners a diagnostic test to see what areas of language need to be in the syllabus. It is common to assert that diagnostic tests are intended to probe the strengths and weaknesses of learners, but there is virtually no description, much less discussion of what the underlying constructs might be that should be operationalized in valid diagnostic tests. In the classroom, progress tests given during the course can also act as diagnostic tests as they help the teacher and learners identify what areas will be looked at next on the course. The purpose of the test is to:

- diagnose students' strengths and weaknesses
- track and report on students' language gains
- be linked to curriculum/ teaching/ materials
- help students to plan their language learning
- inform curriculum development

(2) Achievement Test is designed to measure how much a language learners have successfully learned with specific reference to a particular course, textbook, or program of instruction, thus a type of criterion-referenced test. An achievement test is typically given at the end of a course, whereas when administered periodically throughout a course of instruction to measure language learning up to that point, it is alternatively called a progress test.

(3) Proficiency Test measures how much of a language someone has learned. The difference between a proficiency test and achievement test is that the latter is usually designed to measure how much a student has learned from a particular course or syllabus. A Proficiency test is not linked to a particular course of instruction, but measures the learner's general level of language mastery.

(4) Progress Test may be regarded as similar to achievement tests but narrowed and much more specific in scope. This is an achievement test linked to a particular set of teaching materials or a particular course of instruction. The test is prepared by a teacher and given at the end of a chapter, course, or term are progress tests. The test helps the teacher to judge the degree of success of his or her teaching and to identify the weakness of the learners.

(5) Language Aptitude Test are designed to predict the ability of an individual to learn a foreign language given typical time of study and conditions for learning. Language aptitude refers to the potential that a person has for learning languages. This potential is often evaluated using formal aptitude tests, which predict the degree of success the candidate will have with a new language. Aptitude tests vary but many include evaluation of ability to manage sounds, grammatical structures, infer rules, and memory. Common uses:

- Selection and placement of language learners
- Diagnosis of foreign language learning disability
- Understanding students cognitive strengths and weaknesses pertaining to language learning
- Placement of language learners in the most appropriate instructional settings in colleges/ universities or other formal classroom settings.

02 Principles of Assessment

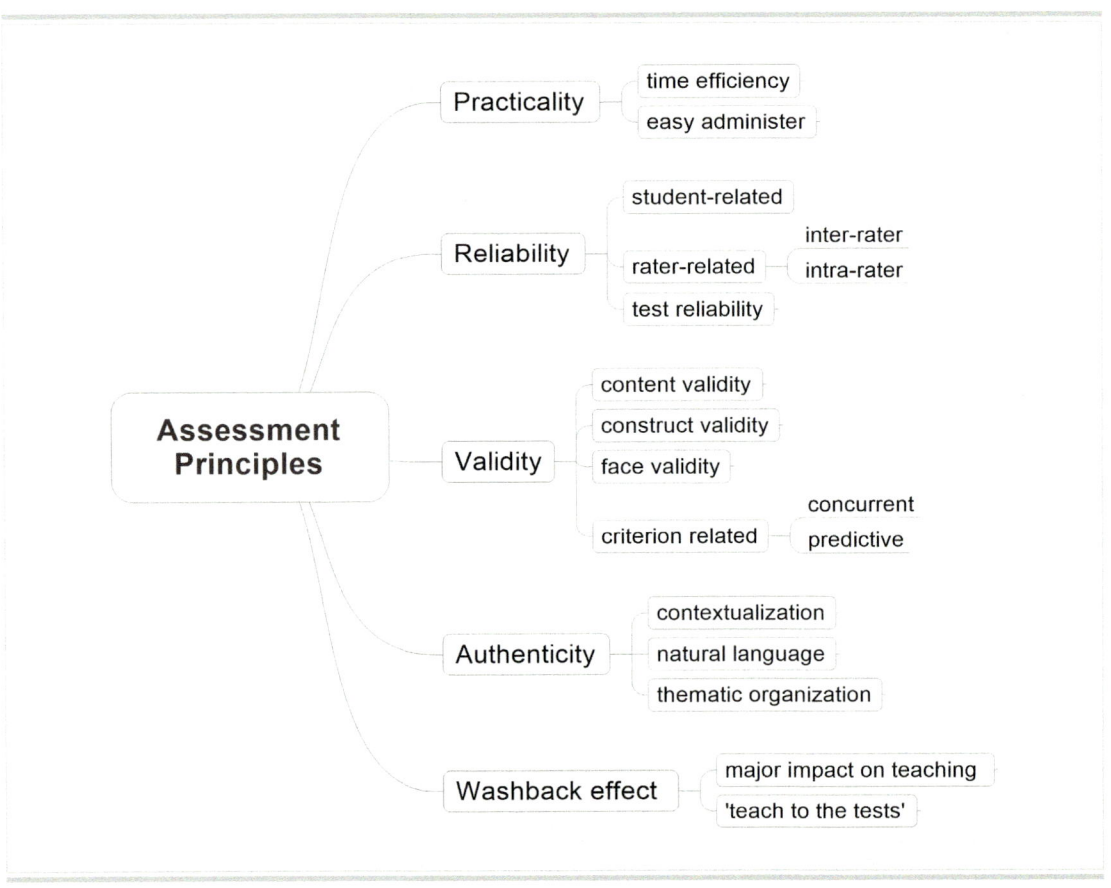

1. Practicality

An effective test should be practical;
- is not excessively expensive
- stays within appropriate time constraints
- is relatively easy to administer
- has a scoring/ evaluation procedure that is specific and time-efficient

A test that takes a few minutes for a student to take and several hours for an examiner to evaluate is impractical for most classroom situations. A test that can be scored only by computer is impractical if the test takes place a thousand miles away from the nearest computer.

2. Reliability

A reliable test is consistent and dependable. If you give the same test to the same students in two different occasions, the test should yield similar results.

(1) Student related reliability

The most common issue in student related reliability is caused by temporary illness, fatigue, a bad day, anxiety, and other physical and psychological factors which may make an "observed" score deviate from a "true" score.

(2) Rater reliability

Human error, subjectivity, and bias may enter into the scoring process.
- inter-rater reliability: Two or more scorers can yield inconsistent scores of the same test, possibly for lack of attention to scoring criteria, inexperience, inattention, or even preconceived bias toward a particular good and bad student.
- intra-rater reliability: The inconsistency a single scorer has within himself when looking at the same data on different occasions.

(3) Test administration reliability

Test administration reliability deals with the conditions in which the test is administered.

예 street noise outside the building, bad equipment, room temperature, the conditions of chairs and tables, photocopying variation

Student-related	Rater-related	Test administration	Test
• test-taker's test • wiseness and strategies	• inter-rater reliability • intra-rater reliability	• conditions of test • administration	• subjective tests • objective tests

3. Validity

By far the most complex criterion of an effective test is validity, 'the extent to which inferences made from assessment results are appropriate, meaningful, and useful in terms of the purpose of the assessment'.

(1) Content validity

- It clearly defines the achievement that you are measuring
- A type of validity that is based on the extent to which a test adequately and sufficiently measures the particular skills or behaviour it sets out to measure.
- A test of pronunciation skills in a language would have low content validity if it tested only some of the skills

> **KEY NOTE**
>
> **Validity 문제성에 대한 학생의 논평**
>
> A. Content Validity : My teacher included too many questions about material that she had not dealt with in class. When she made the exam, I think she used other textbooks that she did not teach from.
> B. Construct Validity: Let me talk about our listening test. Most of the questions were dictation questions. We even had to write a full paragraph for one question. The teacher said it was for measuring our listening skills. But it seemed like a writing test rather than a listening test.
> C. Face Validity : We are middle school students, but the exam looked like one that high school students normally take. The printing was too small, and we had to read five pages in one hour. I really hated it.

(2) Construct validity

- Test should account for the various components of constructs: linguistic constructs (proficiency, communicative competence, fluency), psychological constructs (self-esteem, motivation)
- A type of validity that is based on the extent to which the items in a test reflect the essential aspects of the theory on which the test is based (i.e., the construct).
- The greater the relationship that can be demonstrated between a test of communicative competence in a language and the theory of communicative competence, the greater the construct validity of the test.

(3) Face validity
- The degree to which a test appears to measure the knowledge or abilities it claims to measure, based on the subjective judgement of an observer.
- 예 If a test of reading comprehension contains many dialect words that might be unknown to the test takers, the test may be said to lack face validity.

(4) Criterion-related validity
① (Concurrent validity) Concurrent validity in language learning refers to the extent to which the results or scores obtained from a new test or assessment correlate with those of an established and widely accepted measure used for a similar purpose. Essentially, it assesses the degree to which a new test yields similar results to an existing test that measures the same construct or skill, often administered at the same time. This type of validity is crucial to ensure that the new test accurately measures what it's intended to measure and aligns with established standards or measurements in the field.

② (Predictive validity) The test scores are collected first; then at some later time the criterion measure is collected. For predictive validity, the example is slightly different: Tests are administered, perhaps to job applicants, and then after those individuals work in the job for a year, their test scores are correlated with their first year job performance scores. 예 SAT scores: These are validated by collecting the scores during the examinee's senior year and high school and then waiting a year (or more) to correlate the scores with their first year college grade point average. Thus predictive validity provides somewhat more useful data about test validity because it has greater fidelity to the real situation in which the test will be used. After all, most tests are administered to find out something about future behavior.

4. Authenticity

The degree of correspondence of characteristics of a given language test task to the features of a target language task:
- The language in the test is as natural as possible
- Items are contextualized rather than isolated.
- Topics are meaningful (relevant, interesting) for the learner.
- Some thematic organization to items is provided, such as through a story line or episode.
- Tasks represent or closely approximate real-world tasks.

5. Washback

The positive or negative impact of a test on classroom teaching or learning: In some countries, 예 national language examinations have a major impact on teaching and teachers often 'teach to the tests'. In order to bring about changes in teaching, changes may have to be made in the tests. 예 If the education department in a country wanted schools to spend more time teaching listening skills, one way to bring this about would be to introduce a listening comprehension test component into state examinations. The washback would be that more class time would then be spent on teaching listening skills. When teaching is found to exert an important effect on testing, this impact is called a reverse washback.

03 Classroom Language Tests

1. Classroom Language Tests

Test types	Features
Reading Quiz	Purpose : designed to be an instructional tool to guide classroom discussion formative with purpose of providing beneficial washback
Grammar Unit Test	Objectives : to achieve content validity, your objectives should reflect all four modes of performance and sample all four verb tenses Test specifications : to fulfill your desired principles, validity
Midterm Essay	Test specifications : clear directions, prompt (narrative, description…), time limit, evaluation criteria
Listening & Speaking Final Exam	Test items: elicitation mode (oral & written), response mode (oral & written) Listening comprehension section Oral production section

2. Scoring, Grading, and Giving Feedback

Types	Features
Scoring	to determine the relative weight
Grading	comprehensive treatment of grading
Feedback	• Reading Quiz: to prompt self-assessment and class discussion • Grammar Unit Test: useful feedback is in the form of diagnostic scores, a checklist needing work, class discussion of results • Midterm Essay: peer and individual conferences with beneficial feedback • Listening & Speaking Final Exam: grade and scores and subscores with minimal oral feedback

3. Item Elicitation and Item Response

(1) Item-Elicitation Format

The format for elicitation of the item has to be determined. An item can have a spoken, written, or visual stimulus, as well as any combination of the three. Thus, while an item or task may ostensibly assess one skill, it may also be testing some other as well. 예 A listening subtest in which respondents answer oral questions by means of written multiple-choice responses is testing reading as well as listening.

(2) Item-Response Format

The item-response format can be fixed, structured, or open-ended. Those with a fixed format include true/false, multiple-choice, and matching items. Those which call for a structured format include ordering (예 respondents are requested to arrange words to make a sentence, and several orders are possible), duplication – both written (예 dictation) and oral (예 recitation, repetition, mimicry), identification (예 explaining the part of speech of a form), and completion. Those calling for an open-ended format include composing – both written (예 creative fiction, expository essays) and oral (예 a speech) – as well as other activities, such as free oral response in role-playing situations.

4. Multiple-Choice items

(1) Terms for multiple-choice tests

Methods	Questions	Answers
• receptive response • selective response • supply type of response	• stem • options/ alternatives	• key answer • distractors

(2) Designing multiple-choice tests

- Design each item to measure a single objective.
- State both stem and options as simply and directly as possible.
- Make certain that the intended answer is clearly the only correct one.
- Use item indices to accept, discard, or revise items.

Item facility	Which item is easy or difficult for the group?
Item discrimination	Which item more effectively differentiates between high-ability and low-ability test-takers?
Distractor efficiency	Related to item discrimination, the extent to which the distractors lure a sufficient number of test-takers?

(3) Item Analysis

The analysis of the responses to the items in a test in order to find out how effective the test items are and to find out if they indicate differences between high and low ability test takers.

① Item Facility

A measure of the ease of a test item: It is the proportion of the item test takers who answered the item correctly, and is determined by the following formula: The higher the ratio of R to N, the easier the item.

- Item Facility (IF) = R / N (* R: number of correct answers, N; the number of test takers)

② Item Discrimination

A measure of the extent to which a test item is sensitive to differences in ability among test takers. If a particular item in a test is answered in the same way by both the test takers who do well on the test as a whole and by those who do poorly, the item is said to have poor discrimination. In item analysis, the item-total point-biserial correlation between the answers to an individual item (item) and the scores on the whole test (total) is often used as an estimate of discrimination. Or alternatively, an item discrimination index can be calculated using the following formula: The ID index ranges from −1.00 to +1.00. In a norm-referenced test, test items with low and negative ID indices need to be revised.

③ Item Distractors

Distractors are the incorrect answers for a selected-response item on the multiple choice format. Distractor analysis is conducted to see how distractors are functioning.

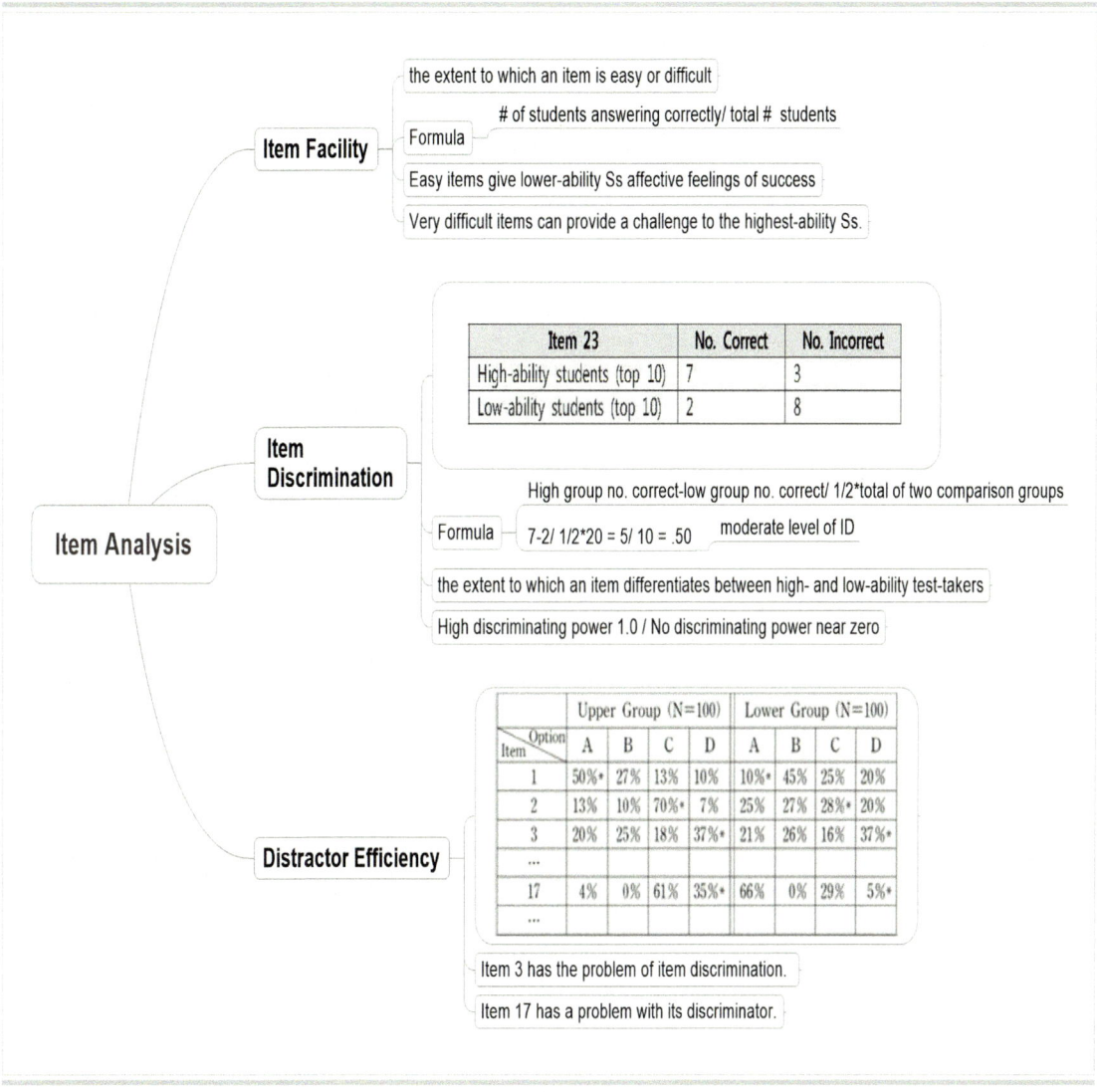

5. Standardized Tests

(1) Advantages and Disadvantages

Advantages	• ready-made, validated product • administration to large groups
Disadvantages	• inappropriate test of assessing an overall proficiency • misunderstanding of the difference between direct and indirect testing

(2) Developing a Standardized Test

Purpose	• to provide high practicality in administration and scoring • to perform a specific gate-keeping function
Test specification	• to identify a set of constructs: construct validation 예 TOEFL: to define the construct of language proficiency
Different kinds of items	• practicality: clarity of directions, timing, adminstration • reliability: scorer • low validity: unclear directions, complex language, obscure topics, fuzzy data, culturally biased information
Scoring procedures & reporting formats	• For speaking, six criteria are set: fluency, intelligibility, conversational development, conversational comprehension, vocabulary, grammar • Rubric makes a test standardized.
Construct validation	• Standardized instrument is expected to have ongoing construct validation.

6. Alternative Assessment

Performance-based Assessment	1) Characteristics • constructed response • Tasks are meaningful, engaging, authentic, open-ended, integration of language skills. • Process and product are assessed. 2) Assessment • to use a reliable evaluation form • systematic feedback • self-assessment and peer-assessment
Rubrics	(Rubric-referenced assessment) • a device used to evaluate open-ended oral and written responses of learners • to focus their efforts, produce work of higher quality, earn better grades, and feel anxious about assignments • to involve scaling, the assignment of numbers to performance • less exact in reality: to ensure all the rigors of validity and reliability that other assessments are
Portfolios	A purposeful collection of students' work that demonstrates their efforts, progress, and achievements in given areas 1) Advantages • intrinsic motivation, responsibility, and ownership • S-T interaction • individualize learning • tangible evidence of students' work • critical thinking, self-assessment, and revision processes • opportunities for collaborative work with peers • washback effect, authenticity, and personal consequential validity (impact) high 2) Disadvantages: low practicality 3) Procedures • Objectives • Guidelines on what to include • Assessment criteria • Review and conferencing • Positive washback

Journals

1) A log of one's thoughts, feelings, reactions, assessments, ideas, or progress toward goals with little attention to structure, form, or correctness

2) Advantages and Disadvantages
   - practice in writing fluently
   - writing as a thinking process
   - emphasizing students' own voice
   - communication with teacher, feedback; most formative, washback effect
   - too free a form to be assessed
   - difficult to set up criteria for evaluation

3) Types for purposes
   - dialogue journals: to carry on a conversation with the teacher
   - language learning logs: to restrict skills, strategies, language categories
   - grammar journals: 'error logs' can be instructive process of consciousness-raising.
   - responses to readings: to use as precursors to freewrites
   - strategies-based learning logs: to learn strategies and to use in their acquisition process
   - self-assessment reflections: a stimulus for self-assessment in a more open-ended way
   - diaries of attitudes, feelings and other affective factors
   - acculturation logs: culture and language are strongly linked

Conferences and Interviews

1) Conferencing
   - Conferencing is to facilitate the improvement of the written work in process writing.
   - Teacher is a facilitator and guide.
   - It should not be scored or graded.

2) Interview
   - Interview is intended to denote a context in which a teacher interviews a student for a designated assessment purpose.
   - For reliability, interview questions should be constructed carefully to elicit as focused a response as possible.

3) Conferencing & Interview
   - Reliability:
     (C) rater reliability not important as it will vary from student to student, to offer individualized attention
     (I) high level of reliability to objectives and procedures
   - Content validity
     (C & I) high level of validity – content validity
   - Washback and authenticity
     (C) high
     (I) moderate

Observations	1) Objective: to assess students without their awareness of the observation so that the naturalness of their linguistic performance is maximized 2) Assessment principles • If the objectives are kept simple, moderate practicality and reliability can maintain. • Content validity gets high marks, because observations are likely to be integrated into the course. • Washback is only moderate with little followup, but is high with a subsequent conference. • Authenticity is high if it goes unnoticed by the student. 3) Devices ① Categories for checklist 　• participation 　• content of the topic 　• linguistic competence (form, function, discourse, sociolinguistic) 　• materials being used 　• skill (listening, speaking, reading, writing) ② Rubrics or rating scales 　• frequency scale 　• holistic assessment scale
Self- and Peer- Assessment	1) Advantages and Disadvantages • direct involvement • autonomy and motivation • subjectivity; not to make accurate assessment 2) Types • Direct assessment of performance: self corrected comprehension quiz, journal, peer-editing, grammar or vocabulary quiz • Indirect assessment of competence: to ignore minor, nonrepeating performance flaws and evaluate general ability • Metacognitive assessment: purpose is setting goals and monitoring one's progress • Socioaffective assessment: motivation, anxiety, emotional obstacles • Student-generated tests: productive, intrinsically motivating, autonomy-building process

CHAPTER 02 Assessing Language Skills

Introduction

평가의 기본적인 원리를 익힌 후에 각 언어 기능에 대한 평가 방법을 살펴 보고, 차이점과 공통점을 중심으로 학교 현장에서 사용될 수 있는 평가를 알아보도록 하자. 이 영역은 평가가 어떻게 4기능과 통합되는지를 볼 수 있으며 그를 통해 수업 평가지나 활동을 만들어 볼 수 있다.

▶ 교육과정

듣기 평가의 방법	듣기 평가상의 유의점
가) 듣기 평가의 내용과 수준은 교육과정의 성취기준을 근거로 선정한다. 나) 듣기 능력을 측정할 수 있는 다양한 자료 및 과업을 활용한다. 다) 평가의 목적에 따라 독백, 대화, 담화 등 다양한 형태의 입력 언어를 사용한다. 라) 평가의 목적과 학생의 수준에 따라 사실적 이해, 추론적 이해, 평가적 이해 문항의 비중을 적절히 조절한다. 마) 선택지의 언어 형태(음성 언어, 문자 언어), 제시 순서 (듣기 전 혹은 듣기 후) 등은 평가 목적과 대상, 내용에 따라 적절하게 선택한다.	가) 입력 언어를 제시할 때는 일관성을 위해서 가급적 녹음 자료를 사용한다. 교사가 직접 제시할 때는 일관성을 유지하도록 노력한다. 나) 듣기 평가를 위한 대본은 대화, 이야기 등의 실제적인 음성언어 자료를 활용하되, 학생의 수준 등을 고려하여 재구성할 수 있다. 다) 말의 속도는 평가 목적과 학생 수준에 따라 적절히 조절하고 가급적 자연스러운 속도로 평가를 실시한다. 라) 영어로 선택지를 줄 경우에 선택지의 길이나 난이도 등이 듣기 능력 측정에 영향을 주지 않도록 한다.

01 Assessing Listening

1. Designing Assessment Tasks

Intensive Listening	• listening for perception of the components (phonemes, words, intonation, discourse markers)
Responsive Listening	• listening to a short stretch of language to make an equally short response
Selective Listening	• listening to scan for certain information • not for global or general meanings but for comprehension of designated information
Extensive Listening	• listening to develop a top-down, global understanding for spoken language

(1) Intensive Listening

Recognizing Phonological & Morphological Elements	• to ask test-takers to identify the stimulus from two or more choices • no context provided 예) Phonemic pair: consonants/ vowels, morphological pair, stress pattern in can't, one-word stimulus
Paraphrase recognition	• to choose the correct paraphrase from a number of choices 예) sentence/ dialogue paraphrase

(test) Stress pattern in 'can't'

> Test-takers hear : My girlfriend can't go to the party.
> Test-takers read : ⓐ My girlfriend can't go to the party.
>   ⓑ My girlfriend can go to the party.

(2) Responsive Listening

- a question-and-answer format
- to provide some interactivity in lower-end listening tasks

예) appropriate response to a question, open-ended response to a question

(test) Open-ended response to a question

> Test takers hear : How much time did you take to do your homework?
> Test-takers write or speak : _____.

(3) Selective Listening

The purpose of such performance is not necessarily to look for global or general meanings, but to be able to comprehend designated information in a context of longer stretches of spoken language (classroom directions from a teacher, TV or radio news items, or stories). 예 to listen for names, numbers, a grammatical category, directions (in a map exercise), or certain facts and events

Listening Cloze	• Deletions are governed by the objective of the test. • exact word method of scoring 예 cloze dictations, partial dictations
Information Transfer	• aurally processed information transferred to a visual representation • to force test-taker to select the correct bits and pieces to complete a task 예 picture-cued items, chartfilling
Sentence Repetition	• to repeat a sentence • to assess the ability to recognize and retain chunks of language and meaning

(test) Listening Cloze : cloze dictations : partial dictations

Test-takers hear :
Ladies and gentleman, I now have some connecting gate information for those of your making connections to their flights out of San Francisco.

- Flight <u>seven-oh-six</u> to Busan will depart from gate <u>seventy-three</u> at nine-thirty P.M.
- Flight <u>ten-forty-five</u> to New York will depart at <u>nine-fifty</u> P.M. from gate <u>seventeen</u>.
- Flight <u>four-forty</u> to Jeju Island will depart at <u>nine-thirty-five</u> P.M.
- And flight <u>sixteen-oh-three</u> to Tokyo will depart from gate <u>nineteen</u> at <u>ten-fifteen</u> P.M.

Test-takers write the missing words or phrases in the blanks.

(4) Extensive Listening

Extensive performance ranges from listening to lengthy lectures to listening to a conversation and deriving a comprehensive message or purpose. Listening for the gist, for the main idea, and making inferences are all part of extensive listening.

Dictation	① Procedure • to hear a 50~100-words passage three times • test-takers write down while listening • finally, they check their work and proofread ② Integrative testing • integration of listening and writing • knowledge of grammatical and discourse expectancies ③ Advantages and Disadvantages • lack of authenticity • practicality of administration, moderate degree of reliability, correspondence of other language abilities
Communicative stimulus-response tasks	• Dialogue and multiple-choice comprehension items: a stimulus monologue or conversation to respond to comprehension questions • Dialogue and authentic questions on details
Authentic Listening Tasks	① Notetaking • an authentic task to focus on in the classroom • valid form for global listening comprehension • criteria of cognitive demand, communicative language, authenticity ② Editing • to require the test-taker to listen for discrepancies • scoring: high reliability ③ Interpretive tasks • to force the test-taker to infer a response 예 song lyrics, poetry, news reports - open ended questions ④ Retelling • reliability, practicality low • validity, cognitive processing, communicative ability, authenticity are well incorporated into the task

02. Assessing Speaking

> 교육과정

말하기 평가의 방법	말하기 평가상의 유의점
가) 말하기 평가의 내용과 수준은 교육과정의 성취 기준을 근거로 선정한다. 나) 말하기 능력을 발현시키고 측정할 수 있는 다양한 발화도출기법을 사용한다. 다) 말하기 평가는 수시관찰평가, 수행평가로 할 수 있다. 라) 말하기 평가는 현장에서 즉석 채점하거나 녹음하여 추후 채점할 수 있다. 마) 말하기 평가를 위한 채점 척도는 일반 말하기 평가 원리에 의한 척도를 응용하거나, 과업에 고유한 척도를 별도로 만들어 사용할 수 있다. 바) 분석적 채점과 총괄적 채점을 적절히 사용한다.	가) 평가 실시 전에 학생이 해당 평가 유형을 충분히 연습을 하도록 지도한다. 나) 과업의 성격 등을 고려하여, 학생들의 발화를 위한 준비 시간을 적절히 준다. 다) 발음, 억양, 강세와 같은 언어적 요소가 다른 주요 평가 요소의 채점에 영향을 미치지 않도록 유의한다. 라) 편안하고 우호적인 분위기를 유지하고 가급적 충분한 시간을 주어 학생이 역량을 최대한 발휘하도록 돕는다.

1. Assessment tasks

Imitative Speaking	• ability to simply parrot back • short-term storage to retain the short stretch of language
Intensive Speaking	• competence in grammatical, phrasal, lexical or phonological 예 directed response tasks, reading aloud, dialogue completion
Responsive Speaking	• interaction and test comprehension in very short conversations
Interactive Speaking	• transactional language & interpersonal exchanges
Extensive Speaking	• monologue 예 speeches, oral presentations, storytelling

(1) Imitative Speaking

While this is a purely phonetic level of oral production, a number of prosodic, lexical and grammatical properties of language may be included in the criterion performance.

- phonologically focused repetition tasks
- to pay more attention to pronunciation – suprasegmentals to help learners more comprehensible

Word and sentence repetition tasks	Test-takers hear: Repeat after me Test-takers repeat the stimulus

(test) Word repetition task

> Test-takers hear: Repeat after me:
>
>   beat[pause]   bit[pause]
>   bat[pause]   vat[pause]
>
> I bought a boat yesterday.
> The glow of the candle is growing.
> When did they go on vacation?
> Do you like coffee?
>
> Test-takers repeat the stimulus.

(2) Intensive Speaking

- limited response-tasks, mechanical-tasks, controlled response
- directed response tasks, reading aloud, sentence and dialogue completion, limited picture-cued tasks, translation up to the simple sentence level

Directed Response Tasks	• limited response task • mechanical, not communicative • minimal processing of meaning to produce correct grammatical output • to elicit a particular grammatical form or transformation of a sentence
Read-Aloud Tasks	• level up to a paragraph • easy scoring • strong indicator of overall oral production ability • advantages: predictable output, practicality, reliability • disadvantages: inauthentic, no pragmatic ability
Sentence/ Dialogue Completion tasks	Dialogue Completion task: a moderate output control, ability to discern expectancies and to produce sociolinguistically correct language

Picture-cued tasks	① ***picture-cued elicitation*** of minimal pairs
	    • of comparatives
	    • of future tense
	    • of nouns, negative responses, numbers and location
	    • of responses and descriptions
	    • of giving directions
	② ***picture-cued multiple-choice*** description for two test-takers

Translation	• the control of the output of the test taker, thus scoring is easily specified • limited discourse

(test) Map cued elicitation of giving directions

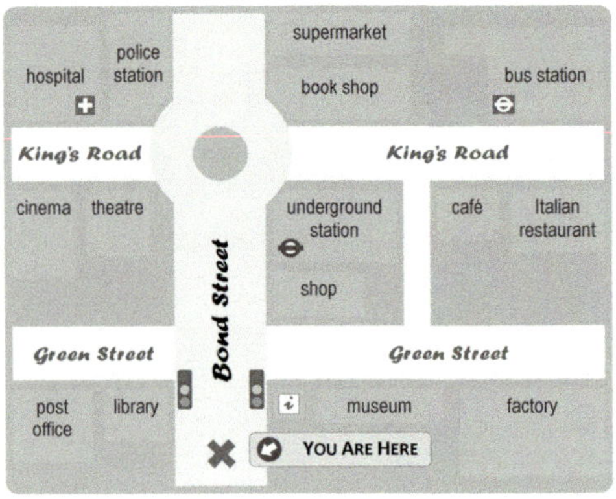

[map showing streets with hospital, police station, supermarket, book shop, bus station, King's Road, cinema, theatre, underground station, cafe, Italian restaurant, Bond Street, shop, Green Street, post office, library, museum, factory, YOU ARE HERE]

Test takers hear:
You are at Green and Bond Streets [point to the spot]. People ask you for directions to get to five different places. Listen to their questions, then give directions.

1. Please give me directions to the cafe.
2. How do I get to the Italian restaurant?
3. Can you tell me how to get to the theatre?

(3) Responsive Speaking

Interaction and test comprehension (somewhat limited level of very short conversations, standard greetings and small talk, simple requests and comments)

Question-and-Answer	• Display Question: to elicit a predetermined correct response • Referential Question: to produce meaningful language in response 예 Questions eliciting open-ended response
Giving Instructions and Directions	• scoring is based on comprehensibility and other specified grammatical or discourse categories 예 Eliciting instructions or directions
Paraphrasing	• to elicit short stretches of output and tap into test-takers' ability • to practice the conversational art of conciseness 예 Paraphrasing a story or description, Paraphrasing a phone message

(test) Paraphrasing a phone message

Test-takers hear :
Please tell Mr. Oh that I'm tied up in traffic so I'm going to be about a half hour late for the nine o'clock meeting. And ask him to bring up our question about the employee benefits plan. If he wants to check in with me on my cell phone, have him call 018-2534-9632. Thanks.

Test-takers respond with two or three sentences.

(4) Interactive Speaking

Interview	① Warmup ② Level-check ③ Probe ④ Wind-down
Role Play	• opportunity for test-takers to use discourse • personal, strategic, and linguistic factors for oral abilities • a level of creativity and complexity in real-world pragmatics
Discussions and Conversations	• formal assessment device: hard to specify and to score • informal assessment device: authenticity and spontaneity
Games	• to specify a set of criteria and practical, reliable scoring method 예 Assessment games

▶ **Functions of language**

- Transactional Language : A, B
- Interpersonal Language : C

<A> Mary : Excuse me, do you have the time?
      Doug : Yeah. Nine-fifteen.

<B> T : What is the most urgent environmental problem today?
      S : I would say massive deforestation.

<C> Jeff : Hey, Stef, how's it going?
      Stef : Not bad, and yourself?
      Jeff : I'm good.
      Stef : Cool, Okay, gotta go.

(5) Extensive Speaking

Oral Presentation	• for effective assessment; specify criterion, set tasks, elicit optimal output, establish practical, reliable scoring procedures
Picture-cued storytelling	• to elicit oral production through visual pictures
Retelling a story	• in a longer stretch of discourse • to assess fluency and interaction
Translation	• control of content, vocabulary, and grammatical & discourse features

(test) Picture cued story-telling task

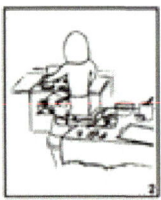

Test-takers see the following six-picture sequence :

Test-takers hear or read: Tell the story that these pictures describe. Test-takers use the pictures as a sequence of cues to tell a story.

03 Assessing Reading

▶ 교육과정

읽기 평가의 방법	읽기 평가상의 유의점
가) 읽기 평가의 내용과 수준은 교육과정의 성취 기준을 근거로 선정한다. 나) 읽기 능력을 측정할 수 있는 다양한 과업을 통해 평가한다. 다) 평가 목적과 대상, 방법에 따라 문자, 낱말, 어구, 문장, 문단 등 적절한 수준의 문자언어 재료를 사용한다. 라) 사실적 이해 능력을 평가하는 문항을 주로 제작하되, 평가 대상에 따라 추론적 이해 문항의 비중을 적절히 조절한다. 마) 문법요소를 직접 측정하는 읽기평가는 지양한다. 바) 어휘에 대한 평가는 맥락 속에서 단어의 의미를 이해하는 능력을 중심으로 평가한다.	가) 낱말, 어구, 문장, 문단을 바르게 소리 내어 읽고 의미를 이해하는 정도를 측정한다. 나) 교과서의 학습 내용과 유사한 수준의 글을 사용할 것을 권장한다. 다) 교과서에 있는 언어 재료를 사용할 경우 적절히 변형하여 사용할 수 있다. 라) 영어로 선택지를 줄 경우에 선택지의 길이나 난이도 등이 읽기능력측정에 영향을 주지 않도록 한다.

1. Types of Reading

Perceptive Reading	• bottomup processing is implied. • letters, words, punctuation, graphemic symbols
Selective Reading	• combination of bottomup and topdown processing may be used. • recognition of lexical, grammatical, discourse features within a very short stretch of language
Interactive Reading	• topdown processing is typical with some instances of bottomup performance • a process of negotiating meaning • schema for understanding a text and intake is the product of interaction
Extensive Reading	• topdown processing • assess to tap into a learner's global understanding of a text

2. Assessment Tasks

(1) Perceptive Reading

It aims to assess letters, words, punctuation, and other graphemic symbols (bottom-up processing).

Reading aloud	to read separate letters, words, short sentences
Written response	to reproduce the probe in writing
Multiple-choice	• minimal pair distinction • grapheme recognition task
Picture-cued items	• word identification • sentence identification • true/false sentence identification • matching word identification • multiple choice word identification

(test) Grapheme recognition task

> Test-takers read: Circle the "odd" item, the one that doesn't belong.
>
> 1. piece   peace   piece
> 2. book   book   boot

(2) Selective Reading

A combination of bottom-up and top-down processing may be used.

Multiple Choice	• (contextualized) vocabulary/ grammar tasks • cloze vocabulary/ grammar task
Matching Tasks	• vocabulary matching tasks • selected response fill-in vocabulary task
Editing Tasks	• multiple-choice grammar editing task
Picture-cued Tasks	• multiple-choice picture cued response • diagram-labeling task
Gap-filling Tasks	• sentence completion tasks

(test) Contextualized multiple-choice vocabulary/ grammar tasks

> 1. Mina : Do you like champagne?
>   Chul : No, I can't _____ it!
>   a. stand   b. prefer   c. hate
>
> 2. Manager : Do you like to work by yourself?
>   Employee : Yes, I like to work _____.
>   a. independently   b. definitely   c. impatiently

(3) Interactive Reading

Top-down processing is typical of such tasks, although some instances of bottom-up performance may be necessary.

예 anecdotes, short narratives and descriptions, excerpts from longer texts, questionnaires, memos, announcements, directions, recipes

Cloze Tasks	• fixed-ratio deletion • rational deletion • c-test procedure • cloze-elide procedure
Impromptu Reading	reading comprehension passages (plus comprehension questions)
Short-Answer Tasks	open-ended reading comprehension questions
Editing (longer texts)	contextualized grammar editing tasks
Scanning	purpose: to quickly identify important elements
Ordering Tasks	sentence-ordering task
Information Transfer	tasks for assessing interpretation of graphic information

(test) Cloze procedure, fixed-ratio deletion

> The recognition that one's feelings of _____ and unhappiness can coexist much like _____ and hate in a close relationship _____ offer valuable clues on how to _____ a happier life. It suggests, for _____, that changing or avoiding things that _____ you miserable may well make you _____ miserable but probably no happier.

(test) C-test procedure

> The recognition th____ one's feel____ of happ___ and unhap____ can coe____ much li____ love a____ hate i____ a cl____ relati____ may of____ valuable cl____ on h____ to le____ a hap____ life. I__ suggests, f____ example, th____ changing o__ avoiding thi____ that you mise____ may we__ make y____ mise____ but prob____ no hap____.

(4) Extensive Reading

Top-down processing is assumed for most extensive task with only occasional use of a targeted bottom-up strategy.

예) professional articles, journal articles, technical reports, longer essays, short stories

Skimming Tasks	• skimming Tasks
Summarizing and Responding	• directions for summarizing • criteria for assessing a summary • directions for responding to reading
Notetaking and Outlining	• informal assessment

(test) Skimming tasks

> What is the main idea of this text?
> What is the author's purpose in writing the text?
> What kind of writing is this [newspaper article, manual, novel, etc.]?
> What type of writing is this [expository, technical, narrative, etc.]?
> How easy or difficult do you think this text will be?
> What do you think you will learn from the text?
> How useful will the text be for your [profession, academic needs, interests]?

04. Assessing Writing

▶ **교육과정**

쓰기 평가의 방법	쓰기 평가상의 유의점
가) 쓰기 평가의 내용과 수준은 교육과정의 성취 기준을 근거로 선정한다. 나) 쓰기 능력을 발현시키고 측정할 수 있는 다양한 쓰기 기법을 사용한다. 다) 쓰기 평가를 위해 포트폴리오를 작성하게 할 수 있다. 라) 쓰기 평가를 위한 채점 척도는 일반 쓰기 평가 원리에 의한 척도를 응용하거나, 과업에 고유한 척도를 별도로 만들어 사용할 수 있다.	가) 평가 실시 전에 학생이 해당 평가 유형을 충분히 연습 하도록 지도한다. 나) 필요한 경우 학생에게 쓰기를 위한 준비 시간을 적절히 준다. 다) 문법이나 기술적인 사항 등 일부 요소가 다른 중요한 평가 요소의 채점에 영향을 미치지 않도록 유의한다.

1. Types of Writing

Imitative	• mechanics of writing • fundamental tasks of writing **letters, words, punctuation,** and **very brief sentences**
Intensive (controlled)	• more focus on form, meaning and context of some importance • producing appropriate grammar and vocabulary within a context
Responsive	• at a limited discourse level • to exercise some freedom of choice among alternative forms of expression of ideas
Extensive	• processes and strategies of writing • focus on purpose, ideas, syntactic and lexical variety, process of multiple drafts

2. Assessment Tasks

(1) Imitative Writing

Tasks in writing letters, words, punctuation	• copying • listening cloze selection task • picture-cued tasks • form completion tasks • converting numbers and abbreviations to words
Spelling tasks and detecting phoneme-grapheme correspondences	• spelling tests • picture-cued tasks • multiple-choice techniques • matching phonetic symbols

(test) Listening cloze selection task

> Test-takers hear :
> Write the missing word in each blank. Below the story is a list of words to choose from.
>
> Test-takers see :
> Have you ever visited San Francisco? It _____ a very nice _____. It is _____ in _____ summer and _____ in the winter. I _____ the cable cars _____ bridges.
>
> | warm | and | is | the |
> |---|---|---|---|
> | cool | like | you | city |

(2) Intensive Writing (controlled)

Dictation and Dictocomp	• controlled writing to rewrite paragraph from recollection • to internalize the content
Grammatical Transformation Tasks	• devoid of meaningful value • easy to administer, practicality, scorer reliability • to measure grammatical competence
Picture-cued Tasks	• short sentences • picture description and sequence description
Vocabulary Assessment Tasks	• form focused • linked with collocations, morphological variants
Ordering Tasks	• reordering words in a sentence
Short-Answer completion	• limited response writing tasks

(test) Vocabulary writing tasks

Test-takers read :

1. Write two sentences, A and B. In each sentence, use the two words given.
   - A. interpret, experiment _____.
   - B. interpret, language _____.

2. Write three words that can fit in the blank.
   - To interpret
     - _____.
     - _____.
     - _____.

3. Write the correct ending for the word in each of the following sentences :
   - Someone who interprets is an interpret _____.
   - Something that can be interpreted is interpret _____.
   - Someone who interprets gives an interpret _____.

(3) Responsive and Extensive Writing

① Features

Authenticity	Scoring	Time
• formative • positive washback	• form and function • quality of writing (impact and effectiveness)	• freedom to process multiple drafts • revising and editing processes are given • (responsive writing) to rely on drafting process

② Task types

Paraphrasing	• scoring criterion: the same or similar message is primary, discourse, grammar, and vocabulary secondary • informal, formative assessment: positive washback
Guided Question and Answer	• Guided writing stimuli • to prompt initial drafts of writing
Paragraph Construction Tasks	• Topic sentence writing • Topic development within a paragraph • Development of main and supporting ideas across paragraphs

Strategic Options	① Attending to task ② Attending to genre • reports • summaries • responses • narration • interpretation • library research paper

(test) Guided Question and Answer

1. Where did this story take place? [setting]
2. Who were the people in the story? [characters]
3. What happened first? and then? and then? [sequence of events]
4. Why did _____ do _____? [reasons, causes]
5. What did _____ think about _____? [opinion]
6. What happened at the end? [climax]
7. What is the moral of this story? [evaluation]

③ Scoring Methods

Holistic scoring	Advantages:	• fast evaluation • high interrater reliability
	Disadvantages:	• little washback • not applied to all genres • very little information about the writing
Primary trait scoring		How well students can write within a narrowly defined range of discourse. • summaries: accuracy • responses: expression • lab report: clarity
Analytic scoring		• according to curricular goals and students' needs • more washback • low practicality

05 Assessing Grammar and Vocabulary

1. Assessing Grammar

① grammatical forms or the structures of a language
② grammatical meanings of those forms
③ pragmatic meaning or use in a given context

Selected Response	• Multiple-choice tasks • Discrimination tasks • Noticing tasks or Consciousness-raising tasks
Limited Production	• Gap-filling tasks • Short-answer tasks • Dialogue-completion tasks
Extended Production	• Information gap tasks • Role-play or Simulation tasks

2. Assessing Vocabulary

(1) Nature of vocabulary

Function and Content words	• function words: more to the grammar of the language • content words: focus on in vocabulary tests
Lexical items	meaning as a whole unit • phrasal verbs • compound nouns • idioms
Prefabricated language (lexical phrase)	groups of words that have a grammatical structure but have a function in communication • poly words • institutionalized expressions • phrasal constraints • sentence builders

(2) Lexical Knowledge

Receptive vocabulary	• Vocabulary in a one-sentence context • Vocabulary matching exercise • Word association
Productive vocabulary	• Fill-in-the blank • Selective deletion cloze

3. Procedure of Assessment tasks

1. Clarify your purpose	• To evaluate the results in relation to the intended use of the test
2. Define your construct	• Ability to measure • Syllabus based: the lexical items and the vocabulary skills to be assessed can be specified in relation to the learning objectives of the course
3. Select your target words	• high-frequency words • low-frequency words • specialized vocabulary • subtechnical words
4. Determine mode of performance	• receptive/ productive vocabulary • vocabulary recognition • vocabulary recall

부록

Glossary

📝 Glossary

analytic scoring

in testing, a method of scoring that separates and weights different features of the taker's performance on a writing or speaking task and assigns separate scores to each feature. The commonly analyzed features in writing tasks include content, organization, cohesion, style, register, vocabulary, grammar, spelling, and mechanics, whereas those in speaking tasks include pronunciation, fluency, accuracy, and appropriateness.

appropriateness

the extent to which a use of language matches the linguistic and sociolinguistic expectations and practices of native speakers of the language. When producing an utterance, a speaker needs to know that it is grammatical, and also that it is suitable (appropriate) for the particular situation. 예 Give me a glass of water! is grammatical, but it would not be appropriate if the speaker wanted to be polite. A request such as: May I have a glass of water, please? would be more appropriate.

artifact study

It is designed to help students discern the cultural significance of certain unfamiliar objects from the target culture. The activity involves students in giving descriptions and forming hypotheses about the function of the unknown object.

automatic processing

the performance of a task without conscious or deliberate processing. In cognitive psychology, two different kinds of processing employed in carrying out tasks are distinguished. Controlled processing is involved places demands on short-term memory. 예 A learner driver may operate a car using controlled processing, consciously thinking about many of the decisions and operations involved while driving. Automatic processing is involved when the learner carries out the task without awareness or attention, making more use of information in long-term memory. Many skills are considered to be 'learned' when they can be performed with automatic processing. In language learning, the distinction between controlled and automatic processing has been used to explain why learners sometimes perform differently under different conditions. 예 a learner may speak a foreign language with relatively few grammatical errors in situations where automatic processing is being used (when talking in relaxed situations among friends). The same learner may speak less fluently and make more grammatical errors when controlled process ing is being used (when speaking in public before an audience). The presence of the audience distracts the speaker, who uses more controlled processing and this interferes with his or her accuracy and fluency.

cognitive strategies

learning strategies that operate directly on incoming information in ways that enhance learning. 예 rehearsal (repeating key words or phrases silently or aloud, organizing (summarizing what has been read or heard), using memory heuristics (a keyword or visual image)), and inferencing.

collocation

the way in which words are used together regularly. Collocation refers to the restrictions on how words can be used together, 예 which prepositions are used particular verbs, or which verbs and nouns are used together. 예 In English the verb perform is used with operation, but not with discussion: "The doctor performed the operation." * "The committee performed a discussion". Instead we say: "The committee held/had a discussion." Perform is used with (collocates with) operation, and hold and have (collocates with) discussion. high collocates with probability, but not with chance: a high probability but a good chance do collocates with damage, duty, and wrong, but not with trouble, noise, and excuse: do a lot of damage do one's duty do wrong make trouble make a lot of noise make an excuse.

communication strategy

a way used to express a meaning in a second or foreign language, by a learner who has a limited command of the language. In trying to communicate, a learner may have to make up for a lack of knowledge of grammar or vocabulary. 예 The learner may not be able to say *It's against law to park here* and so he/she way say *This place, cannot park*. For handkerchief a learner could say a cloth for my nose, and for apartment complex the learner could say building. The use of paraphrase and other communication strategies (gesture and mime) characterize the interlanguage of some language learners.

concordance/ concordancing

a list of all the words which are used in a particular text or in the works of a particular author, together with a list of the contexts in which each word occurs (usually not including highly frequent grammatical words such as articles and prepositions). Concordances have been used in the study of word frequencies, grammar, discourse and stylistics. In recent years the preparation of concordances by computers has been used to analyze individual texts, large samples of writing by a particular author, or different genres and registers. A collection of texts for such purposes is called a corpus. Computer concordances are now often used in the preparation of dictionaries, since they enable lexicographers to study how words are in a wide range of contexts.

connotation

the additional meanings that a word or phrase has beyond its central meaning. These meanings show people's emotions and attitudes towards what the word or phrase refers to. 예 Child could be defined as a young human being but there are many other characteristics which different people associate with child, 예 affectionate, amusing, lovable, sweet, mischievous, noisy, irritating, grubby. Some connotations may be shared by a group of people of the same cultural or social background, sex, or age; others may be restricted to one or several individuals and depend on their personal experience. In a meaning system, that part of the meaning which is covered by connotation is sometimes referred to as affective meaning connotative meaning, or emotive meaning.

consciousness raising

in teaching, techniques that encourage learners to pay attention to language form in the belief that an awareness of will contribute indirectly to language acquisition. Techniques include having students infer grammatical rules from examples, compare differences between two or more different ways of saying something, observe differences between a learner's use of a grammar item and its use by native speakers. A consciousness-raising approach is contrasted with traditional approaches to the teaching of grammar (e. g. drilling, sentence practice, sentence combining), in which the goal is to establish a rule or instil a grammatical pattern directly.

content schema

in theories of reading comprehension, a distinction is sometimes made between two kinds schema that people make use of in understanding texts. Content schema refers o background knowledge about the content of a text, i.e. depending on whether it is a about an earthquake, the economy, French art or cooking This type of schematic knowledge is contrasted with formal schema, i.e. knowledge about the formal, rhetorical, organizational structure of different kinds of texts, such as whether the text is a simple story, a scientific text, a news report, etc, Knowledge of both types of schemata influence how a reader understands a text.

context

the meaning a linguistic item has in context, the meaning a word has within a particular sentence, or a sentence has in a particular paragraph. 예 The question "Do you know the meaning of war?" may have two different contextual meanings: may mean Do you know the meaning of the 'word' war?, when said by a language teacher to a class of students: it may mean War produces death, injury, and suffering, when said by an injured soldier to a politician who favours war.

cooperative learning

collaborative learning as an approach to teaching and learning in which classrooms are organized so that students work together in small co-operative teams. Such an approach is said to increase students' learning since (a)it is less threatening for many students' (b)it increases the amount of student less the of student participation in the classroom, (c)it reduces the need for competitiveness, and (d)it reduces the teacher's dominance in the classroom. Five distinct types of co-operative learning activities are often distinguished:

- Peer Tutoring: students help each other learn, taking turns tutoring or drilling each other.
- Jigsaw: each member of a group has a piece of information needed to complete a group task.
- Co-operative Projects: students work together to produce a product, such as a written paper or group presentation.
- Co-operative/ Individualized: students progress at their owm rate through individualized learning materials but their progress contributes to a team grade so that each pupil is rewarded by the achievements of his or her teammates.
- Co-operative Interaction: students work together as a team to complete a learning unit, such as a laboratory experiment.

C-Test

a variation of the cloze test where beginning with the second in the second sentence the second half of every second word in a reading passage is deleted with the first sentence intact. Only the exact word method is used.

cue

(in language teaching) a signal given by teacher in order to produce a response by the students. 예 in practising questions: cues may be words, signals, actions, etc.

cue	response
time	What time is it?
day	What day is it?

culture capsule

A culture capsule is a brief description of some aspect of the target language culture (예 what is customarily eaten for meals and when those meals are eaten, marriage customs, etc.) followed by, or incorporated with contrasting information from the students' native language culture.

culture island

A culture island is an area in the classroom where posters, maps, objects, and pictures of people, lifestyles, or customs of other cultures are displayed to attract learners' attention, evoke comments, and help students develop a mental image.

decision-making

in teaching, thinking processes employed by teachers in planning, when different instructional choices are involved. Two kinds of decision making are often referred to:

- pre-active decision-making: decisions that are made prior to teaching, such as determining the content of a lesson
- interactive decision-making: unplanned decisions made during a lesson, such as a decision to drop a planned activity

decoding

the process of trying to understand the meaning of a word, phrase, or sentence. When decoding a speech utterance, the listener must:

- hold the utterance in short term memory
- analyze the utterance into segment and identify clauses, phrases, and other linguistic units
- identify the underlying propositions and illocutionary meaning

Decoding is also used to mean the interpretation of any set of symbols which carry a meaning, 예 a secret code or a Morse signal.

deductive learning

also learning to language teaching in which learners are taught rules and given specific information about a language. They then apply these rules when they use the language. Language teaching methods which emphasize the study of the grammatical rules if a language (예 the grammar translation method) make use of the principle of deductive learning. This may be contrasted with inductive learning or learning by induction, in which learners are not taught grammatical or other types of rules directly but are left to discover or induce rules from their experience of using the language. Language teaching methods which emphasize use of the language rather than presentation of information about the language (for example, the direct method, communicative approach, and counselling) make use of the principle of inductive learning.

diagnostic test

a test that is designed to provide information about L2 learners' strengths and weaknesses. 예 A diagnostic pronunciation test may be used to measure the L2 learners' pronunciation of English sounds. It would show which sounds L2 learners are and are not able to pronounce or whether their pronunciation is intelligible or not. Diagnostic tests may be used to find out how much L2 learners know before beginning a language course to better provide an efficient and effective course of instruction.

dialogue journals

written(electronically or by hand) or orally recorded discussions between student and teachers in a writing programme, about school-related or other topics of interest to student. Dialogue journals may be used to develop writing skills, to enable teachers to assess the value of a course of get student feedback and to develop fluency in writing.

discovery learning

(in education) an approach to teaching and learning which is based on the following principles:

- Learners develop processes associated with discovery and inquiry by observing, inferring, formulating hypotheses, predicting and communicating.
- Teachers used a teaching style supports the processes of discovery and inquiry.
- Textbooks are not the sole resources for learning.
- Conclusions are considered tentative and not final.
- Learners are involved in planning, conducting, and evaluating their own learning with the teacher playing a supporting role.
- A number of language teaching approaches make use of discovery based approaches to learning, particularly communicative language teaching.

explicit learning

Explicit learning is a way to teach in a direct, structured way. When teachers use explicit instruction, they make lessons crystal clear. They show students how to start and succeed on a task. They also give students plenty of feedback and chances to practice.

extralinguistic

describes those features in communication which are not directly a part of verbal language but which either contribute in conveying a message, 예 hand movements, facial expressions, etc., or have an influence on language use, 예 signalling a speaker's age, sex, or social class.

form-function relation

the relationship between the physical characteristics of a thing (i.e. its form) and its role or function. This distinction is often referred to in studying language use, because a linguistic form (예 imperative) can perform a variety of different functions, as the following examples illustrate.

imperative forms	communicative forms
Come round for a drink.	invitation
Watch out.	warning
Turn left at the corner.	direction
Pass the sugar.	request

graphic organizer

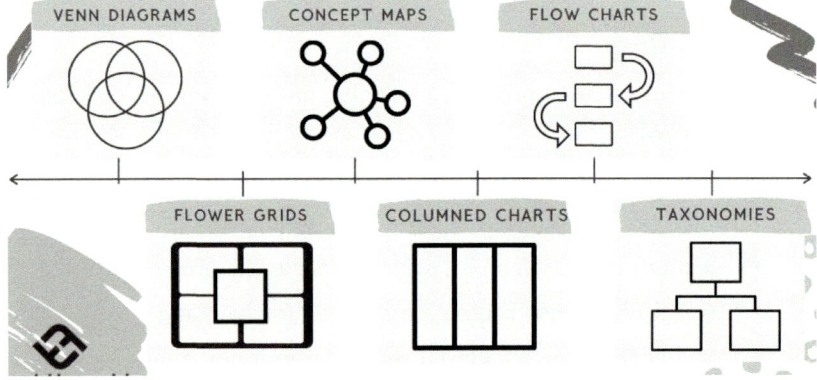

A graphic organizer visually represents ideas, concepts, and relationships between various components. Concept maps and knowledge maps all are types of graphic organizers. You can use any chart or diagram as a graphic organizer to compare facts and depict a story.

holistic approach
an approach to language teaching which seeks to focus on language in its entirety rather breaking it down into separate components, such as reading listening, grammar, etc. This is one of the principles of whole language as well as of some approaches to teaching language arts.

immersion programme
a form of bilingual education and used to describe programmes which serve language majority students and which use a second or foreign language to teach at least 50% of the curriculum during the elementary or secondary grades. 예 There are schools in Canada for English-speaking children, where French is the language of instruction. If these children are taught in French for the whole day it is called a total immersion programme, but if they are taught in French for only part of the day it is called a partial immersion programme.

implicit learning
Implicit learning is acquisition of knowledge about the underlying structure of a complex stimulus environment by a process which takes place naturally, simply and without conscious operations. Explicit learning is a more conscious operation where the individual makes and tests hypotheses in a search for structure.

incidental learning
learning something without the intention to learn it or learning one thing while intending to learn another, for example, unintentionally picking up vocabulary, patterns, or spelling through interaction, communicative activities, or reading for content or pleasure. This can be contrasted with intentional learning, for example learning by following a deliberate programme of study to enhance vocabulary or grammar. In controlled experiments, incidental learning is usually used in a more restricted sense, operationalized as a condition in which subjects are not told in advance that they will be tested after treatment, sometimes contrasted with an intentional condition in which subjects are told what they will be tested on.

intake
a term referring to that part of the language to which learners are exposed that actually "goes in" and plays a role in language learning. Some theorists believe that intake is that part of the input that has been attended to and noticed by second language learners while processing the input. It is also possible to distinguish between preliminary intake, brief notice of some feature of the input, and final intake, integration of knowledge of that item in one's interlanguage.

integrated approach

In the conversation, the two teachers are talking about the integrated approach, which is now typical within a communicative, interactive framework. The approach can give students greater motivation and make them engage more actively, which can convert to better learning outcomes.

integrative test

The procedure used in the contest exemplifies integrative testing in terms of the number of skills assessed. "Listen to a taped radio interview of Barbara Carrel, a famous writer, about her adventure to Africa. While listening, take notes. Then using the notes, write a story about her adventure. You will be given 30 minutes to complete the story."

interactional and transactional functions of language

a distinction that is sometimes made between uses of language where the primary focus is on social interaction between the speakers and the need to communicate such things as rapport, empathy, interest and social harmony (interactional function), and those where the primary focus is on communicating information and different kinds of real world transactions (transactional function). Interactional communication is primarily person-orientated, whereas transactional communication is primarily message focused. Interactional and transactional language may differ in terms of such things as conventions for turn-taking, topics, and discourse management.

inter-rater reliability

One potential problem with the scoring process is low inter-rater reliability, which is most likely due to the subjectivity of the raters.

intra-rater reliability

I don't grade my students' writing assignments when I'm tired. That way, I can avoid being inconsistent. I just put them away until the next day. Another issue is that over time, I tend to stray from the rating criteria. I need to find a way to stick to it for consistency in scoring.

item analysis

(in testing) the analysis of the responses to the items in a test in order to find out how effective the test items are and to find out if they indicate differences between high and low ability test takers.

item discrimination

(in testing) a measure of the extent to which a test item is sensitive to differences in ability among test takers. If a particular item in a test is answered in the same way by both the test takers who do well on the test as a whole and by those who do poorly, the item is said to have poor discrimination. In item analysis, the item-total point-biserial correlation between the answers to an individual item (hence "item") and the scores on the whole test (hence "total") is often used as an estimate of discrimination. Or alternatively, an item discrimination index can be calculated using the following formula: *ID = IF upper − IF lower*

item facility

(in testing) a measure of the ease of a test item. It is the proportion of the test takers who answered the item correctly, and is determined by the following formula:

IF= R/N, where R = number of correct answers, N = the number of test takers

The higher ratio of R to N, the easier the item.

jigsaw activity

a type of information gap activity in which groups of learners have different information that is needed to put together the solution to a task. In jigsaw listening or reading activities, different groups in the class may process separate but related parts of a test and then later combine their information to reconstruct the whole through class discussion or group interaction.

language experience approach

an approach used in the teaching of reading to young children which draws on the experiences children have in their personal lives as well as on the language skills and vocabulary they have developed outside the classroom. In this approach, may recount stories and experiences orally to the teacher, who writes words on charts or other visual devices and uses them as a basis for teaching reading.

language transfer

the effect of one language on the learning of another. Two types of language transfer may occur. Positive transfer is transfer which makes learning easier, and may occur when both the native language and the target language have the same form. 예 Both French and English have the word table, which can have the same meaning in both languages. Negative transfer, also known as interference, is the use of a native-language pattern or rule which leads to an error or inappropriate form in the target language. 예 A French learner of English may produce the incorrect sentence *I am here since Monday* instead of *I have been since Monday*, because of the transfer of the French pattern Je suis ici depuis lundi ("I am here since Monday"). Although L1 to L2 transfer has been investigated most widely, it is also generally recognized that there can also be transfer from an L2 to one's native language, as well as L2 to L3 transfer from one second or foreign language to another.

learning strategy

the ways in which learners attempt to work out the meanings and uses of words, grammatical rules, and other aspects of the language they are learning. In first language learning, the word "strategy" is sometimes used to refer to the ways that children process language, without implying either intentionality or awareness. 예 In trying to understand a sentence, a child may "use" the learning strategy that the first mentioned noun in a sentence refers to the person or thing performing an action. The child may then think that the sentence *the boy was chased by the dog* means the same thing as *the boy chased the dog*. In second language learning, a strategy is usually an intentional or potentially intentional behaviour carried out with the goal of learning. A number of broad categories of learning strategies have been identified, including cognitive strategies such as analyzing the target language, comparing what is newly encountered with what is already known in either the L1 or the L2, and organizing information; metacognitive strategies, which include being aware of one's own learning, making an organized plan, and monitoring one's progress; social strategies such as seeking out friends who are native speakers of the target language or working with peers in a classroom setting; and resource management strategies such as setting aside a regular time and place language study. Learning strategies may be applied to simple tasks such as learning a list of new words, or more complex tasks involving language comprehension and production.

metacognitive strategy

a category of learning strategy which involves thinking about the mental processes used in the learning process, monitoring learning while it is taking place, and evaluating learning after it has occurred. 예 metacognitive strategies a learner may use when he or she is beginning to learn a new language include:

- planning ways of remembering new words encountered in conversations with native speakers
- deciding which approaches to working out grammatical rules are more effective

- evaluating his or her own progress and making decisions about what to concentrate on in the future

minimal pair

two words in a language which differ from each other by only one distinctive sound (one phoneme) and which also differ in meaning. 예 The English words bear and pear are a minimal pair as they differ in meaning and in their initial phonemes /b/ and /p/. The term "minimal pair" is also sometimes used of any two pieces of language that are identical except for a specific feature or group of related features.

multi-word lexical unit

a sequence of word forms which functions as a single grammatical unit. 예 "look into" which is used in the same way as "investigate" Multi word units tend to acquire meaning which are not predictable from the individual parts, in which case they are often described as idioms.

native informant

Native informants can be valuable resources to the classroom teacher, both as sources of current information about the target culture and as linguistic models for students. Students can develop a set of questions they would like to ask before native speakers come to the class.

negotiation

(in conversation) what speakers do in order to achieve successful communication. For conversation to progress naturally and for speakers to be able to understand each other it may be necessary for them to:

- indicate that they understand or do not understand, or that they want the conversation to continue
- help each other to express ideas
- make corrections when necessary to what is said or how it is said. These aspects of the work which speakers do in order to make successful conversation is known as negotiation, in conversational analysis.

outcomes-based teaching/ education

an approach to education and curriculum development which involves:

- describing the learning outcomes that students should know at the end of a course of instruction

- devising a curriculum to help them achieve the outcomes
- using the outcomes achieved as a measure of effectiveness. In some parts of the world, particularly in the US, this approach is thought necessary to ensure that students graduate from high school with the knowledge and skills they will need in real world.

output hypothesis

the hypothesis that successful second language acquisition requires not only comprehensible input, but also comprehensible output, language produced by the learner that can be understood by other speakers of the language. It has been argued that when learners have to make efforts to ensure that their messages are communicated (pushed output) this puts them in a better position to notice the gap between their productions and those of proficient speakers, fostering acquisition.

performance-based assessment

an approach to assessment that seeks to measure student learning based on how well the learner can perform on a practical real-world task such as the ability to write an essay or carry out a short conversation. This approach is thought to be a better measure of learning that performance on traditional tests such as multiple-choice tests.

polysemy

having two or more closely related meanings. 예 *foot in*: *He hurt his foot.* She stood at the foot of the stairs. The foot is the lowest part of the stairs just as the foot is the lowest part of the human body. A well known problem in semantics is how to decide whether we are dealing with a single polysemous word (like foot) or with two or more homonyms.

process syllabus

In teaching, a syllabus that specifies the learning experinces and processes students will encounter during a course, rather than the learning outcomes. Objectives developed for such a course are known as process objectives. 예

- to conduct classroom discussions in which learners learn to listen to others as well as express their own views
- to provide opportunities for learners to reflect on their own learning strategies

A framework for classroom decision-making based upon negotiation among teachers and students applied to any chosen aspect of the curriculum.

prominence

(in discourse), greater stress on the words or syllables which the speaker wishes to emphasize. Prominence may be given to different words according to what has been said before by another speaker. 예 He may come tomorrow.(as a reply to "When is Mr Jones coming?") He MAY come tomorrow. (as a reply to "Is Mr Jones to come tomorrow?") Prominence may be accompanied by pitch movement on the prominent syllable.

realia

In this lesson, the teacher is using a type of supplementary materials called realia to teach key vocabulary. Along with other visuals, these materials are expected to attract students' attention and to aid understanding and retention of vocabulary.

scaffolding

the support provided to learners to enable them to perform tasks which are beyond their capacity. Initially in language learning, learners may be unable to produce certain structures within a single utterance, but may build them through interaction with another speaker.

speech act

an utterance as a functional unit in communication. In speech act theory, utterances have two kinds of meaning:

- propositional meaning (also known as locutionary meaning): This is the basic literal meaning of the utterance which is conveyed by the particular words and structures which the utterance contains
- illocutionary meaning (also known as illocutionary force): This is the effect the utterance or written text has on the reader or listener. 예 In "I am thirsty" the propositional meaning is what the utterance says about the speaker's physical state. The illocutionary force is the utterance says about the speaker's physical state. The illocutionary force is the effect the speaker wants the utterance to have on the listener.

standardized test

which has been developed from tryouts and experimentation to ensure that it is reliable and valid for which norms have been established which provides uniform procedures for administering (time limits, response format, number of questions) and for scoring the test

usage

a distinction made by Widdowson between the function of a linguistic item as an element in a linguistic system (usage) and its function as part of a system of communication (use). 예 The progressive aspect may be studied as an item of grammar or usage (i.e. to consider how it compares with other aspects and tenses in English and the constructions in which it occurs) and in terms its use (i.e. how it is used in discourse of performing such communicative acts as descriptions, plans, commentaries, etc.).

wait time

(in questioning) the pause after a teacher has asked a question before a student is asked to respond. The effectiveness of questioning is said to be partly dependent on the use of wait time. Teachers tend to use insufficient wait time and to either answer questions themselves or call on another student to answer the question. Increasing wait time both before calling in a student to respond and after a student's initial response (i.e. before the teacher comments on the response) often increases the length of students' responses, increases the number of questions asked by students, and increases student involvement in learning.

washback

(in testing) the positive or negative impact of a test on classroom teaching or learning. In some countries, 예 national language examinations have a major impact on teaching and teachers often "teach to the tests". In order to bring about changes in teaching, changes may have to be made in the tests. 예 if the education department in a country wanted schools to spend more time teaching listening skills, one way to bring this about would be to introduce a listening comprehension test component into state examinations. The washback would be that more class time would then spent on teaching listening skills. When teaching is found to exert an important effect on testing, this impact is called a reverse washback.

zone of proximal development

From a socio-cultural perspective, effective learning takes place when what a student attempts to learn is within his or her zone of proximal development. This is the distance between what a student can do alone and what he or she can do with scaffolded help from more knowledgeable others like teachers or more capable peers. For learning to be effective, such help should be provided to a student through interaction like the teacher's utterances offered to aid the student in the dialogue.

참/고/문/헌

Brown, D. (2015) *Teaching by Principles (4th ed)*. Pearson Education.

Brown, D. (2014) *Principles of Language Leaning and Teaching (5th ed)*. Pearson Education.

Brown, D. (2013) *Language Assessment: Principles and Classroom Practices* (2nd ed). Pearson Education.

Celce-Murcia M. & Hilles S. (1988) *Techniques and Resources in Teaching Grammar*. Oxford: Oxford University Press.

Davies, P. & Pearse, E. (2000) *Success in English Teaching* Oxford: Oxford University Press.

Ellis, R. (2003) *Task-based Language Learning and Teaching* Oxford: Oxford University Press.

Harmer, J. (2007) *The Practice of English Language Teaching (4th ed)*. Pearson Education.

Harmer, J. (2007) *How to Teach English*. Pearson Education.

Hedge, T. (2000) *Teaching and Learning in the Language Classroom*. Oxford: Oxford University Press

Hughes, A. (2003) *Testing for Language Teachers* (2nd ed). Cambridge University Press.

Richards, J. (2013) *Techniques and Principles in Language Teaching* (3rd ed). Oxford: Oxford University Press

Larsen-Freeman, D. (2013) *Teaching English as a Second or Foreign Language (4th ed)*. Oxford: Oxford University Press

Lightbown, P., & Spada, N. (2014) *How Languages are Learned*. Oxford: Oxford University Press.

Nunan, D. (2003) *Practical English Language Teaching*. New York: McGraw-Hill Contemporary

Nunan, D. (1999) *Second Language Teaching & Learning*. Newbury House Teacher Development

Nunan, D. (2003) *Syllabus Design*. Oxford: Oxford University Press

Richard-Amato, P (2003) *Making it happen*. NY: Pearson Education.

Richards, J., & Rodgers, T. (2014) *Approaches and Methods in Language Teaching*. Cambridge University Press.

Richards, J., & Renandya, W.(Eds) (2002) *Methodology in Language Teaching*. Cambridge University Press.

Richards, J. (2001) *Curriculum Development in Language Teaching*. Cambridge Language Education

권영주 임용 전공
영어 교육론
TEACHING ENGLISH

초판 1쇄 발행 2022년 12월 15일
개정 1쇄 발행 2025년 01월 02일

편저 권영주
발행인 공태현 **발행처** (주)법률저널
등록일자 2008년 9월 26일 **등록번호** 제15-605호
주소 151-862 서울 관악구 복은4길 50 (서림동 120-32)
대표전화 02)874-1144 **팩스** 02)876-4312
홈페이지 www.lec.co.kr
ISBN 978-89-6336-963-1 (13740)
정가 26,000원